Inevitable Grace

Also by Piero Ferrucci:

What We May Be

The Child of Your Dreams
(with Laura Huxley)

Inevitable Grace

Breakthroughs in the Lives of Great Men and Women: Guides to Your Self-Realization

Piero Ferrucci

Translated by David Kennard
in association with First Edition

JEREMY P. TARCHER, INC.
Los Angeles

Library of Congress Cataloging in Publication Data

Ferrucci, Piero.
Inevitable grace / Piero Ferrucci.
p. cm.
Includes bibliographical references.
Includes index.
ISBN 0-87477-550-7
1. Transpersonal psychology. I. Title.
BF204.7F47 1990 89-27425
150.19—dc20 CIP

Jeremy P. Tarcher, Inc.
5858 Wilshire Blvd., Suite 200
Los Angeles, CA 90036

Distributed by St. Martin's Press, New York

Design by Deborah Daly

Manufactured in the United States of America
10 9 8 7 6 5 4 3 2 1

First Edition

. . . simplicity, and beauty, and inevitable grace.

William Wordsworth, *The Prelude*

Contents

Acknowledgments

First of all, I would like to thank Roberto Assagioli, the founder of psychosynthesis. The themes in this book are to a great extent inspired by his teachings. Assagioli was one of the first to study peak experiences empirically and to emphasize their importance in the field of psychology. In the last years of his life Assagioli was preparing a book on the central idea of psychosynthesis—the existence of a transpersonal Self as the Center of our being and source of our most beautiful and meaningful experiences, and the various ways of realizing this Center. It was to be the culmination of his life's work.

Unfortunately that book was never written. Assagioli died in 1974, when the project was still in its initial stages. I had the opportunity of studying and collaborating with him during those last years of his life, and of speaking in depth with him about these themes: the Self, transpersonal experiences, the ways and means of Self-realization. This is not the book Assagioli would have written; however, it tackles the same subjects. The structure of this work, the empirical data, the reflections, and the developments are mine. The main ideas are Assagioli's. To him I express, deep and unchanged through the years, my gratitude.

Writing is a solitary adventure. But completing and perfecting what one has written demands the collaboration of several minds. This is what happened in my case. The help of various people was crucial, and I want to thank them one by one. My wife Vivien almost rewrote my own rewriting of the English translation. No husband was ever so happy to be corrected 5,000 times. Laura Huxley reminded me that readers were not going to be eggheads only, but people. From Stuart Miller I understood the necessity for a book to have a coherent architecture. My editor, Allyn Brodsky, helped me understand the importance of flow, the continuity from one subject to the next. Maria Rosa Marchi's observations reminded me that the process of Self-realization is full of dangers, distortions, and problems. Talking with Alberto Alberti, I realized this book should be more a work of psychology than of literature. Together with Diana Whitmore, I have presented this material in countless workshops, and delved in depth into its practical usefulness. Andrea Bocconi encouraged me to rely less on quotations, and more on my own thought. Nives Favero and Chiara Uderzo showed me the importance of details. My aunt, Emilia Rossi Ferrucci, made me even more enthusiastic about the subjects on which I was writing. My mother, who read the manuscript when close to her death, taught me to stick to the essential. Each one of these contributions has revealed to me cardinal values in writing.

Finally, other people have also helped and encouraged me: Aredana Amadori, Silvia Cerchiai, Sascha Doenges, Francesca Meucci, Fernando Rossi, and Fiorella Rossini.

Introduction

Throughout the course of human history, a number of individuals have shown exceptional capacities. They have perceived realities to which other people were blind, invented the unimaginable, or ventured into unknown worlds. They have seen, and created, things of extraordinary beauty, and loved in a selfless, genuine way. They have soared to the heights of human experience.

I have made a study of more than five hundred such people: some of the greatest artists, scientists, sages, philosophers, educators, mystics, men and women of action, pioneers, political leaders, actors, and athletes.

In my selection these individuals had to meet certain criteria:

> They must be considered exceptionally competent and creative in their fields;
>
> They must belong to as wide a variety of cultures, historical times, and arenas of human endeavor as possible;
>
> They must represent both sexes;
>
> The information available on them (autobiographies, biographies, diaries, letters) must carry a high degree of historical certainty, barring all spurious writings and testimonies.

My purpose was to identify their moments and periods of greatest happiness—the states of grace they felt to be supremely significant and beautiful. I was looking for the answers to these questions:

> What are the highest expressions of human nature?
>
> How did these individuals become capable of such feats?
>
> What can we learn from them and apply to our own lives?

I made some very encouraging findings. The attitudes and techniques adopted by the people I studied have an identical form in different ages and civilizations. This means that to a certain extent they transcend the confines of history and the diversity of cultures. These attitudes and techniques are simple and natural ways of being. We see them at work in ourselves, too, and in the people around us. We all have them, although in an embryonic, dormant, or repressed form, and it is quite likely that we could all develop them.

Because of our conditioning, the topmost expressions of humankind appear to us as rare occurrences or unreachable peaks. Here we will consider them as examples of what each one of us may become. To deny such a possibility is to belie our humanity. We may find it difficult, even impossible, to jump higher than the athletic champion who clears two meters, but learning to jump well is something we can do.

Since this book studies the peaks of human consciousness, it is not uncommon to find words like *God* or *divine* used by those who described these experiences. For us this means they were a climax in the lives of those who had them. We will not be led to any metaphysical or theological statements here: whether or not God exists, and what his nature may be, are not subjects we will tackle.

We will study human experience as such, just as we study

any other phenomenon in the universe: the vortices in a river, the roots of a tree, the flight of an eagle, or the structure of a comet. The experiences described in this book no doubt happened: they are *facts*—and therefore a legitimate field of empirical inquiry. From these facts we will extract principles about human nature and indications of possible behaviors and practices. There we will stop, at the threshold of the mystery.

We will study widely different people and phenomena. We will also study traditions because, when not fossilized into dogmas and superstitions, they represent the quintessence of human wisdom, attained after innumerable trials. At first glance it may seem as though we are looking at a jumble of experiences having no link with one another. Soon, however, we will realize how they reveal their significance and interconnectedness as we look at them side by side. By viewing them in this light, we will inevitably think of them as having a single origin. We will call this origin the Self, for we are dealing with the essence of each human being, his or her Center.

To speak of the Self is a difficult enterprise, because it cannot be expressed in words or defined by abstract concepts. It is easier, as people have done through the ages, to represent it with symbols: a diamond, a spring of pure water, a flower coming into bloom, a flame, a mountaintop, the breath of life, a cloudless sky, or a light that shines brighter than a thousand suns. In more technical terms we could describe it as a *field*, similar to a gravitational or electromagnetic field: a space in which certain phenomena are possible and others are not. In our present case these phenomena are higher ways of feeling and being.

According to the thesis of this book, everyone has a Self; everyone, in fact, *is* a Self. In order to grasp this concept, we need only think back to the best moments of our lives: moments when our brightest ideas came to us, or when time stood still, or when we were unusually sensitive to beauty, times when we felt our confines expanding to include another person or other people, and we were filled with feelings of solidarity and genuine self-forgetting. The Self is the substance of who we are at those times when we feel truest and most alive.

This area of study has been called *transpersonal psychology*, that is to say it extends beyond the boundaries of a person's own individuality, covering such phenomena as the expansion of consciousness, creative inspiration, peak experiences, the intuition of archetypes, ecstasy, and enlightenment. A large body of information and ideas has been collected on these subjects. Researchers and scholars in a whole spectrum of disciplines have directly or indirectly contributed—from comparative religion to the psychology of creativity, from physics to philosophy, from sociological analysis to systems theory, from anthropology to neuropsychology, from animal communication to mythology, from the study of altered states of consciousness to research on near-death experiences.

Transpersonal psychology is more a way of thinking than a creed. It has no dogmas, labels, or rigid confines. Those who are part of it, though they represent a multiplicity of perspectives and methodologies, all subscribe to one central thesis: our ordinary conscious experience is not the most representative of who we are, but other ways of being more appropriately express our real nature—broader, truer, and happier ways.

Among those who have anticipated, created, or enriched these concepts we can list the following as only a few examples among many: William James, Frederic Myers, Rudolf Otto, Richard Maurice Bucke, Sri Aurobindo, Evelyn Underhill, Martin Buber, Daisetz Teitaro Suzuki, Carl Gustav Jung, Erich Neumann, Sarvepalli Radhakrishnan, Aldous Huxley, Teilhard de Chardin, Pitimin Sorokin, Mircea Eliade, Roberto Assagioli, Abraham Maslow, Gregory Bateson, Elizabeth Kübler-Ross, Ram Dass, Ken Wilber, and Stanislav Grof.

In parallel with transpersonal psychology, another significant development in the human sciences has matured during the 1970s. Brought about mainly by the work of Erich Jantsch and Ervin Laszlo, it is a new way of regarding evolution. In this view, cosmic, biological, and sociocultural evolution are a form of self-organization and self-transcendence occurring at different levels but following the same laws. Evolution is not merely the survival of the fittest in the biological world but also a paradigm that can explain a variety of phenomena ranging from the formation of nebulas to the development of animal species or human societies.

This paradigm is highly relevant in our context, because it shows that transpersonal states are not just singular and random events, but expressions of future stages in human consciousness. Yet if we look at contemporary culture we seldom find traces of these ideas. Its models of the human being are far poorer, often based on the great revolutions of thought in the nineteenth century and the early twentieth century. A number of factors have conspired to reinforce this neglect:

- ◊ In a world where wars, crime, and the exploitation of men and women appear to predominate, it seems absurd, almost offensive, to speak about higher aspects of human nature.
- ◊ For the great majority of individuals, the Self is beyond the reach of ordinary awareness.
- ◊ The prevailing cultural models in the Western world are reductionist: A human being is nothing more than a series of electrochemical reactions, a computerlike information system, a statistical figure, the result of economic and social interactions, or an organism that seeks pleasure and fears death.
- ◊ For many people it is difficult to accept higher or transpersonal levels. These intense, revolutionary states of consciousness, though desirable, may often seem terrifying.

◇ Over the centuries the Self has at times been expressed in dogmatic, one-sided, even insane ways. Therefore, through no fault of its own, the Self has acquired an ambiguous reputation.

Here we will bring about a Copernican revolution by examining the highest manifestations of humanity not as isolated facts, but as the most realistic pattern of what we are. We will be sustained in this enterprise by irrefutable evidence: throughout human history various individuals have had these experiences—and current theoretical models are unable to adequately explain them. From this new perspective, to speak of human beings without mentioning the Self is like speaking of the solar system without mentioning the Sun; it is the most complex and laborious sleight of hand one could ever dream up.

We will look at people's lives in motion—and see that their goal is the Self. Each one moves forward in a different way, and each has a different path. The analogy of a path is accurate, for it reminds us that we are all in the process of *becoming*. We may, of course, crystallize. At times, however, we move forward, make discoveries, and change. We venture into unknown territory, looking for something we long for without knowing—and yet recognize the moment we encounter it. During our search we come up against obstacles. As anyone who sets out on a long, arduous journey, we may lose our way, grow weary, become disheartened. And perhaps fail.

The various paths we will encounter are grouped together under different headings to better facilitate their description. A brief preview of these "Ways" may help to outline the plan of the book (the order is arbitrary; start with the Way that attracts you most—or least):

◇ The Way of Beauty is based on aesthetic enjoyment, inspiration, and creativity. In it we find artists of various types.

- ◇ The Way of Action leads to the Self through disinterested service and tireless involvement in the world. It is the path of benefactors and philanthropists.
- ◇ The Way of Illumination is founded on the practice of meditation and is taken by the great contemplatives, philosophers, yogis, and sages of all times.
- ◇ The Way of Dance and Ritual covers physical, externalized, and communal approaches to the expansion of consciousness. It is comprised of dancers, performers of rituals, and actors.
- ◇ The Way of Science leads to attainment of the sublime through research, observation, and speculation. Here we find scientists and inventors.
- ◇ The Way of Devotion is practiced by mystics and saints of all religions. Prayer is its main vehicle, relationship with God its central theme.
- ◇ The Way of the Will is the path of all who dare: explorers who venture into the unknown, inspired political leaders who confront hostile social forces, and also some athletes who challenge the limits of human capacities.

These are not rigid categories. We may well come across the same person on more than one of these paths, and no single individual mentioned embodies all the characteristics of a given Way. Each of them, and each of us, follows his or her individual course—a unique, unrepeatable process. The Ways described in this book, therefore, are general developmental models based on observation of certain exceptional individuals. They are prototypes a particular life may approximate, but never fully realize.

A Way, then, is not a predetermined course; rather, it is a process that engages us in ever new situations. With its surprising developments, it by far surpasses the most imaginative of novels. Treading a Way does not consist in mechanically applying a technique until liberation is achieved. There are no magic formulas or assembly line techniques. Each person must come up with *his* or *her own* Way—by giving up most dearly held convictions and habits, by making use of all resources, by doing the most extraordinary spiritual somersault. And with no guarantee of success.

The Ways toward the Self are not only individual undertakings but also aspects in the evolution of the human species. We may look at our highest capacities as expressions of an evolutionary pathway and as indicators of its future developments. From the primal soup of five billion years ago, to the emergence of the first monocellular living organisms, to our primate ancestors, to Homo sapiens, all the way up to the Sistine Chapel, the Fifth Symphony, the theory of relativity, and the great achievements of human civilization, our evolutionary history has witnessed a series of dramatic breakthroughs.

Certainly, there have been, and still are, tragic errors and failures. Furthermore, we have acquired the power to destroy all forms of life on this planet, so our history could come to an abrupt end. Were this not to happen, however, must we think that our extraordinary curriculum will go no further? The answer to this question is that the seeds of our future evolution are already visible here and now.

An analogy may help: sometime toward the end of winter we come across an early tree that already shows its first buds, standing among other as yet bare trees. In the same way, people like Buddha, Leonardo da Vinci, Mozart, and many other people less prominent have characteristics that humankind is perhaps destined to develop on a large scale in a future stage of its evolution. Any appearance of new faculties in a given individual, rather than being a private, solitary phenomenon, is an event that concerns humanity as a whole.

Let us now return to individual growth. As one proceeds along a Way toward the Self, one comes into contact with an entirely new realm that transcends the confines of individuality —the transpersonal level. Encountering this world can be an ecstatic experience, but it can also upset the mental balance of someone who is not prepared for it. Immature individuals may use transpersonal glimpses as an excuse for covering up their own weaknesses and avoiding the difficulties of life.

Alternatively, having perceived sublime realities, individuals may construe them as a criterion for absolute perfection, thus splitting themselves within, setting themselves apart from others, even condemning life as it is. Then again they may use their own experiences in order to claim superiority. The Self can cause us to come to our senses. But if we are not ready for it, it can also have the effect of multiplying our neuroses.

Myths from the past warn us. The story of Phaëthon is an example. Phaëthon was the son of a woman, Clymene, and Helios, the god of the sun. Schoolmates ridiculed and ill-treated him, refusing to believe in his divine origin. Phaëthon was deeply hurt and angry. One day he set out for the shining palace of his father. The great god promised to do whatever his son wished, and Phaëthon took advantage of his father's generosity. He asked that he should be allowed to take Helios' place for one day in the chariot that bore the fiery sphere across the sky. Hearing his son's request, Helios regretted the promise he had made. But *noblesse oblige*, the gods do not go back on their word, and he had to consent to his son's request.

Happy and proud, young Phaëthon rises up in the chariot as the horses pull him into the sky. He climbs higher and higher, shedding light and heat. He flies through space with a heady feeling of power and majesty. What a triumph! And what a sweet revenge on those who had taunted him! But then the horses, realizing that a different hand is at the reins, leave their usual path and fly at random, too close to the earth. Fields burst into flames, rivers dry up. In order to avoid further catastrophe, Zeus, the king of the gods, shoots Phaëthon down with a thunderbolt. A meteor flies through space to its death:

that meteor is Phaëthon, a poor, unhappy boy who believed he had conquered the infinite.

Phaëthon represents all those people who, upon reaching the transpersonal world, wish to use it to their own advantage in order to compensate for their inferiority feelings and to increase their status in the eyes of others; but this only results in disaster.

The opposite, however, can also happen. Through apathy, for the sake of convenience, or out of fear, people sometimes do not want to have anything to do with the Self.

The Self is, after all, an uncomfortable subject. It asks us to revolutionize our lives; it may temporarily make us more vulnerable; it gives us more responsibility; it demands hard work and exposes us to danger. Ignoring the whole matter and getting on with our everyday lives may be far easier. This response is the greatest form of betrayal—the denial of what we really are. The consequences take many forms: a vague sense of uneasiness, cynicism, various psychosomatic troubles, depression, or despair.

In one of his short stories, H.G. Wells gives a symbolic representation of this drama. Nunez, a mountain guide, falls into a valley that has been inhabited for centuries by a community of blind people. They are completely unaware of anything that has to do with sight, and oblivious of the civilized world. Nunez attempts to describe to the blind people the beauty of the clouds, flowers, and light, but they think him mad. Little by little, he is forced to accept the rules of their culture. He then falls in love with a woman and wants to become accepted as a part of the community. But the price is very high—he must lose his eyes and become blind like them.

Faced with this tragic choice, Nunez hesitates and almost gives in. At the last moment, however, he changes his mind. He courageously forsakes the country of the blind and climbs back up the mountain from which he had fallen. When he reaches the summit he looks around. He sees the facets of a crystal, a green vein of exposed ore, a tiny orange lichen, the mysterious purple and turquoise shadows deep in the valley, the fiery sunset, and then the star-studded sky. Everything appears to him as an extraordinary vision of freedom and beauty.

Nunez' predicament is one we all have to face, particularly now, in our present civilization, marked as it is by restless confusion as well as novel opportunities. We can be blind to the most beautiful realities, ask others to join us in our blindness—or grow accustomed to their form of blindness—and take this attitude as a basis for organizing our lives, our relationships with others, and society as a whole. Or, alternatively, we can bet on the qualities and the resources within ourselves.

This book is based on the second alternative. Although it is not a manual of techniques, it can be of practical help to those who read it. The study of transpersonal states changes our concept of what it means to be human, and therefore changes our image of ourselves and other people. To recognize the varieties of transpersonal experience may widen too narrow a conception of what has value in human life. To consider the richness and the diversity of the various Ways is a useful exercise in self-transcendence.

Moreover, by coming into contact with the happiest moments in the lives of great people, we will be stimulated and inspired. As with all ways of being—from apathy to zest—transpersonal states, too, are communicated and resonate in those who are exposed to them, even in written form.

Knowing about the experiences of enlightened and creative people also enables us to become better attuned to the greater potential of each human being. We realize that these experiences do not strictly belong to individuals far removed from us in space and time but that, at least potentially, they reside in us as well. Descriptions of higher states evoke in many the desire to experience them. This desire is not a passing whim, but a deep aspiration that may take the shape of a Way to the Self.

Deciding to set out on a spiritual Way is a crucial event. Life becomes a field offering innumerable new possibilities of transformation. A true *sadhana* can be born—a systematic work on oneself. Thus, with a new clarity, we are all faced with the same choice: denying what we are or trying out new ways of feeling, thinking, and being. And then, perhaps for a moment, we may find joy.

1

◊

◊ **The Way of Beauty**

◊

◊

Who can afford to live without beauty? Beauty fills us with passion; it graces us with joy and lights up our existence. A landscape, a piece of music, a film, a dance—suddenly all dreariness is gone, we are left bewitched, we are dazzled. If we get lost in dark despair, beauty takes us back to the Center. With its colorful spontaneity, it regenerates our lives. Beauty challenges the force of gravity. It is the promise of a world where all contradictions and pain have vanished. Embrace it, and all greed disappears, for in that moment you are completely disinterested, you are innocent. To savor the beautiful means to glimpse complete goodness, an unconditional yes to life.

Plato was the first to speak of beauty as a Way. According to him we can reach infinite beauty by climbing a ladder of increasingly refined aesthetic experiences and, starting from the more tangible and fleeting realities, reach up to universal, timeless levels.

We begin with beauty in its easiest and most spontaneous mode—physical attraction. The central motivation here is enjoyment; the main obstacle, attachment. The first steps of the Platonic ladder are so pleasurable that we may be tempted to settle here and forget about climbing any higher. But what a pity! For we would fail to see that each level of enjoyment prepares us for the next one, and invites us there.

Those who proceed beyond physical beauty find realities

visible only to the eye of intuition: they find the inner beauty of a person. This is an essential transition because the qualities of people are far less fleeting and far more transparent than their physical appearance, which, on the other hand, changes with time and often fails to fully reveal one's inner being. A person's qualities—for instance, intelligence, ability to love, or sincerity—can be appreciated even when that person is far away, has changed, or is dead. Even if those qualities are no longer actively expressed, they can still nourish and inspire us—they can still live.

Climbing higher on the Platonic ladder, we find the world of intellectual beauty—its crystalline harmony, its truth and power. This beauty is independent of personal factors, available to all who are willing to take part in it and ready to make the necessary commitment. Here we find the beauty of mathematics, philosophy, and science.

The last and highest step on the scale is pure beauty, independent of any qualification or structure whatsoever. Plato described it thus, through the words of Diotima, in the *Banquet*:

> A beauty whose nature is marvellous. . . . This beauty is first of all eternal; it neither comes into being nor passes away, neither waxes nor wanes; next, it is not beautiful in part and ugly in part, nor beautiful at one time and ugly at another, nor beautiful in this relation and ugly in that, as varying according to beholders . . . [it will be seen as] absolute, existing alone with itself, unique, eternal, and all other beautiful things as partaking of it.

In the light of our knowledge today, we find that the Way of Beauty is, in practice, much less hierarchical, much more varied and unpredictable than Plato thought. Moreover, Plato largely undervalued the experience of beauty in nature and art, and also the hidden paradoxical beauty in the prosaic, the coarse, and the painful. However, his main point is unquestionably valid: Beauty has a formidable, liberating effect on the human spirit.

We may verify Plato's hypothesis by studying the aesthetic experience in the real lives of great artists. All genuine experience of beauty begins with confidence in one's own judgment and close contact with one's unique sensitivity. That is our point of departure. We then move on to the complementary ability of empathy—getting in touch with other beings and identifying with them. A section on nature follows, because identification with the wonders of the natural world is a primary source of enjoyment and learning in this path. We then give attention to the many modes in which creative people use memory and imagination as fundamental resources in their work. Two sections—on the discovery of innocence and the transformation of pain—deal with the nonrational aspects in the Way of Beauty. The final topic—inspiration—shows in greater detail the dynamics of creativity.

Let us begin now with a specific experience of beauty. Anton Chekhov, the Russian dramatist, arrived in Venice in the summer of 1891 and there (as we can read in his letters) he spent several blissful days. The canals, St. Mark Square, "as smooth and clean as a wooden floor," the palaces of the doges, everything stirred in him the same strong emotions he would feel with music. He was conscious of an "extraordinary beauty":

> And the evenings! Good God in heaven! Then you feel like dying with the strangeness of it all. You move along in your gondola. It is warm, calm, the stars gleam. . . . There are no horses in Venice, and so the silence is that of the countryside. All about you drift other gondolas. . . . Here is one hung about with little lanterns. In it sit bass viol, violin, guitar, mandolin and cornet players, two or three ladies, a couple of men—and you hear singing and instrumental music. They sing operatic arias. What voices! You glide on a bit farther and again come upon a boat with singers, then another; and until midnight the

> air is filled with a blend of tenor voices and violin music and sounds that melt one's heart. Merejkowski [a Russian writer], whom I met here, has gone wild with rapture. It is not hard for a poor and humble Russian to lose his mind in this world of beauty, wealth and freedom.

We see a combination here of Chekhov's particular aesthetic sensitivity, the newness of the place for him as a foreigner, and the enchantment of Venice. Perhaps this description has a somewhat touristy air about it; but we should not undervalue it. We can see in it two main characteristics: the "losing of the mind"—the release from one's familiar way of thinking—accompanied by the "melting of the heart"—the "dying" or fading away of all the structures that normally encumber the psyche. Into this wider space of awareness enters the Self.

Chekhov was thousands of miles away from home. Distance and novelty may have helped him to forget himself. Beauty, however, also may be perceived in the ordinary home setting, or just around the block. The Italian poet Giacomo Leopardi notes:

> On my walks alone through the town the most delightful sensations and beautiful images are awakened in me when I look inside of rooms through their open windows. These rooms would not have the same effect on me were I to look at them from the inside. Is not this a picture of human life, a picture of its pleasures and delights?

These words show how fragile the aesthetic experience can be—a slight shift in viewpoint, and it is all over. We also see how a commonplace scenery can suddenly change to reveal an unexpected charm.

Now let us take a look at the experience of an interpreter, the conductor and composer Leonard Bernstein. His words describe how beauty enables us to transcend our personal world, and yet be even more present to ourselves at the same time. For him, conducting a big orchestra is the most powerful experience of love:

> At the end of such performances, performances which I call good, it takes minutes before I know where I am—in what hall, in what country—or who I am. Suddenly, I become aware that there is clapping, that I must bow. It's very difficult. But marvellous. A sort of ecstasy which is nothing more and nothing less than a loss of ego. *You* don't exist. It's exactly the same sort of ecstasy as the trance you are in when you are composing and you are inspired. You don't know what time it is or what's going by.

At a much more fundamental level, the principle that beauty opens the mind has at times been taken up in psychotherapy, though many possibilities in this area are still undiscovered. Beauty—especially the beauty of music—evokes serenity, speaks to our feelings in much more profound and effective ways than therapeutic verbiage, and reveals new ways of thinking and being. Creation is even more beneficial than mere enjoyment. Learning to draw, paint, or make sculptures is useful because it encourages self-expression in clients, teaches them a new skill, and ultimately allows them to produce pleasing forms. Being creative, even at a very elementary level, harmonizes the mind.

We would be wrong, however, in thinking that the Way of Beauty is only ease and delight. One of the traps to be avoided in this Way is, first of all, aestheticism—the divorce of beauty from other values such as solidarity, intelligence, or justice. Aestheticism becomes a way of isolation from others and estrangement from oneself. We see an instance of it in John Ruskin, the great English art critic of the nineteenth century. There can be no doubt that Ruskin traveled a long way on the path of beauty. Read his letters, and you will find wonderful examples in the observation of nature and art. His travels in Italy have provided us with enchanting watercolors of Venice and other cities, as well as drawings of rocks, trees, even hailstones, all testifying to his keen perception of beauty everywhere. Ruskin had an extraordinary facility for genuine aesthetic experience, but this very ability occasionally betrayed him. Once he was in Bologna, drawing a woman with a baby in her arms. Merely looking at the light and shade in the folds of her dress made him ecstatic. In a letter, Ruskin describes his delight. Then, incidentally, he mentions another fact: the baby, wrapped in those beautiful folds, was dying of hunger. Here we find beauty and ecstasy—but no heart.

Another danger pertaining to each of the Ways, but more pronounced in the Way of Beauty, is mental disintegration. When consciousness expands, countless possibilities open up. However, the ability to integrate new feelings, images, and ideas must grow apace. Otherwise, the result is madness. A case in point is Robert Schumann, the German composer, who at the end of his life was haunted by terrifying hallucinations. His wife Clara wrote in their *Journal Intime* that one day he heard every noise as wondrous, celestial music, but instead of delight he felt only horror. The following night Schumann had visions of angels alighting on him and bringing him divine inspiration. Then, toward morning, the angels changed into demons and wild animals, attacking and threatening him with every form of suffering, and causing him to cry out in pain. Surely other factors were involved in Schumann's psychosis, but his excessive sensitivity played a major role.

The crisis of duality is another pathological phenomenon found in all of the Ways but especially prevalent in the Way of Beauty. The envisioned beauty—pure, perfect, impossible—contrasts painfully with the coarseness of the ordinary world. The exquisite harmony of the transpersonal levels seems to mock the clumsiness of our limited and imperfect existence. This contrast, when extreme, produces depression and despair.

In the specific area of artistic creation, the crisis of duality often coincides with the torment of the blank page, blank canvas, or raw marble. How can I, as an artist, translate into sounds, shapes, or words the vision of overwhelming beauty I have been able to glimpse? How can I give it public, definitive expression? Monet felt this problem was causing him to become "furiously mad"; Van Gogh was hypnotized by the blank canvas, which seemed to say to him "You can do nothing"; Thomas Mann's creative efforts found comfort in repeating the words Flaubert expressed when writing *Salammbô*: "My book causes me much suffering." Chopin was quite calm as long as he was improvising but had trouble when he had to recapture the original thought in all its details to write it down. One of his pupils wrote about him: "He spends days of nervous strain and almost frightening desperation. He alters and retouches the same phrases incessantly and walks up and down like a madman."

Finally, too much beauty can become intolerable. It is natural that beauty should overwhelm us. But when the aesthetic experience is too intense and the personality insufficiently stable, one is in trouble. Strange as it may seem, enjoyment—not only rage, despair, or terror—can violently upset personality balance. Consider the French composer Hector Berlioz. One evening in Paris, as a young man, he saw *Hamlet* for the first time. Shakespeare, says Berlioz, revealed to him the "paradise of art," and made him understand the meaning of "true greatness" and "true beauty." However, this awareness so shocked Berlioz that he became restless and could no longer work or sleep but instead fell into depression. All this beauty was too much. A long period of distress followed, until one day he wrote his *Élegie*, where he felt he had reached a rare truth of musical expression. His torment was over, the crisis resolved.

Estrangement, depression, despair, and even madness are possible dangers along the Way of Beauty. Insight, ecstasy, and enthusiasm are among its rewards. It is worthwhile, from time to time, to ask oneself: What would my life be like with more beauty?

TO BE ONESELF

Sooner or later, we all come up against the old dilemma, What is and what is not really beautiful? Perhaps some "immortal masterpiece" left us cold—and how guilty we felt! Maybe we liked a painting only after reading the painter's name, or enjoyed a piece of music after we knew it was Beethoven. Or perhaps, uncertain of our judgment, we allowed others to guide us in choosing a house, a car, a suit. Afterward, we felt uneasy—deep down we knew we had lacked faith in ourselves. At other times, when we really saw and appreciated beauty, the feeling born in us was sincere—it was unmistakably our own. After all, what can be more indisputable than pure enjoyment?

True aesthetic experience is uncompromising and spontaneous. It is never brought about by tradition, logic, opinion, or social pressures. In fact, the basic condition in the Way of Beauty is freedom from such impediments. This is a rigorous search for the ultimately genuine response.

But what an easily hindered search it is! Everyone wants beauty, and this is where the trouble starts. Relationships between people, productive activities, economic interests, and power relationships—in one way or another, all are influenced by how we perceive beauty. It is inevitable that society, rather than let beauty be prey to transitory and unpredictable criteria, should set up and impose stable and commonly accepted standards. This pressure is one of the many prices we pay for living in a civilized community. It is in most cases tacitly accepted, partly from indifference and partly because challenging such pressure would elicit anxiety and tension.

Those who want to follow the Way of Beauty must break

away from cultural dictatorship and move out into a no-man's-land where everything is new and unknown. Only then can they find beauty in its full force. They must learn to live outside of stereotypes and worn-out attitudes, and free themselves from any bonds—roles, ties, ideologies, interests, or habits—that might hold them back. They must learn all over again, without fear or hesitation, to be themselves.

This is how the caricature of the eccentric artist was born (the same applies for the rebel and the misfit). Artists may seem strange because, through their wish to be true to themselves, they do not fall in with others' expectations and their culture's accepted roles. Let us listen to Flaubert's words:

> A thinker must have neither religion nor country, nor even a social creed. . . .
>
> To participate in anything, become part of an entity, fraternity or group, even to assume a title of any sort, is to dishonor and lower ourselves. . . .
>
> When we are caught up in life, we will not see it clearly, we will suffer from it as well as enjoy it too much. The artist, in my view, is a monster—something outside of nature.

Alongside the common criticism that they are eccentrics, artists have at times been accused of narcissism. They are seen as totally absorbed in their own world, oblivious of real problems and real people, preoccupied only with their fantasies and visions. More often than not, however, theirs is not so much narcissism as careful inner listening. And, rather than being unproductive and superfluous, this attitude is the very source of their best work.

Indeed, those treading the Way of Beauty become finely tuned instruments, able to sense minimal variations. They perceive color and line, sound and space, with the keenest attention; they feel the subtle emotions no one is able to describe. They substitute the guidance of their own sensitivity, coupled with an exceptional degree of alertness and exactitude, for the slavery of social consensus. Truly open to beauty, they do not blindly follow choruses of assent or dissent but instead look with their own eyes, hear with their own ears, feel with their own hearts.

In advising a young friend, the American writer F. Scott Fitzgerald affirmed the idea that a good writer is able to find within what no one else has thought or dared to say. Thus, he increases the "range of human life." However, in having to decide what to say and what not to say, he is tempted to go along with general consensus—a much easier and more relaxing alternative. A deceitful voice inside warns him that the subjects to which he most personally relates are of little general interest. Fitzgerald went on:

> But if the man's gift is deep or luck is with him, as one may choose to look at it, some other voice in that crossroads makes him write down those apparently exceptional and unimportant things and that and nothing else is his style, his personality—eventually his whole self as an artist. What he has thought to throw away or, only too often, what he has thrown away, was the saving grace vouchsafed for him.

This capacity of inner listening is the basic precondition for creativity. For how else could inspiration come unless you trust it? You listen. You capture an inner impulse. It is compelling, or perhaps it is faint and vague. Should you follow it? You let it guide you into territories as yet unknown, you break new ground. You believe in your impulse. You believe yourself. The French writer Simone de Beauvoir described her method of writing:

> I keep to my plan, but I leave room for my moods; if I suddenly want to write a certain scene, treat a particular theme, I do so, without holding myself rigidly to a pre-established sequence. Once the main body of the book exists, I willingly trust myself to chance. I let my thoughts wander, I digress,

> not only sitting at my work, but all day long, all night even. It often happens that a sentence suddenly runs through my head before I go to bed, or when I am unable to sleep, and I get up again and write it down.

Sometimes withdrawal from consensus to find oneself again becomes physical withdrawal from society. In order to break away from all social influences at once, one simply packs up and leaves. The French painter Paul Gauguin, for example, found his truest inspiration after he had left his own land and gone to live in Tahiti. A short time after his arrival he described his return to innocence:

> Between me and the sky there is nothing more than the wide roof of pandanus leaves, light and diaphanous, where lizards live. In my dreams I can imagine the free space above my head, the great celestial way, the stars. I am far, far removed from those prisons which European houses seem to be. . . . Little by little civilization is leaving me. I am beginning to think with simplicity. . . . I live a free life. . . . I shun the artificial and identify myself with nature, knowing that tomorrow will be like today, as free and beautiful. Peace is taking possession of me.

Much more often, however, moving away is not necessary —all one needs is solitude. The idea is to unlearn old patterns, move away from society's myths and lies, and regain lost innocence. Solitude is a most effective working tool. Petrarch, the Italian poet, sums up its advantages well:

> [Solitude] is not out to deceive anyone; it does not pretend nor embellish; it has nothing to hide and invents nothing. It is completely naked and without adornment; it knows nothing of shows or the applause which poisons the mind. It has God as sole witness of its life and actions; as such it places no

confidence in vulgar, deceptive people, but only in its own conscience.

Petrarch was not alone in finding solitude congenial. But being fully oneself is also possible while mixing with other people. The French painter Gustave Courbet, more of an extrovert than Petrarch or Flaubert, would often paint in the presence of other people, while still recognizing his need to express his uniqueness. These were his instructions to pupils:

I. Do not do what I do.
II. Do not do what other people do.
III. If you do what Raphael did in the past you will not survive. Suicide.
IV. Do what you see, what you feel, what you want.

Being oneself in no way implies isolation or antagonism to others and to the world. Goethe's motto in his *Dichtung und Wahrheit (Poetry and Truth)* was "to preserve my internal nature according to its peculiarities, and to let external nature influence me according to its qualities." In Goethe's words we see a beautiful synthesis in which self-discovery coincides with openness to all living beings. A twofold attempt is at work here. First: "I endeavored to free myself inwardly from all that was foreign to me." Second: "[I endeavored] to regard the external with love; and to allow all beings, from man downwards, . . . to act upon me, each after its own kind." To shake off what is alien to us, to open ourselves up to the universe —these are the secrets in the Way of Beauty. The result can be sublime: "Thus arose a wonderful affinity with the single objects of nature, and a hearty concord, a harmony with the whole."

If we are to embark on this enterprise, we will require courage, confidence, and openness. Courage, because we will be exploring and expressing the unknown in ourselves, thereby opposing commonly accepted norms. Confidence, because we will say yes to everything that lives in us, simply because it exists. And openness, because we will be cultivating the mental ability to notice everything, even seemingly irrelevant details.

Umberto Saba, the Italian poet, wrote about "literary honesty." In his view, to be original we need to be humble and honest—only thus can we be receptive to fresh inspiration. Saba recounts that one day he was passing by a mirror, and in a glimpse he saw himself as different from how he had always imagined himself to be. Immediately he recalled a dream that had revealed aspects of himself about which he had never known. Then he wrote this poem:

> I thought dreaming was play;
> but dreams are a fearsome God,
> one who only unmasks
> what truly I am like.
> *(Credevo sia un gioco sognare;*
> *ma il sogno è un temible Iddio*
> *è il solo che sa smascherare*
> *l'animo mio.)*

When he reread this poem a few days later, Saba felt something did not sound quite right; the verses did not truly express what he wanted to say. The words *fearsome God* did not agree with the idea of dreaming, since a dream is not a vindictive divinity. Repeated attempts only served to take him even farther away from his original insight. He then retraced, one by one, the steps of the poem's development, noting even the most insignificant details. At this point he remembered the mirror episode that had been the starting point. Saba decided to replace *fearful God* with *mirror*. This was the result:

> I thought dreaming was sweet;
> but dreams are a mirror, making me whole,
> revealing

my intimate truth.
(Credevo sia dolce sognare;
ma il sogno è uno specchio, che intero
mi rende, che sa smascherare
l'intimo vero.)

A far more beautiful version. Saba says he felt as though a speck had been removed from his eye. This version's success lies in its honesty; whereas the other analogies, such as God and judge, were more high-sounding, the mirror metaphor was the one most faithful to what his actual experience had been. According to Saba, one must always show "heroic meticulousness" in noticing any discrepancy between the thoughts and the words, and never try to make it appear that one's inspiration is "more vast and transcendent than it happens to be." This faithfulness to one's mental process, says Saba, should look more like scientific research than literary activity.

There have been artists who were able to clearly describe how they lost the innocence of beauty. Thomas Traherne, the English religious poet who lived in the seventeenth century, has left us wonderful descriptions of his childhood visions, in which the dusty stones on the street were as precious as gold, children playing appeared as jewels in motion, old people seemed like immortal cherubim, and eternity was everywhere present. Then Traherne was able to see in the world "a mirror of infinite beauty."

As he grew up the vision faded. But he did not forget, and later wondered about its loss. He realized that his capacity for ecstasy had been eclipsed by people's customs, by a host of irrelevant matters, by wrong desires, and by an ill-guided education. Small and vulnerable like most children, he had followed the authoritative dictates of grown-ups and had become alienated from himself. Thus he learned the "dirty devices of this world," and he began to prefer a smart suit, a gilded book, or a drum. "As for the heavens and the sun and stars they disappeared," recalls Traherne, "and were no more unto me than the bare walls."

Being oneself is a rare and difficult path to tread. It is far easier to fit in with the accepted order. In one of his letters Van Gogh muses on what constitutes the recipe for mediocrity. We forfeit our uniqueness

> by compromising and making concessions, today in this matter, tomorrow in another, according to the dictates of the world—by never contradicting the world, and by always following public opinion!

EMPATHY

In order to see beauty it is essential that we allow ourselves to be touched by things and by people, and that we be able to identify ourselves with them. All barriers between us and the world have to go. When looking at the beauty of a flower or listening to music, we are no longer ourselves: we become the flower, we become the music.

The situation, however, is often quite different. The kingdom of our personal individuality is a citadel in which we are securely locked. Messages from outside reach us through the filter of our beliefs and emotions, our defenses are deployed, the treasure is safeguarded, and the secrets are concealed. Even when seemingly confused and powerless, our personality is much sturdier than it looks—strong, in fact, even in its weakness. Its disorganization is highly organized. This system we have built through the years becomes our home, we look at reality from its perspective, and nothing else remains for us to see or hear.

Empathy is the exit from this watertight system. For however short a time, it delivers us from our mental habits and brings us into contact with new values and meanings. Thus we feel the vitality of other beings and learn to enjoy what is beautiful in various forms of existence. For only if we allow ourselves to be shaped and changed by what is alien to us, rather than remaining rigid and untouchable, will we succeed in perceiving beauty. According to Shelley, this is the poet's intrinsic ability, and the basis on which both love and the aesthetic perception rest:

> A man, to be greatly good, must imagine intensely and comprehensively; he must put himself in the place of another and of many others; the pains and pleasures of his species must become his own. The great instrument of moral good is the imagination. . . . Poetry strengthens that faculty which is the organ of the moral nature of man in the same manner as exercise strengthens a limb.

Surely, all living beings are capable of empathy. If someone becomes injured, we try to help. We identify with children, friends, sports champions, people in the news—even with our pets. When we watch a film or read a novel, we identify with the protagonists: it is we who fight their battles, live their loves, and enjoy their triumphs. But at times empathy becomes a conscious attitude rather than an instinctive response. Thus, stepping out of our citadel, we sight new, surprising landscapes; we feel vulnerable, but also closer to others. If, in turn, someone else enters into our world, weeps and laughs with us, and understands what we think and dream about, we feel regenerated, and we have won a victory over loneliness.

But make no mistake. Our empathy is rarely total. Our identification with other people is often imperfect and based on self-interest. In putting ourselves in their shoes our aim is actually to meet some need of our own—and to leave intact the whole panoply of our personality structure. In fact, learning to acquire new perspectives is a goal on the way to maturity, and a lifelong job.

From our earliest years we learned to see the world from our point of view. As children, for instance, we believed that when we closed our eyes other people would not be able to see us. Then, little by little, we understood that other viewpoints existed. Yet this development is seldom complete, and our identification with others is often fleeting, superficial, and fortuitous. In creative people, however (not only on the Way of Beauty, but in the other Ways as well), the empathy evolves until it reaches the very pinnacles of intelligence and love.

Empathy seems to be the opposite of the capacity we saw in the previous section—being fully oneself. Is there a contradiction between the two? It might look as if there were. One attitude reinforces what we are; the other weakens it. Here is a description of empathy in the words of John Keats:

> A Poet . . . has no Identity—he is continually . . . filling some other Body—the Sun, the Moon, the Sea and Men and Women.
>
> When I am in a room with People if I ever am free from speculating on creations of my own brain, then not myself goes home to myself: but the identity of every one in the room begins so to press upon me that, I am in a very little time annihilated.

We would be mistaken, however, if we were to consider empathy a weakness. Keats's passive attitude is actually deliberate and conscious and is accompanied by full contact with his feelings and sensations. Certainly, excessive empathy and the premature transcendence of one's individuality are a danger. Unlike Keats, one may identify with others without first knowing what it is to be oneself. But that is pseudoempathy, for how can we truly live in others if we do not first develop our personal sensitivity? To be capable of experiencing the joys, pains, dreams, and secrets of another, we must first know our own. Ultimately, there is no real conflict between being ourselves and identifying with others.

Empathy is an act of inner discipline and a temporary surrender of our personality. It is a conscious act: we become impregnated with the other until we know his or her essence. The great French writer Honoré de Balzac wrote:

> Listening to people talking I could enter into their lives, feel their tattered clothes on my back, walk with my feet in their shoes; their desires, their needs, all passed into my soul, or my soul passed into theirs. It was the dream of a man awake.

In addition to being a vehicle for awareness, empathy is also an instrument for transformation. It temporarily changes the structure of our being by taking us to an entirely different wavelength. Thus we overcome the attitude of judging, one which more than any other erects barriers between us and our neighbors. Indeed, when we become the other we forget our own criteria of judgment. Moreover, empathy frees us from our private maze and shows us new and unenvisaged modes of being, greatly enhancing our imaginative and creative abilities.

In empathy one may not only use the mind but the entire organism. The French poet Paul Valéry wrote that his close acquaintance Edgar Degas had the ability of perfectly reproducing anyone he had observed. When he felt lonely, says Valéry, Degas went out and spent his evenings traveling on open tramways. One evening, immersed in the crowds, Degas observed a woman who stepped in the tramway and sat near him:

> She ran the fingers over her dress to uncrease it, contrived to sit well back so that she fitted closely into the curve of the support, drew her gloves as tightly as possible over her hands, buttoned them carefully, ran her tongue along her lips which she had bitten gently, worked her body inside her clothes, so as to feel fresh and at ease in her warm underwear. Finally,

> after lightly pinching the end of her nose, she drew down her veil, rearranged a curl of hair with an alert finger, and then, not without a lightning survey of the contents of her bag, seemed to put an end to this series of operations with the expression of one whose task is done.

Degas, writes Valéry, mimed this woman without missing the smallest detail. With these words in mind, it is easier to understand his "ironing woman" or the "danseuses," their muscular tensions and nervous movements. Whoever wants to paint an image cannot represent it without first being it.

At other times empathy can occur at a mental or spiritual level—as a communion of spirits. Such was the case with Niccolò Machiavelli, the Italian writer, who, in a famous letter to his friend Vettori, tells of how during the day he would waste his time playing dice at the tavern, but in the evening he would come home, enter his study, leave his everyday clothes at the door, and wear "royal garments." Then he would imagine himself to be in the company of great people from ancient times. This, wrote Machiavelli, was his favorite occupation, the one for which he felt he was born, "and during four hours I do not experience any boredom, I forget all cares, I do not fear poverty, death dismays me not: I transfer myself entirely in them [the great people of ancient times]."

Here empathy reaches a climax, leading an individual beyond the anxieties of life and the terror of death. These words describe precisely the transpersonal realm, and the metaphor of the change in clothing illustrates the detachment from ordinary consciousness and the ascent to a world immeasurably richer, more serene, timeless.

Empathy, however, is no solitary event. On the contrary, it is that which permits artists to feel and express the most concealed needs, pains, and dreams of a whole society. The aim of the poet, says Pablo Neruda, is to embody hope for the people, to be one leaf in the great tree of humanity:

> My reward is the momentous occasion when, from the depths of the Lota coal mine, a man came up out of a tunnel into the full sunlight on the fiery nitrate field, as if rising out of hell, his face disfigured by his terrible work, his eyes inflamed by the dust, and stretching his rough hand out to me, a hand whose calluses and lines trace the map of the pampas, he said to me, his eyes shining: "I have known you for a long time, my brother." That is the laurel crown for my poetry, that opening in the bleak pampa from which a worker emerges who has been told often by the wind and the night and the stars of Chile: "You're not alone; there's a poet whose thoughts are with you in your suffering."

By allowing other beings to live within us, we feel that each individual is linked to the whole. For if your pain is also mine, and I recognize your joy in myself, every barrier between us is dropped. "We weep with those who weep, laugh with those who laugh and suffer with those in pain," said Leon Battista Alberti, thereby expressing the nature of the universal human being as it was understood by the Italian Renaissance.

Universal human beings—men or women—are at ease with the whole cosmos, and nothing in all creation is alien to them. They are inwardly open to any experience, ready to adapt to any situation without reservations or prejudices. They are universal because they are available, and will not let themselves be limited by roles, history, or creed. They have access to every possible experience and recognize in themselves the many different aspects of life, male and female, rational and irrational, dark and light. They are also universal because they find in the capacity to suffer and rejoice with all other living beings the ultimate affirmation of their humanness. More than just being a Renaissance ideal, they are the human beings of the future, who will be born into a worldwide civilization, beyond the barriers that separate people and nations.

Empathy, then, is an expansion of consciousness. Through

this faculty we are able to become one with trees, ants and elephants, birds, rivers and seas, children and old people, men and women, suffering and joyful people, rainbows and galaxies. Thus we become able to breathe and live in other beings—or to find them within ourselves as in a living microcosm. In the most unlikely face, in the strangest of situations, in the remotest places, we discover ourselves. And once we reach this point there need never again be the feeling that we are strangers in a strange land.

NATURE, TEACHER OF TEACHERS

Think of the thick black smoke from chimneys rising to the sky. Think of the litter that strews our beaches, the soda cans, cigarette butts, and picnic leftovers cast about a meadow. Think of cement constructions devastating green scenery, billboards profaning a landscape, or loud, vulgar music booming into the sounds of nature. Think of the machines that uproot trees and raze a forest to the ground, of seas and rivers swamped with pollution. Think of these disasters, and you will feel a violation, because the wrong done to nature is also done to you.

When nature is intact and innocent, on the other hand, we discover ourselves in it, because its innocence and purity exist in us too. In everyday speech the term *natural*, as opposed to *artificial*, means "genuine, having its own rhythm, in harmony with itself and everything around it." The word contains an appeal to our sense of trust—if it is natural, you can rely on it. Nature never makes a mistake.

These are common feelings, but some people experience them with a greater intensity. They faithfully love and study nature, dedicating their lives to it. Thus they find a supreme justice, a perennial beauty unchanged by fashions. Perhaps they have known the "Adamic" ecstasy of nature as an earthly paradise abounding in a thousand wonders. Thus they have found their transpersonal realization. The Way of Beauty always passes through nature.

Many painters and poets teach us this art. We have to let nature take us by the hand, and allow ourselves to be stripped of all artifice. It is hard to be false when surrounded by unspoiled nature. There is no place here for human affectations. When standing on top of a mountain or precipice, when walking through a field in bloom or watching the night sky, it is more difficult to keep up pretensions, either with others or with ourselves. When we turn to nature, greed and fear vanish; our defenses drop and we rediscover the sincerity we so easily lose in our everyday struggles and compromises. And through an unfathomable resonance, the spontaneity of nature reawakens the spontaneity of our innermost being.

Paradoxically, in the natural world we lose ourselves, dispensing with our habitual mind-set, and we discover ourselves in a glimpse of true happiness. When the French poet Alphonse de Lamartine was fifteen, and studying at Jesuit school, he would look forward to the clear, moonlit nights. As soon as everyone else was asleep, he would climb up to the dormitory window and look at the valley patched with meadows, framed by trees and pale blue mountains rising between the mists of distant waterfalls:

> I would perch for hours on that window ledge, lovingly contemplating the horizon of silence, solitude and recollection. My soul flew out with inexpressible transport to those meadows, forests and waters; and it seemed to me that being able to roam there, as my eyes and thoughts were already roaming, must be the greatest happiness imaginable.

William Wordsworth, too, describes in a letter his journey through the Alps, in which his mind crossed over "a thousand dreams of happiness":

> Among the more awful scenes of the Alps, I had not thought of man, or a single created being; my whole soul was turned to him who produced the terrible majesty before me.

We sense a numinous presence in Wordsworth's description. (*Numinous*, from the Latin *numen*, 'god', is a word first used by the German philosopher Rudolf Otto, to describe the feeling of awe and mystery evoked by the presence of divinity.) Nature is impersonal. With its vast sceneries, its age-old rhythms, and its infinite inventiveness, it carries us beyond our narrow sphere of concerns and reveals to us its "terrible majesty."

How does one look at nature? Studying the lives of those who have understood it best, we consistently find the same attitude: to look, free of aims or prejudices, noticing everything. Henry David Thoreau, who made solitude his lifestyle and nature his path, wrote pages in his diaries that serve as an excellent guide to contemplation:

> That aim in life is highest which requires the highest and finest discipline. How much, what infinite leisure it requires, as of a lifetime, to appreciate a single phenomenon! You must camp down beside it for life, having reached your land of promise, and give yourself wholly to it. It must stand for the whole world to you, symbolical of all things. The least partialness is your own defect of sight and cheapens the experience fatally. Unless the humming of a gnat is as the music of the spheres, and the music of the spheres is as the humming of a gnat, they are naught to me.

Contemplation enabled Thoreau to assimilate nature into himself. For instance, when looking at a stream (his diary tells us), he sensed it flow through his veins. When lost in the mist, he felt as though he were being carried back to the origin of creation. He perceived the cosmic order in the hexagonal structure of all snowflakes.

And what about the human body? Many painters and sculptors have been enthralled by its agility and graceful movements. The French impressionist painter Pierre Auguste Renoir, for instance, only had to look at it to be transported into a "state of grace." Others have been fascinated by the energy and buoyancy of the limbs, by the sensuality emanating from the skin, or by the intelligence shining in the eyes. Some—like Michelangelo, who used it as an architectural model—have discovered in the body the ideal structure. Many have seen in it the mystery of being a man or a woman, or the expression of a reality that transcends both the body itself and its individuality.

The human body, like the rest of nature, must be studied with the highest degree of attention. For instance, the French sculptor Auguste Rodin would look at the human body in order to assimilate its lines and movements. While drawing, he would focus not on the picture, but on the body, so as not to interfere with his own vital flow:

> I am accustomed to having my models wander naked about the studio. They walk or rest. . . . I familiarize myself with all of their movements. I constantly note the association of their feelings and the line of their bodies, and by this observation I accustom myself to discover the expression of the soul, not only in the features of the face, but in the entire human form.

Anyone closely studying nature will learn much from it. In the colors and shapes of flowers, in the fields of grain, in the forests, in the birds and insects, in the streams and rivers, in the waves of the sea, and in the clouds, the countless treasures of the universe await discovery. A cursory look, however, is not sufficient. We need a patient eye, and a lot of hard work. When patience and discernment are lacking, the perception of nature will be false. It may be a literary image of nature, overloaded with cultural references; an anthropomorphic model, built in our own likeness; a sentimental caricature; a Hollywood stage set; or, finally, like the photographs in glossy magazines, nature may appear a little *too* perfect.

For anyone breaking free of his or her own prefabricated ideas, nature becomes a true teacher. "Those who took as guide anything other than Nature herself, the teacher of teachers, laboured in vain," wrote Leonardo da Vinci. And the German artist Albrecht Dürer, who depicted crystal-clear scenes and scrupulously exact bodies, is uncompromising: "Art is steeped in nature; whoever can extract it will possess it." The Chinese painter Chang Tsao, who painted landscapes in which humanness is seen in the perspective of infinity, said that "outwardly, nature has been my teacher, but inwardly I follow the springs of inspiration in my heart." Camille Pissarro, the French impressionist painter, echoed his words: "One must have only one master—nature; she is the one always to be consulted." In the contemplation and study of nature, artists of all times—and a number of scientists as well—have extracted from her sounds, shapes, ideas, and inspiration, as though from an immense mine of creative material.

Day after day, the observation and study of nature in all its aspects reveal its unimaginable riches. The French painter Paul Cézanne often insisted on the importance of this work. In a letter to his son, he talked about the profusion of material that nature offers to the trained eye:

> Here on the edge of the river, the motifs are very plentiful, the same subject seen from a different angle gives a subject for study of the highest interest and so varied that I think I could be occupied for months without changing my place, simply bending a little more to the right or left.

John Constable, the English landscape artist, saw nature as a system of hieroglyphics that the painter must learn to decipher. Its meanings are not immediately apparent, but the more one persists, the more one discovers. A friend of his wrote that he sometimes saw Constable admiring a tree with the same ecstasy of joy he felt as when he took a child into his arms. For Constable, painting was not only an art but also a branch of natural science to be pursued as a search for universal laws. The path of true painters, according to Constable, is extremely slow, but the painstaking study of nature offers them the opportunity of being original by revealing aspects and qualities never seen or drawn before by others:

> The landscape painter must walk in the fields with an humble mind. No arrogant man was ever permitted to see nature in all her beauty. . . . The art of seeing nature is a thing almost as much to be acquired as the art of reading the Egyptian hieroglyphics.
>
> Selection and combination are learned from nature herself, who constantly presents us with compositions of her own, far more beautiful than the happiest arranged by human skill.

In the slow perfection of seeing into nature's depths, an unexpected fact emerges—what once seemed familiar becomes alien. This happens because instead of looking at a personal concept of nature one looks at nature itself. Then the richness it contains becomes an invitation to a disquieting adventure into the unknown, at times into the sublime. Shapes take on surprising new senses. English artist and poet William Blake said, "I can look at a knot in a piece of wood till I am frightened at it." Petrarch saw the outlines of a threatening face in the trunk of an oak, in a clear fountain, or in the clouds. When looking at rocks, French painter Eugène Delacroix saw human forms, bulls' heads, elephants, and fantastic creatures, and in the tidal patterns on the shore he perceived trees or the lines of a tiger's skin.

Such effects are not only visual but can also be auditory.

In the silence of night Tchaikovsky would hear a deep bass note that he imagined coming from the movement of the earth through space; Debussy heard the song of mermaids in the splashes of sea waves; and Wagner, in a fever, had the inspiration for his prelude to the *Rheingold* when listening to the flow of an imaginary river.

Nature is able to enchant, teach, and astound us. And we, all too often alienated from a world once ours and now violated by pollution, lost as we are among a thousand illusions, and prisoners in an artificial universe, must never forget it.

MEMORY AND IMAGINATION

Memory: the ability to re-create the past. We recall shapes and colors, faces and emotions, voices and smells. Past events live again in us, perhaps even more intensely than when they initially occurred. Through memory, beauty is remembered and savored again.

Imagination: the ability to create. Breaking the bonds of the known, the mind generates new forms—ideas or images, music or prose, mathematical insight or mechanical invention. A gifted imagination, rather than re-creating, *originates* beauty.

At first, memory and imagination may appear to be two antithetical functions of the human mind, but an accurate examination reveals that they belong to a wide continuum. Imagination feeds on stored experiences and then elaborates on them. Memory may take some liberties and assimilate fantasy. In this section we will examine both functions.

When memory is born out of careful observation, it abundantly supplies ideas and inspiration; thus, it can be a true source of aesthetic experience. For this purpose memory must be as rich with detail as possible, and faithful to reality. Dürer, for example, always so thorough in his observations, used his memory as a working tool. He regarded his experiences as a data bank to which he might turn at any time:

> No one can create a beautiful image from the imagination if he has not filled his mind with many pictures from life . . . a skilled artist does not have to copy every image from life: he need only produce what he has gathered from the outside world over the years.

Memory may also surface when a present sensation evokes a similar one we had in the past, and from the coincidence of the two an aesthetic emotion is born. For instance, the French novelist Marcel Proust had only to place his foot on uneven polished pavement and was instantly taken back to a similar pavement he had walked on years before in Venice. The gondola waiting for him on the canal, the precious hours spent there, the happiness of those days—these recollections he relived all at once. This type of memory made him feel as if he were "free from the order of time":

> We have only to re-experience in the present a sound once heard or a smell once sensed, and immediately our "I," which may have seemed dead for a time, but was not completely dead, comes back to life as it takes in the celestial nourishment offered to it.

On other occasions, memories emerge unsolicited and may be even more intense than the corresponding past experience. The American novelist Thomas Wolfe had extraordinarily vivid memories that continually engrossed him in myriads of different sensations. One day, for instance, he was sitting in a café in Paris, watching people pass by, when he suddenly remembered, of all things, an iron railing in Atlantic City:

> It was all so vivid and concrete that I could feel my hand upon it and know the exact dimensions, its size and weight and

> shape. And suddenly with a flash of blinding discovery, I would realize that I had never seen any railing that looked like this in Europe. And this utterly familiar, common, and perhaps ugly thing would suddenly be revealed to me with all the strangeness and wonder with which we discover a thing which we have seen and lived with all our lives and yet have never known before.

Some individuals consciously move back and forth along the road to the past, reinforcing each milestone on the way. Dim images take on substance and import, and their outlines, once vague, become sharp. Forgotten riches are discovered. Digging out such memories means familiarizing ourselves with the stuff of which our lives are made—a material often of inestimable aesthetic and creative value. For it is *our* reality, it happened to *us*; and even if it happened a long time ago, it is still warm and alive, possessing the unmistakable mark of direct experience. When Goethe proposed to some friends that they drink a toast to the memory of past days spent in good company, he added:

> Everything great, beautiful and significant that we encounter in our lives must not be regarded as if it were being transfused into the heart from the outside. The moment it arises it weaves itself into the heart, becomes one with it, forges in us a new and better me; and it continues, perpetually creating, to live and act in us. There is no such thing as a past that has to be recalled with longing—only a perpetual present, which blends with the heightened elements of the past.

We all have memories, of course. What counts is the use we make of them:

◇ Some people turn memory into torture, wallowing in regret, resentment, or nostalgia.

◊ Memories can also be a frame that defines and limits any possible event. The present is only seen in terms of former experiences, and the future is nothing but a further reflection of the past.

◊ For others, memories are like messy, dusty objects piled up in a cupboard. All living relationship with them is gone.

◊ Others still vigorously deny their memories, thereby divorcing themselves from the past.

Leaving aside these negative possibilities, we also find that, as in the examples quoted earlier, a fertile attitude toward one's past is possible. Memories are contemplated, studied, elaborated, enjoyed and, above all, assimilated. Thus they contribute to the wholeness of a person's history and inner world. In this practice we encounter the fundamental *principle of economy* recurrent in all transpersonal Ways: Nothing is wasted or regarded as useless; each inner or outer event is the stuff we have to work with, and an opportunity for growth.

Besides being an archive—albeit a living one—memory can be a laboratory where past events are skillfully manipulated and developed. Delacroix wrote in his diary that creative artists are engaged in the selection and elaboration of their memories:

> I admired the soul's involuntary work, recalling happy moments, discarding and suppressing whatever may lessen the delight of the happiness in which they were lived. . . . The great artist concentrates the emphasis, omitting useless, distasteful or trivial details.

Degas affirmed a similar concept:

> It is all right to copy what you see, but it is much better to draw what you can no longer see except through your memory.

> This is a transformation in which imagination collaborates with memory. All you reproduce is what struck you.

Memory, according to Gauguin, is the occasion for stripping the past of all that is inessential. He elaborates:

> When you observe a scene and remember it later in your studio, do not paint the scene exactly as it was, but rather its essence. Imagination simplifies what the eye sees, rejecting all non-essential details. Shapes become the clear lines of a geometric architecture, and tones are reduced to the seven colors that make up white light.

Clearly we have moved away from memory as a complete and exact reproduction, to memory as a function that selects and re-creates. This is only one step away from imagination —the faculty that takes off from recorded reality in order to combine the various images available to it, changing them to invent new ones.

We all imagine; and we can all conceive of imaginary events to torment, console, distract, deceive, or enrage ourselves. We can also use our imagination to prepare for action. The cook preparing a dinner, the crook premeditating a crime, the driver determining which road to choose, the mechanic carrying out a repair, or the surgeon performing an operation—all use imagination; that is, the capacity to create a subjective representation of the world and of their action in this world. All action is born in the laboratory of the imagination.

Some people who take this faculty to its greatest heights become able to experience its extraordinary power. In the words of Leonardo da Vinci we sense his marvel at the fact that all things are possible:

> If the painter wishes to see beauties that charm him, it lies in his power to create them, and if he wishes to see monstrosities that are frightful, buffoonish, or ridiculous or pitiable, he can

> be lord and creator thereof; and if he wishes to produce inhabited regions or deserts, or dark and cool retreats from the heat, or warm places for cold weather, this too is within his reach.

When Georgia O'Keeffe discovered that painting did not necessarily mean imitating and that she could freely invent what she wanted, she felt this was a basic personal skill—"like learning to walk." It was an ability that would enable her to change shapes and colors at will, to create worlds never before seen. During the days when this inspiration came to her, O'Keeffe thought she would go mad, as so many new, strange shapes filled her mind. So visualization became for her a basic tool: "I know what I am going to do before I begin, and if there's nothing in my head, I do nothing."

Creative imagination does not belong solely to the realm of art and beauty. With its ability to combine and recombine diverse elements, to break rules, to represent even unlikely and disconcerting situations, to create possible universes, it is an instrument of great relevance to science and technology. Here are some examples:

- ◇ By means of his "thought experiments" (*Gedankenexperimente*), Albert Einstein would create imaginary situations and draw aid from them for theoretical work. For instance, he once imagined an observer in free fall from the roof of a house. This person—though subject to gravity—has no gravitational field around him. In this way Einstein arrived at the "happiest thought" of his life—that gravitational and electric fields have a relative existence. And this thought led him to formulate his theory of general relativity.
- ◇ Biologists Francis Crick and James Watson had to use their utmost powers of visualization for representing the double-spiral three-dimensional DNA molecule. "[On

the night of discovery] I happily lay awake," wrote Watson, "with pairs of adenine residues [an amino acid that forms part of DNA] whirling in front of my closed eyes."

◊ Heinrich Schliemann, the archaeologist who discovered the ancient city of Troy, visualized people and activities as they must have been thousands of years before while looking at ruins, and he used these images to guide him in his exploration.

The story of Nikola Tesla, the great Slavic-American inventor, deserves special consideration. From childhood Tesla suffered from an unpleasant condition: whenever anyone spoke of an object in his presence, he would involuntarily visualize it, and so intense, clear, and persistent was the image that he felt he could touch it with his hand. In order to rid himself of this obsession, Tesla began deliberate visualizations of all sorts of subjects, among them landscapes, towns, people, and journeys in unknown lands. He wanted to master this ability and to be capable of excluding undesirable images. At about seventeen, Tesla began to devote himself to his inventions and discovered that he had a new method at his disposal:

> Before I put a sketch on paper, the whole idea is worked out mentally. In my mind I change the construction, make improvements, and even operate the device. Without ever having drawn a sketch I can give the measurements of all parts to workmen, and when completed all these parts will fit, just as certainly as though I had made the actual drawings. It is immaterial to me whether I run my machine in my mind or test it in my shop.

Just as it supports speculative and inventive work, imagination is also an aid to meditation. In a Tantric visualization, for instance, you imagine a divinity seated on a solar disk, which in turn rests on a lunar circle on a lotus flower in the heart area. You then imagine becoming small, identifying with this divinity, and experiencing its state of consciousness. Lastly, you imagine this divinity becoming a single point until it disappears—and nothing else is left but the ecstasy of emptiness.

In the Tibetan tradition the subject of visualization is not regarded as a neutral, passive form, but as a living entity with a psychospiritual force of its own. And accurately so. Everything the mind creates, as though by some magic spell, comes to life. The French painter Jean Baptiste Corot wrote:

> After my excursions, I invite my friend Nature to spend a few days under my roof. Once she is there, I give free rein to my imagination. Brush in hand, I start out in the forest of my studio. I hear right there the songs of birds and the murmur of the branches agitated by a ghost wind.

Jung called this phenomenon the "reality of the soul" (*Wirklichkeit der Seele*). Internal images are not inert, but have an independent life of their own, and are as real as living beings. What Jung had discovered as an instrument for inner exploration was not unfamiliar to many artists—Corot among them—who had already been using it as a means for increasing their creative powers. In some cases images themselves appear and speak, as another French painter, Jean Auguste Ingres, tells us: "A figure or a group continually appear to me as ghosts and say 'make me like this, make me like that.' " Wagner would hear the "spiritual voices" of the protagonists in his operas. And Johann Schiller, the German dramatist, found that the characters he created became "living beings who confide [to me] their joys and trials."

In these and other ways, imagination activates our psychological and transpersonal resources. First, by inventing possible worlds, the mind learns to transcend its own stereotypes. Second, when we use our imagination we are not bound to duties or stopped by obstacles—we are free to play. No longer weighed down by the real world, we can let chance and the unconscious do their part—above all, we can laugh. At the same time, inhibitions loosen up and the resources that everyday life perennially restricts can reach full flower. In this way imagination becomes a way to freedom.

INNOCENCE AND MYSTERY

What would the world be like if it appeared to us without the filter of our thoughts—completely bare? What if faces, bodies, objects, houses, trees, and machines were to become things we had never seen before, inexplicable and unnamed? What if a friend's countenance became nothing more than a series of lines and colors, if words reached our ears as sounds without meaning, if the most common places were transformed into enchanted scenes—as though everything we have ever known had vanished?

Frightening. We would wander around aimlessly, lost in strangeness. Dangerous—we could not survive for a moment in such an improbable place. But think again. Perhaps, stripped of all predictability and staleness, the world would appear in its virgin state. Prodigious. Every perception would be a discovery, and, free of all we believe and know, we could find beauty.

To forget all we believe and know may be impossible. But we can, at least for a miraculous moment, put all explanations aside and look with innocent eyes. For many, this is where the Way of Beauty leads—striving to look at the world as though one had never seen it before. It is a search for pure perception. Monet once told a friend that he wished he had been born blind and then suddenly gained his sight, so that he could paint his subjects with totally fresh vision:

> When you go out to paint, try to forget what objects you have before you, a tree, a house, a field or whatever. Merely think,

> here is a little square of blue, here an oblong of pink, here a streak of yellow, and paint it just as it looks to you, the exact color and shape, until it gives you your own naïve impression of the scene before you.

On other occasions, naked perception happens unexpectedly. One sunny autumn afternoon, the Italian painter Giorgio de Chirico, convalescing from a long illness, was sitting on a bench at Piazza Santa Croce in Florence. He looked around —Dante's statue, the church facade, the marble of the buildings and fountains: "I had the impression that I was seeing those things for the first time, and the composition of the painting revealed itself to my mind's eye." Thus was born *The Enigma of an Autumn Afternoon*, a wonderful metaphysical painting full of magic and ageless nostalgia.

More than a trend in art, innocence is an intrinsic aspect of inspiration. We also find it in certain sculptors. Henry Moore, for instance, liked to contemplate objects stripped of their familiar connotations:

> Suddenly the most commonplace objects came to have for me such significance that they no longer existed as just objects, but as shape and form in space. It has been the same with nature and the human figure, both sources of unending interest for me.

This innocence, this nudity, can lead to very high states. Eugène Ionesco, the Rumanian-born dramatist, spoke in his diary about seeing familiar reality as if it were unfamiliar. He describes the following experience:

> I sometimes wake up, become conscious, realize that I am surrounded by things and by people, and if I look closely at the sky or the wall or the earth or the hand writing or not writing, I have the impression that I'm seeing it all for the first time. Then, as if it were the first time, I wonder, or I ask,

> "What's that?" I look all round me and I ask, "What are all these things? where am I? who am I? what do these questions mean?" And then sometimes a sudden light, a great blinding light floods over everything, obliterates all meaning, all our preoccupations, all those shadows, that's to say all those walls that make us imagine limits, distinctions, separations, significances.

Others delve inside for the eternal child living in a universe forever new. Perhaps better than anyone else, the Italian poet Giovanni Pascoli has expressed the beauty of the innocent eye:

> Poetry is seeing something that everyone looks at without ever seeing, so that when the poet points it out, it seems that he has discovered it and people can say: "It didn't take much to see it!" Yes, but you didn't see it! You were unable to either think it or express it, and he, the little child *[il fanciullino]*, is the Adam who gives a name to everything he sees and feels, discovering everywhere the most ingenious resemblances and relations.

In innocence abides love. Those traveling along the Way of Beauty have an erotic attitude toward life. Like all true lovers, they do not ask for explanations or impose conditions, but simply embrace life in its mystery. Do not ask them for a formula or theory—that is not their specialty. Look, instead, at the way they face the world. Rather than trying to decipher it, they open themselves to it and perceive beauty in its subtlest and most poignant aspects.

But watch out! Reason has strong defenders. After all, this precious faculty offers a number of advantages: it provides coherent explanations, foresees the future, gives a sense of security, resolves contradictions, and makes life easier to tackle. Reason is one of the greatest triumphs of human evolution and a highly refined tool at our disposal. But let it step over its boundaries, and it will explain away the mystery.

Allow it to take over, and all passion, all enthusiasm, will vanish—and so will beauty.

Anyone who wants to experience beauty must first of all abandon all preconceived ideas and perceptual frameworks. This stage in the process—however unsettling—is necessary, and each person goes about it in his or her own way. Some, like Baudelaire, propose quite radical measures:

> You need to become drunk. It all depends on this, it is the only key to the problem. In order not to feel the terrible burden of time weighing you down to the point of oppression, you must unremittingly get drunk. But on what? Wine, poetry, or virtue—the choice is yours. Yet drunk you must be. . . . In order not to be slaves or victims of time, you must get completely drunk!

Baudelaire's stance was not just the expression of a particular artistic fashion. Actually, the rejection or transcendence of reason can assume different faces and may at times resemble a method. This is the case with Schiller, when, in a famous letter, he advised letting ideas flow freely without first subjecting them to scrutiny. A literary critic friend, who was also a frustrated artist, had asked him for advice on how to get past a blockage. Schiller replied:

> Apparently, it is not good—and indeed it hinders the creative work of the mind—if the intellect examines too closely the ideas already pouring in, as it were, at the gates. Regarded in isolation, an idea may be quite insignificant, and venturesome in the extreme, but it may acquire importance from an idea which follows it; perhaps, in a certain collocation with other ideas, which may seem equally absurd, it may be capable of furnishing a very serviceable link. The intellect cannot judge all those ideas unless it can retain them until it has considered them in connection with these other ideas. In the case of the

> creative mind, it seems to me, the intellect has withdrawn its watchers from the gates, and the ideas rush in pell-mell, and only then does it review the multitude.

It is important to notice that Schiller does not do away with the intellect. Reason does not necessarily have to be destroyed; it must simply be held in check. Schiller's method is the same as the one used in brainstorming—namely, producing a large quantity of thoughts and images and not stopping the flow with critical judgments. These should come later.

Thoughts, then, can adulterate experience. In fact, explanations can spoil everything. Just listen to someone trying to explain lovemaking, the starry sky, or a joke. But how difficult it is to refrain from the vices of intellect! And how often do we try to interpret and formulate! Reason is a reassuring prop, and without it we feel anxious. So we are ever ready to find ideas to neatly label an intolerably puzzling universe. It is hard to accept that our life may be a mystery—that the whole thing goes on without any explanation. If we ponder on it for a while, we get dizzy, perhaps even fall into terror.

In the Way of Beauty, on the other hand, we embrace life's ambiguities without having to interpret and explain them. We *enjoy* the mystery and transform its terror into awe. Obscurity and ignorance are positive factors here, because they help us to get rid of cumbersome opinions and relish the enigma. For some this attitude is a way of being; for everyone it is an invitation to take one's thinking less seriously. The result is the ability to accept life's contradictions without feeling we have to resolve them. Keats calls it the "negative capability":

> Several things dovetailed in my mind & at once it struck me, what quality went to form a Man of Achievement especially in Literature & which Shakespeare posessed *[sic]* so enormously —I mean *Negative Capability*, that is when man is capable of being in uncertainties, Mysteries, doubts, without any irritable

reaching after fact & reason . . . with a great poet the sense of Beauty overcomes every other consideration, or rather obliterates all consideration.

Usually we manage to fully conceive or feel only one reality at a time: joy or pain, good or bad, dark or light, movement or stillness. The simultaneous presence of two opposites is difficult to endure, because it is illogical, and our mind, with its tendency to sort things out, finds it easier to choose just one of the two polarities at any given time: How can a person be both malicious and charitable at the same time? How is it possible to experience simultaneously both pleasure and pain? Yet life is full of surprising contradictions the rational mind cannot unravel. This is its richness.

Yale University's Albert Rothenberg conducted a research project (published in the book *The Emerging Goddess*) based on more than one thousand interviews with creative artists and scientists. According to his findings, an essential factor in creativity is "Janusian thinking" (named after Janus, the ancient Roman god with two faces looking in opposite directions), the ability to conceive actively two opposing ideas or images, or to feel two opposing emotions.

Many great works of art contain these contradictions: Leonardo's *Mona Lisa*, for instance, is both virginal and sensual, gentle and cruel; Rembrandt, in many of his paintings, succeeds in uniting a strong, preternatural light with an almost complete darkness; the dramatic tension of Picasso's *Guernica* depicts the slaughter of war bombings in a scenery that is both external and internal, suggesting that war permeates our inner and outer worlds.

A fine example of Janusian thinking comes from Mozart. He once spent an enjoyable evening with some friends in Leipzig. It had been a happy meeting, and his friends, after much insistence, managed to get him to write a few notes as a memento of their cheerful time together. In just a few minutes Mozart produced two three-part canons, one light and sparkling, the other characterized by the poignant sadness of farewell. Imagine the surprise of Mozart's friends when they learned that the two canons were to be performed simultaneously, representing the enigma of life as a microcosm of opposing feelings. Mozart himself was moved and, bidding them a hasty good-bye, disappeared into the night.

THE TRANSFORMATION OF PAIN

Have you ever seen a young child hurt himself? Perhaps he was running along, tripped, and fell down. But he did not cry immediately. For a few moments his eyes registered a puzzled look. He had encountered something he could not understand. Then the neurological reality of pain overcame him, and he cried—partly because we, who had hastened to reassure him, provided him with our anxious interpretation. As adults we are far more prepared for the emergency of pain. We have at our disposal a host of past experiences and tested reactions to draw on, not to mention philosophies and superstitions, bandages and aspirins. What happens to children, however, also applies to us, albeit to a smaller degree: suffering thrusts us into the realm of the inexplicable.

When suffering becomes too strong, it imprisons our attention with its impersonal brutality, kills our enthusiasm, turns our hopes into empty dreams. Its incomprehensibility undermines the psychophysical structure we have come to know as ourselves. In pain, be it mental or physical, we are faced with the concrete possibility of our own annihilation.

But just when the personality structure is about to crumble and disintegrate, an unexpected chink of light opens up. "Suffering is permanent, obscure and dark," said Wordsworth, "and shares the nature of infinity." Pain shows us our limitations and at the same time evokes in us a desperate desire that we might transcend them. The realities that have long absorbed us now crumble, become unreachable, or turn out to be illusory. We are rudely turned away from them, and we shift our focus on survival. Our sensitivity is stretched to the limit, and our most deeply ingrained certainties are shattered. Distressed and overwhelmed, we yearn for a peace we cannot anywhere envision. And yet these very hardships may reveal to us the greatest potentialities of the human spirit.

Often pain brings only destruction. We become rigid, fall into despair, die a thousand deaths, never rising from the ashes. Senseless and terrible as it may be, however, pain can also become a Way to transpersonal realization. In each path described in this book pain is present and can be changed into grace. In the Way of Beauty the transformation of pain is described most clearly. Like a coarse, dark rock that breaks in the middle and shows a stupendous crystal at its center, pain may bring insight and even peace.

Consider Oscar Wilde. Accused of homosexuality, abandoned by everyone, imprisoned and condemned, alone and suffering, he had an enlightenment which he described in a long letter to his lover, subsequently published with the title *De Profundis*. The beginning of his prison term was horrendous. He was put through "every possible mood of suffering." Then, little by little, Wilde began to understand the meaning of pain. Before being sent to prison he had sought only pleasure and had avoided suffering at all costs. But he had not been truly rooted in life. Now, after terrible struggles and difficulties, he was able to "comprehend some of the lessons hidden in the heart of pain."

Before his imprisonment Wilde had told a lady friend that there was enough suffering in a small London lane to show quite clearly that God did not love humanity: "Now it seems to me that Love of some kind is the only possible explanation for the extraordinary amount of suffering that there is in the world." Wilde, alone in betrayal and poverty, was able to say in the darkest moment of his life:

> He who can look at the loveliness of the world, and share its sorrow, and realize something of the wonder of both, is in immediate contact with divine things, and has got near to God's secret as anyone can get.

Wilde fell to his point of greatest despair when, during his imprisonment, they took his oldest son away; but precisely this event enabled him to understand that the only solution was "to accept everything." In the same letter he also wrote:

> Since then—curious as it will no doubt sound to you—I have been happier. It was of course my soul in its ultimate essence that I had reached. In many ways I had been its enemy, but I found it waiting for me as a friend.

We see here that acceptance of reality as it is coincides with being oneself—being the "soul in its ultimate essence." When we accept what is, we accept joy and pain, good and bad, without distinction. This is the ability to enter into a full and direct relationship with everything in life.

Acceptance is the key word here. If we resist pain, it will tighten its hold and strengthen its intensity; but the moment we fully accept it, we may overcome its stern dictatorship. The path from resistance to acceptance, however, is long and slow. In the case of Beethoven, we find at first a bitter, ambivalent resignation. In 1801 he wrote in a letter: "I have cursed my pain many times already. Plutarch has shown me the way of *resignation*." The pain of deafness, to this man who lived for music, was appalling, and forced him to isolate himself in a silent universe, cut off from society. It brought him to the brink of suicide. But in 1802 he wrote in the *Heiligenstadt Testament* that "*patience* . . . is what I must choose as my guide." As the years passed, a deeper transformation took place in Beethoven. In 1818 he wrote in a letter: "We finite creatures with an infinite spirit are born to suffer and to rejoice. One might almost say that the chosen few receive their joy through pain." The life of Franz Schubert followed a similar course. Some of his greatest compositions sound happy and carefree, yet a few years before his death he wrote in his diary: "My creations have been produced by my understanding of music and by my sorrow."

Like a ruthless intruder, pain digs, pushes, and breaks into our being. But the travail involved produces a new capacity for insight. In his early twenties, the great Spanish cellist Pablo Casals experienced a crisis in his life. He saw the misery around him—selfishness, oppression, and violence—and he hated it. He felt desperate. Although he was already a celebrated musician, he felt he could no longer surrender to music. Eventually Casals understood that music could not by itself be a final answer, but could become meaningful only if it became "part of humanity." This conviction, born out of despair, remained with him for the rest of his life and was the foundation for his art:

> To see people gathered in a concert hall came to have a symbolic significance for me. When I looked into their faces, and when we shared the beauty of music, I knew that we were brothers and sisters, all members of the same family. Despite the dreadful conflicts of the intervening years and all the false barriers between nations, that knowledge has never left me.

Once pain has been faced, it is easier to rise to a wider, perhaps universal, perspective. One is no longer bound by one's own taste or personal advantage. According to Rodin, for the artist

> all is beautiful . . . because he walks forever in the light of spiritual truth. Yes, the great artist, and by this I mean the poet as well as the painter and sculptor, finds even in suffering, in the death of loved ones, in the treachery of friends, something which fills him with a voluptuous though tragic admi-

> ration. At times his heart is on the rack, yet stronger than his pain is the bitter joy which he experiences in understanding and giving expression to that pain. . . . When he sees people everywhere destroying each other; when he sees all youth fading, all strength failing, all genius dying, when he is face to face with the will which decreed these tragic laws, more than ever he rejoices in his knowledge, and, seized anew by the passion for truth, he is happy.

What is true of pain equally applies to ugliness. A vision of beauty that excludes the grotesque and the hideous is weak and false. Far more real and convincing is the vision that accepts ugliness and, in some way, transfigures it. One need only think of Dante's *Inferno*, or Bosch's haunted scenes, or Goya's *Caprichos*, to name but a few well-known and widely divergent examples.

A true artist's temperament can be recognized in his or her attitude to what is ugly or banal. Neither repulsion nor judgment is present, nor, on the other hand, morbid pleasure; rather, we find an attitude of universality—the ability to love and appreciate even the most unlikely subject—as in the "old women's throats," to which Leonardo devoted hours of attention and observation for several of his drawings; or even in cigarette butts, in which the Russian painter Wassily Kandinsky claimed he could see "the secret soul" of things. To be interested in everything, to find beauty everywhere—what a feat! Van Gogh wrote in a letter:

> It is true that I am often in the greatest misery, but there is a calm pure harmony and music inside me. I see drawings and pictures in the poorest huts, in the dirtiest corner. And my mind is drawn toward these things by an irresistible force.

Things are seen with new eyes. Thus Pissarro viewed beauty in the streets of Paris:

> It is very beautiful to paint! Perhaps it is not aesthetic, but I am delighted to be able to paint these Paris streets that people have come to call ugly, but which are so silvery, luminous and vital.

Monet, irritated by the criticism that the mists he painted were not a suitable subject for a picture, responded by painting the smoke from a train. According to Renoir's son, Monet set up his easel "like a tyrant" at Saint Lazare station, and, though not as yet a well-known artist, convinced the astonished station master of the Western Rail Company to stop the trains at his request, burn extra coal so they would produce more smoke, and change the timetable so that he could catch the sunlight on the billowing steam: "It is an enchantment, a true phantasmagoria," Monet told Renoir. Who would have guessed that train smoke and a dirty station would generate a masterpiece?

O'Keeffe, on the other hand, was interested in bones: bones from antelopes, horses, cows, and mules living at the edge of the New Mexico desert. She collected a great many samples and used them to produce a whole series of paintings:

> To me they are as beautiful as anything I know. To me they are strangely more living than the animals walking around—hair, eyes, and all with their tails switching. The bones seem to cut sharply to the center of something that is keenly alive on the desert tho' it is vast and empty and untouchable—and knows no kindness with all its beauty.

Beauty is visible to those who have looked at life in all its forms, including the most horrifying or the most inane. Contact with beauty, indeed with the whole of the transpersonal world, is authentic only when it is preceded by contact with the shadow—the pain, the ugliness, and the banality in the inner and outer worlds. Were this not the case, every transpersonal experience would be nothing more than an escape.

Let us think of two people who have been together in a warm and truthful relationship. They have seen each other's weaknesses, shared difficulties, lived with what they could not stand in the other, and learned to accept it. They have shown trust at times when it would have been easier to doubt and withdraw; they have taken the risk of loving each other with no guarantees or superficial promises. In this way friendship and love are born and grow. Our relationship to life can be the same: Joy and pleasure enrich it; pain may mold and deepen it.

Indeed the more we examine the difference between ugliness and beauty, or between pain and joy, the more mysterious it seems. In the most intense pain, such as that of a woman giving birth, there can be ecstasy. The greatest joy, in contrast, can be so intense as to be painful. Similarly, the finest example of beauty can suddenly appear false and empty, just as stark ugliness can arouse sympathy and, with its sincerity, relief. Beauty and pleasure refuse to have a definitive form. With their mysterious, almost ironic dance, they elude us, suddenly confronting us with their opposite, reappearing again where we least expect them. We see this in the case of Russian novelist Fyodor Dostoyevski who, during the moments immediately preceding an epileptic fit, would experience a feeling of great happiness:

> I feel a happiness impossible in ordinary conditions, unknown to others. I feel a perfect harmony in myself and my surroundings, and this sensation is so strong that for a few moments of such bliss I would give ten years of my life . . . perhaps my whole life.

Wordsworth provides another example. When reproved by a reader for writing a poem about an "idiot boy," an inappropriate and distasteful subject according to the conventions of the day, he replied in a letter that when he sought to contemplate lofty and virtuous subjects, he had a reaction of disgust.

When, on the other hand, he saw a retarded child (and the way in which such a child was treated in lower-class families), he felt he was in the presence of "the great triumph of the human heart" and "the strength, disinterestedness, and grandeur of love."

INSPIRATION

It arrives with an independent life of its own, overflowing with energy and newness. So light and unexpected, it seems to come from nothing and then disappear into nothing. Apparently generated by a superior intelligence, it is indescribable and can only be represented by metaphors, such as lightning, the breath of life, a divine voice. Creative inspiration shows us the thousand faces of beauty. In Greek mythology the nine Muses, the goddesses of the arts, are given to song and have free spirits. With the inspiration they bestow, they take away the problems and pain from whomever they wish, making that person happy.

These are strong words indeed. Yet with the study of inspiration we touch the farther reaches of the mind. Read the descriptions of its beneficiaries—or of those close to them—and you will find evidence of extraordinary happenings. We will mention just two of them, beginning with Gauguin:

> Where does the creation of a painting begin, where does it end? When intense feelings merge deep within a person and the idea bursts forth as lava from a volcano, is this not the emergence of a suddenly created work, brutal if you want, but certainly great, and bearing a superhuman aspect?

In Gauguin's words we sense the numinous power of creation. Chopin's work, described by George Sand, shows us how inspiration arrives with total autonomy and ease:

> His creation was spontaneous, miraculous. He found it almost without seeking or anticipating it. It arrived at his piano unannounced, complete, sublime, or it would sing itself in his head during a walk, and he would hurry back to play it on his instrument.

The experience of creative inspiration sounds quite similar to enlightenment, as we know it from the descriptions of mystics and sages throughout the centuries. There are, however, two important differences. First, creative inspiration has its roots in a particular culture and employs that culture's material and language. Enlightenment, in contrast, has very few or no cultural connotations and is the same for all societies at all times.

Second, enlightenment is the recollection of a truth one has always known, a return to a timeless source. In creative inspiration, conversely, we see the extraordinary inventiveness of the spirit, its ability to continually come up with something new. Enlightenment and inspiration belong to the same family of events but they are not identical.

Inspiration appears not only on the Way of Beauty but also in a variety of other fields—from sports to science, from religion to gastronomy, from business to everyday life. In the Way of Beauty, inspiration has an aesthetic quality whereby beauty is perceived and expressed on a higher plane, and with greater intensity and coherence.

As with many other transpersonal phenomena, inspiration has both exceptional and ordinary versions—namely, the inspiration of great geniuses and the inspiration of all common men in everyday life. And although the difference between the two is enormous, it is useful to note what they have in common.

We all have moments of inspiration—a sudden flash of understanding, the solution to a problem, a state of grace, a brilliant thought about a future project, a witty remark. These are the moments in which we experience original thoughts accompanied by euphoria and energy, sometimes even by manic agitation; we forget about tiredness, and spontaneity puts an end to doubt and tension.

Inspiration comes whenever it wants—even at the most unlikely times and in the most inappropriate situations. Often it arrives bit by bit. Therefore it must be anchored, and this is where a most valuable item makes its appearance: the notebook.

Much could be said about the notebook. Tchaikovsky would scribble down a melody on the first piece of paper that came to hand. French painter Toulouse-Lautrec would take out his sketch pad at any moment, during a walk or in the middle of a conversation, jot down a few lines for a second or two, and then return it to his pocket. Another French painter, Georges Braque, always kept an exercise book within reach so that he could seize any thought that passed through his mind and record it. He said that his sketch pad was as useful to him as a cookbook when one wants to prepare food: he would open it and the smallest sketch would provide him with the starting point for a painting.

Beethoven jotted down in notebooks his musical ideas, but often made use of any scrap of paper available, even a restaurant bill. Most of the musical ideas jotted down in his notebook never materialized into a significant work. As one leafs through them, wrote his biographer Alexander Thayer, one discovers countless compositions in draft form, musical masterpieces that have remained in the limbo of the unfinished.

The use of the notebook serves as a reminder that the transpersonal world is subtle and elusive—and can be forgotten in a moment. How many valuable ideas, one wonders, have been glimpsed and have then sunk into oblivion? In the lives of creative people moments arise when gleams appear, then vanish forever. That is why *anchoring* is a must.

Creative work is a full-time job. It happens during the day when we are awake, but it goes on at night as well in the world of dreams. To dream means to fancy improbable realities, to bypass limits and logic, or to envisage the fulfillment of our highest hopes—all aspects of inspiration. Indeed, many artists have used dreams as a starting point. One of the most interesting examples is Keats. One day he was reading the fifth canto of Dante's *Inferno*, where the two lovers, Paolo and Francesca, in the circle of the lustful, were blown all over the place by a violent wind. The following night Keats dreamt that he himself was in that part of Hell. But, instead of horror, the dream gave him "one of the most delightful enjoyments" he ever had in his life. Keats recounts his vivid dream:

> I floated about the whirling atmosphere as it is described with a beautiful figure to whose lips mine were joined as it seem'd for an age—and in the midst of all this cold and darkness I was warm—even flowery tree tops sprung up and we rested on them sometimes with the lightness of a cloud till the wind blew us away again—I tried a Sonnet upon it—there are fourteen lines but nothing of what I felt in it—o that I could dream it every night. . . .

It is a very beautiful sonnet, but the complaint of being unable to fully express the ineffable is a recurring one. We find it, for instance, in the Italian composer Giuseppe Tartini, who heard in a dream the Devil playing the violin. When he awoke he wrote his *Devil's Trill*, which, though exquisite, could not faithfully reproduce the extraordinary melody he had heard.

Here are additional examples of creative dreams:

- ◊ Albrecht Dürer had a nightmare about a great flood and painted it when he woke up.
- ◊ Igor Stravinsky dreamed of a young gypsy girl playing a violin to amuse a child, and he included the motif in his *Petit Concert*.
- ◊ Robert Louis Stevenson completed *The Strange Case of Doctor Jekyll and Mr. Hyde* after receiving the inspiration in a dream.

◊ The Italian painter Giambattista Piranesi, while suffering from malaria fever, had a nightmare in which he saw his famous *Prisons*.

◊ Wordsworth, who had fallen asleep on the beach reading *Don Quixote*, dreamed of an Arab in the desert offering him a shell. When he put it to his ear, Wordsworth could hear "a wild prophetic blast of harmony" in an unknown tongue, which, nevertheless, he could understand. He then used this image for one of his poems.

These are the moments of grace—in sleep or in wakefulness. After inspiration, however, comes perspiration: the finished product calls for skillful application. Speaking to Eckermann, Goethe described this fundamental distinction in the creative process. About the truest and highest inspiration, he said, one can do nothing. One is chosen by a "divine influence" to which one yields as an instrument, even though one may deceivingly believe one is in control. Then, at a lower level, one gives the work of art its visible substance, and that is where aptitude and mastery come into play. Goethe elaborates by means of example:

> Thus the first idea for *Hamlet*—the moment when the spirit presented itself as unexpected intuition to the poet's soul and when, in a state of exaltation, he saw each circumstance, the characters and the overall plot—came to Shakespeare as a pure gift from above, without his having any immediate influence over it, although the ability to receive such inspiration naturally presupposes a spirit like his. But the arrangement of the different scenes, the dialogues between the characters, all of this was within his power, so that he was able to spend on them as many hours, days and even weeks, as he liked.

Goethe could not have known how Shakespeare's mind worked, but his hypothesis is useful, and we have every reason to believe that he was actually speaking about himself and his own creative process.

Another basic phenomenon involved in the process of inspiration is unconscious elaboration. Many creative people have discovered that if they leave their work alone for a time, they return to find it modified and enriched, as though another part of their mind had been working on it while they were busy with other matters. Entrusting their material to this invisible coworker in the unconscious is for them a highly effective and energy saving method. Brahms, who took ten years to complete his first symphony, wrote:

> Once I have found the first phrase of a song, I can shut my book there and then, go for a walk, engage in some other activity, and perhaps not even think about it for months. None of it is lost, however. If I then go back to it, I can be sure that it will have taken shape. Then I can truly start working on it.

Beethoven wrote in a letter that he would carry a theme around in his head for years, and at some point it would begin to "develop and grow in all directions." Renoir maintained that one needed to put the canvas away and let it rest; little by little the work would then ripen itself. Joan Miró, the Spanish surrealist painter, said that the "spark" came to him when he least expected it:

> The most unlikely incident can suggest to me the most unexpected ideas. Then, when the first moment has passed, I put the canvas aside, facing the wall, and get on with living; but I can feel that it is "working" within me. Then one day, and in a completely unexpected way, something is triggered: I pick up the painting again and, as I proceed, a host of new ideas come in. It is like being in a state of drunkenness. This is how I paint.

This process of elaboration is as useful for creation as it is for the artist's inner balance. As both Berlioz and Wagner agreed when they met, one's impressions of life are assimilated as in the digestive process. And while we are using physiological analogies, we should also consider images of childbirth used by several artists in describing their work. Speaking of his short story "The Sentence" ("*Das Urteil*"), Kafka wrote in his diary: "It came out of me as though in childbirth, covered with dirt and slime, and my hands were the only ones able and willing to take hold of its body." In Schumann's words about the birth of his first symphony, the physiological realism is equally precise:

> The overall sketch was produced in four days, and that means a lot. But now, after many sleepless nights, comes the labour. I feel like a young woman who has given birth to a baby: light, certainly, and happy, but suffering and aching.

For creativity to bloom, one condition seems to be essential in most cases—the pursuit of perfection. Bad news for bunglers and amateurs: inspiration rarely comes without hard work and a tireless search for perfection. Where others stop—overlooking a discordance or an incoherence, pretending everything is all right, bored with thinking and retouching, happy with a mediocre product—is where the truly creative start their work, trying again and again, refusing to accept compromise, relentless in their dissatisfaction and their care for detail. Here is Brahms's advice to a young composer:

> Put it [a musical piece] aside, then keep coming back to it, and work on it many times until its completion as a finished work of art; until there is not one note too many nor too little, nor a line you can still improve. . . . You see I am lazy, but I never let go of a work once I have started, till it is perfect, unexceptionable. One should never forget that, by truly perfecting one

piece, one learns more than by starting ten and leaving them half done.

What influence does an ideal of perfection have on the psyche? As innumerable psychotherapists never tire of repeating, an ideal can torment and even paralyze us. But for creative people an ideal is a end in itself, worth pursuing for its own sake, without aspiration to further rewards such as fame or riches. Perfection is itself the ultimate fulfillment. In the rare moments when one perceives it, the ideal gives a sense of rightness and completeness. Anna Pavlova, the great Russian ballerina, said:

> To strive tirelessly and at all times to reach one's goal—therein lies the secret of success. But what, actually, is success? I do not find it in the applause of audiences, but in the satisfaction of having realised an ideal.

The quest for perfection serves—in art as well as in ethics or in science—to stimulate our latent faculties, to guide us, to inspire us. An ideal elevates us and enlarges our perspective; without it, we would feel sad and empty. When it is present and alive, we have a vision, a dream that stimulates us to move forward. Wanda Landowska, the Russian musician, wrote about her work as a concert pianist:

> When I begin to dream up a new program, a fever of happiness seizes me. I want that concert to be an extraordinary event as the result of the atmosphere I hope to create. I spin an enchanted thread, a web that must envelop us all. I forget everything, all previous pains and torments, and I start anew. All day, all night I work, and I feel—I always do—that I need many more days and nights to modify, retouch, improve, and go deeper into the meaning of the works I play. Oh! The hours of folly, of oblivion, of happiness—my hours of work in the middle of the night!

> It is best to work the most difficult parts in the evening because they will ripen during the night.

Landowska's comments here are interesting, because they show the search for perfection to be a stimulus for unconscious elaboration—an implicit, vigorous demand for new ideas and new solutions. What is the difference, then, between the neurotic and the creative ideal? Whereas the neurotic ideal is a device for self-condemnation, the creative ideal is felt as our own. It is not an enemy that haunts us but a reality we love and care for more than anything else; it is an answer to our questions.

The search for perfection, however, should not interfere with subtle unconscious activity. In a letter to Pierre Bonnard, the French painter Henri Matisse shows how important it is to insist on perfection, and how equally important it is to stop:

> I never get to finish, I continually start all over again—after 40 sessions I have completed a sleeping figure which I started a year ago next January, and I have an unfinished still life which is already about a hundred sessions old, and since my return to Nice I work every day. Surely, our constant anxiety harms the unconscious work which habitually holds us while we are not in front of the easel. Once more, one has to wait.

Thus they persevere, those incorrigible perfectionists—they polish and revise, spend sleepless nights, overthrow everything to begin anew, without ever feeling quite content. And perhaps they will never be satisfied, because they have glimpsed a beauty that no form can express. Yet, without this elusive, undefinable beauty, there is no true art. In an interview the German contemporary composer Karlheinz Stockhausen spoke about beauty:

> It has always been a goal—my goal. Beauty should not be separated from the idea of perfection: however, human beauty

> in front of primordial, cosmic beauty is but a modest miniature. Cosmic beauty reveals itself in moments of grace, its principle is harmony, the exact equilibrium of the planets. . . . And it is precisely the supreme beauty of cosmic order which constitutes and encapsulates the vital nucleus of any authentic work of art.

What can we learn from these inspired people? Certainly not their talent, for that is unique and cannot be communicated. But we can glean from their methods and breakthroughs some useful points on creative work:

1. They place great importance on their inspiration and take a keen interest in it, realizing that any mental process regarded with interest grows and develops, whereas if it is ignored or treated with suspicion, it shrivels and dies.
2. They pay close attention to the twilight phenomena of the psyche, such as dreams and sudden intuitions.
3. They take hold of and record at once any elusive ideas, knowing how easily they may vanish.
4. They use the unconscious as a faithful, diligent helper, entrusting it with tasks and problems to solve, and later finding the work completed.
5. They relentlessly search for perfection.

2

The Way of Action

No action leaves us the same as before. Whether it be stealing or making a gift, heroism or eroticism, restraint or spontaneity, everything we do produces its mark on us. The murderer is stamped by his crime; the posture of a miser reveals his greed; the face of a benefactor radiates kindness. But in addition to its external manifestations, every action leaves a trace on the cellular record of an organism as well as in the deepest layers of the psyche. Just as streams engrave their course into the earth, so our actions mold our character. We are what we have done.

Whether we know it or not, we all are already familiar with this Way. For to live is to act—even breathing makes us part of life's process. We cannot help but be engaged in action. The choice of *what* to do, and *how* to do it, is nonetheless for us to decide. Will our action bring well-being to ourselves and others, or will it make its own poisonous contribution to the world's misery? Will it be mechanical, or will it spring from our conscious presence? Will we feel the force of circumstance or the freedom of responsibility?

In this path to the Self we will encounter individuals who have made of action an instrument of awareness and realization—people like Albert Schweitzer, Florence Nightingale, Mother Teresa of Calcutta, and Raoul Follerau, who have elevated action to its highest levels. And we will not overlook traditions, particularly Oriental ones, in which the experience of certain individuals has found its sublime expression in timeless laws. Thus we see how everyday action, even the most humble of tasks, can rise to the rank of a true yoga. Zen Buddhism, Taoism, and Hinduism have consistently shown that the way we do what we do can itself be a path to freedom.

Alas, human life frequently falls short of such peaks. Action is often an obstacle to inner development: through it we are hypnotized by events, seduced by success, or destroyed by failure. We become entangled in minor setbacks and lose ourselves in infinite details. In order to defend our ground, put right any damage, or pursue what we value, we keep generating the need for further doings, in an endless chain of activities. Yes, action can sometimes be the easiest way for us to lose sight of what really counts.

Fortunately, the opposite can happen too. Through action we can become more capable, stronger, freer. We can also learn. This has been the case ever since, in the early stages of human evolution, the quadrupeds that we were stood upright, leaving their hands free to act on the environment in an enormous variety of ways. Thus we learned new skills and took a decisive step in the evolution of consciousness. In ways large and small this phenomenon continues to operate in our everyday lives. Through involvement in action—be it cooking, fixing the car, or playing the violin—we develop new abilities and refine old ones.

Action overcomes the heavier side of our nature. Inertia often holds us back, and life becomes insipid and empty. Or else fear stops us. We dread being wounded or beaten. We are tempted to give up. Yet if, despite these difficulties, we engage in some form of action, whether we are beaten or not, we will have won a victory.

Action works upon objective reality. It is the means we have for affecting the world, communicating, and sustaining our own lives and the lives of others. In action we are able to express what we are. By refusing to act we abandon our potential in the gray, perpetual waiting room of unrealized projects. Action is the inexorably sincere measure of our abilities. We may make grandiose promises with our words, but actions cannot lie.

The most widespread and necessary form of all action is work. In other times and cultures, work was in harmony with the cycles of nature, and rather than abusing people it enhanced relationships among them. These times are perhaps lost forever. Nowadays, work often destroys playfulness and the joy of life, encouraging exploitation rather than collaboration, or substituting the slavery of the assembly line for the craftsman's pleasure in creating. Nevertheless, one fact remains: Work is the way in which a human being transforms chaos into order, gives meaning to his or her actions, and makes it possible for life to continue.

It is natural, therefore, that work should have become the first form of psychotherapy. Ergotherapy, long ago conceived by the Greek physician and writer Galen ("work is nature's best physician and essential to human happiness"), was rediscovered in Europe at the end of the seventeenth century as an effective way of treating the mentally ill. The principles of ergotherapy are simple, full of common sense, and valid for all people. In work

> the mind is diverted from its obsessions and is used constructively;
>
> the body is exercised (in manual labor);
>
> attention is drawn away from the ambiguous, formless world of emotions to the tangible world of action;
>
> we are able to see the results of what we have done, thereby measuring our own competence; and
>
> we can collaborate with others and are thus freed from the vicious circles of self-preoccupation.

A question arises at this point: If action awakens strength and awareness, can it become a valid Way to the higher realms of awareness? The answer is yes, because through action it becomes possible to truly know. As Albert Schweitzer said: "Thought and analysis are powerless to pierce the great mystery that hovers over the world and over our existence, but knowledge of the great truths only appears in action and labour."

We come up against a paradox here. Action, we have seen, molds us in its own image and likeness. But in a deeper, unexpected sense the opposite happens. If we listen to people who tread this Way, we find that the Self they realized was not affected by action. Their core, they discovered, is not altered by life's events. It was their true Self, which remained the same in busyness and in quiet, in defeat or victory, in joy or despair. Beyond action, they found *Being*.

As we study the experiences of those who have followed this Way, we find that it has two main characteristics. First, it changes our *attitude* toward our own actions. Usually we identify ourselves with what we do. Even when I act against my will or unthinkingly, each action is *mine* and something *I* do. This is not the case in the Way of Action. Here the label "mine" is removed from the action itself, and every link with personal expectations is severed. We release action from ego, and thus find inner freedom.

Second, the *content* changes. Action is directed at a beneficial end that transcends selfish aims. Instead of acting in order to feel wiser, richer, or greater, we engage in action in order to benefit others. Instead of reinforcing the egotistic responses of personality, we make action a channel through which love can flow.

In the Way of Action, data about the people involved and their experiences, though clear, are scarce. These individuals find greatest worth in what is of no value to most people. They do not dream of great undertakings or seek immortal fame. They are too humble—or too busy—to speak of themselves.

Furthermore, men and women of action have often distrusted the subjective dimension, subordinating it to active participation in the world. Transpersonal vision is important, of course, but one needs to keep one's feet firmly on the ground. Nightingale once said: "I think that feelings waste themselves in words; they ought to be distilled into actions, and into actions which bring results."

Thoughts, emotions, fantasies—all these are secondary, if not contrary, to the urgency of action. How important are my inner experiences when people at large are suffering, when things need to be done right away? Also, the really necessary words are few, since actions speak for themselves. Thus, in the forge of life, with no help from introspection, untrammeled by theories, one realizes the Self.

For the people on this path insights are immediately converted into activity. Mother Teresa, for instance, was headmistress of a girl's school in India before she embarked on her great service with the "poorest of the poor." While she was traveling on a train, the inspiration came to her like a flash of lightning, and before long she was in action.

One day Schweitzer was reading a magazine article on the need for medical help in Africa and decided then and there to make the trip. The way in which these individuals start out on their chosen path is often marked by the same simplicity typical of all their behavior. Faced with an imperative, they do not waver for a moment. They must act—now.

DOING WITHOUT DOING

Imagine you are taking part in an archery competition, says the Chinese philosopher Chuang Tzu. If the prize is a mere trinket, you will shoot to the best of your ability, free from any worries. If, on the other hand, gold is at stake, you will suddenly find yourself nervous and end up missing the target. Why should this be? In both cases your skill and the objective conditions of the contest remain the same. However, when a substantial sum is at stake, your mind becomes plagued by all sorts of interference.

In order for action to have its freeing effect, nothing must impinge on it—neither hope of success nor fear of failure. Chuang Tzu advises:

> Do not be an embodier of fame; do not be a storehouse of schemes; do not be an undertaker of projects; do not be a proprietor of wisdom. Embody to the fullest what has no end and wander where there is no trail. Hold on to all that you have received from Heaven but do not think you have gotten anything. Be empty, that is all. The Perfect Man uses his mind like a mirror—going after nothing, welcoming nothing, responding but not storing. Therefore he can win out over things and not hurt himself.

The Way of Action does not begin with action, but with mind. One has to think of action in a new way. Chuang Tzu provides various examples: the butcher who danced as he worked, without needing to sharpen his knife in nineteen years, while his fellow butchers had to sharpen theirs every month; the swimmer who dived into a waterfall, while tense onlookers panicked, and who then reemerged with a song on his lips, explaining that he simply allowed himself to flow effortlessly with the swirling current; or the craftsman who carved wonderful pedestals—he would shrug off all thought of either praise or criticism, of ability or clumsiness, and merely go off into the forest. There, his vision purified, he was able to gaze at the shapes of trees and select a form suitable for a pedestal, if he found one; if not, he would simply return home.

Unfortunately, this state of grace is a rare occurrence for most of us. When we act, we constantly strive and come up against one thousand obstacles. This happens because we are acting to satisfy our desires or to get rid of our fears. We thus become entangled in an endless series of events. If, for example, we are out to achieve fame, once we have it we attempt to defend or renew it, either hoping to increase it or fearing lest we should lose it. If our actions are aimed at obtaining wealth, affection, power, or pleasure, we fall prey to the same mechanisms. We will be doomed to

1. Believe in the reality and value of what we are seeking.
2. Immerse ourselves in that search.
3. Create around it a whole world of images, fears, desires, and behavior patterns.
4. Take part in the instability and vulnerability of that world.
5. Work continuously to maintain it.

In this way we build, brick by brick, the prison in which we find ourselves trapped. Can we, on the other hand, create through action a path to freedom? We can, according to the *Bhagavad Gita*, India's sacred poem, but only if we meet certain conditions. This extraordinary piece of writing opens with the predicament of Arjuna, the warrior prince who, overcome by the horror of war, throws down his arms in despair. He is then joined by the divine Krishna, who guides him through this crisis.

Krishna exhorts Arjuna to combat. This is the first lesson: Life is a battle—you must enter into it fully, and do what needs to be done. You cannot shrink from your duty. Life presents difficult, sometimes horrendous, situations, unwelcome tasks, and obstacles of every sort. Despite this harsh reality, you must resolutely go forward.

When we were born we entered the world. But did we *really* enter it? We often dodge situations that seem too threatening or demanding. We run away, hoping things will improve. We are no longer truly present. Krishna says reality is precisely what it is, albeit stark and frightening. The time has come for accepting it as it is, then overcoming all hesitation and entering into the fray.

Equally important is the attitude with which we act. According to Krishna, it must be one of equality, or *samatvam*. This term is used to describe the ability, also mentioned by Chuang Tzu, to remain in equanimity under all circumstances. Do people despise or threaten you? Or do they applaud you and throw flowers at your feet? Does life smile on you, or does misfortune bedevil your existence? Have you been raised on the altar or thrown down in the dust? Whatever may be happening, you always have an enduring point of reference—your inner Center or Self. If you are able to fix your awareness on the quiet Center, the eye of the hurricane, you will be saved. You can then do what needs to be done, concentrating on the action and not on its fruits. In this way action no longer imprisons you, because the mind is impartial to the outcome and is therefore free.

Impartiality does not in any way mean apathy. Arjuna must engage in combat, just as we must commit ourselves fully to our own battles. However, Arjuna must be detached from the results of his action. He may die at any moment, but he is aware that he, and all those who face him, are one timeless Spirit. He knows that the tumult of war and the flowing of blood are an unreal phantasmagoria. At the same time, this is his duty now: the battlefield is real and the fight requires all his resources. This is how we should view our own action—by acting as if we want to win at all costs but at the same time remaining equally aloof from victory or defeat.

When attention is withdrawn from the results of action, it can be better focused on action itself, thereby achieving the highest performance. In the Hasidic tradition it is said that every action creates in the invisible worlds an angel or a psychic being that resembles it. Thus an unharmonious action produces a disagreeable being that frets and shrieks; a hasty action gives rise to a being forever breathless and darting around; a confused action gives rise to a creature that leaves chaos in its wake; but a disinterested action creates a being endowed with the tranquillity and the gentleness of the pure. This is a beautiful analogy for showing us that our actions produce clear-cut effects in our inner world.

We must focus on the present action in order to make every aspect of it conscious and beautiful. No fantasies, distractions, or sloppiness should derange it. It becomes a work of art. Nightingale wrote:

> Nursing is an Art; and if it is to be made an art, it requires as exclusive a devotion, as hard a preparation, as any painter's or sculptor's work; for what is the having to do with dead canvas, or cold marble, compared with having to do with the living body—the temple of God's spirit . . . [Nursing] is one of the Fine Arts; I had almost said, the finest of the Fine Arts.

Various parallels other than art have been used to represent perfect action, all pointing out some supremely valid and beautiful aspect: ritual, for example, is the performance of an action with no purpose beyond itself, and is therefore sacred. Meditation and prayer also involve turning the attention inward, toward the Self or toward God. Thus action and meditation—or prayer—become one and the same thing. Krishna advises Arjuna to focus his attention inwardly and to dedicate all of his actions to the divinity, performing them not for himself, but for God.

This was also the Way of Brother Lawrence, a contemplative who lived at the time of the Thirty Year War in the seventeenth century. Brother Lawrence had always been predisposed to transpersonal experiences. Once, as a young man, looking at a dry, lifeless tree in winter, he contemplated the thought that before long the tree would be renewed, producing flowers and fruit, and he felt a love of extraordinary intensity that brought to him a profound enlightenment. Brother Lawrence's capacity for abstraction in prayer was very keen, but his Way was not one of prayer alone; rather, it was the practice of the presence of God in everyday actions. One of his contemporaries wrote:

> In the greatest hurry of business in the kitchen he still preserved his recollection and heavenly-mindedness. He was never hasty nor loitering, but did each thing in its season, with an even, uninterrupted composure and tranquillity of spirit.

For him, the writer goes on, the time engaged in action was no different from the time given to prayer. And in the noise and heat of the kitchen, when several people simultaneously asked for different things, his tranquillity was the same as in the deepest state of contemplation.

How can we put this ideal into practice? It is difficult yet simple. Here I am, about to perform an action. It may be managing a big sum of money or fixing the kitchen sink. It could be meeting with the president of the United States to decide the world's future, peeling potatoes for the regiment, or embroidering fifty table mats by next Monday. Whatever the task before me, I do what I do. In this way I eliminate, in one stroke, any interference. I am not out to beat my rivals or satisfy a thirst for greatness, nor am I out to grow rich or show how clever I am.

Distracted neither by the past nor by the future, I devote myself to what I am doing—and I do it to the best of my ability. At the same time, I do not look for any particular outcome. It is as though what I am doing did not belong to me. It is then I discover, for a moment, that no longer am I performing the action, but the action is taking place by itself without effort, as if a force greater than my own were doing it. There is an extraordinary feeling of lightness—what Chuang Tzu called *wei wu wei*, "doing without doing."

SERVICE

Africa, 1915. A young doctor from Alsace had been living for a year in a small lost village, caring for the natives. Although he was quite young, he already had two careers behind him. Albert Schweitzer had been a university lecturer in Strasbourg and had become known throughout the world for his book on Bach and his organ recitals. After that, against everyone's advice, he decided to become a doctor and go where the greatest need was, in the middle of the African jungle.

During the horror of World War I, Schweitzer was committed, in a remote corner of the earth, to a solitary and silent activity—he was busy thinking. He was asking himself two questions: Why did the ideals of our civilization fail? In what way can we affirm life and reach the highest ethical levels without repeating the same mistakes that had previously brought catastrophe to the world? For months Schweitzer reflected on these problems without ever reaching a convincing conclusion.

Then came the turning point. One day, during a trip to visit the sick wife of a missionary, on board a small steamboat laboriously making its way up a river, Schweitzer again pondered his questions. In order to focus his mind on the problem, he filled one notebook after another with his thoughts, without following any logical thread. On the third day, as the boat was passing through a herd of hippopotamus, the words *reverence for life* ("*Ehrfurcht vor dem Leben*") flashed through his mind, and Schweitzer knew he had found the answer.

Reverence for life means deep respect for the mystery of existence, the commitment to preserve and help life in all of its forms and to raise it to its highest level. Reverence for life, according to Schweitzer, finds its clear, tangible expression in the reality of daily living:

> You ask me to give you a motto. Here it is: SERVICE. Let this word accompany each of you throughout your life. Let it be before you as you seek your way and your duty in the world. May it be recalled to your minds if ever you are tempted to forget it or set it aside. It will not always be a comfortable companion but it will always be a faithful one. And it will be able to lead you to happiness, no matter what the experiences of your lives are.

This is a fine-sounding idea, but does it work? Are we really ready to help others? And if we are, does our desire spring from a genuine motive or from a sense of obligation? A study carried out in the United States, although it does not reach any absolute conclusion on human nature, offers some notable findings. A number of mothers were asked to record the immediate reactions of their children (ages 18 to 24 months) to another person's suffering. A total of 1,500 everyday incidents —most of them minor—were recorded: a parent returning home from work tired, someone getting burned on the stove or expressing discouragement, and so on. In the majority of cases the children participated in the pain and wanted to help or console the hurting person. They did this, of course, in their own way, by offering their bowl of cereal, displaying affection, or otherwise showing concern.

According to the researchers, children reach a turning point toward the age of two. Beginning to appreciate the difference between themselves and the world about them, they arrive at a crossroad: they can either continue along the way of spontaneous empathy or opt for selfishness. Much will depend on how their parents encourage—or at least do not repress—their altruistic feelings.

These findings are exceptionally relevant. Before this research was conducted, the widely held view on child development was that altruism only becomes possible when children approach seven years of age. Then, according to

Freud, they begin to participate in those duties and values that society, in contrast with our own impulses, imposes on us; or, according to Jean Piaget, they use their cognitive ability to see things from another person's point of view, an ability not yet developed in younger children. The data we have seen deny this view. Empathy and a spontaneous feeling of concern for others are not imposed from outside, nor are they factors of mental maturity. Instead, they are natural, original attitudes of our being.

Taking our lead from this research, we will draw up a few hypotheses:

◊ In each of us lives a natural disposition—though it may often be forgotten or held back—to care for others and identify with them.

◊ We can learn much from genuinely altruistic people about mental health, openness, and inner strength.

◊ Service is one of the most effective ways of overcoming frustration and loneliness, and of bringing us closer to the Self.

We have all experienced the satisfaction that comes from having been useful, even if it is only showing the way to a passerby who got lost, cheering up a friend, or giving a well-chosen present. Such actions produce warmth, perhaps happiness, and a special quality of feeling flows between two or more people. This is a simple fact of everyday life. Some people have raised this quality to the status of an ideal upon which to base their entire life. They give their whole self for the benefit of others, expecting nothing in return. Mother Teresa, speaking to her sisters, advised:

> Be kind and merciful. Let no one ever come to you without leaving better and happier. Be the living expression of God's kindness; kindness in your face, kindness in your eyes, kind-

> ness in your smile, kindness in your warm greeting. In the slums we are the light of God's kindness to the poor. To children, to the poor, to all who suffer and are lonely, give always a happy smile. Give them not only your care, but also your heart.

Here things become more difficult; for there is only one true form of service, while there are countless caricatures. We may stoop in condescension to help people; we may try to serve because we feel the pressure of guilt, or the secret wish to control, or the pang of loneliness. But only true service affirms, in a completely selfless way, the fundamental value of others and of oneself. A revolution springs into action, affecting all of our values, beliefs, habits, and states of mind.

To begin, each of us is fundamentally alone—alone when we are born, alone in our uniqueness, alone in never being able to fully communicate our experience, alone in the intensity of our desires and pleasures, and alone when we suffer and die. This is true even of the most protected and loved individuals, because what they feel and want is, after all, theirs alone.

Service turns this situation upside down. In it we direct all our resources at the well-being of other people, and it is then that the gloomy wall of separation crumbles away, pulverized.

Being fed, cared for, protected, and loved are the first experiences for many people. For the fortunate among us, upbringing took place in an atmosphere of joy and plenty. For others it did not, and this fact, as much research has shown, has devastating repercussions in adult life. Care, then, is a reminder of happiness and unity. Whenever we help someone, we re-enter that sort of relationship, now as the provider of service rather than the recipient. And we repeat the experience of unity, this time more consciously.

In his autobiography Schweitzer writes that strangulated hernia, which could be treated promptly in Europe, was considered a terrible sickness in Africa because of the lack of medical knowledge. The intestines became blocked and swelled up with gas until, after days of torture, the abdomen burst, leading to a dreadful death. Schweitzer, having helped many people suffering from this illness, describes both his and the patient's reactions after the operation:

> Scarcely has he recovered consciousness when he stares about him and ejaculates again and again: "I've no more pain! I've no more pain!" His hand feels for mine and will not let it go. . . . The African sun is shining through the coffee bushes into the dark shed, but we, black and white, sit side by side and feel that we know by experience the meaning of the words: "And all ye are brethren." (Matt. xxiii:8)

Those who undertake to serve others come into contact with unfulfillment and pain. This experience changes them. Their boundaries expand to include another person, perhaps many other people, and this extension is felt as a beneficial, positive event. By directing one's attention to the world of another, servers forget themselves and their worries. In this way, without even seeking it, they find their own realization.

Mary Carpenter, who lived in England in the nineteenth century, dedicated her life to the poorest and most underprivileged youth, the children of Irish immigrants. Because of famine in Ireland, many desperate people sailed to Bristol, in England, for survival. But there they were also hungry and helpless, forced to live in overcrowded huts with only straw beds—amid squalor, broken windows, and stagnant water. Their children soon became involved in delinquency and ended up in jail. Even for children, English prisons in those days meant long sentences and solitary confinement in the dark.

Carpenter was a sensitive, delicate woman, given to introspection. Her friends and family united in trying to dissuade her from her social activities. It was dangerous for any adult to have anything to do with delinquents. But she took care of these young people and loved them as her own children. She felt guided in her activity by a "greater consciousness" of her "existence and powers." Carpenter founded the "ragged school," a derisive title given to it by self-righteous citizens.

Many beautiful things happened at the school. Carpenter describes a few special moments: the day when she brought a shell to school and the children, fascinated by it, passed it around; the time when they saw the magic lantern's colored projections; or again when they went to the zoo; or when they together learned how to use a map. It is important, said Carpenter, to make school a happy place, impart general knowledge, teach the children a useful trade and, above all, give them self-respect through trust and loving kindness. In this work, Carpenter found "unspeakable joy."

Here again we see the paradox in the Way of Action: in the lowliest pits known to the world, Carpenter rose to the shining summits of consciousness. Although fully immersed in the fray, she remained in the silent calm of the central core. Even when passionately engaged in human affairs, she lived at the same time in a detached, serene sphere, a "central peace subsisting at the heart of endless agitation," as she herself described it.

Of course, in service one risks perpetuating the very condition one is out to transform, as well as the roles that define it—the benefactor and the derelict. That, however, is not service, but alms. True service is not merely concerned with temporary relief for the individuals one is helping but rather is based on the ability of the server to step into the shoes of those people, understand their situation, lead them to believe in themselves, and help them to stand on their own feet.

Cesar Chavez pioneered the social campaign on behalf of Hispano-American farm workers. Theirs was not simply an economic dispute. Chavez wanted, through nonviolent means, to transform these poor, exploited, and resigned people into a community of individuals who would have confidence in their opportunities and be aware of their own worth:

> One of the most beautiful and satisfying results of our work in establishing a union in the fields is in witnessing the worker's bloom—the natural dignity coming out of a man when his dignity is recognized. Even some of the employers are seeing this point. Workers whom they previously had treated as dumb members of a forgotten minority suddenly are blooming as capable, intelligent persons using initiative and showing leadership.

Service is much more than mere activity; rather, it is a way of being and entering into a relationship. Of all the ways in which we can relate with others, service is the most fertile and harmonious. An analogy may be of help here. In thermodynamic physics and information theory, *entropy* is the measurement of disorder. It measures, for example, how much information has been lost in a message when a garbled telegram arrives or when interference appears on a television screen. The greater the loss of order and meaning, the greater the entropy. Transfer this concept to the realm of human interactions: Entropy exists when a relationship detracts from an individual's independence, when it damages his or her self-image, when it decreases faith in life, and when it causes feelings of inadequacy, guilt, or unworthiness—in other words, when it lowers the level of consciousness.

Then we have *syntropy* (a term coined by the Italian mathematician Fantappié), the opposite of entropy—order, coherence, harmony, meaning. A syntropic relationship has many positive effects: it enhances inner freedom, satisfies real needs and eliminates fictitious ones, increases one's sense of responsibility, enlivens attention, communicates energy, reinforces appreciation of individual worth, stimulates positive potential, opens the mind, lightens the spirit, and raises the level of consciousness.

Syntropy is the result of true service. In this sense, it transcends the Way of Action and belongs to all the Ways. It is the spontaneous radiation of a person who lives in the world of the Self. Transpersonal experience is contagious. The creativity, love, strength, and beauty of the Self do not remain in the enclave of private enjoyment; rather, they are communicated to others in an infinite variety of ways.

In the Way of Action, service takes a more explicit and concrete form than in the other Ways. In the midst of a cutthroat world, weighed down by countless anxieties and problems, ensnared by the chimeras and the nightmares of life, immersed in the mystery of existence, surrounded by cosmic loneliness, a human being takes the time to understand and help another human being. And this fact alone fills us with wonder.

THE SUPREME IMPORTANCE OF THE INDIVIDUAL

Raoul Follerau was a journalist when he first saw lepers in Africa. This was the beginning of a long, painful revelation:

> I found lepers in prison, in asylums, shut up in desecrated graveyards, interned in desert camps surrounded by barbed wire, searchlights and machine guns. I saw them naked, hungry, crying out in despair. I saw their sores swarming with flies, their infected hovels and their armed keepers. I saw a world of unimaginable horrors, pain and despair.

Follerau set to work. He spent six months each year with the lepers of the world, helping them to get better, to return to society and find work. The other six months he spent with nonlepers, traveling from one place to another, holding conferences, writing articles, and doing everything he could to bring their tragedy to the attention of a distracted humanity. During fifty years of hard work, traveling more than a million miles and collecting vast sums of money, he succeeded in curing a million lepers in the aid centers he had established around the world. Follerau would embrace these despised, abandoned individuals to show that they were not contagious, saying he could see Christ in them—infinite value.

Those who follow the Way of Action affirm the supreme value of the very individuals ignored or despised by society. Thus, in order to climb up toward the Self, they descend to the lowest levels of the social hierarchy and there encounter outcasts, lepers, and derelicts. By this reversal of normal preferences, these individuals express their freedom to alter meanings and values. It is as though they were saying, "What we love or hate is not based on automatic preferences. It depends on us, on our own choices." These people reinterpret the world and affirm the existence of an invisible reality—infinitely rich and beautiful—alongside a visible reality that is sometimes poor and repugnant. It is the Christian teaching of seeing Christ in each person, or the *Bhagavad Gita*'s message of looking to a single indestructible immortal Self, the Light of Lights, at the heart of each living creature.

True service, as we have seen, does not act merely on the surface aspects of the individuals to be served but also effects changes deep inside them. This is only possible when we are prepared to see great beauty in these individuals, even when their outward appearance may be repulsive. Any person who chooses to follow the path of humanitarian action will be master of this paradox.

In Florence Nightingale's time, during the Victorian era, those who were wounded, sick, and dying as a result of battle were left to themselves in unhygienic and overcrowded hospitals. Who, it was thought, could possibly be interested in this mob of uncouth soldiers? Yet, indeed, someone cared. During the Crimean War, Nightingale brought about a revolution in health care and created the nursing profession. By treating the wounded she reduced the death rate from 42 percent to 2 percent.

Despite the prejudiced attitude held by the military hierarchy, who feared she would invade their territory, Nightingale worked without respite, bringing to thousands of wounded men her friendliness and competent medical care. The picture of this woman holding a lamp in her hand, moving through dark hospital corridors, became a legend. Some soldiers would kiss her shadow as she passed, so grateful were they for her care.

In these miserable soldiers Nightingale saw beauty and dignity:

> The tears come into my eyes as I think how, amidst scenes of loathsome disease and death, there rose above it all the innate dignity, gentleness and chivalry of men . . . shining in the midst of what must be considered the lowest sinks of human misery.

Great courage is required in this work. One is confronted with the horrors of life: suffering, misery, ignorance, sickness, death. Consider the Abbé Pierre. One day he came across an ex-convict of the terrible French Guiana prisons. This man, returning to his homeland after twenty years of confinement, had been rejected by everyone, even his wife, and had attempted to kill himself. The Abbé Pierre took him into his home.

From then on, the Abbé began to look after individuals on the fringes of society. He would collect junk from people's attics, sell it, and use the meager proceeds to continue helping vagabonds. His work received a great boost in the terrible winter of 1954 when, because of the exceptional cold, the Ministry of Health allowed him to broadcast an appeal over the radio. He met with an overwhelming response that enabled him to organize aid and touch the hearts of many French people.

Aided by a team of volunteers, the Abbé Pierre bought land, built huts for the homeless, erected tents, and went about the streets at night with a lorry full of food and drinks to help those in need. One day he was called in to help a homeless family who had been forced to live in the fields with an oilcloth for a roof. Two children had already died and a third one was seriously ill. The Abbé Pierre recalls the experience:

> It was then that I realized some terrible things. I realized that so long as people who were supposed to be apostles, as long as a priest like me was incapable of saying to that poor woman, "Come on, get your things, pick up your child and come along with me and your husband and sleep in my room. I'll take your place in the tent and tomorrow we'll find some way of solving this." Until then, well, fundamentally I was simply an impostor.

Abbé Pierre realized that it is all too easy to make fine-sounding speeches when we have enough to eat in a properly heated room all to ourselves. Instead, we have to enter the arena ourselves. Only then will the people we are trying to help understand how important they are to us—that is, only when we place ourselves on an equal footing with them.

This is the *principle of equivalence*: What happens to another person happens to me. His or her poverty, suffering, or isolation is mine, and I am ready to take it on myself without reservation. According to the Abbé Pierre, by forgetting our selfish interests we find "universal joy."

This is also the story of Mother Teresa. The first person she helped in Calcutta was a woman in the street, whose dying body was being gnawed by rats. Shortly afterward Mother Teresa managed to obtain the use of the temple consecrated to the goddess Kali as a refuge for the dying. She wanted these people to know that they had value and that they were loved; and she wanted to give them the chance to die in peace. Mother Teresa and her team of caring sisters search for the poorest of the poor. With a song on their lips, they clean them, feed them, and help them find their own dignity.

Mother Teresa tells how one day she saw a fellow worker

smiling and full of joy. She asked her why, and the sister told her that she had found an old man who had fallen into a drain and had been there for some time. He was completely covered in dirt and maggots, and suffered open wounds. She cleaned him and took care of him. Then something very beautiful happened: "I knew I was touching the body of Christ." Mother Teresa and her helpers see in the people they care for—beneath the pain of the sores, the dirt and the rat bites, the loneliness and the despair—a splendor that can only be found by those who are willing to look for it in its dark hiding place.

As in the case of all the Ways, we commence from afar—in fact, from the opposite disposition. Deep within our personality pulsates a basic desire to exist, to be satisfied, to be at the center of everything.

There is nothing wrong with this phenomenon. Our individuality is a conquest won over the eons; it is no wonder we value it so highly. The danger, however, is that we devalue others, turning them into objects for satisfying our own desires, threatening enemies, or insignificant shadows. Thus violence is born—not only the more obvious, dramatic violence, such as social injustice, war, the denial of civil liberties, rape, and abuse of the weakest, but also the indifference we all take for granted, the "I am too busy seeking my own happiness to even notice you" attitude.

Recognizing the absolute value of another person is one way to escape the prison of the ego. An individual traveling the path of humanitarian action is saying, "You matter; for you I am prepared to live in difficulty and poverty, under the threat of contagion, placing my personal integrity at risk, forgetting my own plans and affairs. You, the criminal, the leper, the old man covered with vermin, you, the miserable tramp—you have an infinite value. You mean more to me than all the potentates, all the riches, all the respectability in the world."

This is a deep change. We shift attention from ourselves to other people and redirect our inclination from the attractive to the unwanted. This is a useful form of inner training for anyone, including those who are not out to reach the spiritual heights we have just seen—and that is the majority of us. It is a shift that could be evoked at all times, to free ourselves from deeply ingrained mental habits. In the people we meet we can see, beyond the roles we all play, a beauty less visible yet more real than that which society has conditioned us to perceive. To ignore something beautiful and great makes us less than we are. To recognize it uplifts and regenerates us. We benefit ourselves and others at the same time. The distinctions between selfishness and altruism ultimately disappear.

Seeing the true value in a person, however, is only the first step. We must then decide what needs to be done—and here we strike the keynote in the Way of Action. To understand this point we need only consider Elizabeth Fry, the great English prison reformer of the nineteenth century. But first, let us enter a prison of that day. The initial impressions are darkness and stench, and the cells are not ventilated. Prisoners are either locked up alone or housed together in incredibly overcrowded cells. (In Wakefield prison, for example, there were at one point 1,700 prisoners instead of the 110 for which the building was made.) The most uncontrollable inmates are chained to the wall, while those sentenced to death are locked up in a large wooden box and exposed to curious visitors for the price of one shilling. The "lunatics" are shut up alone and chained, made to vomit and bleed, then beaten and thrown into cold water.

All these practices are generally accepted. The basic concept here is, punish the culprit and prevent the crime. At this point a single voice breaks in with a cry of protest. Is it the voice of a great politician, philosopher, or artist? No, they are too busy elsewhere. The voice belongs to a mother of ten children, a Quaker by the name of Elizabeth Fry. One day, with only her goodwill to assist her, she ventures into a women's prison, a place where the inmates have said good-bye to the human world and entered a subhuman one. Many have brought their children in with them, without the slightest chance of educating them. They have become hardened, desperate, and wild, and when they see visitors they kick up a din, uttering abusive curses and threats.

The occasional individual having to enter the gaol must be accompanied by armed guards for protection. But Fry presents herself to the keeper and asserts her wish to go in alone. After some hesitation the keeper opens the barred doors, then shuts them behind her. The prisoners, their curiosity roused, suddenly fall silent and surround her, like tigers stalking their prey. From the outside all you can see now is the white quiff of Elizabeth's Quaker hat among all the inmates. But she is not intimidated. She looks around and, seeing a child, takes it in her arms and says, "What shall we do for the children?"

This question entirely transforms the atmosphere. Fry has reached at once the hearts of women who only a moment before showed hardness and cynicism. Together they now make plans for the children's education in order to prevent them from following the ominous path ahead of them. The inmates now realize that someone cares enough to meet them in the darkest and most frightening place, and they feel grateful. Fry has seen at once what needed to be done. With her courageous bet, she had made the unhappy women realize that they *counted*.

THE INFINITE VALUE OF THE ORDINARY

One day, during his first visit to the United States, Schweitzer found himself at Pennsylvania Station in New York, waiting for a train that would take him, his wife, and some friends to Colorado. It was the first time he had seen a big American station, and there was much to do and look at while they waited. Schweitzer saw a broom and, in the middle of this big crowded place, quietly began to sweep up the rubbish on the ground. After a little while he realized that in the meantime the crowd had thrown down more rubbish. Without getting angry or criticizing, he went on sweeping until departure time arrived.

An insignificant episode, perhaps. But insignificance is precisely what counts in the Way of Action. A humble action is performed in the daily round, accomplishing whatever is required. In this episode Schweitzer was obeying a rule he had expressed on another occasion:

> Only a person who can find value in every sort of activity, and can devote himself to each one with full consciousness of duty, has the inward right to undertake some out-of-the-ordinary activity instead of that which falls naturally to his lot.

All Ways toward the Self must destructure our mental framework in order for consciousness to expand. The strategy adopted in the Way of Action consists in affirming values in contrast to our dreams and desires. From the dizzy heights of future gratification we descend into the valley of the anonymous present. From fantasies of pleasure or greatness we return to the jagged contours of everyday life. We learn, in other words, to give ourselves to reality as it is. We practice the virtue of humility.

The word *humility* (also *human*) is derived from the Latin *humus*, meaning "the soil." Perhaps this is not simply because it entails stooping and returning to earthly origins, but also because, as we are rooted in this earth of everyday life, we find in it all the vitality and fertility unnoticed by people who merely tramp on across the surface, drawn by distant landscapes.

It is not by chance that in stories from many different traditions we encounter characters who discover extraordinary treasures in the most ordinary of places—in the home kitchen, for instance, rather than in the king's palace where the treasure was first imagined to reside; or in the cornfield where one was made to plough, only to find that the treasure was actually the ploughing of the field. What all this means is that if we explore the ordinary instead of disregarding it, we discover our true richness. It also means that the proper place for our transpersonal growth is not elsewhere, but here and now, in daily work.

One winter evening, Thérèse of Lisieux, a French nun later to become a saint, was looking after a sick woman, as she was used to doing day after day. Hers had been a cheerless life. From school Thérèse had gone straight into a convent. Naturally she daydreamed about the pleasures she had never enjoyed: "One day I heard the harmonious sound of a musical instrument in the distance and I imagined a drawing-room shining with lights and gold; I saw elegant young women gaily conversing, a worldly expression on their faces."

But this was only for a moment. Thérèse's attention was suddenly brought back from her fantasy to the harsh reality around her: "My eyes then fell on the poor sick woman I was tending. Instead of music I could hear her intermittent moans, instead of gold I saw the bricks of our sombre cloisters, barely lit up by a pale light." This was the turning point:

> I cannot express what happened in my soul: God illuminated it with the rays of truth, which so much surpassed the gloomy blaze of worldly celebrations that I could hardly believe my happiness. I would not exchange ten minutes of my humble work of love for the pleasures of a thousand years of worldly feasts.

The Way of Action is characterized by precision, respect, and presence. Precision is a victory over approximation and amateurishness, haste and forgetfulness, the tendency to leave things half-finished or to cheat oneself. It means answering letters right away, keeping things tidy, washing dishes carefully, dusting even where it does not show. In other words, completing work in all its aspects, whatever the task might be, and finishing it well. God, it has been said, is in the details!

Respect means treating the present situation with care rather than with indifference or tacit hostility. It is about giving to ordinary circumstances the attention we would spare for the most eminent and powerful, and facing every moment as though it carried the significance of a millennium.

Presence is giving one hundred percent of ourselves to a situation without allowing our thoughts to be distracted by the lure of future events, or by the regurgitation of unassimilated experiences. Every act serves to focus the mind on the present reality.

Indeed, the reality of everyday life is a maze of alleys that would seem to carry us far from the main road of relevant projects. We can never manage to do everything: time passes, duties multiply, plans meet with the unexpected, further projects come to mind. A feeling of incompleteness is engendered —the perennial incompleteness of human life. Then we react, we become anxious and do more, but the cure is worse than the sickness. The only way out of irrelevance and incompleteness is to do whatever we do with total commitment.

After all, it is common enough to put on a good show for special occasions. When the spotlight is on us, our resources are stimulated and our pride pushes us to rise to the occasion. But what happens in the less important though more frequent matters, when perhaps no one is watching us, and when, having taken off our Sunday best, we set our sights lower? It is quite likely that we just get by. This is where we are put to the test, because it is easier to be distracted and forgetful. To demonstrate precision, respect, and presence in this context is worth twice as much, because we are driven by no motivation other than the wish to do things well.

Oriental traditions abound in comments on the infinite value of each act and each moment of life. They point out that in the commonplace is concealed a supremely meaningful reality:

> Where is the Tao [the essence of life]?
> —There is no place it does not exist!—

You must be more specific!
—It is in this ant!—
Can you give me a humbler example?
—It is in this blade of grass!—
Anything lower than that?
—It is in this pebble!—
Is this its lowest point?
—It is in this excrement!

These are the words of Chuang Tzu, who often likes to remind us of the importance in everything that is not important. For this reason his works, and in general the whole Taoistic and Zen tradition, are populated with cripples, stunted trees, fools, dead cats, and anything else that, from a practical point of view, is supremely useless.

When the king's emissaries approached Chuang Tzu with the suggestion that he become the royal adviser, he replied by asking them which was happier—a live tortoise dragging its tail through the mud, or a dead tortoise whose shell had been adorned with diamonds. The live tortoise, replied the emissaries. Then allow me to keep dragging my tail through the mud, replied Chuang Tzu. This response epitomizes his ironic rejection of the officially recognized values in favor of ordinary everyday life—much humbler, but much truer.

A person who is able to appreciate the value of every situation is free, because he or she is using the mind in the most open way. In his autobiography Han Shan, the Chinese Ch'an or Zen master, recounts one of his dreams. Having been lifted up into the heavens, he floated for some time in the cosmos and then descended into a wonderful place, paved with crystal. In the distance he could make out a splendid castle, so big it filled the sky. In this palace the whole universe was mysteriously reflected. All things and people were there, intertwined —including the most insignificant events of everyday life. The splendor of this palace surpassed all imagination.

At this point a doubt came into Han Shan's mind: How

could it possibly be that the tainted, trivial things of life could be displayed in this pure world above the heavens? Suddenly the palace receded into the distance: it had become inaccessible. Then another thought came to him: pure or tainted, it all depends on how our minds perceive it. At once the palace returned and he was able to enter it. There inside he met Maitreya, the future Buddha, who told him that wisdom is to be found in not making divisions and comparisons. Feeling empty and light in body and mind, the master awoke from his dream.

Finding value in the ordinary also means respecting the objects surrounding us. Every thing, even the smallest, is a microcosm, so nothing should be wasted. When a Zen master reproved a disciple for wasting a few drops of water, in that moment the young man attained enlightenment.

That is why we should use objects with care: If the Infinite Spirit is somewhere else, then we could break, misuse, and mishandle anything that comes our way. We would live in an obtuse material world. But suppose the Spirit is right here—in this book of which we have earmarked a page, in this cup of coffee we lay on the table where it will leave a stain, in these shoes we would like to throw away although they could be repaired, in this clock that has been showing the wrong time for a year now, in this car that we treat as if it were our worst enemy. Aurobindo wrote the following words in a letter to one of his students:

> What you feel about physical things is true—there is a consciousness in them, a life which is not the life and consciousness of man and animal which we know, but still secret and real. That is why we must have respect for physical things and use them rightly, not misuse and waste, ill-treat or handle them with a careless roughness. The feeling of all being consciousness or alive comes when our own physical consciousness—and not the mind only—awakes out of its obscurity and becomes aware of the One in all things, the Divine everywhere.

Just as each object has value, each moment is precious and unique. The Zen monk Kyogen took copious notes on the teaching of his masters. Then, one day, he realized that all this enormous material was completely useless. Discouraged, Kyogen burned his notes, turned his back on everything, and went to live in the country as a cemetery attendant. As he was sweeping the ground one day, his broom hit a small stone that struck a nearby bamboo cane. The sound it made brought him instant enlightenment. Where years of study had failed, one ordinary moment succeeded.

"Life delineates itself on the canvas called time," writes Suzuki, "and time never repeats: once gone, forever gone; and so is an act: once done, it is never undone." This is the meaning of the Zen affirmation "When I am hungry I eat, when I am tired, I sleep." If we give actions the attention they deserve, each one is purely itself, without corrections, regrets, or second thoughts.

It might appear that Nightingale, back in Victorian England, is immeasurably remote from Zen; yet if you read her manual for nurses you are immediately struck by its complete agreement with the principles we have been discussing. The book is based on the idea of carefully observing details. According to Nightingale, for instance, a nurse must take note of any weakening in her patients because often they themselves will not talk about it. A nurse must therefore note what her patients can and cannot do now, in comparison with, say, a month before. The face is the last part of the body to show signs of a deteriorated condition; it is far better to look at the hands, taking into account, of course, the "physiognomy of illness."

Nightingale goes on to give several definitions of paleness in the face. Questions, too, are of the utmost importance, and they must be precise. Asking, "Did you have a good night?" is inadequate. Far better would be to ask, "How many hours did you sleep? Which hours of the night were they?" Equally relevant are such issues as how to arrange the bed; how to monitor feeding; and the importance of the nurse's cleanliness, accuracy, and punctuality. How true all this is! Of far greater significance for the patient, more important than all the theories and spiritual visions, is the correct position of his pillows.

At a certain point Nightingale mentions as an example the following exercise: let a child stand for a while in front of a toy shop window; then ask him to recall everything he has seen. The aim here is to train observation, and nurses are invited to practice with similar techniques. Her book, however, is not merely a practical manual. On every page you sense a genuine interest in the life of the patient, a belief in the dignity of each human being, a feeling for everyday action as a primary expression of men and women in their life.

The path to the Self passes through the familiar sceneries of daily life. In a letter describing the illumination she had experienced, Nightingale speaks about seeing "God in all things, and all things in God, the Eternal shining through the accidents of space and time."

3

The Way of Illumination

The starting point is simple and at the same time prodigious: it is the fact of being conscious. *I am*—this is in itself a great mystery. Being conscious is the basis for all my feelings, emotions, or thoughts; it is the first datum. Thanks to it I know I exist. It is so elementary a fact that we all take it for granted. Yet who can define it, who can truly understand it?

I am conscious—and here starts the show. As though by some extraordinary legerdemain, my consciousness stretches to include stars and galaxies; or instead it narrows down to a single point; it turns to the remote past or to possible futures; it generates imaginary faces, scenes, dreadful or splendid events, whole universes. But suppose I eat too much, and my consciousness is dulled. I have a toothache, and it is overwhelmed. I fall asleep, and it is gone.

It is only natural that this mystery should invite us to explore our inner world and turn it into a laboratory for carrying out a host of experiments. As one starts out in this search, one soon realizes that among the various states of consciousness some are more convincing and complete, indeed more true. One discovers that consciousness can be a continuous source of revelation, a Way toward the Self.

Each Way, of course, is an expansion of consciousness. But other Ways have an external focal point: action, scientific research, ritual, the observation of nature, dance. In this path the focal point is internal, and it is the most rarified and puzzling one: consciousness itself.

Just as there are geniuses in art, science, politics, so there are geniuses in consciousness: Buddha, Patañjali, Eckhart, Sankara, Ibn al-Arabi, Ramana Maharshi, and numerous others, including philosophers and educators. Their main instrument has been meditation. Many have not only explored the remote regions of the spirit for themselves but have also given precise indications for others who embark on this adventure.

The first stage in this path is groundwork—simply clearing oneself of everything that clutters, clouds, or weighs on consciousness.

First, we tackle bodily problems such as tiredness, psychosomatic disturbances, and ill health. That is why the Way of Illumination at times emphasizes the relationship with the physical world. The food we eat, the way we breathe, how we treat our bodies, can produce either heaviness or lightness. This is the beginning.

Second, emotions can adversely affect our consciousness. We can, for instance, be slaves to anger, fear, guilt, or despair. Burdened with such weights, consciousness can hardly open and expand. We must learn to free ourselves from the tyranny of emotions. Sometimes, in order to make consciousness more agile and attentive, feelings themselves are paradoxically taken as subjects of meditation.

The same can be said about desires. If we are obsessed by them, consciousness will assume a centrifugal tendency—that is, it will be continually drawn toward something other than itself. Of course, it is neither right nor even feasible to try and eliminate all desires. By taking too strong a stand we may repress desires and involuntarily end up intensifying them. It is essential, however, that life should not be reduced to a continual and exclusive pursuit of self-gratification. We need to learn how to be content with little. We must discover inner simplicity.

Ideas, too, can be an obstacle to expansion of consciousness. First, their content may hinder. For instance, it is not possible to be racist and at the same time intuitively perceive the essential unity of all living beings. Thus, in the Way of Illumination we start out by accurately looking into our own assumptions. Also, ideas themselves, whatever their content, can become an obstacle. Too strong a reliance upon any conviction—even the noblest and most universal one—can prevent us from looking further. Indeed, the Way of Illumination ventures into states of consciousness that are above and beyond even the greatest idea. That is why in this path we come to reexamine our relationship with the mental world.

This is the groundwork. We may come across it in various forms in all the Ways. On this path, however, because an unbalanced psychophysical state could interfere with meditation, it is more evident and it has often been summed up in rules and principles.

Once we reach a certain level of transparency, the specific work may start. Many experiments can be done with consciousness. Special techniques have been developed over the centuries, and the variations are infinite. There are three main avenues, however, and they all start from the conscious "I":

◊ I may open up consciousness with a panoramic view over both inner and outer worlds. Attentive and present, I am conscious of everything without filters or preferences.

◊ I can, instead, focus on a single object, to the exclusion of everything else, taking consciousness to a level of maximum intensity.

◊ Through introspection, I can retrace consciousness to its source and let it merge back into itself. In this way I become conscious of my Self as empty of all content, unconfined by space or time.

These are, respectively, the subjects of the following sections. They may seem to be contradictory approaches, but they have at times been successfully combined to develop a balanced outlook. After discussing these three basic methods, we will move on to other themes in the Way of Illumination: the technique of reframing, in which one discovers the mind's power to change one's reality; education as the task of liberating people's consciousness; and love as a form of enlightenment.

In this path, as in the other ones, there is no lack of dangers and sidetracks. The inner world is vast: It will devour anyone not strong enough or prepared for it. In the Way of Illumination individuals may become unable to distinguish between dream and reality, become lost in visions, mistake minor insights for supreme revelation, deceive themselves into thinking they are sages, disintegrate the conscious field into a thousand pieces, and wander aimlessly along remote, eerie pathways—far, very far from anything that has meaning and value for other men and women.

Gopi Krishna, for example, was a true and earnest seeker who devoted himself to exploring the visionary worlds through Kundalini yoga. At a certain point he was caught up in a series of frightening experiences:

> Whenever my mind turned upon itself I always found myself staring with growing panic into the unearthly radiance that filled my head, swirling and eddying like a fearsome whirlpool; I even found its reflection in the pitch darkness of my room during the slowly dragging hours of the night. Not infrequently it assumed horrible shapes and postures, as if satanic faces were grinning and inhuman forms gesticulating at me in the blackness. This happened night after night for months, weakening my will and sapping my resistance until I felt unable to endure the fearful ordeal any longer, certain that at any moment I might succumb to the relentlessly pursuing horror,

> and bidding farewell to my life and sanity, rush out of the room a raving maniac.

Gopi Krishna moved way beyond his predicament. Others get stuck in their dreamlands. How are we to distinguish between delirium and enlightenment? The answer is that true enlightenment brings serenity and joy, never excitement or fanaticism; it always regenerates and never injures; it helps us to expand beyond the limits of our personal world; and, in its highest manifestation, it is probably the same for everyone. *Satori*, *samadhi*, *nirvana*, *mystic union*, *fana*, *wu*—the terms vary from one tradition to another, but the experience is the same in all cultures.

It is hard indeed to describe enlightenment. We can cite the case of Hildegard of Bingen—an unusual, lively German woman of the twelfth century, who was writer, theologian, scientist, and musician. Hildegard corresponded with the popes and emperors of her day; founded the Rupertsberg convent on the Rhine; wrote books on theology, philosophy, botany, zoology, and medicine, as well as several biographies of saints; and composed music of exceptional artistic and historical importance. She was unquestionably an eminent person of the times and a true visionary. In her mystical writings she describes episodes of her rich spiritual life. Among other things, Hildegard saw a great light that dispelled all her sadness, causing her to return to the simplicity and innocence of a child:

> And my soul ascends in this vision, as God wills, to the height of the firmament . . . and extends itself to many different peoples who live far from me in distant lands and spaces. . . . The light I see is not local; it is far, far brighter than the cloud that carries the sun. And I cannot see depth or length or breadth in it. . . . And as sun, moon, and stars are reflected in the water, so in this light the images of the writings and the speech

> and the forces and many works of men shine forth to me. . . . And the words in this vision are not like the words that sound from the mouths of human beings, but like a vibrating flame and like a cloud moving in pure air. . . . And what I see and hear in that vision, my soul draws up as from a spring that still remains full and unexhausted.

Light, release, total openness: This is illumination. This state, more than any other, deserves to be called love.

ATTENTION

At about age fifteen young Prince Siddhartha, the future Buddha, was sitting by a river one day, observing. The current was carrying small and large pebbles along with it. Some insects sought to make their way upstream on the surface of the water, but, after a while, they too had to yield. Only a few large, majestic boulders remained still, unmoved by the vehemence of the stream.

This, thought Siddhartha, is a metaphor for human existence. The great mass of people allow themselves to be swept along, like small pebbles, by the current of life, tossed here and there by circumstances and chance. Others, like the insects on the river, attempt to escape but end up being carried along like the rest. Is it possible to be like those immovable rocks, standing out from the flow of unconsciousness and death?

Human beings, thought Buddha, are blind and powerless, condemned to a life full of errors and suffering, which stretches out into an endless series of further errors and suffering. What can we do to escape from this nightmare? Young Prince Siddhartha did not yet know. It was to take him many years of searching and experimenting to find out. The answer, as is true of all creative answers, was simple:

> Attention is the path of immortality, lack of attention is the path to death. Those who are attentive do not die, those who are not attentive are as if already dead.

Conscious attention shows us the world with ruthless sincerity, stripped of the illusions and the fabrications with which we usually clothe it. Our dreams and nightmares vanish: we are awake. At a basic level, conscious attention is a therapeutic tool. Roger Vittoz in Switzerland and Frederick ("Fritz") Perls and Charlotte Selver in the United States have used it for curing neurosis, the habit of reacting to an imagined situation as though it were real. Being conscious in the here and now encourages us to see the world as it is, not as we would like it or fear it to be. This attitude—rather than a lengthy analysis—is a powerful way of dispelling anxieties and obsessions.

In order to be accurate and truthful, awareness must be receptive. Instead of producing formulas and applying them to the world, as we usually do, we *receive* the world into ourselves. As Aldous Huxley, who practiced this type of meditation, wrote in a letter, we need to be "alert and open and empty." According to Huxley, the state of grace at any level—be it physical, emotional, aesthetic, or spiritual—can only be achieved by cultivating "alert passivity . . . to the point of complete humility and selflessness." The great protagonist within us, cynic or moralist, rational or romantic, cheerful or depressed, steps aside. Then life appears, in the words of Vittoz, as if seen through the eyes of a child waking up from sleep, innocent.

When we free ourselves of stereotypes and abstractions, we live in a richer and more interesting world. What Buddha called "attention," Georges Gurdjieff, the Greek Caucasian spiritual teacher, referred to as *self-remembering*—that is, remembering at all times that we exist and that we are awake. He made this attitude the cornerstone of his teaching methods.

Peter Demianovich Ouspensky, his Russian disciple and collaborator, described one occasion on which he himself experienced self-remembering:

> I saw that self-remembering gave wonderful sensations which, in a natural way, that is, by themselves, come to us very seldom and in exceptional conditions. Thus, for instance, at the time I used very much to like to wander through St. Petersburg at night and to "sense" the houses and streets. St. Petersburg is full of these strange sensations. Houses, especially old houses, were quite alive, I all but spoke to them. There was no "imagination" in it. I did not think of anything, I simply walked along while trying to remember myself and looked about; the sensations came by themselves.

This is all well and good, but what about practicing it? I am conscious, say, while walking in the street, looking at passers-by; I am conscious while eating, and even in the simplest meal I experience a symphony of tastes; I am conscious while listening to music, and a multitude of intense new sounds come to my attention; I am conscious while brushing my teeth, driving the car, or setting the table, and I feel better than ever. But then I am distracted, and my consciousness is suddenly a thousand miles away; I judge, and thereby separate myself from reality; I compare the present situation with a past one, and immediately feel divided within; I start daydreaming, and already I am asleep, absent, carried off to another world.

Any time I lose awareness, however, I can recover it at once. Over and over, I again become awake. The laboratory is always at my disposal. This wastepaper basket, the cracks in the wall, the happy shouts of children playing in the distance, the flow of thoughts through my mind or the flow of clouds across the sky—everything is spiritual and everything is perceived, as the great Indian teacher Krishnamurti said, "choicelessly," without any valuation or comparison. Woe to those who think they know it all beforehand. According to

Zen master Sunryu Suzuki, freedom belongs to the person who knows nothing. In the beginner's mind there are many possibilities, in the expert's, only a few.

In this state of consciousness it is easier to comprehend true love, free of judgments and demands. In his biographical writings Krishnamurti described one experience, among many, that came to him in this state of complete openness. He was in India, the rice fields were a golden-yellow color, large white birds flew while the sun was setting, bullock carts creaked as they moved along the road, and frogs were croaking:

> What was beautiful was now glorified in splendor; everything was clothed in it; there was ecstasy and laughter not only deeply within but among the palms and the rice fields. Love is not a common thing but it was there in the hut with an oil lamp; it was with that old woman, carrying something heavy on her head; with that naked boy, swinging on a piece of string a piece of wood which gave out many sparks for it was his fireworks. It was everywhere, so common that you could pick it up under a dead leaf or in the jasmine by the old crumbling house.

There are, alas, few individuals who are aware. The major problems of humanity—famine, violence, injustice, and pollution —seem to be generated by people who are unaware, and subject to crazy dreams. On the contrary, only a person who is aware can hear the people's mute lament, understand their needs, recognize when someone is discriminated against, see how nature is being violated—and consequently act in the most appropriate way. In a society obsessed by its illusions, awareness—like love and beauty—should become a foremost value. In a world where the imaginary is more important than the actual, where genuine contact between people is on the wane and illusory needs are compulsively pursued, awareness is a must.

One of the consequences of being aware is the "fall of the

gods": ideals crumble, words lose their persuasive fascination, reason is omnipotent no more. This should be no cause for dismay, however. Gods tumble when we no longer need them. There is no wish for intermediaries or external points of reference, and our relationship with reality is transparent.

The most illustrious victim is an old acquaintance—the ego. Indeed, according to Buddha, practicing awareness elicits the fundamental intuitive realization of *anatta*, or impersonality. Our personal identity bursts like a bubble. Specific techniques—such as conscious walking—are also used to enhance awareness. You walk slowly, conscious of the foot leaving the ground, lifting, then lowering and touching the ground again; then you become aware of the intention of lifting the foot, of the transition from intention to act, and so forth. You can also be conscious of breathing. Awareness of this subtle process makes you realize that every breath is different and that each moment between breaths is timeless.

These are not concentration exercises. Every distraction, instead of being chased away, is received as subject itself for meditation—a thought or a physical sensation, a wave of discouragement or boredom, the wish to swallow or to scratch. This work helps us to see things with greater clarity. What looked like our individual identity turns out—thanks to a keener attention—to be nothing more than a series of impersonal interactions.

The intuition of impersonality is well described by Alan Watts, the brilliant British writer who popularized Zen in the United States. Here is his description of an experience he had during a visit to Kyoto, Japan:

> Zen meditation is a trickily simple affair, for it consists only in watching everything that is happening, including your own thoughts and your breathing, without comment. After a while thinking, or talking to yourself, drops away and you find that there is no "yourself" other than everything which is going on, both inside and outside your skin. Your consciousness, your

> breathing, and your feelings are all the same process as the wind, the trees growing, the insects buzzing, the water flowing, and the distant prattle of the city. All this is a single many-featured "happening," a perpetual *now* without either past or future, and you are aware of it with the rapt fascination of a child dropping pebbles into a stream.

Propounding these ideas, the monk Nagasena went to the court of the Greek king Milinda, who reigned in the Indus Valley in the century before Christ. "There is no individuality," he said, "there is no soul."

"How can this be!" exclaimed the king. "Who are you, then, who are we, how can we be responsible to one another, and with whom am I speaking right now?" Disputing the idea of an individual soul in Greece, its very homeland, was at best a metaphysical faux pas. The king must have been upset.

But Nagasena was unperturbed. "Imagine a cart," he replied. "What is its essential part—the shaft, the wheels, the axle, the reins? None of them, of course; the cart is simply a grouping of pieces." We, too, are a grouping of pieces. Our individuality is a convention, a word. As Buddhism sees it, reality resembles a pointillistic painting by Georges Seurat or Paul Signac. We see the ladies sitting on the bank of the Grande Jatte on a summer's day, or the ballerina dancing on the back of a horse running around the circus ring. But upon a closer examination of the painting, one realizes that there are no ladies or ballerinas, only soulless points of color.

In practicing Buddhist meditation, we discover to our surprise that the protagonist we thought ourselves to be does not exist: we are only a momentary, impersonal combination of mental states. In fact, there is nobody there to be tortured by problems and anxieties. From this perspective, everything takes place in a state of indescribable lightness, no longer fraught with dramas or terrors. This is what release means, this is nirvana.

CONCENTRATION

We have all had the experience of fixing our attention on a single object, forgetting everything else. Concentration is a natural faculty, and children use it too when they play. The beauty of concentration is the beauty of everything that is pure and strong, undiluted by uncertainty and ambiguity. The universe around us, however, is rich with distractions and temptations, and no sooner are we concentrating on a given subject than we find ourselves being even more readily diverted away from it. To focus is a spontaneous action. To keep focused is a discipline.

Our whole being is involved in concentration. Indeed our consciousness is the most precious and individual faculty available to us—it is our very self. To give consciousness is to give of ourselves; to allow it to be captured is to allow ourselves to be captured. In this age of thought manipulation on a mass scale, this is a point we must not forget.

Whereas in conscious attention awareness choicelessly opens to everything that is, in concentration all realities in the universe are excluded except one, and we apply ourselves to it completely. Thus we learn to limit ourselves and to ignore distractions. The advantages of concentration are considerable:

- ◊ By preventing our attention from wandering, we free it from distraction and chaos.
- ◊ All our mental faculties are brought to bear on a single point, and thus the mind becomes united.
- ◊ Unity intensifies; the mind, instead of being scattered or listless, becomes alive and full of energy.

These three factors—release from distraction, unification of the mind, and increased mental vitality—enable individual consciousness to attain silence and gain access to a higher level of consciousness. The *Yoga Sutras* of Patañjali, a classic written in 200 B.C., tell us that "cessation of the mind's waves is liberation." This is the fundamental affirmation of *raja* or royal yoga. Its aim is to discipline—through concentration—the activity of the mind, traditionally compared in India with a mad monkey. One directs the mental waves to a point of convergence and then allows them to subside. In their wake follows the transparency of inner silence: union with the Self.

Any object or process can be the subject of concentration:

◊ In Tibetan Tantric Buddhism, visual images are used: shining, multicolored shapes of divinities; Sanskrit words; geometric shapes; or images of the subtle body.

◊ In the Indian yoga tradition one focuses, among other things, on a *yantra*—a geometric figure representing the metaphysical structure of the universe.

◊ In *mantra* yoga one repeats over and over again "like oil flowing incessantly," a sacred word or *mantra* such as *Aum*, *Ram*, *Soham*, etc., which tunes the person repeating it to the corresponding state of consciousness.

◊ In Zen, one is sometimes invited to count one's breaths or to repeat over and over in one's mind a *koan*—a paradoxical formula suitably chosen for its ability to short-circuit the mind and thereby open it up to *satori*, or enlightenment.

◊ In *laya* yoga one listens to inner sound:

> The mind lost in that sound forgets everything outward, and merges itself into the sound, as milk mixes with water, finally to dissolve with it in the ether of consciousness. Controlling his mind, the yogi, by constant practice, becomes indifferent to everything else and is attracted by such sounds as transport him beyond the mind.

We can also concentrate on an idea. This method has often been preferred in the West: one focuses attention on a given subject, looks at it from different viewpoints, perceives its meaning, and identifies fully with it. Reflection, after all, is nothing more than a succession of thoughts. But instead of letting thoughts run their natural course, one brings them back to a predetermined subject so as to dig into it and discover its very essence. Michel de Montaigne, the French essayist, was a master of reflection. He wrote:

> Meditation is a rich and powerful method of study for anyone who knows how to examine his mind, and to employ it vigorously. . . . The greatest men make it their vocation, "those for whom to live is to think." Moreover, nature has favoured it with this privilege, that there is nothing we can do for so long a time, nor any action to which we can apply ourselves more frequently and easily. It is the occupation of the gods, says Aristotle, the source from which comes their beatitude and ours.

Why would disciplined thought help us to catch a glimpse of the transpersonal world? The reasons are many. First of all, through concentration mental habits are deautomated. Usually ideas repeat themselves automatically within the psyche, becoming what Hindu tradition refers to as *samskara*, the mental processes we repeat thousands of times until they concretize to form the structure of our personalities. Reflection makes a big difference. Instead of being repeated mechanically, thoughts are examined one by one. We learn to weigh them, not to take anything for granted, to come up with alternatives, and to produce paradoxes. There is no longer room for automatic thinking.

Thought, therefore, contains the essence of freedom. When we think, we can take off in a thousand different directions. (This is in contrast with action, which is subject to the laws of physical reality.) We can create and unmake universes, arrive instantaneously anywhere, generate new realities, conceive the infinite.

In this process of reflection it is necessary to separate oneself from thoughts of others, even those of great thinkers, and be confident about what emerges from one's own intimate mental processes. Ralph Waldo Emerson, the famous American poet and essayist, has given us a useful tip on this subject:

> To believe your own thought, to believe that what is true for you in your private heart is true for all men,—that is genius. . . . A man should learn to detect and watch that gleam of light which flashes across his mind from within, more than the luster of the firmament of bards and sages.

How often have we discarded an original thought in favor of unconvincing but sufficiently reassuring ideas? In contrast, being ready to gamble on one's own thoughts, however outlandish they may seem, is the mark of the creative thinker, and it is more readily displayed in those who enjoy some familiarity with the mental world, those who move in it with ease and confidence.

Another reason why thought can elevate the center of consciousness is that the human mind models itself on its contents. If the mind is focused on transpersonal themes, it assimilates them, the center of consciousness rises, and one may perceive fundamental truths. Thus did Tolstoy resolve a crisis in his life:

> At that time—when I was living in the Caucasus—I was solitary and unhappy; I started to reflect as people have the power to reflect only once in their lives. . . . It was both a stormy and a blessed period. Never, neither before nor after, have I reached such heights of thought; never have I looked as deeply as I did then, during those two years. And everything I then discovered will remain a firm conviction in me for the rest of my days . . . in two years of work with the mind, I discovered a simple, age-old truth, but one I know as no one else can know: I found that there is immortality, there is a soul, and

that one needs to live for another, in order to be eternally happy.

There is disagreement, however, on the issue of thinking as a path to the transpersonal world. The mind has repeatedly been made the culprit for shutting out the transpersonal vision. And by no means has it been the only defendant in the dock. The blame has been brought in turn against nearly all aspects of human nature—body, sexuality, emotions, desires. The charges have often been influenced by cultural factors, by traditions, as well as by the personal characteristics of the accuser.

In the mind's case, reservations are twofold: First, elements of a higher level cannot be explained in terms of a lower level; thus the rational mind cannot explain the world of the Self, which transcends it. Second, the mind may crystallize into dogma and prejudice and thereby preclude us from any new experience, including the experience of the transpersonal world.

This bad press has tempted many to do away with the mind altogether. Often, however, concentrated thought has been a source of vitality, sometimes even a springboard toward higher levels of consciousness. Germaine Staël-Holstein (known as Madame de Staël) was a nineteenth-century intellectual giant and one of the leading figures in the Romantic movement. She opposed Napoleon ("Intellect does not attain its full force unless it attacks power"), and as a result of the extraordinary vigor of her intellect, she was compared by her contemporaries to a blinding light and to an explosion equal to all storms and earthquakes put together. Madame de Staël said, among other things, that "it is in making some intellectual advancement from day to day that the consciousness of one's own moral existence becomes a happy and vital feeling" and "from the exercise of his mental faculties man receives an enhanced belief in the immortality of the soul."

Others in the West preferred simply to concentrate on silence. This approach is like starting at the end rather than at the beginning. Only the most gifted individuals are able to use such an approach, and when they do, a lot happens. Let us take two examples: Tommaso Campanella and Jacob Boehme.

Campanella, the Italian philosopher, was an unusual person. Thanks to his prodigious memory, anything he read was recorded indelibly in his mind. When he wrote a letter, he would contract his facial muscles to assume the features of his correspondent in order to understand him better. Campanella had paranormal intuitions, such as hearing an inner voice alerting him to danger. He considered himself a forerunner of a new era, and his contemporaries compared him to an erupting volcano. To meditate, Campanella would withdraw to a silent, dark place, leave aside his worries and problems, find a comfortable position, and shut his eyes. He would then clear his mind of thoughts, chasing away any that still survived, until he became "immobile like . . . a plant or a rock." In this way he achieved "philosophical ecstasy."

Resembling Campanella was Boehme, his contemporary, a man also endowed with paranormal faculties such as clairvoyance and psychometry. Boehme called plants and animals by name and knew several languages without ever having studied them. Above all, he was a great mystic. Since childhood he had transpersonal visions, and in 1610, at the age of thirty-five, he had a full-blown illumination in which he became aware of the divine order in nature. What he had previously seen in a fragmentary way appeared to him to be harmonized like the many strings of a harp. At various times in his life Boehme had problems with the theological establishment of his day, and he was forced to earn his living as a cobbler in his native German city of Görlitz. His method of meditation is reminiscent of the Zen instruction to discover your face before you were born. Boehme advises:

> If thou canst, my son, for a while but cease from all thy thinking and willing, then shalt thou hear the unspeakable words of God. . . . When thou art quiet and silent, then are thou as God was before nature and creature; thou art that which God then was; thou art that of which he made thy nature and creature. Then thou hearest and seest even with that wherewith God himself saw and heard in thee, before even thine own willing or thine own seeing began.

Practicing inner silence, however, is not easy. Many people have discovered that it is easier to reach this state by degrees. Saint Teresa of Avila, for example, differentiated four successive levels of meditation, comparing them to four different ways of watering a garden—the garden of the human soul, to be irrigated in order that it might produce flowers and fruit.

The first stage, corresponding to discursive meditation (reflection on a subject), is also the most strenuous: one must fetch the water oneself, drawing it in a bucket from a well. This is arduous and tiring work, because one relies entirely on one's own strength and continually struggles with distractions. After some time, however, the benefits begin to show; indeed, many new buds sprout.

The second stage occurs when the well is fitted with a winch, and the gardener thus obtains more with less effort. This is the "orison of quiet." After so much work, meditation is easier, the intellect is suspended, the faculties of the soul are united, and only the will is used; the plants in the garden yield flowers and perfumes, but the gardener must get rid of the weeds.

In the third stage, referred to as the prayer of union, personal effort is dispensed with—a canal waters the garden. This stage is associated with sleep and rest in that the faculties of the soul are dormant—although memory and imagination, which by this time have become useless, may still cause trouble. The fruits in the garden are ripening.

In the fourth and final stage, corresponding to union, there is nothing more that the gardener has to do, because the water showers directly from the sky like divine grace. One experiences bliss and dies to all one has been. Teresa describes one of her illuminations in this way:

> It is a light that does not dazzle, a brightness full of gentleness, an infused splendor which enchants and delights the eyes without tiring them, just as they are not made tired by the clarity of that sublime beauty. It is as though . . . one saw the clearest water flowing across a crystal lit up by the sun . . . [it is] a light that knows no waning and which nothing can disturb because it is eternal; it is so boundless that no one could imagine it, not even if he possessed the greatest mind and thought about it all his life.

INTROSPECTION

India, 1896. In a small village, a seventeen-year-old boy named Venkataram suddenly feels he is about to die. He is the middle brother of three. Their father is dead. Until now he has been a very ordinary boy, somewhat undisciplined and negligent at school but alert, lively, and in perfect health. Instead of calling the members of his family or a doctor, Venkataram does a strange thing: he lies down on the ground, shuts his eyes and mouth, tenses his muscles, and pretends he is already dead. He then enters into his inner world. What is death? he asks himself. It means that this body is going to perish and be burned to ashes. And now comes the all-important insight. The body is inert, realizes Venkataram, but I can sense the "I" that is me, independent of body and death, an immortal spirit:

> All this was not dull thought. It flashed through me vividly as living truth which I perceived directly, almost without

> thought-process. "I" was something very real, the only real thing about my present state.
>
> Fear of death had vanished once and for all. Absorption in the Self continued unbroken from that time on. Other thoughts might come and go like the various notes of music, but the "I" continued like the fundamental *sruti* note that underlies and blends with all the other notes.

The young boy later took the name of Ramana Maharshi and became one of the greatest sages in Indian history. In his discovery he had spontaneously adopted a method of meditation that had been used in India for hundreds of years. Rather than opening oneself up panoramically onto everything, or concentrating on a single subject, consciousness is redirected to its origin and becomes aware of itself.

Our individual consciousness, or "I," becomes identified in the course of our life with the various elements of the personality. It becomes one with the body, with emotions and desires, with opinions and roles. This is its universe; this becomes its being. Once it coincides with a structure, consciousness is limited by it: I am my body, my emotions, my ideas, my roles, and so on. So credible and compelling, the dream of our identity becomes a reality shared by everyone, a public and definitive statement.

In this meditation technique the "I" is detached from everything with which it is usually identified—in other words, I am *not* my body, my emotions, my roles. One does not condemn or despise all these aspects. Instead, one dispassionately and objectively observes them from a distance. Thus detached, consciousness turns back to itself and finds itself. Consciousness is *being*, not becoming—pure being, without form and without limits, beyond the flux of time, free.

Centuries before Ramana, Sankara had made this method the basis of his teaching and the symbol of India's spiritual renewal. Two main events brought Sankara onto the path of self-realization: first, the death of his father, which led him to reflect on how ephemeral and illusory life is; then, a meeting with a *chandala*, or untouchable, on the banks of the Ganges. Walking along with a group of disciples, Sankara, following the normal custom, signaled the untouchable to move aside —an ordinary, unthinking gesture. But the untouchable confronted him: God is one, he objected, all distinction of caste and creed is absurd. Sankara, overwhelmed by this idea, prostrated himself before the *chandala*, and affirmed that anyone who had learned to see the One everywhere should be his master. A legend maintains that the untouchable was none other than the god Shiva, who had assumed human form in order to teach Sankara the unity of all beings.

According to Sankara, discernment—or *viveka*—cuts through our identity like a sword, severing it from all that is not timeless. In this way we understand that the realities to which we attribute value and significance are but phantoms. Would you identify yourself, says Sankara, with the shadow cast by your body, or with the image of your body in sleep? Of course not. In the same way, it is absurd to believe that our countless emotions, ideas, and sensations in their many different forms are our true being, the Self.

The Self, in contrast with the ever-changing nature of the universe, is immutable. Meister Eckhart, the great German mystic, used the analogy of a door: the world is a swinging door, and the Self is the unmoving hinge. Sankara compared the *Atman*, or Self, with the hub of a wheel that remains still while the wheel turns, and described it thus:

> The *Atman* is supreme, eternal, indivisible, pure consciousness, one without a second. It is the witness of the mind, intellect and other faculties. It is distinct from the gross and the subtle. It is the real I. It is the inner Being, the uttermost, everlasting joy.

Some psychotherapists have realized that this insight may not only occur to a few yogis but can benefit all of us. In Assagioli's psychosynthesis, the client is helped to see his or her fears, anger, guilt feelings—in fact, to see all psychological contents, negative or positive, as distinct from the true Self. Through the exercise of *dis-identification*, without repressing, forcing, or judging, you learn to take a new spatial attitude to the various elements of your personality. You distance yourself from them and see them in perspective—as no longer overwhelming or absolute. From this new outlook it is easier to answer the ever-recurring question we all carry inside: Who am I?

Assagioli discovered that having a clearer perception of the "I" makes us feel better. Usually, when we are not thinking too much, we feel we know quite well who we are. It only takes a moment of attention, however, to realize that nothing is more elusive and mysterious than our own identity, and the many contrasting theories psychology has formulated about the "I" testify to the confusion. If, on the other hand, we continue to probe, everything becomes clearer. The clutter of ready-made ideas and programmed mechanisms is swept aside. We even penetrate through the layers of our most intimate feelings and meaningful ideas. Then we arrive at a Center, a geometric point without dimensions.

As in the case of all powerful techniques, this approach involves some risks, especially for unbalanced personalities. These are the dangers referred to in psychology as an excessive "field independence"—namely, too strong a separation from the internalized social norms (the "superego") and from one's environment. The result can be a feeling of omnipotence, absolute freedom, and the absence of limits. On the other hand, separation from everything can be sought as a means of escape or denial. If I do not feel at home in my body, I am frightened by other people; the world out there is complicated and hostile. Then I shut my eyes, decide it is all an illusion, and withdraw into myself. Neither of these two attitudes, of course, is genuine realization.

The breakthrough comes as the result of a search in the

dark. Another Indian sage, Ramakrishna, likens it to the experience of a burglar feeling his way around a room in the dark, touching one object after another; he says *neti neti* to himself—"not this, not that." He then comes across the gem he had been looking for and, recognizing it at once, rejoices: "This is it!"

This point of arrival, we realize, is our original point of departure. It is not an artificially contrived concept; rather, it is our innermost "I," the Self which we have always been. In finding it we experience relief; we feel centered. It is a beautiful discovery to which we can frequently return. Who would have thought it could all be so simple?

A few rare individuals arrive at this discovery almost by chance, or perhaps with the help of an exceptional sensitivity. Helen Keller became blind and deaf at the age of nineteen months as a result of contracting scarlet fever. Helped by her patient and skillful teacher, Ann Sullivan Macy, she learned to understand words and to communicate. But blindness and deafness were forever.

What was Keller's inner world like? Compared with ours, it was probably more independent of the external environment. In the silent darkness of her inner universe, there must have been a consciousness able to separate itself from space and time with greater facility than that of a seeing and hearing person. One day Keller, accompanied by Sullivan, was in the library reading Braille. "A very strange thing has happened," she suddenly told her teacher. She had experienced vivid sensations of being in Greece:

> Scarcely were the words out of my mouth when a bright, amazing realization seemed to catch my mind and set it ablaze. I perceived the realness of my soul and its sheer independence of all conditions of place and body. It was clear to me that it was because I was a spirit that I had so vividly "seen" and felt a place thousands of miles away. Space was nothing to spirit!

> In that new consciousness shone the presence of God, Himself a Spirit everywhere at once, the Creator dwelling in all the universe simultaneously.

Plotinus also adopted the introspective approach, perhaps because he himself had received instructions about it at the age of thirty-nine when on a visit to Persia, following the Roman Emperor Gordian III. We have clear evidence that this philosopher had an extraordinary natural capacity for transpersonal experience. This is what Plotinus writes about it in a letter to his friend Flaccus:

> You can only apprehend the Infinite (*ἄπειρον*) by a faculty superior to reason, by entering into a state in which you are your finite self no longer—in which the divine essence is communicated to you. This is ecstasy. It is the liberation of your mind from its finite consciousness. Like can only apprehend like; when you thus cease to be finite, you become one with the Infinite. In the reduction of your soul to its simplest self, its divine essence, you realize this union, this identity.

Here Plotinus speaks of "reduction of the soul to its simplest self." Indeed he strips the soul of all its structures until it is left naked. This is the path of supreme simplicity. For many people this process is described by the metaphor of entering into oneself. One enters one's most intimate self, withdrawing from everything that has a form, from anything that changes. What we have grown accustomed to thinking of as "inner" then becomes "outer." Even our most cherished emotions, unexpressed thoughts, and secret fantasies, instead of being perceived as harbored within, appear as distant entities, objective landscapes distinct from ourselves. Friedrich Schelling, the German philosopher, knew this path well:

> We all possess in fact a secret, wonderful faculty of withdrawing from the changes of time into our inner being, into our

> self denuded of ourselves under the form of changeability. This perception is the innermost, most individual of experiences, on which depends everything which we know and believe of the supersensual world. This perception convinces us that something *is* in the true sense of the word, while everything else merely appears.

It may be disconcerting to hear the same spiritual path being described in different ways. On the one hand, the method of panoramic awareness that we examined in the first section is based on a destructuring of identity—nothing has substance, the "I" is an illusion. On the other hand, as we have seen in this section, by means of an inward journey one arrives at an exaltation of the "I"—the "I" not only exists but is immortal and infinite.

We can explain these differences by an analogy. Let us imagine that the same movie is shown to a group of deaf and blind people. When asked what happened, the two subgroups would describe it in completely different terms. The blind would say they heard dialogues and sounds, while the deaf would maintain they saw pictures in motion. We can say the same about the Self (as we call it in this book)—an unutterable reality is perceived and described in remarkably different, perhaps even opposite ways, depending on the point of view and personal traits of whoever makes the description.

But beyond the differences, similar approaches stand out in the two methods. Both employ the subtlest and most intimate part within us—consciousness—as a tool for transformation. Both warn us not to put faith in our identity as we have grown to understand it, encourage us to rely less on the ever-changing world of phenomena, and praise detachment and equanimity in the face of what life brings our way. Above all, both methods stress the same goal—supreme freedom.

The technique of introspection which, layer by layer, takes us to the immutable Self, is elegant in its simplicity. The Self is poor and naked. In order to understand it we do not need complicated techniques, rituals, or tortuous thought processes. On the contrary, all these devices belong to the world of becoming, and thus form part of its illusions. Rather than operating in the field of experience and finding in it the means for transfiguring it, we are led to transcend it altogether. Then we discover there is no longer any reason for worry, anxiety, or effort. The infinite is already within us; it has always been there and always will be.

REFRAMING

Consider the following situations:

◊ You are feeling fine; then a friend, concern in his voice, says "You look tired," or "Are you all right?" Immediately you feel weak and weary.

◊ Someone makes a judgment in your presence: "What a lovely tie," "This fish is rotten," or "He's a terrible actor." At once the tie is no longer dull, the fish stinks, the actor is stumbling.

◊ A person is pointed out to you: "That man is famous" (or a tax dodger, a rich man, a suspected murderer, a transsexual). From then on, you perceive that individual through new eyes.

◊ You see a TV ad for a new type of car, stereo system, drink, or cookie. Immediately that product, of no interest to you before, seems attractive, perhaps indispensable.

In each one of these examples your perception of reality has undergone dramatic change. "Suggestion," someone will say. But that is to undervalue the psyche's exquisite flexibility. Much more is at stake here—our relationship with the world, our criteria for truth, perhaps the very essence of mind. More important, these same mental processes that in the previous examples were triggered by chance or commercial purposes can be consciously utilized to attain inner freedom. Let us see which principles are at work here:

1. *The reality we live in is mental.* Working with the subjective world, as anyone treading the Way of Illumination inevitably does, one soon realizes the extent to which the mind gives shape to the reality surrounding us. Everything we see around us—objects, people, events—is filtered, colored, organized, or eliminated by the mind. "People are agitated and disturbed not by things, but by the opinions they have about things," said the Greek philosopher Epictetus in his *Manual*.

2. *The framework through which the mind interprets reality can be a source of illusion, fear, and pain.* In the Indian tradition, two examples are proverbial: the rope wrongly perceived as a serpent, and the stone dogs, thought at a distance to be real. Both were harmless inanimate objects brought to life by our fears. The mind may distort reality and imprison us in an illusion. Our fundamental and most ingrained assumptions may be at stake here—the distinction between the "I" and the world, the substantiality of things and people, the passing of time, perhaps even the existence of evil and death.

3. *Mind patterns repeat and reinforce themselves.* Thoughts tend to attract corresponding emotions and images, repeat themselves, and solidify. Thus are forged our basic traits—generosity or avarice, shyness or audacity, weakness or strength.

4. *All thoughts are possible.* Despite the mind's tendency to imitate itself, we can play with it and perceive its essentially arbitrary nature. In Naropa's Tibetan yoga, adepts train themselves during sleep to transform mental images—for instance, they turn an animal into a man, water into fire, earth into space, the one into the many, and the many into the one. They change their body into a bird, tiger, lion, king, house,

rock, or forest; or they multiply it into millions until it fills the whole universe. The aim, says Naropa, is to "realize that all things are manifestations of the mind."

5. *By shaping and transforming thoughts we free ourselves from their control.* We are usually lived by our thoughts. They come to us, we accept them, and they control us. Working on them, instead, gives us a sense of mastery and objectifies the mental world. Ideas are no longer intangible, undefinable entities that govern us without our even realizing it. Now they are out there, so to speak—mental objects we can observe, weigh, question, and transform.

Working on our thoughts shows us that the mind is an instrument, not an oracle. From this vantage point it is easier to transcend the mental plane and rise to higher levels of consciousness.

The foregoing five statements (commonly found in various cultures and traditions), all lead to the sixth one, the most practical:

6. *We can change our reality by changing our thoughts.* We can transform our thoughts and thereby reframe our world. This does not necessarily mean that the mind changes the external world, assuming that such a world exists. It means that we change *our* world—the world in which we live and move and breathe—and thus we are responsible for change.

Let us begin with examples from Greek and Roman philosophers. Epictetus suggested that we look on life as a theatrical performance in which roles are assigned to us without our consent. Our task is to perform them to the best of our ability. Seneca, in a letter to his friend Lucilius, advised him to accept everything that happens as a decree of the gods. Marcus Aurelius, the emperor-philosopher, imagined that he was watching human vicissitudes—including his own life—

from a seat in the clouds, in the context of the whole world. This wider perspective enabled him to see things with greater wisdom and serenity.

Thoughts can be applied to various entities: ourselves, others, things, life. Here are some examples from the Christian tradition:

◊ Jean Pierre de Caussade, a French mystic, advised that we see every event that happens to us as "that which is the best and most divine for us" at that particular moment.

◊ The *Theologia Germanica*, the work of an anonymous fourteenth-century German author, suggests that we regard everything as not our own, so that we are free of all attachments.

◊ When Saint Catherine of Siena recoiled from taking care of a sick and purulent person, a vision of Christ appeared and told her to transform "sweet into bitter and bitter into sweet."

◊ When Saint Francis kissed a leper, he no longer saw a repulsive being, but instead a brother and an immortal soul.

These are all precise instruments for reframing, because they invite us to see reality from a new perspective. In the same way, the yoga precepts of the Kargyupta Tibetan sect exhort us to regard our enemies with the thought that in one of thousands of our previous incarnations they were our friends and relatives (thereby changing our hostility into affection); to regard misfortunes and pain as a guru (because we may learn from suffering even more than from pleasure); and to look at the world as though it were a dream or a mirage, a prevalent theme in all Buddhism, as we can see in these words attributed to the Buddha:

> The phenomena of life can be compared to a dream, a ghost, an air bubble, a shadow, glittering dew, the flash of lightning —and they must be contemplated as such.

In the Hasidic tradition, everyday existence—filled as it is with tasks and challenges—is seen as the true field of realization. With its banalities and awkward moments, everyday life—not another and better life—is regarded as the only true opportunity for transformation.

But, one might object, is not reframing a way of manipulating consciousness and restricting our perception of reality? In the hands of religious, political, or commercial powers, isn't it likely that this technique could become a method for controlling minds? This danger does indeed exist and we are all affected by it—all the more reason for becoming familiar with it. In the Way of Illumination, in any case, the thoughts to be used are never chosen arbitrarily, nor do they bow to the dictates of gain or power. Rather, the thoughts employed in conscious reframing are

◊ *Provocative*: They question our commonplace attitudes.

◊ *Significant*: They express hypotheses that, though seemingly paradoxical, make sense and inspire.

◊ *Heuristic*: They lead to new perspectives and unexpected answers.

◊ *Liberating*: By showing us the universe in a new light, they reduce our burden of ignorance, bondage, and pain.

Do we, for instance, take the events of life too seriously? We are told to look on them as dreams or mirages. Are we bound by suffering? We can learn to look on it as an opportunity for using resources we would not otherwise tap. Are we afraid of people? We can think of them—and ourselves—

as players in a game, or actors in a theatrical performance. On the other hand, do we find ourselves undervaluing them? We can learn to see in them their infinite value.

This is no magic formula, of course. However, from ancient times the moldable nature of the mind has been put to good use in all the great civilizations. Reframing is a kind of gymnastics that increases our inner flexibility, mental mastery, and ability to reverse a situation. As many psychotherapists are discovering, it is also a basic therapeutic tool, because it helps us to understand that we are responsible for how we shape our perception of ourselves, our relationships, and life in general.

In certain cases, when the mind is sufficiently transparent, reframing can lead to a genuinely transpersonal experience. Thus it is used in the Way of Illumination as a support for some of the techniques we saw in the previous sections. Reframing has a powerful effect on a person already open to the transpersonal world. When Aurobindo was shut up in prison for political reasons, he looked at other prisoners and at everything else around him, while thinking at the same time, "All this is Brahman," and superimposing this thought onto the reality he perceived. Then came a time, he wrote in his memoirs, when prison was no longer prison:

> The high wall, those iron bars, the white wall, the green-leaved tree shining in sunlight, it seemed as if these common place objects were not unconscious at all, but that they were vibrating with a universal consciousness, they loved me and wished to embrace me or so I felt. Men, cows, ants, birds, are moving, flying, singing, speaking, yet all is Nature's play; behind all this is a great pure detached Spirit in a serene delight. . . . The hard cover of my life opened up and a spring of love for all creatures gushed from within. . . . After this for many days I did not have to suffer any troubles in the jail.

EDUCATION

We will now speak about the most influential people of all.

Educators. No one is as important as they are, because no one is more responsible for shaping tomorrow's world. Indeed, they play a greater role in our future than politicians, financiers, or industrialists.

We might well devote a separate treatise to educators, as distinct from all other individuals we will encounter in this book. Rather than being primarily concerned with progress in their own lives, these people focus on the path other individuals tread. Educators are like the *bodhisattvas* of the Buddhist tradition who, rather than seeking nirvana for themselves, renounce it until all other beings, to the last blade of grass, are also set free.

All the people we meet in this book are educators in some way. This is because transpersonal experiences rarely remain a private enjoyment; rather, their radiance and power are more or less deliberately communicated to others. Ultimately, we are all educators. Mostly without realizing it, we all have an educating—or mis-educating—effect on one another. How we drive a car, what we say to a stranger in the elevator, how we tell a joke or read a newspaper, what clothes we wear, how we laugh, what we do in the thousand circumstances of life —everything reveals who we are and subtly transmits to others our flaws and qualities.

In this section, however, we will focus on educators in the literal sense of the word—all those explicitly concerned with other people's growth and understanding. Educators themselves tread a Way as well. And just as anyone else who proceeds along a Way, they too come up against problems, they search and suffer, discipline themselves, and sometimes have peak experiences. Their main tool is perhaps the ability to perceive intuitively another person's inner world and potentialities. For this reason they may be seen as belonging to the Way of Illumination, because they work with eliciting greater insight.

We can differentiate transpersonal experiences of educators into two broad categories: those coming from an initial understanding about the nature of education; and those arising from actually working with children and students.

We shall start with a few examples in the first category. Like many great educators, Friedrich Froebel, the nineteenth-century German pedagogue, was frustrated with the poverty and fragmentation of traditionally oriented education in the schools of his day. Moreover, in order to earn his living he had chosen the profession of architecture, which was of no real interest to him. The breakthrough came unexpectedly. One day, Froebel writes, "there broke upon my soul, in harmony with the seasons of nature, a springtime such as I had not before experienced; and an unexpected life and life-aim blossomed in my breast." While on a business trip in Germany, he had arrived in Mainz, where the Main and the Rhine rivers meet:

> Here there budded and opened to my soul, one lovely bright spring morning, when I was surrounded by Nature at her loveliest and freshest, this thought, as it were by inspiration: That there must exist somewhere some beautifully simple and certain way of freeing human life from contradiction, or, as I then spake out my thought in words, some mean of restoring man to himself, at peace internally; and that to seek out this way should be the vocation of my life.

As with all paths, the starting point is always the same: life poses an enigma. How are we to resolve it? Froebel's predicament was a disappointing education and a job he disliked. For Jean Jacques Rousseau, the great French philosopher, the problem was an even deeper and more painful one. Some critics contend that Rousseau was not so great an educator because, despite having written *Émile* (perhaps the greatest pedagogical work ever published), in the reality of his private life he let his children end up in an orphanage.

Were we to judge Rousseau from the immediate evidence, our verdict would be severe—and we would not see in *Émile* anything more than a literary exercise. But ours would be an unfair conclusion. Abandoning his children made Rousseau the most tormented pedagogue of all time. Indeed, remorse haunted him for the rest of his life, causing him, as he himself admitted, to shed many "bitter tears." It was from this torment that *Émile* was born. This was the great manifesto which, for the first time in the history of education, celebrated the spontaneity of the human spirit and basic goodness of our original nature, and stressed the value of nurturing the child's inherent potentialities as opposed to the artificial imposition of alien notions and norms.

Another important factor—the observation of children—played a part in the birth of Rousseau's pedagogy. "If I ever made any progress in knowledge of the human heart," wrote Rousseau, "it was because of the delight I felt in observing children." As he grew older, Rousseau realized that his ghostly form frightened children, and he then had to be content with watching them from a distance. Luckily, this distance enabled him to understand them even better and to observe in them the first spontaneous "movements of nature," of which, he wrote, the experts know nothing.

Yet another factor contributing to the genesis of Rousseau's work was his initial inspiration. This striking experience illuminated the whole of his subsequent intellectual output. One day Rousseau had gone to visit French encyclopedist Denis Diderot, who was held in prison in Vincennes. During the journey he began to read the newspaper, *Mercure de France*. At some point he stopped and sat under a tree. Then inspiration suddenly hit him like a thunderbolt: "All at once I felt my spirit illuminated by a thousand lights; a host of living ideas were presented to me with such force and confusion that I was thrown into a state of indescribable bewilderment." Rousseau felt as if he were drunk; he wept and felt violent palpitations for about half an hour. In those moments the central ideas of his most important works—including his treatise on education—flashed through his mind:

> Had I ever been able to write down one quarter of all I saw and felt under that tree, with what clarity would I have been able to show all the contradictions of the social order, with what force could I have expounded all the injustices of our institutions, and with what simplicity could I have demonstrated that man is naturally good and that it is only as a result of these institutions that people become bad.

Rousseau and Froebel are examples of intuitions apparently coming out of the blue. More often, educators are inspired by their work with children. Children are as close to the Self as one can ever be; with them, we have no need to compete or defend ourselves—and when we lower our guard access to the Self is easier. Their joy, spontaneity, and innocence remind us of a world we adults have long ago suppressed or forgotten. For instance, after his initial inspiration Froebel took a post at a school in Frankfurt. It was his first teaching experience. He faced a class of forty children, ages nine to eleven, but he was neither uncertain nor anxious. Instead, he felt an "indescribable happiness."

The great Swiss educator Johann Heinrich Pestalozzi, in a fortuitous meeting with a child, looked into his eyes and was instantly saved from despair:

> I forgot the judgements of God and of men and experienced the bliss of human nature and its sacred innocence while losing, or finding, myself in the child on my knees. . . . So a deep feeling of love which was stronger than everything that troubled me, saved me from utter ruin.

Tolstoy had similar experiences when he set up a school at Yasnaya Polyana. Rather than prepare people to be better exploited by the powerful, he thought, school should bring about equality and brotherhood. The master should only act as an assistant to his pupils, and the key to education, rather than in compulsion, lies in the child's desire to learn. Over the entrance door to Tolstoy's school were the words "Come and leave freely." No tasks were to be completed, and the children came voluntarily, eager to learn.

One of Tolstoy's greatest discoveries was that these peasant children had remarkable artistic talent. He would give them a proverb around which they had to create a story. At one time the whole class took part, dictating and suggesting ideas that Tolstoy wrote down word by word. So interested were the children that they went on until eleven o'clock at night, finally exploding in joyful laughter. One of Tolstoy's many pupils, Fedka, showed outstanding talent. Tolstoy describes his feeling for him in these words:

> I cannot express the mixed feeling of joy, fear and even remorse I felt that evening. I felt that from that day on a whole new world of delight and suffering would open up for him: the world of art. It seemed that I had taken by surprise what no one has the right to see: the birth of poetry's mysterious flower. I experienced . . . joy because I had suddenly and unexpectedly discovered the philosopher's stone I had been looking for in vain during two years: the art of teaching thought and its expression.

Let us look at another example of transpersonal experience elicited by contact with children. Maria Montessori began teaching at the psychiatric clinic at Rome University, working with children who had been labeled "unteachable." In a short time they learned how to read and write with correct spelling, so that they were able to pass tests along with normal children.

Montessori realized it was not so much that her own methods were exceptional but rather that the methods used in ordinary schools were disastrous—to the point of keeping "normal" children at an artificially low level of development.

After this insight, Montessori was able to organize teaching activities in San Lorenzo, at that time one of the poorest districts in Rome. There she developed several techniques for bringing out the latent resources of children and for "giving order to their personality." To mention a few:

◊ Exercises to develop the sense of smell, using flowers and herbs from the garden.

◊ Silence, or moving around in the room without making a sound, a great exercise for developing the child's self-discipline.

◊ Walking along an elliptical line drawn on the floor, to develop concentration.

◊ Keeping pets and plants, to cultivate care and foresight.

◊ Walking along a line while holding a bell, and never letting it ring, an excellent way for training psychophysical coordination.

In Montessori's poor school within a wretched district, amazing things happened: the emergence of spontaneous discipline, effortless learning of reading and writing, free and responsible social interaction. These events exceeded all of Montessori's hopes. She was filled with wonder:

> One day, in great emotion, I took my heart in my two hands as though to encourage it to rise to the heights of faith, and I stood respectfully before the children, saying to myself: Who are you then? Have I perhaps met with the children who were held in Christ's arms and to whom the divine words were

spoken? I will follow you, to enter with you into the Kingdom of Heaven.

We have looked at a few transpersonal experiences of educators. Even more important are the attitudes and faculties that great educators elicit within themselves when they work.

For many of them the starting point is a conscious, often painful realization of the educational mistakes suffered by children in families and schools. For instance, the Indian poet Rabindranath Tagore set up a school in Santiniketan that was free of the restraints of conventional discipline. Every day the students would be introduced to musicians, poets, and thinkers from all over the world in an open, nonsectarian atmosphere. Children were led to "see fire, air, water, land and the whole universe as pervaded by a universal consciousness."

What had led Tagore, at age forty, to engage in this demanding experiment? It was a painful memory of the school he had been obliged to attend as a child—and from which he ran away at thirteen. Traditional education in schools is like a parrot's training, said Tagore, a form of torture that alienates children from nature and kills their sensitivity and joy. Everything Tagore learned, he claimed, had been learned outside of school.

Other attitudes often found in great educators are complete availability and love for their pupils. When he began teaching, Pestalozzi worked with eighty uneducated children, and had neither teaching materials nor assistance. He was present with them from morning to evening, slept in the same room with them, and even taught them while they were in bed until they fell asleep. He believed that school education should be the same as the education one receives from a parent, who is able to observe continually every step in the child's progress. So Pestalozzi dedicated himself to the children completely:

> On these principles I built my procedure. I wished my children to realize at every moment that my heart was theirs, that I was

sharing their luck, and that their joy was my joy. . . . My hands were in their hands, and my eyes rested on their eyes. I laughed and cried with them.

Moment by moment observation enables the educator to notice even the subtlest changes in the child's abilities as he or she grows and develops: intelligence, psychophysical coordination, emotional growth, curiosity, self-discipline, and so forth. This process resembles the development occurring in other living creatures. Biological metaphors are among the most frequently used by great educators, because they recognize in their pupils a living, autonomous evolution that follows its own intrinsic rules and unfolds at its own pace.

Pestalozzi used the analogy of a growing tree to represent the educational process, seeing in this process the mark of an infinite intelligence. He suggested that in order to do a better job, educators observe the way in which trees grow. At first, nothing seems to be happening in a seed; then it sprouts into a delicate sapling. Nature ensures the unfolding of each part. The flower blossoms out of the bud's heart, and then the fruit ripens and at last falls to the ground. Each part of the tree—from roots to trunk to branches to buds—plays an important role. The whole tree is harmonious and well-proportioned, and relates to the environment with no waste of energy. For Pestalozzi, the development of a tree and the growth of a child were both subjects for attention and cause for wonder.

Perceived in this way, a developing child evokes deep respect and confidence. An autonomous process ensues in him or her, without the educator needing to force it. Nothing has to be added: all wisdom and goodness are already in the child. It is the educator's task to learn from the pupil, not vice versa. According to Froebel, we need only to place children—without intermediaries—in front of what they are to learn:

Be guided by the children's questions, for they will teach you, and they will not be content with half-truths. It is true you

> cannot answer them all, for children ask questions which nobody can answer. But either they take you where the earthly and the divine meet, or they simply go beyond your own knowledge and experience.

A less obvious ability—though nonetheless crucial—is the capacity to see universality in a child. A child, learning and growing, is not merely an individual engaged in doing his or her duty and satisfying the teacher's expectations. Rather, each child is *all* children, just as a star moving through space in accordance with universal laws mirrors in itself the whole cosmic order. A growing child, while also a unique individual, is the expression of a universal harmony. Pestalozzi said: "I saw an inner power awake in the children, the universality of which far exceeds my expectations." Montessori, too, observing the emergence of spontaneous self-discipline in children, wrote:

> Had these children, maybe, found the orbit of their cycle, like the stars that circle unwearyingly and which, without departing from their order, shine through eternity? . . . A natural discipline of this kind seems to transcend its immediate environment, and to show itself as part of a universal discipline ruling the world.

These are among the most fertile attitudes to be found in great educators. What are their results in practice, in the experiences as lived by the children and students themselves? What makes a good educator? Some will know the answer to this question at once; they need only look back through their childhood and school memories. Others will have only their dreams and wishes from which to answer. A good educator is someone who

◊ helps us to experiment as we choose, and explore the world without fear. And if we make mistakes or get into trouble, we know we will not be judged.

◊ shows us what we can do and be—and how much joy the discovery can generate.

◊ brings to life even the most banal subjects and fills them with fascination.

◊ encourages us to dig things out for ourselves and connects us with our own resources, helping us realize that what we have learned is our own doing.

◊ never allows us to grow bored or fall asleep, only letting us dream the right amount, always ready to awaken our attention and stimulate us.

◊ helps us to learn without effort, so we sense that what we are learning is something that, deep down, we have known all along.

In addition to all these factors, however, an intangible element lives at the heart of all the great moments in education. In the presence of this element it matters little what you, the pupil, have been learning—whether tennis or Greek, embryology or calligraphy, singing or fashion. If the educator was good, you will have extended yourself, and become more independent, more confident, and more in harmony with yourself, others, and the universe.

At the end of a course one can measure how much a student has learned about a given subject. But at a deeper level, the teaching of the subject was really only a pretext for a beautiful event to be shared by two or more people. The number of topics for study is immense. But the greatest masters all teach the same thing.

LOVE

Martin Buber's recurring dream would always start with a lonely, barren setting like a desert or a cave. At first something unusual would happen—for example, he might be mauled by a lion cub that tore strips of skin from his arm. But the initial events, however dramatic, took place at some speed, as if to say the essence of the dream was yet to come. Then the pace would suddenly slow down, and Buber would let out a cry. Depending on the dream's content, this might be a cry of joy, pain, or triumph, but always a cry coming from deep within his being, and almost too strong for his throat to express it. Then, from far away, another cry would reach his ears—the same type of cry, but emitted by another voice. It was not an echo, but an answer. It meant that another being had heard him, had understood and responded. Now he knew that he was not alone. The dream would end with an intense certainty: *Now it has happened.*

What had happened? What was so important? This: two beings had come into contact. In this dream Buber discovered the following themes that inspired him throughout his life: All true living is relating; love is "the cosmic force"; the primary characteristic of human nature is a readiness for relating with another person; we become an "I" through a "You"; and this relationship is the only one capable of giving "intuitions of eternity."

Despite the many forms of injustice, falsehood, and banality so often present in human interactions, it is possible for two people to truly meet each other. A true meeting is free from greed, fear, or prejudice. Each person is completely open to the other. When it happens, love becomes possible, and one human being can become a Way for the other. And that Self which some reach through introspection, people like Buber discover through the other, rather than in themselves.

The fact that love—even in its most commonplace manifestations—is the most effective vitamin for psychological and spiritual growth is a truth we can all recognize. We need only think of a circumstance when we were treated kindly, or we were understood, or when someone stood by us or appreciated a quality of ours to at once feel better. This is an elementary fact. From a wider perspective, the Russian sociologist Pitimin

Sorokin—whose outstanding work is not known as widely as it deserves—shows in such well-documented books as *The Way and Power of Love* and *Altruistic Love* that love is the best remedy for anxiety, loneliness, and hostility; that there are ways and techniques for developing it; that it makes people saner and longer-lived; that it is the best tool for resolving chronic interpersonal problems; that it stimulates creativity; and that it opens the mind to the "supraconscious."

Why do we speak of love in the Way of Illumination? Love in its many forms is actually to be found in all the Ways. It is too big and manifold a reality to be confined to one path alone. In the Way of Illumination, however, love takes a more explicit role. A seeker on this path will use consciousness as an instrument of exploration and will work toward making awareness as transparent as possible, releasing it from false assumptions, passions, and attachments. In this manner, consciousness is refined, clarified, and freed from envy and shame, regrets and fantasies. One feels united with other people and the universe and knows that this very state can genuinely and legitimately be called true love.

We will start our inquiry in this section by looking at love as the highest form of encounter between two individuals. Unfathomable affinities can emerge between two people, although rarely is the entire potential in a relationship fully manifest. In the exceptional examples we shall be looking at, as in those cited in the previous section, we can begin to get some idea of the tremendous promise inherent in all encounters. It is worthwhile to study and understand these examples, because a meeting between two beings is the pattern for all possible relationships—in the family, in society, and in the planet.

Since love can be seen as a mutual resonance, let us begin with the musical field. Few relationships are as intense as that between composer and interpreter. The violinist Yehudi Menuhin was playing a Béla Bartók composition in the latter's presence:

> Immediately with the first notes there burst forth between us, as an electric contact, an intimate bond which was to remain fast and firm. In fact, I believe that there can exist between a composer and his interpreter a stronger, more intimate bond, even without the exchange of words, than between the composer and a friend he may have known for years. For the composer reserves the core of his personality, the essence of his self, for his works.

After this concert, Bartók wrote a violin sonata, the last work before his death, and dedicated it to Menuhin. Why was their rapport so intense? Menuhin explains it clearly: He had succeeded in reaching the essence of Bartók, and Bartók had felt it. The two men had achieved a resonance.

Let us take another example, although quite a different one, because it is about the relationship between a man and what, to all outward appearances, was a vegetable. At the age of thirty-six Rudolf Steiner, the founder of anthroposophy, met Friedrich Nietzsche in Weimar. Nietzsche, however, was no longer conscious of his surroundings. Steiner found him laid out on a couch, his eyes lifeless, his gaze passive and empty. Nonetheless, Steiner's inner eyes were able to perceive Nietzsche's "soul":

> And so there appeared before my soul the soul of Nietzsche, as if hovering above his head, already boundless in its spiritual light, surrendered freely to spiritual worlds for which it had yearned before being benighted but had not found. . . . I had, before this, *read* the Nietzsche who had written; now I beheld the Nietzsche who bore within his body ideas drawn from widely extended spiritual regions—ideas still sparkling in their beauty even though they had lost on the way their primal illuminating powers.

From the very onset of their encounter, Steiner was at a disadvantage, for how can one enter into a relationship with a human vegetable? And yet he was able to meet Nietzsche at higher levels of consciousness, where vitality, beauty, and intelligence continued to exist even when the ordinary personality had disintegrated. It is possible to see the beauty of the soul even in a wreck.

The third example comes from the religious field. In meditation and prayer, the seventeenth-century French mystic Madame Guyon achieved at times a form of wordless communication. She would remain in silence for hours with her confessor, but much was going on in the stillness:

> It was then that I learned a language I had never known before. I gradually realized that when they brought in Father La Combe to hear my confession and to give me communion, I was no longer able to speak to him and that his presence produced in me the same silence I experienced when in God's presence. . . . Little by little I started speaking to him only in silence, and at that point we understood each other in God, in an inexplicable, divine mode. Our hearts spoke and communicated a grace which defies words. It was a new country for him and for me, but so divine I cannot express it.

Here we see two individuals communicating "in God"—that is to say, on the basis of a higher principle. They were not interested in each other as personalities. Instead, their attention was fully absorbed by a reality that transcended them, and for this reason their encounter was not weighed down by those vicissitudes so common in ordinary relationships. No filter, no shadow, no expectation limited this rapport. Two beings were face-to-face, each reflecting to the other the one Self they both were.

Let us look at how a particular experience, originating in an individual's pain, can expand to be of universal relevance. It happened in 1901 to the prince of mathematics, Bertrand Russell. The wife of his friend and colleague Alfred North Whitehead was suffering intense physical pain. Russell stood by her for a while and then took hold of Whitehead's young son and led him out of the room. Seeing distress in another person revealed to Russell the basic isolation of each human being:

> Suddenly the ground seemed to give way beneath me, and I found myself in quite another region. Within five minutes I went through some such reflections as the following: the loneliness of the human soul is unendurable; nothing can penetrate it except the highest intensity of the sort of love that religious teachers have preached; whatever does not spring from this motive is harmful, or at best useless; it follows that war is wrong, that a public school education is abominable, that the use of force is to be deprecated, and that in human relations one should penetrate to the core of loneliness in each person and speak to that.

In this instance, a relationship to an individual extends to all others. Also, in the period before his "sort of mystic illumination," Russell had lived—as he tells us in his autobiography—in a rather tranquil and superficial way, oblivious of all the more important aspects of his life. After this turning point, Russell felt dramatic changes taking place in him: he could read people's most intimate thoughts—even people he met in the street; he became a pacifist; he took a passionate interest in children, felt much closer to all his friends and acquaintances, and experienced a desire "almost as profound as that of the Buddha" to find a way of making human life more bearable.

As we move on to relationships wider than the encounter between two individuals, love takes on new richness and meaning. Beyond the great variety of its forms, love can be seen as *the realization of oneness*. At an emotional level this realization eradicates self-preoccupation and engenders extraordinarily intense feelings of care, affection, and warmth for all beings. Intellectually, it generates insight into the simplicity underlying the apparent diversity of the universe. Spiritually, it reveals imperishable unity with a greater whole.

In studying the lives and the experiences of those who traveled the Way of Illumination, we shall find that at the peaks of human awareness, loving and knowing are one. A brief look at how some of these people have felt and thought about love shows us that our own experience of love, however beautiful and significant, is like a small leaf in an enormous tree spreading out in all directions. It may help us to realize that love has infinite possibilities for branching out and blossoming:

- ◊ According to Plato, the human soul is like the sea god Glaucus, who, as a result of remaining too long under the sea, became covered with seaweed, shells, and rocks until he was unrecognizable and looked like a monster. In the same way the soul is debased when it pursues what it deceivingly takes to be a source of happiness. Absorbed by transitory desires, lost in a thousand cares, it becomes gross and thick. For us to emerge from the sea of unconsciousness and shake rocks and seaweed off, only one thing can help: love (ἔρως) for what is timeless.
- ◊ At the height of his journey in the *Divine Comedy*, Dante Alighieri experienced himself as an effortlessly turning wheel, moved by cosmic love, "the love which moves the sun and all the stars ("*l'amor che move il sole e l'altre stelle*"). Dante had reached this peak after a long journey of transformation. In Hell and Purgatory he had visited the souls ensnared in the fetters of greed, hatred, and folly. In Paradise he explored ever-higher states of consciousness until he reached the realization of universal love.
- ◊ Rumi, the Islamic poet, stated that everything in the universe is a rhythmic drumbeat—only love (*ishq*) is a melody. According to Rumi, anyone who does not love is like a fish without water or a bird without wings. There are three arduous requirements for attaining the state of

perfect love—to be free from greed, to disdain the intellect, and to transcend all social roles and find one's true Self. Love, says Rumi, is the creative essence of the universe. Through love, thorns are turned to roses, sickness is transformed into health, and anger softens into gentleness; good fortune is seen in the bad, and the ugliest prison becomes a rose garden.

◇ According to Spinoza, the humble Dutch philosopher who chose poverty and solitude as a way of life, the highest state a human being can reach is the "intellectual love of God (*amor intellectualis Dei*)." It is reached when, free from emotional control, one perceives oneself and the world in their necessary order and arrives at "consciousness of the unity of mind with universal nature." In his book *De intellectus emendatione (The Improvement of the Mind)*, Spinoza starts with a biographical note, saying that at one point he made the decision to love that which is eternal and infinite, because only this kind of love can yield true joy.

◇ Saint Francis of Assisi made universal love the cornerstone of his life. He felt a deep love for all—not only for his friends and companions but also for the more unfortunate, and even for the dangerous brigands; not only for human beings but also for every living creature. He would pick up worms in the street lest they be trodden on, and in winter he would feed the bees with honey and wine; when the monks cut down trees for wood, he would ask them not to remove the whole trunk, so that the tree could grow again. He felt a deep sense of love for all creation, and when he looked at a stream, an animal, or the starry sky, he was filled with joy.

◇ Buddha affirmed that one of the most important qualities for attaining nirvana was loving-kindness (*metta*) for all beings. This is how he spoke in the *Sutta-nipata*:

Just as with her own life
a mother shields from hurt
her own, her only, child,
let all-embracing thoughts
for all that lives be thine,
—an all-embracing love
for all the universe
in all its heights and depths
and breadth, unstinted love,
unmarred by hate within,
not rousing enmity.
So, as you stand or walk,
or sit or lie, reflect
with all your might on this;
—'tis deemed "a state divine."

4

◇

◇

◇

◇

The Way of Dance and Ritual

The Ways to the transpersonal Self are tentative answers to profound, vital questions that every one of us, consciously or not, has to face. The Ways use forms and patterns that are both common and spontaneous; there is nothing artificial or abstruse about them. The starting point is always some aspect of life with which we are all familiar—awareness or aesthetic enjoyment, for example, or thought or involvement in action. These aspects are taken to their ultimate level of purity and universality and often surpass their original functions to become something new and entirely different from what they originally were.

Dance and ritual are common aspects of life found in all cultures, and even in certain animal species. They have various uses and meanings. Dance serves the purposes of recreation, self-expression, and the release of surplus energy. Ritual promotes social control, adaptation to the environment, and reinforcement of relationships within a group. Both are ways of responding to the fundamental questions: How do we relate to our bodies? How can we express a private experience in a visible and public way? How can we share with others—with a whole community, perhaps—the higher states of consciousness? In attempting to answer these questions with ritual and dance, many people throughout the ages have discovered the possibility of new states of being, and sometimes they have attained the splendid perspective of the Self.

At this point, however, a question arises: Why are we dealing with such apparently diverse practices as dance and ritual under the same heading? No doubt about it: Dance and ritual are two distinct fields of human endeavor. But look beneath the surface, and you will find they share many characteristics:

- ◊ They both use visible, material means (the human body and its movements) and then its extensions (clothing, setting, and accessories of various kinds) to aspire to an invisible, immaterial reality.
- ◊ They are ways of affirming and displaying that reality at a concrete level, and of participating in it with one's own body.
- ◊ They usher in a new relationship with our physical organism. The body, rather than being the expression of our individuality and of our precariousness, becomes the interface between the finite and the infinite.
- ◊ They are based on the principle that gestures and movements produce corresponding images, thoughts, and emotions and can therefore be used to induce transcendental serenity, lucidity, and presence.
- ◊ They are based on rhythm and the repetition of gestures. Movements repeated indefinitely can bring about altered states of consciousness. Rhythmical uniformity puts the rational mind to sleep, relieves the psyche from the burden of having to choose, and causes corresponding physiological changes.
- ◊ They are intensified by forceful psychophysical changes, caused either by movements (especially when they are vigorous and repeated) or by the intake of substances or drinks (wine, soma, etc.).
- ◊ By means of movements and gestures they generate a subtle, nonphysical reality—a field.

◊ They are public events: one enters their arena, if not as protagonist, then as spectator. The transpersonal world changes from a remote, unexplored area into a meeting place for a community.

◊ They sharply sunder ordinary life—so unpredictable, jumbled, and prosaic—from the sublime dimension of the sacred.

On this path, therefore, we will find practices and people belonging to various categories: traditions and rituals whose creators are lost in the anonymity of ancient traditions, bodily techniques such as Hatha Yoga and T'ai Chi, as well as dancers and actors. At this point, however, another question naturally arises: Do not many of these activities belong to the Way of Beauty? The essence here—expressing the intangible, invisible reality of the Self through material means—is indeed the same in both Ways. A dance may primarily be beautiful and the dancer may think of himself as an artist; and a ritual may be more forceful if enhanced by art—music, for instance.

True, the two Ways are often combined. Also, talking about "Ways" is an abstraction. Like colors, the Ways we are considering can merge and be combined in an infinite number of subtle variations. Moreover, in their higher and more universal aspects, all the Ways are similar and mirror one another.

We can, however, make a clear-cut distinction between the Way of Beauty and the Way of Dance and Ritual. Some dances are not art forms, and ritual is primarily intended to evoke not an aesthetic experience, but a sense of the sacred. The Way of Dance and Ritual has unique aspects that differentiate it from the Way of Beauty—namely, a deepening of body awareness and control over physiological processes; the repetition of gestures and movements; the creation of a subtle field; and the forming of a community of people who temporarily share the same state of consciousness.

As in all the other Ways, dangers and risks abound. When one attempts to express an elusive state of grace in an ordered, predictable fashion, how easy it is for the substance to vanish, leaving behind an empty shell. One needs only to recall a boring ritual or a clumsy dance. Rituals may rigidly program individuals and even whole communities. In dance, the struggle to transform bodily heaviness into ecstatic lightness may lead to narcissism and exclusive interest in one's own private physical pleasure. Finally, trying to make an invisible splendor visible may invite delusions of omnipotence.

Every Way is an attempt to solve a problem. As in every Way, in addition to dangers, one must face obstacles and blind alleys. The main difficulty here is to find a means to demonstrate the state of grace through the opacity of matter. One comes up against resistance from all that is inert or awkward. Here begins a long, hard discipline aimed at achieving a miracle.

The American dancer Isadora Duncan, for instance, was looking for the secret source of beauty. She found it in the pure form of the Parthenon. But it was not enough for her to contemplate it; she wished to express it through dance. The sober, static simplicity of the Doric columns, however, could hardly be represented in the fluid forms of dance. In a letter, Duncan relates how she meditated for several days at the foot of the Greek temple, experiencing her body as nothing and her soul as lost. Even when she succeeded in hearing in the silence the "voice of the Temple," she did not dare to move.

Her paralysis was, fundamentally, the paralysis we all feel when our way is blocked. Deep within ourselves we know and are able to conceive of harmony and grace—perhaps in the form of distant memories, or as dreams that have never broken through into reality, or as formless ideals. We would like to make them real, but we feel only blocked and paralyzed.

Duncan realized that of all the body movements she had made until then, none deserved to be performed before a Doric temple. And while standing motionless, she understood that she must find a dance worthy of this Temple, or never dance again. For many days no movement was born in her. Then, one day, the inspiration came: She realized that those columns which had seemed so straight and immovable, in reality were not straight; each one had an endless undulating movement, each moved in harmony with the others. As soon as she had this thought, her arms rose slowly toward the Temple and she bowed. She realized then that she had found her dance: it was a prayer.

Every path is the answer to a question. Life confronts us with problems, crises, and tasks. We must face them and in some way resolve them (this may simply mean to accept them, or even transcend them). We are then ready to move forward and tackle the next predicament.

Every Way is defined by the difficulties it presents. The problems, in turn, are the expression of what is close to our hearts. For if nothing mattered to us, we would have no more problems.

Our problems need not be a disgrace. When seen from the right perspective, they reveal what is most important to us, what we love most of all. They may be hidden, not readily apparent on the surface, but they are always present. And in the problems before us, whatever their nature or origin, we may happen upon the most advanced point of our lives, the point where, for the time being, we had to stop. That point also shows us to our next step.

THE TRANSFIGURATION OF THE BODY

How beautiful it is to fly in our dreams! Fearlessly we soar, feeling light and powerful; entire landscapes float by beneath us, and we glide in weightless joy. This type of dream may symbolize the age-old human desire to transcend the organism and its limitations—its needs, heaviness, isolation, illness, old age, death. Indeed, many people have considered the body an obstacle to spiritual evolution, as though they needed to leave behind the ballast of matter so that they could rise to subtler, vaster dimensions of the spirit.

Just think of our common experience: the body is the storehouse of tensions and fatigue; it dominates us with the urgencies of hunger, thirst, sleep, sex; it falls ill and deteriorates, reminding us of our mortality; it wraps us in a fleshy envelope and thus marks the confines of our solitude; heavy and dense, it slows down thought; and, with its vulgarity, its unbearable grossness, its smells and rumblings, it shatters all illusions of grandeur. As Nietzsche wrote, it is having a paunch that makes it impossible for us humans to believe we are gods.

But does it have to be this way? From a transpersonal outlook, categorical statements are often a mistake, and paradoxes are ubiquitous. Everything can be turned on its head once you are on a spiritual path: The ugly becomes beautiful; in suffering you find joy; wisdom is won through ignorance; the ephemeral reveals eternity. Surely, many people experience their body as a prison. But for others the pure, wide, creative world of the Self finds its most complete realization *in* matter. "We believe," said a dancing dervish of the Mevlevi sect when talking to American dancer Ted Shawn, "that soul and body are alike divine—that the soul grows, like a flower, on the body's stem. We accept material beauty as the true mirror of divine beauty. And we seek this divine beauty, this ineffable harmony in which all things become as one, through the most nearly perfect of sensuous forms—the rhythm of music and the dance."

This Way toward the Self, then, is not undertaken despite the body, but through it. The obstacle becomes a means: from being a mark of individuality and isolation, the body becomes a symbol of universality—the universality of humankind and its unity with cosmic life.

The goal is far and may seem beyond reach. Yet it all starts in everyday life, in our ordinary body consciousness. Everyone knows that stretching relieves tension and produces well-being; that after a brisk walk we feel more alive; that we can change our state of mind by simply breathing deeply; that dancing, if we are fond of it, helps us forget our worries; that an erect, relaxed posture, or a tense or slouching one, express different moods and attitudes to life. These are commonly accepted facts that all point to one basic truth: Using our bodies in certain ways not only reconciles us to the physical world but also changes our state of mind.

Some people in the course of history have raised these simple, everyday experiences to an art form, discovering in the body a mine of new resources and sensations, transforming the body into an instrument through which they could gain access to new states of consciousness. Sometimes they have even used their organism as a laboratory in which to alter their chemical balance and physiology—particularly in the case of yogis, dancers, and actors, especially mime artists (Jean-Louis Barrault once said: "I feel the divine Presence through a *carnal* perception").

From a detailed study of the experiences of sports champions, recorded in their book *The Psychic Side of Sports*, Michael Murphy and Rhea White show that athletes as well, without having actually made it the explicit aim of their discipline, have experienced states of intense well-being and freedom; altered perceptions of size and field; acute well-being; floating, flying, weightlessness; exceptional energy; and out-of-body experiences.

The starting point in body-work is always the physical experience itself. But many individuals also look for—and find—a model outside themselves by observing nature and imitating its movements. This was the case with Isadora Duncan, who studied the flight of birds, the dance of elephants, and the movements of the clouds in the wind, of waves, of swaying trees, of blooming flowers:

> These flowers before me contain the dream of a dance; it could be named "the light falling on white flowers." A dance that

would be a subtle translation of the light and the whiteness. So pure, so strong, that people would say: it is a soul we see moving, a soul that has reached the light and found the whiteness.

Many postures in Hatha Yoga bear the names of creatures or natural events: tortoise, peacock, cobra, camel, lotus, mountain, embryo, half moon, lightning. Something similar happens in T'ai Chi, which can be defined as a dance, even if its origins are martial. Many of its movements refer to natural entities or processes—for instance, "embrace tiger and return to mountain," "wave hands among clouds," "walk towards the stars," "the stork spreads its wings," and so forth. In watching T'ai Chi one sees in it an expression of the Tao, the natural flow of life. In his teaching, Al Huang Chiang, a master of T'ai Chi, places particular emphasis on spontaneity and ease of movement. He describes the highest experience of T'ai Chi with the words of the Chinese Taoist philosopher Lieh Tzu:

> It was then that the eye was like the ear, and the ear like the nose, and the nose like the mouth; for they were all one and the same. The mind was in rapture, the form dissolved, and the bones and flesh all thawed away; and I did not know how the frame supported itself and what the feet were treading upon. I gave myself away to the wind, eastward or westward, like leaves of a tree.

The basic principle in these body-approaches is that posture and movement are ends in themselves. T'ai Chi movements are not aimed at manipulating; dance is not for seizing or grabbing. And Hatha Yoga *asanas* remove an individual from the turbulent, unpredictable, precarious flow of daily life, and return them to the serene, luminous world of being.

The same happens in *maithuna*, the Tantric practice in which the sexual act is transformed from the mere gratification of a need into a meditation. The tenth-century temple of Khajuraho in India displays statues of men and women in various kinds of explicit sexual activity. These intertwined bodies show no sign of sin or shame. Simple sexual pleasure or personal affection are also absent. These human forms are hieratic, their expressions timeless. They represent beings who are not merely satisfying their own personal desires. Sexuality, here, is transformed into sacrament.

In this yoga, libido is perceived as the creative essence of the universe; suspension of male orgasm during copulation is a means of gaining control over desire and unawareness; the partner becomes the incarnation of a god; the bodies united represent the unity of all beings; and sexuality, instead of enslaving us with the force of unrestrainable impulse, becomes a means to liberation. "While being caressed, sweet princess," chants the God Shiva to his wife Devi in a Tantric text written four thousand years ago, "enter *the caressing* as everlasting life."

Everyday reality, as we know, is quite another thing—the body learns to act in socially acceptable and culturally conditioned ways; it mechanically performs habitual movements (eating, getting dressed, driving the car); it gradually forms an armor—a network of muscular chronic tensions reflecting one's emotional history; it accumulates the dreary marks of illness and time. Each body therefore becomes a constellation of memories and tensions, an individually and socially defined emblem. But transpersonal body techniques use movements and postures that have nothing to do with our personal history or with the practical gestures we make in everyday life. They are actions and gestures whose significance transcends our present situation, and thus they have the power to set us free.

In some cases—Hatha Yoga, for instance—the aim is "cosmicization" of the body, as Mircea Eliade called it. The body is the universe: the sun, the moon, the planets, every entity in the cosmos finds its counterpart in it. For each *chakra*, or energy center, there is a god, a sound, and a spiritual quality. In this view, such centers and currents of subtle energy in the human body, far from being symbolic, are a physiological reality. The body is not only flesh and bones, nerves and organs but also an energy system—intangible and invisible to the naked eye, likely to escape the instruments of scientific inquiry but accessible to a few open, sensitive individuals, who receive visionary impressions of its vital existence.

Postures and breathing techniques enable the body to be more than the incarnate summary of our history, with our weaknesses, our triumphs and failures. It can, instead, become a concentrated manifestation of the universe with the magnificence and grandeur of cosmic harmony. The correspondence between microcosm and macrocosm is no magic or superstition. As we shall see in the Way of Science, analogies are a device for freeing the human spirit. The analogy of the body with the universe is a way of transforming chaos into order, the particular into the universal, the transitory into the eternal.

Sometimes the style is Apollonian; at other times, Dionysian. Some techniques are highly structured, others follow a freer approach. The basic factor, however, is always control. Adept yogis, dancers, and athletes have attained it to a high degree through patient discipline and contact with even the remotest parts of their bodies.

The first stage in this work is often the ability to imagine and be in touch with one's body in all its aspects and movements, even the subtlest. When his wife Romola told him it was a pity he was unable to watch himself dancing, Vaslav Nijinsky answered:

> You are mistaken. I always see myself dancing. I can visualize myself so thoroughly that I know exactly what I look like, just as if I sat in the midst of the audience.

Visualization is a widespread technique in body discipline, and it is often used in sport as well. A study of the greatest sports champions of our day, *The Pursuit of Sporting Excellence* by David Hemery, showed that approximately 80 percent of all athletes habitually visualize their performance. By imagining with precision and in every vivid detail what they want to accomplish, athletes familiarize themselves with their practice, mobilize the organism's psychophysical energies, alert and prepare the nervous system, come to believe that what they want to do is feasible, and perfect their performance.

Equally important is the broadening and refining of expressive possibilities. According to the renowned ballet dancer Rudolf Nureyev, the relationship between dancers and their dance parallels the one between actors and the poems they recite. Many different readings, he explains, are possible:

> Of course this involves a lot of research, but it is endlessly fascinating. It means studying for hours the exact way of placing a shoulder, a chin, or certain stomach muscles. Each part of the body must be studied separately as one might examine the different parts of a machine. Then all those bits of the puzzle must be put together, glued together, one might even say—and submerged into the artist's personal expression. Thus our dancing, which the public often imagines to be made up of easy, spontaneous movements, is most often the result of days and days of study, of patient long hours spent in front of the mirror severely criticizing oneself for the slightest wrong attitude.

Over and over again in this search we find some basic facts: Learning to control a given function frees us from unconscious slavery to habits, conditioning, and vicious circles; it extends our range of possibilities; it raises us above the function we intend to control; it gives us a position of greater balance and freedom toward the psychophysical processes of our organism; it makes possible the invention of new harmonies and new rhythms; and, after a long purgatory, it offers well-being and ecstasy.

Martha Graham, the American pioneer of modern dance, once stated in a lecture that in order to achieve the mastery of the body necessary for becoming a dancer, a long period of training is required. At the end of this period, something very beautiful happens:

> You see, to begin with, it takes about ten years to produce a dancer. That's not intermittent training; that's daily training. You go step by step by step. In ten years you'll be dancing—probably even before that time—but by ten years, if you are going to be a dancer at all, you will have mastered the instrument. You will know the wonders of the human body, because there is nothing more wonderful. The next time you look into the mirror, just look at the way the ears rest next to your head; look at the way the hairline grows; think of the little bones in your wrists; think of the magic of that foot, comparatively small, upon which your whole weight rests. It's a miracle. And the dance in all those areas is a celebration of that miracle.

Physical training, of course, is merely the first step. When ready, the body becomes an instrument of inspiration, without which dance is little more than gymnastics. According to Duncan, there are three types of dancers: those for whom dancing is physical exercise, those who dance to express emotions, and those who hand over their bodies to the inspiration of the "soul":

> This . . . sort of dancer understands that the body, by force of the soul, can be in fact converted to a luminous fluid. The flesh becomes light and transparent, as shown through the X-ray —but with the difference that the human soul is lighter than these rays. When, in its divine power, it completely possesses the body, it converts that into a luminous moving cloud and thus can manifest itself in the whole of its divinity.

But what about us—we who are not dancers of the third kind, or athletes, or yogis; we whose bodies are not finely tuned and who are breathless going up a flight of stairs—what can we learn from these ideal models? A crucial lesson: We learn that "matter," rather than being an ontological category, is a state of consciousness: a way of feeling heavy, alienated, and bitter—nothing more. We learn, too, that it is possible to reconcile ourself with our body; that we can give it a rhythm and a discipline; that it is possible for us to learn to live in the body, use it as a means of expression in the world, and perceive it as a source of energy, lightness, and euphoria— No longer an enemy to bother and bog us, but an ally, perhaps a friend.

DANCE

The reflection of the sun on a stream, a flower unfolding, trees moving in the wind, a baby wailing, the cycle of day and night—according to Indian tradition, the universe is movement as an end in itself, the delight of creation, a vitality continually renewing itself. Everything is a dance.

This idea contains an implicit message: However precarious, isolated, or desperate you may feel your existence to be, you are nevertheless taking part in the dance; and you are part of a universe that is fundamentally all right. The message then becomes more specific: If you want to perceive the deepest aspects of this reality, you must dance.

Throughout the ages, and in all civilizations, dance has been used as an aid to higher knowledge and to mystical union with the cosmos. In dancers' biographies we find ample proof of this fact. Those who dance are able to step outside the confines of personal existence, transcend linear time, dive into ecstasy. For example, American dancer Ruth St. Denis describes the moment when she realized dance would become the focal point of her life:

> I see myself standing on a hill behind our old farm house in New Jersey, lifting my arms in an unconscious gesture of

> oneness towards the round silvery glory of the moon. At the same time I'm listening to the whisper of a faint breeze as it gently sways the tips of the tall pines. I begin to move. It is my first dance urge to relate myself to cosmic rhythm. With a motion of complete joy, as a free being in a world of infinite depth and beauty, I surrender myself to the unseen pulsation of the Universe.

Dance unravels the mental and emotional patterns that have crystallized over the years in an individual's makeup. This is particularly evident in the case of imitative dance, where one is invited to identify oneself with an animal, a spirit, a god, or a natural phenomenon such as fire, wind, or rain. Every type of dance, however, transforms dancers into something other than themselves, enabling them to escape from a predefined physical, mental, and social structure, and thus become free—free from themselves above all.

This release takes place when dance follows a repetitive rhythm and every movement in it is foreknown. The mind is no longer weighed down with the responsibility of deciding which movements to make and which not to make—that is, one simply surrenders to the rhythm. But release also happens for the opposite reason, when dance, devoid of prearranged sequels, can develop freely. In this case, as the movements change and renew themselves, so does the mind.

By multiplying the movements they are able to make, dancers also multiply their mental and spiritual possibilities. Because each gesture and posture evokes a state of mind, a greater repertoire of movements corresponds to an expanded inner repertoire. Reading Einstein's statement that there are no fixed points in space was a breakthrough for dancer and choreographer Merce Cunningham: in a fluid space with no fixed points, the possibilities for movement are enlarged; indeed, they are countless. The Argentinean dancer Edward Villella feels that his inner repertoire is fully realized only when he is dancing:

> That saying, "dancing for joy"—I know exactly what that means. I am only half alive when I am not dancing. I am fully alive only when I dance. When I'm dancing at my best, I feel exposed, and confident in that nakedness. I feel that life is wonderful, that everything is possible.

To discover new possibilities means to have one's life transformed, and this principle also applies off the stage, and to people who do not dance professionally. One day the French choreographer Maurice Béjart decided to organize a course that would introduce dance to, as he put it, "Mr. and Mrs. Anyone," that is to say, to total amateurs. For three weeks they had a two- to three-hour lesson every evening. At the end of the course, according to Béjart, the students were "transfigured." Many of those who took part had found courage, confidence, and a joy in living.

It often happens that a method for spiritual growth is adopted as a technique in psychotherapy. Dance offers many benefits in this regard: by releasing muscular and psychological tension, it lightens the load of inhibitions; it stimulates and frees the emotions; it enables people to move beyond their habitual experience and to give themselves over to a rhythm other than their own; it awakens new potential for life and thought; it unites body and mind; and, when done in a group, it enhances communication. These are all factors of transformation, and anyone facilitating them in the context of psychotherapy will discover that they can be much more powerful and direct than verbal communication, because they quickly reach and change otherwise inaccessible skeletomuscular patterns we learned in our remote past.

Temporarily loosening our ancient psychophysical habits can bring relief and a sense of well-being. We are left, however, with the disorganization of a system which, albeit limited and neurotic, until this point has been the only known and tested reality. In some cases the abrupt change can render a person vulnerable to eruption of unconscious forces that the "I" is too weak to control, resulting in delirium.

We have historically documented cases of collective madness and excesses of various kinds. The Roman writer Apuleius, for instance, described the ecstatic dance of Syrian priests who danced and cried out like madmen, biting and lashing themselves, cutting their arms with swords. In the Roman Empire, until the fourth century A.D., devotees of the goddess Cybele arranged a special day they called the "day of blood" (*dies sanguinis*) when, at the end of a wild dance accompanied by cymbals, drums, flutes, and horns the participants would cut their own bodies and sprinkle their blood on the altar. During the fifteenth century, Italy was swept by a dancing frenzy such that whole communities, particularly among the poorer classes, would dance until they lost their senses. This mania became known as tarantism, or Saint Vitus' dance.

There is a physiological basis to dance-induced madness. Dance, especially when it is intense and unrestrained, leads to a state of trance and produces significant changes in a person's psychophysical balance. According to anthropologist Erika Bourguignon, a trance is an altered state of consciousness in which one's perception of time and space, color and brightness, sound and movement, taste and smell—as well as sensations of touch, pain, heat, and cold—are altered; there can even be changes in memory and in the awareness of one's own identity. Dance also affects a person's breathing rhythm, causing hyperoxygenation. Rotating movements alter the sense of balance and contribute to the feeling of losing control of one's body—and, therefore, of oneself.

In this temporary disorganization of the personality some people lose, and others discover, themselves. As always, the first element in a Way toward the Self—the destructuring of existing patterns—must be accompanied or followed by the possibility of a new and higher synthesis. Mere chaos cannot in itself guarantee enlightenment. Anyone who genuinely follows the Way of Dance gains, from deep or light trance, a new understanding of oneself and of the world. Listen, for example, to the great American dancer Mary Wigman:

> And the secret of the never ending turns around yourself—how I battled for it! Time and again I gave myself up to the intoxication of this experience, to this almost lustful destruction of the physical being, a process in which, for seconds, I almost felt a oneness with the cosmos. I turned and turned until I succeeded in tracing this secret; to know how I had to place my feet, to displace my hips, to regulate the posture of the torso in order to achieve the abstract form of rotation and to be able to bring these turns back into the sphere of their ecstatic experience.

Even in an ecstatic state of consciousness, Wigman was able to make mental notes on the technical nature of the movements she wanted to perform. This is surrender to the flow of dance, accompanied by an attentive, conscious presence. The words of the Indian dancer Ram Gopal also show how a state of trance, rather than leading to disintegration, brought him to the blissful beginnings of time:

> I remember the first time I danced on the black cylindrical marble floor of Belur, that ancient Hoysala monument built by a king and queen for both of them to pray, meditate and dance on during various temple rituals. What a trance I fell into! I was conscious of the music, and of the silent faces of the Indian spectators for a few brief moments, and then gradually they seemed to dissolve, and in their place I saw only mists and I was back at the very beginning of creation when man's body sang in an ecstatic trance through the mute language of the dance.

Dance, as Ram Gopal puts it, is a return to our primordial origins. Everyone agrees on this point. Dance evokes a feeling of oneness with the very source of movement, with energy in its pure form, with the gods at the time of creation. The Roman poet Lucian wrote that the movements of the stars reflect the original dance of the universe. In more recent times Ted Shawn has echoed these same thoughts from a more personal point of view:

> Through rhythm we are in closest contact with the universe for, as we all know, the universe is based on rhythm and we identify ourselves with the universe by rhythm because we collaborate in its work; what we do is backed up by infinite and absolute power.

In its highest and most beautiful forms, dance is the activity of the gods: light, carefree celebration of life. Those who dance are not working, are not imprisoned by daily routine, and are free from the usual pain and worry. Dance reminds us of a lost world or a world we have long yearned for; it is the ideal representation of the unimaginable joy we glimpse only in our moments of greatest happiness. Nijinsky's wife wrote of her husband:

> He wanted to show there was more in life than the momentary satisfaction of a craving towards beauty . . . he wanted to show his public the meaning of life, the way lasting happiness could be obtained.

And he succeeded. "He was so light," wrote the critic Valentine Hugo, "and so graceful in his costume that we thought we were looking at a being from another world. No other dancer, however great, has since given me a similar impression of flight, of amazing elevation . . . and complete absence of heaviness. Never did I hear the sound of his steps on the stage. It was as if something supernatural occurred before the transfigured audience."

This description refers to *Les sylphides*, a ballet in which

Nijinsky danced (to the music of Chopin) with Anna Pavlova and Tamara Karsavina, as well as a corps de ballet that for the first time played a significant role instead of merely a decorative one. Nijinsky's leaps have become legendary. While flying through the air he gave the impression of stopping for a moment in space, and this defiance of gravity, this miraculous lightness, symbolized the triumph of spirit over matter and sent the audience into rapture. In the *Spectre de la rose* there is a scene in which Nijinsky circled the stage, skipping like a child. The critic Peter Lieven recalls the scene:

> I can remember the audience of the Metropolitan Opera in New York—one of the most stolid and immovable audiences in the world—letting out, at the sight of him, something which was between a sigh and a groan. There was no applause—just that strangled cry. Nijinsky travelled through the air, just above, but never seeming to touch the ground. Like an autumn leaf he came lightly down.

On other occasions there was an explosion of enthusiastic applause. Nijinsky's wife wrote:

> With complete abandon the audience rose to its feet as one man, shouted, wept, showered the stage with flowers, gloves, fans, programs, pell-mell in their wild enthusiasm. This magnificent vision was Nijinsky.

Dance is not a private event occurring only in the dancer's body. Dancing is public. Spectators participate empathically, and they too feel the lightness of dance. They behold a world of grace and harmony, and understand that they have been allowed to take part in it. That is why audiences can be so enthusiastic and grateful toward great dancers. Duncan's sister-in-law wrote:

> When she [Duncan] danced the *Blue Danube*, her simple waltzing forward and back, like the oncoming and receding waves

> on the shore, had such an ecstasy of rhythm that audiences became frenzied with the contagion of it, and could not contain themselves, but rose from their seats, cheering, applauding, laughing and crying. . . . We felt as if we had received the blessing of God.

One evening, at the beginning of her career, Pavlova was followed after a show by a group of spectators, mostly lower-middle-class laborers. They followed her in silence, all the way to her home, and when she appeared on the balcony to wave to them they exploded into a spontaneous ovation and began to sing in her honor. They stayed there until the early hours of the morning, unable to leave. Pavlova, thinking out loud, asked what she had done to produce such an intense, enthusiastic response. Her maid, a Russian peasant girl, replied with words Pavlova never forgot: "Madam, you have made them happy by enabling them to forget for an hour the sadness of life."

As Valéry says, dance creates a world of its own, having nothing to do with the world of everyday life. In our daily lives, every movement meets some practical need; in dance, on the other hand, there is no ulterior motive—each movement is *gratuitous*. For this reason, dance creates a magical space in which something unthought of and full of wonder can take visible form. Sometimes the stage alone can have this effect, even the atmosphere of the theater itself. Nureyev thus describes his first impact with this enchanted world as a child:

> I shall never forget a single detail of the scene that met my eyes: the theater itself with its soft, beautiful lights and gleaming crystal chandeliers; small lanterns hanging everywhere; colored windows; everywhere velvet . . . gold—another world, a place which, to my dazzled eyes, you could only hope to encounter in the most enchanted fairy tale. That first visit to the theater has left behind a unique memory, something

> illuminated within me in quite a special way, a very personal privilege. Something was happening to me which was taking me far from my solid world and bearing me right up to the skies. From the moment I entered that magic place I felt I had really left the world, borne far away from everything I knew by a dream staged for me alone. . . . I was speechless.

Dance is a Way to knowledge because it breaks up our familiar universe and transports us to another universe, a world of pure understanding and awareness. According to a Chinese story, a young prince did not wish to follow the teaching of his preceptor. The abstract lessons of Buddhism held no interest for him—words, nothing but words. For this reason everyone called him the lazy prince. Then, as he was looking out of the window one day, he saw a group of butterflies flying past. He ran after them, crying "There's Buddha, among the butterflies," and he began to dance among them. When he returned to the palace, runs the legend, he was no longer the lazy prince but instead the Knower of the Mystery.

SACRED DANCE

Christ was at the center. In a circle around him were the twelve apostles. Soon the enemies would arrive to crucify the son of God, and darkness would descend on the world. But before that happened, Christ invited his disciples to dance with him. From the center of the ring he said:

> I shall be saved and I shall save.
> I shall be freed and I shall free.
> I shall be wounded and I shall wound.
> I shall be born and I shall bring forth life.
> I shall be consumed and I shall consume.

The disciples danced around him, holding hands. To each of Christ's statements they replied "Amen." Then Christ continued:

> I am a torch for you who see me.
> I am a mirror for you who look at me.
> I am a door for you who knock.
> I am a way for you who walk.

Christ then explained that dance can bring us to the very center of life, to that full involvement without calculation or reserve, which means freedom.

Let us now move to the thirteenth century. We are in the Auxerre cathedral to watch the Dance of the Angels. Christ is now represented by a golden sphere; he is the Sun of resurrection. At the center is the dean, and all around him in a ring the other priests dance, each rotating about his own axis. The dean throws the golden ball to one of the priests, who catches it, spins round and throws it back, and so the dance goes on—the dance of the Sun (Christ) in the cosmos, through the months of the year. At the same time everyone sings a hymn. The dance happens around the image of a maze on the ground, representing the world and matter, in which the soul is lost. Christ helps the soul to find the right path again through the labyrinth of forgetfulness.

These are two examples of sacred dance. The first, taken from the apocryphal writings of John, is dubious and is more likely to describe an initiation dance of second-century Gnostics; the second example is authentic. In both cases the participants concentrate on the highest reality and their bodies express it in visible form. This is precisely the essence of sacred dance.

Usually the sacred is associated with stillness and silence, perhaps because such modes sharply contrast with the mind-scattering hustle and bustle of daily existence. Sacredness, however, can also be expressed through sound and movement, with a burst of vitality and a blaze of lights and colors. The transpersonal world is not necessarily a quiet one; it is also endless festivity and tireless energy. It can aptly be represented by rhythm and dance.

Many of the characteristics we have examined in dance as art or as entertainment are also present in sacred dance. There are some differences, however. In sacred dance

◇ the ritual aspect is more explicit. One is dancing in order to honor the divinity, to raise oneself to its level, perhaps become one with it;

◇ the themes of the dance concern universal realities more than personal vicissitudes and emotions;

◇ less space is allowed for individual creativity and originality of either choreographer or dancer;

◇ the whole community sometimes participates, drawn irresistibly into the dance;

Because sacred dancing readily adapts to any culture, meets real needs, and brings about strong, beneficial effects, it is found in all the great traditions, often appearing at times when a religious movement is enjoying its greatest flowering. We have already seen two examples. Let us look at a few more:

◇ In ancient Egypt a river procession, connected with the worship of the god Amon and portrayed in the reliefs of the temple at Luxor, is halfway between a ritual and a show. The procession is headed by a priest followed by soldiers. Then come three black dancers turning somersaults, while a fourth beats the drum. All four dancers are dressed in animal skins and wear earrings and bracelets. A number of Libyans follow, dressed in ostrich feathers. Some brandish small curved sticks, while others shake rattles. Next come the systrum players, seminaked women dancers performing acrobatic movements, and singers. Some of the dancers' heads are thrown backward, a universal sign of frenzy and ecstasy in dance.

◇ Pictures painted on vases and other ornaments from ancient Greece show the dance of the Maenads or Bacchantes, the followers of the Dionysian cult, holding flowers and serpents, beating drums or playing bagpipes and flutes, raising their clothing, pouring out wine, their heads adorned with laurel wreaths. Dionysus is Lysios, the liberator. The purpose of these wild dances is to relieve the dancers—with the aid of wine—of all frustrations and inhibitions. According to the myth, Dionysus was torn to pieces by order of Zeus, his father, but was then revived by his mother, Demeter, who put all the pieces back together again. This was probably a symbolic way of showing the extraordinary effects of dance—first, disorganization of existing psychophysical rhythms; then temporary chaos and disappearance of all points of reference—ultimate dismemberment; and, finally, rebirth into a world of vitality and harmony.

◇ We have descriptions of shamanic dances based on nineteenth-century eyewitness accounts of missionaries and others in central Siberia, the region with which shamanism is originally linked. Shamanic dances are circular, accompanied by a rhythmic drumbeat, and are based on the shaman's identification with an animal (a bird, horse, or dog) through which he divests himself of ordinary human limitations. These dances are characterized by leaps and darting movements, always culminating in the ecstatic flight of the shaman to the world of the spirit.

◇ In an Indian dance from the Bharata Natyam tradition, a woman—known as a *devadasa*—is dedicated to the temple at a young age, and the dance she performs before the altar of the god is an act of pure devotion. The dancer represents the essence of all beings who honor divinity. In the ecstasy produced by the dance, the god becomes her lover. An ancient text states that

> he who worships the Supreme through dance, fulfils all desire and unfolds the way to salvation. The dance destroys misery and brings peace and fulfillment.

◊ The nineteenth-century Shakers moved "like clouds agitated by a mighty wind." They were the descendants of the Albigensians, heretics of the thirteenth century who had embraced dance as a means of worship. Their movements consisted of energetic shaking of the arms and hands (hence the name "Shakers"), stooping, and turning. Their most suggestive dance had lines of men and women interweaving like threads in a fabric. It should be noted that, in contrast with the society of their day, the Shakers cultivated a feeling of equality with blacks and Indians, who freely participated in their dances.

◊ The rotating dances of the dervishes from the Mevlevi sect were created by the great sage and poet Rumi. One day, as he was passing a goldsmith workshop, Rumi heard the rhythmic beating of a hammer and began dancing in the street. At the sound of music—whether drums, flutes, or singing—dervishes first extend their arms, the right hand facing upward, the left hand facing down. Cosmic energy supposedly enters through the right hand, passes through the body and leaves from the left hand, on which the dervishes' eyes are focused throughout the dance; it then flows out over the world, like a blessing. Dervishes dance, gyrating about their axis and concentrating on the name of Allah. They repeat it inwardly, in step with the lifting and lowering of their right foot, which turns the body round, while the left foot, firm on the ground, acts as a pivot.

"He who knows the power of dance, lives in God,"

said Rumi. We have eyewitness accounts by Westerners describing the effects of dervish dance, showing that it can lead to higher states of consciousness. An English researcher, for instance, saw the dervishes dancing at an ever-greater speed, the look on their faces becoming more and more remote until they fell down with a cry. The researcher himself took part in the dance and later described his experience:

> The circles moved faster and faster, until I (moving in the outer circle) saw only a whirl of robes, and lost count of time. . . . I began to be affected, and found that although I was not dizzy, my mind was functioning in a very strange and unfamiliar way. The sensation is difficult to describe, and is probably a complex one. One feeling was that of a lightening: as if I had no anxieties, no problems. Another was that I was a part of this moving circle, and that my individuality was gone, was delightfully merged in something larger.

The story of Black Elk, the last great Sioux Indian, would deserve a chapter to itself. This extraordinary person had a vision at the age of nine, in which a black horse danced and sang with a voice so strong that it filled the whole cosmos, like an invitation to universal dance. In Black Elk's description, the leaves of the trees and the grass on the hills and valleys were dancing, and so were the waters of streams, rivers, and lakes, as well as people and animals. Black Elk then felt himself to be at the center of the world. His words reach the highest levels of beauty and intensity:

> Then I was standing on the highest mountain of them all, and round about beneath me was the whole hoop of the world. And while I stood there I saw more than I can tell and I understood more than I saw; for I was seeing in a sacred manner the shapes of all things in the spirit, and the shape of all shapes

> as they must live together like one being. And I saw that the sacred hoop of my people was one of many hoops that made one circle, wide as daylight and as starlight, and in the center grew one mighty flowering tree to shelter all the children of one mother and one father. And I saw that it was holy.

As the vision faded, Black Elk became aware of a vast plain; in that plain was his village, in the village his tepee, in the tepee his parents bending over a sick child—and that sick child was himself, a poor child who had had an experience bigger than himself, now returning to his senses, a child powerless to explain the wonders he had witnessed.

When he returned to himself, Black Elk felt alone, ill, and full of fear. He thought he must be mad, and his parents were worried about him. Only when he reached the age of seventeen did he decide to speak about his vision and his malaise to a wise old healer. The sage understood that the boy had come into contact with stupendous spiritual energies that he could not explain; he had the potential charisma for becoming the leader of his people, but, having never expressed his vision, the boy was ill and helpless. The solution: Black Elk must dance his vision before the entire tribe. All the details should be represented, using men and women, horses, face paint, song, and every possible aid. This was done and, at the height of the dance, Black Elk again had the vision he experienced in childhood. Now, however, the whole tribe was taking part in it, and this served to redeem the pain his people suffered under the white invader, and to unite the community. Black Elk explained how he felt:

> It seemed that I was above the ground and did not touch it when I walked. I felt very happy, for I could see that my people were all happier. Many crowded around me and said that they or their relatives who had been feeling sick were well again, and these gave me many gifts. Even the horses seemed to be healthier and happier after the dance.

> The fear that was on me so long was gone, and when thunder clouds appeared I was always glad to see them, for they came as relatives now to visit me. Everything seemed good and beautiful now, and kind.

Such altered states of consciousness are often facilitated by physiological factors. Sacred dance, with its rhythmic repetition and the extensive use of physical resources, brings about significant changes in the organism. According to some researchers, these reactions serve to tune the organism as one might tune a musical instrument. Moreover, this neurobiological earthquake produces a deautomatization of the neurological patterns and makes way for ecstasy.

More important than the physical effect of movement, however, is its symbolic significance. Every movement in sacred dance has a meaning that not only is understood with the mind but is also realized with one's whole being—body and soul. The movements used in sacred dance can have many meanings: They can include human beings in the harmony of celestial spheres; interconnect each dancer with the All; join humans with the divine world; or represent progression from multiplicity to unity. A swirling rotation can symbolize the process of becoming, around the still Center of Being, and so on. But mental understanding is incomplete. The realities represented in sacred dance cannot be fully expressed in words. Sacred dance speaks the ineffable. It has the function of reawakening intuition and of opening one's organism to a vaster world, at the moment of heightened receptivity.

In conclusion, we might ask ourselves whether dance, more than an exhilarating activity, is not itself a state of consciousness. The sacred dances we have been considering have largely disappeared with the passing of time. Others will appear in the future. However, it is perhaps right at the Center of the human spirit that we will be able to rediscover dance as an inner condition, as a metaphor for a way of being. Saint Ambrose wrote:

> Just as he who dances with his body, rushing through the rotating movements of the limbs, acquires the right to a share in the round dance, in the same way he who dances the spiritual dance, always moving in the ecstasy of faith, acquires the right to dance in the ring of all creation.

Sacred dance, then, is not just physical activity, but a way of realizing the Self in the depths of one's own being, as boundless exultation, joyfulness, inextinguishable energy.

RITUAL

Immensely richer than our minds are able to conceive, governed by rules beyond our comprehension, so subtle it eludes all definition, the transpersonal Self is the unfathomable essence of our being. Any attempt to represent in space and time this invisible, unimaginable reality risks clumsiness or rhetoric. Our means of expression are inadequate for representing that which infinitely transcends them.

Yet to experience a fleeting awareness of the Self is not enough. Many people throughout history have felt the need to connect with it repeatedly, to celebrate it, and to share it with others. They wanted liberation from the drudgery of everyday life; they wanted periodical regeneration and reminders of the numinous. Ritual reaches these aims by using sensory means, such as architectures, shapes, gestures, scents, food and drink, song and music, light and color. When ritual is performed well, external representation becomes an inner reality, consciousness expands, and a purely private experience is shared by all.

We need only think of a solemn mass in a Gothic cathedral. The vaulted arches give a sense of emptiness and elevation, facilitating detachment from daily life. The rhythmic sound of the human voice and chant puts the rational mind to sleep; familiar voices become solemn echoes in a vast space. The fragrance of incense takes us far away from the everyday smells. The fantastic imagery of stained-glass windows reveals a visionary world and raises the level of consciousness, as do the music and the voices of the choir. In this setting the colored, glittering vestments of the priest, his movements and actions, are a concentrated expression of the sacred. The visible world of matter and the invisible world of spirit become one.

Every gesture produces precise mental events. One cannot remain unchanged, for instance, after raising one's arms to heaven, or after kneeling, or even after joining the thumb and index finger in the circle that symbolizes union of the finite with the infinite. Body postures and movements evoke a corresponding state of mind in a person who observes them, and even more in the person who performs them. Sunryu Suzuki describes the significance of the bow:

> By bowing we are giving up ourselves. To give up ourselves means to give up our dualistic ideas. So there is no difference between zazen practice [Zen meditation] and bowing. Usually to bow means to pay our respects to something which is more worthy of respect than ourselves. But when you bow to Buddha you should have no idea of Buddha, you just become one with Buddha, you are already Buddha himself. When you become one with Buddha, one with everything that exists, you find the true meaning of being. When you forget all your dualistic ideas, everything becomes your teacher, and everything can be the object of worship.

We can find rituals in daily life, too: reading the newspaper, a cup of coffee after a meal, or the usual television program. Even the keenest advocates of improvisation end up with rituals of their own, for we all need some order and structure. These sequences of predetermined actions are distributed throughout the day. They serve to mark out the passage of time, enable us to take a mental break, and to confirm us and others in our chosen way of life. They give our lives a reassuring rhythm, reinforce a relationship, and generate a desired atmosphere. There is nothing sublime in these routines; they are simply external means for generating a subjective universe.

The gestures and movements of ritual, however, are quite different from those of everyday life. Whereas the Way of Action is carried out in the everyday world, the Way of Ritual is a sharp departure from that world. The words *temple* and *contemplation* are derived from the Greek τέμνω, meaning "to cut," to indicate the separation between the sacred and the secular. The enclosure surrounding the temple protects it from the foolish and the worldly. Sacred gestures are not responses to actual circumstances. They are set apart from the commonplace and are gratuitous, because they are not aimed at obtaining a specific result. Precisely for this reason, they express the fullness of being.

As children's games, observes the Catholic theologian Romano Guardini, rituals—though they serve no practical purpose —are governed by precise rules; and by their calm, steady rhythm they help to free people from the restlessness of utilitarian activity. Rituals never change—they are independent of life's circumstances and can be repeated in times of war or in times of peace, in poverty or in wealth, in youth or in old age, in happiness or in despair. They represent a timeless dimension, untouched by chance, doubt, or decay—a true stronghold. Furthermore, the deliberate attention with which they are carried out, their solemnity, the concentrated attention of the participants, and the movements of the body suggest a suprasensible reality. All these factors generate a situation in which consciousness is naturally led to transpersonal levels.

Let us take an example: Friar Giovanni of Alverna (about whom we read in the *Little Flowers* of Saint Francis) was celebrating mass, and when he came to the central words *Hoc est corpus meum* ("This is my body") he became ecstatic. He could see Christ in his glory, together with all the angels, hovering above the host, waiting to enter it at the moment of consecration. Giovanni's ecstasy was so intense that he said the first words, *Hoc est*, but was not able to finish with *corpus meum*. At this point many of those present realized what was happening and were filled with awe. Some wept. Finally brother Giovanni succeeded in saying the words *corpus meum* and at that moment saw Christ entering the host. Then, as he raised the chalice he felt his own soul being lifted out of his body and lost all physical awareness, while his body—being left to itself—fainted and became cold, even though (as the chronicler tells us) it was summer. It took some time for Giovanni to come back to his senses.

A ritual creates a microcosm, a reality that somehow becomes a whole universe complete in itself. In order for this to happen, it is necessary that all the appropriate elements in the environment are present. For example, in the Zen tea ceremony as described by D. T. Suzuki, the place in which the ritual is performed must contain the right ingredients to induce tranquillity. A little house in a bamboo wood or beneath the trees—near a stream, rocks, and bushes—is the ideal setting.

The room must be laid out so as to restore the serenity of those who have been invited; it must avoid anything that might distract them and should express that simplicity (*wabi*) which, by freeing the mind from the desires that besiege it, gives joy. Flowers in a vase are the only permitted ornament. The art of the tea ceremony, then, becomes a transpersonal discipline in which all the senses are purified—sight and smell, by the color and scent of the flowers; hearing, by the sound of the water boiling in the pot; touch, by the handling of items with which the tea is prepared; taste, by the flavor of the tea. Finally the mind itself, which Buddhism regards as the sixth sense, is purified by the meditative tranquillity (*jaku*) produced by the ritual.

Other requirements are sincerity and respect for the person with whom one is taking the tea; after all, this is not an everyday encounter, full of chatter and pretense. Even the desire to show off one's good taste or wealth melts away. This ritual is about opening oneself to another from the heart. Suzuki asks: "Who would then deny that when I am sipping tea in my tearoom I am swallowing the whole universe with it and that this very moment of my lifting the bowl to my lips is eternity itself transcending space and time?" Horst Hammitzsch, a German scholar who practiced the tea ceremony in Japan, likens the experience from this discipline with a previous one he had back home some years before, when an organist in a small country church began to play Bach:

> And suddenly, with the music filling the whole body of the church, I felt that space ceased to exist and only the flood of notes still remained. I, too, seemed as though divested of all materiality, totally absorbed in the music. And here in Japan I had now had a similar experience. The effect of the Tea-Ceremony was so strong as to engender a feeling of self-surrender, a feeling of oneness with all others, and extraordinary feeling of satisfaction with myself and with my surroundings.

The Way of Ritual contains many echoes of other Ways. Like the Way of Beauty, it aspires to give a material representation of the intangible Self. Like the Way of Action, it teaches to act with disinterest. Like the Way of Illumination, it trains attention. Moreover, in ritual we see personality—the mixture of needs, fantasies, problems, and plans with which we usually identify—slowly disappear. Gestures and actions are predetermined; therefore they are empty and release us from the need to decide. Every ritual is a discipline to follow without allowing any scope for individual originality.

Precisely in this aspect of ritual we see both its strength and its weakness. Its predetermined gestures can produce an inflow of transpersonal strength and open a window to an unknown, extraordinary world. But they can also turn the ritual into a soulless, mechanical routine. The ritual then becomes tedious and oppressive, its constricting sense of duty then negating the Self. Rituals can evoke and affirm the transpersonal dimension, making it available to each of us, but they can also be a method for reinforcing dogma and social control; or become a mere fossil-remain, devoid of any meaning.

At still other times, rituals are animated and effective, but their aim is dubious to say the least—as in certain cults. Rituals are powerful tools: they elicit strong emotions and bodily changes, generate visions, and give participants a sense of belonging and a structured meaning. For this very reason they may be used in perverse ways. The emotions they elicit may originate in the *lower* unconscious rather than in the higher—in the repository of all that is more primitive and unregenerated within us. They may offer illusory new strength by taking advantage of people's weaknesses and demanding surrender to one individual's charisma. Thus they gratify adepts while depriving them of the autonomy and responsibility true growth always entails. Finally, these rituals may induce altered states of consciousness and powerful sensations, whose only function may be to complement and perpetuate the psychopathologies of an individual or a group.

Now let us return to creative, life-giving rituals—specifically, the ceremony of initiation, which heralds the passage from one limited state of consciousness to a more expanded one. The initiate undergoes tests that are sometimes painful and terrifying, even faces death, and emerges a transformed being. The initiation rite is the outer manifestation of an inner process; it is the clearest way of expressing the end of a life that has become outworn and the entrance to a better, truer, and more beautiful world.

Perhaps one of the most fascinating accounts of this process is Apuleius' *Metamorphoses*, popularly known as *The Golden Ass*. Despite the fact that he seems to be telling a story, Apuleius is symbolically describing the course of his own development and his experiences with the initiation cult of the goddess Isis. On a voyage the protagonist Lucius falls in love with a slave—a foolish, unreliable girl—and forgets to return to his native land (celestial origin of the soul and downfall into matter and darkness). Because of his curiosity, he is changed into a donkey (degeneration due to ignorance). Then, after a period of hard testing (vicissitudes of the spiritual path), Lucius is helped by Isis and becomes a man again during a sacred river procession (attainment of personal maturity). Now he is ready to be initiated into the Isis cult.

During the ten days leading up to the ritual Lucius must not eat or drink wine, but keep to a strict diet. The priest, reciting from a book that contains mysterious characters and the shapes of various animals, reads the instructions to him. Lucius is immersed in water and divine grace descends upon him. He is then dressed in a linen robe and led into the innermost part of the sanctuary. Here the most esoteric part of the ritual takes place, about which Lucius is advised to remain silent. However, he describes his experience of death and rebirth:

> I reached the boundary of death; I placed my foot on Persephone's threshold [the goddess of the underworld]; when I returned I was brought through all the elements of the cosmos; in the middle of the night I saw the sun shine with its blinding light; I appeared in the presence of the gods of the underworld and of heaven; and I performed acts of adoration at their very feet.

During the twelve hours of the night Lucius had to wear a special vestment. Thus he identified himself with the sun and embodied its course across the subterranean hemisphere. The following morning he was presented to everyone wearing a magnificent robe decorated with Indian dragons and animals from the other world known as gryphons. In his right hand he held a flaming torch and on his head was a crown of palms whose shining leaves extended like rays in all directions. Lucius was hailed by everyone as the rising sun.

In some cases ritual uses psychedelics (etymological meaning: "revealers of the soul") in order to reach the transpersonal state. One example is the ancient Vedic ritual in which *Soma*, probably a psychedelic mushroom, played a central part. The ritual centered around three sacrificial fires and was enacted by seven priests who prepared the potion—considered to be the very soul of the god Indra—and then offered it to the gods and drank it in order to reach the state of transpersonal rapture. In a Vedic prayer, the unknown author calls on *Soma* to transport him into everlasting light, to an indestructible, immortal world filled with flowing fountains, glittering stars, and infinite joy. Those who drink *Soma* cry out, "We have drunk *Soma*, we have attained immortality, we have reached the light, we have met the gods."

Many rituals fit into the basic situations of human life. There are times in our existence—birth, puberty, marriage, and death—when we are more vulnerable and more open. It is easier for our masks and affectations to disappear. Roles become blurred, hidden emotions reach their greatest intensity, and the mystery, precariousness, and beauty of life appear with all their power. At such times ritual is employed to make the most of the occasion and to offer a glimpse of the transpersonal world.

In the pre-Buddhist *Bön* funeral ceremony in Tibet, for instance, the priest guides the dead or dying person (the body having been placed in the fetal posture as a symbol of future rebirth), encouraging him or her to avoid the snares and illusions of the after-death state and to make full use of this experience for spiritual growth. According to the *Bardo Thödol*, or *Tibetan Book of the Dead* (*bardo* means "after-death state"), an individual who has just died is confused, has visions derived from earlier actions and thoughts, and is confronted by demons and gods of all sorts. The guide's task is to accompany the spirit of the dead person through the illusory realms toward freedom, encouraging him or her to forgo all attachments, so as to enter the pure, timeless Light of the Void.

In the stages described with great technical precision in the

Bardo Thödol, it is easy to find parallels with more recent data on near-death experiences. Perhaps the most important aspect, and the one least affected by cultural variables, is the vision of a preternatural light of great intensity and beauty. Those who have come back to life after being close to death describe it as an experience of profound regeneration, which leads to a rethinking of one's existence. For the dead, according to the *Bardo Thödol*, such an experience is the final goal of every aspiration. It is nirvana.

The Tibetan ritual, however, does not only benefit the dying. To be guided through the world of afterlife is the same as being guided in this world—beyond the obstacles we find every day in our path, the ties that bind us, the inner ghosts that terrify us. The ritual then becomes a meditation on the essential meaning of life and death. And the words the priest whispers in the ear of the dying are actually directed to us all:

> O nobly born, the time has come for you to find the Path. Your breathing is about to stop. Your master has placed you face to face with the Clear Light. Now you will know it in its Reality, in the state after death in which all things are as an empty, cloudless sky, and naked, spotless awareness is like transparent emptiness, having neither circumference nor center. At that moment, know yourself, and remain in that state.

THEATER

Why is it that so many cultures in the course of human history have considered actors and actresses to be close to divinity, if not actually divine? Even in our own time, when gods are not in fashion, this attitude persists—film stars are immortalized. Perhaps it is because, like divine beings, actors have access to a wider range of possibilities than do the rest of us. Actors may be heroes or rogues, saints or murderers, kings or jesters, elders or youths, men or women. Therefore, they are not restricted to a single existence, as is the case with us. Their consciousness extends to include many different beings and ages. And who but a god is able to live so many different lives?

There is also another reason for this situation: an actor is able to express visibly the dramas that haunt us, the secrets we conceal, the problems we are unable to face. We see them all portrayed, perhaps even resolved, on the stage or on the screen. The same happens with our most dreaded nightmares and most unlikely fantasies. We see them represented with the purity and intensity of an archetype—the emotions of every man and every woman, but also our very own. Who but a god could show us ourselves as we really are?

Actors and actresses are no gods, we know. But doubtless they tread a transpersonal Way—a Way rich in aspects and techniques. Apart from the ones we have just examined—access to a greater range of possibilities and archetypal representation of the human world—other elements are present in this path. Above all, an ability to evoke images and emotions powerfully and precisely. The German actor Mitterwürzer, speaking of his most successful roles, said:

> I experience a peculiar condition in which I see, not before me, but within me, the characters, especially those which I should like to play; I see them in person, palpable, definite in all of their manifestations of life, those described and those left undescribed. The character I am to be and how I am to be it, in its essential forms, charged with its collective emotions, stands all at once actually before my soul.

Actors, then, re-create different states within themselves and then express them. To achieve this aim, many have stressed the importance of observation. David Garrick recommended observing people and studying characters in various situations. "It is the noblest and best study," he said, because it leads to the understanding of human nature, as essential to the actor as observation of nature is to the painter. Others recommend reading as much as possible, so as to be able to identify more readily with other worlds and types of existence. Sometimes, in order to learn how to extend the limits of the possible, actors practice by generating random situations. Lee Strasberg, for instance, asked his students to recite Hamlet's monologue "To be, or not to be" as if they were drunk.

Often actors make use of specific techniques to draw on emotional memory banks. Laurence Olivier, for example, was playing the role of Sophocles' Oedipus. He would come to the terrible moment when an old shepherd revealed to Oedipus the cruel reality of the situation, and he finally understood: the man he had killed was his father, the woman he had slept with was his mother.

At this point Oedipus-Olivier had to cry out, expressing an anguished combination of shock and pain. In order to reproduce this feeling within himself, Olivier would imagine an ermine caught in a trap. (An ermine is trapped by the cruel method whereby salt is sprinkled on hard snow. The ermine licks it, and the mixture sticks to its tongue, thus preventing the ermine from escaping, however hard it tries to tear itself free.) Imagining this horrible experience helped Olivier to evoke in himself the feeling appropriate for the tragic scene and to emit that awful cry.

Sometimes masks are used. Usually we think of masks as devices to conceal our true being. Not so in theater, at least in the case of traditional masks, argues director Peter Brooks. The use of the mask, according to Brooks, is a technique for instantly eliminating all defenses, all those expressions with which we represent ourselves to others, and which we have always been accustomed to. The moment we wear a mask, these defenses have no more reason to exist, and actors can identify themselves with that which is truest in them. Says Brooks, "It's the most electrifying impression . . . the most extraordinary sense of liberation."

Familiarity with one's own inner world; a quick, vivid imagination; and an accurate, ready access to possible universes—these are the basic tools in this path. But there are other elements too. At various times the actors must learn how to

◊ concentrate with maximum intensity;
◊ eliminate all mental and muscular blocks to spontaneous expression;
◊ master gestures, and voice and facial expressions;
◊ plunge into the world of emotions without being dominated by them;
◊ allow themselves to be taken over by the role to be played—that is, to act as a medium;
◊ develop a highly tuned mode of expression.

Discipline, truth, and inspiration are characteristics of all the Ways. But why should we speak of actors in conjunction with the Way of Ritual and Dance? Acting stands on the indefinable ground between two major aspects of the Self: the beautiful and the sacred. From our contemporary viewpoint, ritual is the vehicle of the sacred. Theater evokes beauty. In the past and in other civilizations, however, theater and ritual were one and the same reality. Indeed, some would claim that theater has its origins in ritual. It is not by chance that they employ similar methods—gestures and movements, costumes and masks, a public and a stage.

Ritual and theater share a central characteristic: *the creation of a field*. Both create fields in which time, space, events, and emotions are different from those in our ordinary world. And it is not only the actors—or the officiant, in the case of the ritual—but an entire community of people who enter that enchanted universe and for a brief moment live within it and are transformed by it.

We all create fields in our lives (even if they are much weaker than those of ritual or theater) by means of our very presence and the material objects we use: the family coming together around the dinner table; the doctor visiting a patient; a class studying at school; football fans watching a match: these are all fields with a structure and an atmosphere of their own. A *field* is a temporary universe made up of ideas, emotions, and a physical setting. It may be casual and unintended, or, on the contrary, its elements may be deliberately chosen to create an impression or evoke a feeling.

In the case of good theater and of ritual, the coherence and meaningfulness of a field elicits order within us; its beauty renews us; its enthusiasm sets us on fire. This happens when the field imparts an atmosphere beyond its mere utilitarian function—as in the tea ceremony, where one is not simply offered a drink but also assimilates a way of being. In many situations the emotional and spiritual climate is left to chance, but in ritual and in theater it is raised to the level of an art.

The field created in the theater may depend on the stage set and on various props, but it is primarily the result of the actor's presence. Duncan tells of an evening in 1899 when she saw Eleanora Duse performing in Paris. It was a second-rate play, *The Second Mrs. Tanqueray*, and Duncan was amazed that Duse should lower herself to take part in such a trivial work. At the end of the third act, Mrs. Tanqueray, played by Duse, is threatened by her enemies and decides to kill herself.

At that point the magic happened: Duse, alone on stage, was standing motionless. Without any particular effort on her part, she looked as if she were growing and growing until her head might touch the ceiling in the theater. She was no more a woman, writes Duncan, but had become a goddess. That transformation into a divine being was one of the greatest artistic events she had ever witnessed.

Before her performance Duse would meditate and visualize the characters she was to play. Another great Italian actor, Salvini, would spend hours in silence before acting. These actors were able to distill in themselves the indefinable quintessence of their charisma. One evening Konstantin Stanislavski saw Salvini play *Othello* at the Bolshoi. At first the actor did not impress Stanislavski at all: he was plump, with a large moustache and no makeup—far too much Salvini and not enough Othello. Then Stanislavski changed his mind:

> Salvini approached the tribune of the *doges*, stood a moment in thought, focused himself, and, without our even noticing, he already had the whole of the Bolshoi audience in his hand. It seemed as though he had done it with a single gesture, as though without even looking at the spectators, he had stretched out his hand towards us and taken hold of us all as if we were mere ants; we were held spellbound during the whole performance. . . . But we were now in his power for ever, for our whole life. . . . It was then that a certainty was born within me: Othello-Salvini was . . . a statue embodying an immutable law.

The conscious creation of a field also occurs in other areas. The German conductor Wilhelm Furtwängler said that, between the composer, himself as conductor, the orchestra, and the audience, "a communion of love" would occur in the most inspired moments. Those who knew Father Pio of Pietralcina relate that his masses would last hours and that he would take the congregation with him in his ecstasy.

The audience is almost as important as the protagonist in the creation of a field. As in the case of Bishop Berkeley's tree, which, when it falls in the forest, only makes a noise if someone is present to hear it, the field is created only if a public is there to participate in it. Before the play (or dance, concert, ritual), a number of different people were separately involved in their individual lives, preoccupied with all sorts of problems and dreams. On arrival they were linked by a common aim and tuned into the same wavelength. Then the sacred, dramatic, musical, or dance performance began, and they were all transported to the same universe—not an illusory world, as some have described theater, but a world that is just as real as our normal lives, in a sense, more real.

It is not easy to grasp hold of the ethereal substance that emanates from a charismatic actor when he or she performs. On one occasion Duse was among the Turin audience when Sarah Bernhardt appeared on stage. Duse explains her reaction to Bernhardt's performance:

> She came irradiated by her great aureole, her worldwide fame. And as if by magic the theater was suddenly filled with movement and life. . . . She was there, she played, she triumphed, she took possession of us all, she went away . . . but like a great ship she left a wake behind her . . . and for a long time the atmosphere she had brought with her remained in the old theater.

Sometimes the state of grace erupts on the film set, later to be indefinitely multiplied and extended to a thousand movie halls all over the world. But the original situation is closest to the theatrical one. In 1948 the Japanese director Akira Kurosawa was shooting *The Quiet Duel*. In this film Toshiro Mifune plays a young doctor who refuses to marry a woman he loves, so as not to infect her with a terrible sickness he had incurred while curing a patient. In the climactic scene, Toshiro Mifune breaks down and reveals his secret. Discussing the protagonists, Kurosawa recounts:

> As the seconds ticked by, their acting reached a fever pitch of tension, and sparks seemed to fly as from fireworks display. I could feel the perspiration forming in my clenched fists. Finally, when Mifune broke down in tears with the misery he was confessing, I heard the lights next to me rattle.

This shaking, found Kurosawa, was his own doing. He himself was transmitting it to the lamp by trembling, so strong was the emotional intensity conveyed to him by Mifune. Meanwhile, the cameraman was crying like a child and every few seconds had to wipe off his tears, jeopardizing the shooting of the whole scene. At the end, says Kurosawa, "while everyone on the set remained caught in the extreme tension of the scene, I felt like a man inebriated."

Some people may consider it sacrilege to say that ritual and acting are one and the same Way. But we have seen their common mode of expression—the creation of a field through various materials, gestures and movements, a relationship with an audience, and above all, presence. What is being expressed can vary infinitely: It may be the collective delirium of a rock concert; a vaudeville show; a Gregorian choir; the drama of a human soul; or the eternity of the Self in space and time. There is an infinite number of possibilities for field creation. And each one can be sacred or profane, comic or tragic, banal or sublime.

5

The Way of Science

We have all experienced the frustration of not understanding. We feel uneasy and helpless—perhaps we are obsessed by our incomprehension.

We have all experienced the pleasure of understanding, even if it is only deciphering the dishwasher instructions, finding a mistake in a sum, or knowing why summer is hotter than winter. We feel uplifted and interested, more alive. Every piece of knowledge has the effect of a tonic.

Now let us take this elementary form of understanding and imagine it to be far wider and more profound. Let us suppose that in order to obtain it, instead of a few seconds we have devoted a whole life of effort and concentration, and that this comprehension is in turn the result of hundreds of insights, as well as of long periods of search and doubt. Finally, let us imagine the power this intuition will have. Then we will have begun to grasp what the Way of Science is like.

This Way—in contrast with other Ways, such as the Way of Devotion or the Way of Illumination—is not explicit. Few scientists, if questioned, would be likely to affirm that they were on the "Way of Science" or even to recognize the existence of such a Way. In our civilization science is associated more with technological progress and the achievement of well-being than with the adventure of knowing. And when scientists speak of knowing, they almost always refer to specific, exterior knowing—not the ineffable, intuitive realization we encounter in transpersonal experience.

Yet when we study the work of great scientists, we discover that it stems from a curiosity prompted by a far deeper and more universal questioning than pertains to any material need: How is the universe made, and how does it work? We discover that any answer to this question uplifts the mind. We also find that scientific research shares many characteristics of a spiritual Way.

Along each Way certain lessons lie awaiting to be learned: we need to know how to overcome our own limited point of view; how to be strong in the face of external pressures; how to persist despite disappointments; how to get rid of erroneous views; and how to step back from our own experience and give up immediate gratification. These are the basics of every Way and are necessary because the individual consciousness would otherwise not be strong enough to evolve toward the Self, or, if it were, it would be incapable of sustaining its energy or of comprehending its nature.

In the Way of Science this training is perhaps more visible than in any other Way. Science is a rigorous discipline: it teaches individuals to persevere even in the absence of enthusiasm, to avoid self-deception, and to gain control of their thoughts and attention; it trains them to persist until they grasp a principle rather than stopping at partial solutions; it teaches them to notice how events are linked, to identify structures and rhythms not immediately apparent, and to leave behind a familiar world in order to visit another one, strange and impersonal.

This chapter's first section discusses a basic attitude in this path—intellectual honesty. The following two sections, on analogy and chance, show that scientific work is a much subtler process than mere logical reasoning and systematic observation—that there *is* madness in this method. On the other hand, tackling the next subject, discipline, brings to light the more balanced and systematic side of science. Finally, by looking into curiosity and wonder in scientists, we reach the transpersonal roots of scientific research.

The pathway along which a scientist travels is not only slow and demanding but can often go through periods of despair. These are the dark moments in which one feels lost among barren hypotheses, and the universe seems to have lost all meaning. Einstein said that when he was working on his theory of relativity he was prey to every kind of conflict: "I used to go away for weeks in a state of confusion," Einstein recounted, "as one who at that time had yet to overcome the stage of stupefaction."

Sometimes the first approach may be easy—the difficulties follow. Margaret Mead wrote in a letter that at the beginning of a field trip she would feel that she understood everything. Later, she recalled, the problem would start, "a period of despair, a sense that all is unknowable." At other times, confusion comes from the incapacity to make contradictory facts fit together in a coherent model. The German physicist Werner Heisenberg had many passionate discussions on quantum and wave theories with his Danish colleague Niels Bohr. Heisenberg recalled:

> I remember discussions with Bohr which went on until late at night and ended almost in despair. At the end of one discussion I went alone for a walk in the neighboring park. I remember repeating to myself again and again the question, "Can Nature possibly be as absurd as it seems to us in these atomic experiments?"

Anyone who follows this difficult Way through to the end cannot help but be changed by it. And this change is radical, affecting one's whole way of living and interpreting reality. In some cases it opens a person up to the transpersonal world. More than one scientist has had intuitive glimpses that transcended the immediate subject of his or her research and has experienced the "cosmic religious feeling" which, according to Einstein, is the "strongest and noblest motive for scientific research."

But is expansion of consciousness really akin to scientific inquiry? You think of science and you inevitably think of the problems and the cruelties it has caused—among them, nuclear and chemical warfare, vivisection, pollution, genetic monsters, technological alienation, and many other horrors. Yet it would be unfair to say that all scientists have exploited or violated reality. Many have obeyed it, studied it, and understood its deepest structure. And some scientists, starting out from the reassuring coordinates of the tangible and logical sequence of principles, have come face-to-face with a reality beyond matter and logic. In the brain or in a mineral, in the atomic structure or in the abstractions of mathematics, in flowers or in geological strata, in the play of dolphins or in the formation of crystals, in a microorganism or in a galaxy, they have found knowledge of the ineffable.

The French astronomer Camille Flammarion was on a hillside at sunset. He felt entranced by the beauty of nature as the sun sank beyond the horizon. Then, as the stars began to appear, his thoughts turned to the immensity of the cosmos:

> The sublime harmonies and immense movements of the heavenly bodies were unfolding above my head; the earth became an atom floating in infinity. But between this atom and all the suns in space, those whose light takes millions of years to reach us, and those which move, unknown, beyond the power of our human sight, I felt there was an invisible bond which links all universes and all souls in the unity of a single creation. . . . The grandeur of this spectacle was too much for me to contemplate. I felt my personality vanishing before the immensity of nature. Soon I felt as though I could neither speak nor think—this vast sea stretched to infinity—I no longer existed and something like a veil descended over my eyes.

Flammarion's testimony is lyrical and, for that reason, rare. Scientists of all times have tended to be far more cautious in describing their inner experiences. When publishing a discovery they illustrate their theoretical and practical conclusions; anything else is anecdotal and therefore irrelevant. To the reasons for their reticence we must add a sense of professional modesty and a general suspicion of anything nonrational. Fortunately, their restraint has occasionally yielded, and in the letters, notes, or interviews of some scientists we are able to get a glimpse of their inner worlds filled with passion and wonder.

Sometimes the pure concept of infinity is the trigger. The German mathematician Hermann Weyl commented that

> purely mathematical inquiry in itself . . . by its special character, its certainty and stringency, lifts the human mind into closer proximity with the divine than is attainable through any other medium. *Mathematics is the science of the infinite.*

On other occasions, the human mind is lifted above its limits as it discovers the presence of a greater Mind in the subject it is studying. Jean-Henri Fabre devoted his life to the study of insects and other small animals. His books contain the most beautiful descriptions of this enchanting world—the cicada that builds its home of bubbles and foam; the amazing architecture of the orange eggs from which the cabbage caterpillar is born; the glowworm that anesthetizes small snails with chloroform before eating them; the spider that efficiently constructs its web at night; the sacred beetle that surrounds its eggs with a sphere of dung so that the larvae can feed off it; the pine caterpillars that move along in single file, one behind the other, leaving a trail that glistens in the sun—all are reasons for interest and delight.

One day Fabre was studying the hairy ammophila wasp. He was fascinated by this insect's ability to sting as though it were perfectly knowledgeable of its victim's nervous system.

So precise and effective, it seemed almost an act of inspiration. With great wonder Fabre perceived the presence of a Mind in this tiny activity of animal life, noting that "the more I see, the more I observe, the more this Intelligence shines forth behind the mystery of things."

Intelligence, perfection, harmony—these words differ but the substance remains the same. In an interview, Einstein told one of his biographers all true searchers of Nature find it impossible that they have been the first to conceive the laws they discover. A greater Mind must have conceived before them "the exceedingly delicate threads" that connect their perceptions. He also said that

> this deep intuitive conviction of the existence of a higher power of thought which manifests itself in the inscrutable universe represents the content of my definition of God.

What Einstein intuited in his study of the laws of the cosmos, Swedish botanist Carolus Linnaeus had seen in plants and flowers. In the face of all the colors and shapes of the vegetable kingdom, its immense variety suggestive of inexhaustible inventiveness, the harmony of plant development, and the splendor of blossoms, it is natural to feel wonder. Linnaeus would go into rapture over the discovery of each new plant variety. In the preface to the second edition of his *Systema naturae*, he wrote:

> I saw the eternal, all-knowing, all-powerful God from the back when He advanced, and I became giddy! I tracked His footsteps over nature's fields and found in each one, even those I could scarcely make out, an endless wisdom and power, an unsearchable perfection.

Wonder also springs from the observation of human physiology. The great British neurophysiologist Charles Sherrington perceived an ineffable element in the human brain, "a residue which is the source of all of its splendid 'realities' as well as of its dreams. A residue which contains *all* the 'values'—for space is irrelevant to 'values'. In a word, the conscious 'I', called in the abstract 'mind'." And Candace Pert, who discovered neurotransmitters, said: "I see in the brain all the beauty of the universe and its order—constant signs of God's presence."

Teilhard de Chardin saw the emergence of the "human phenomenon" in the fossil remains of our remote prehuman forebears. After studying the structure of a Neanderthal skull, he had examined the jawbone of a member of the genus *Australopithecus* and had explored the geological deposits of Northern Rhodesia. Teilhard was returning to New York by ship from Africa, when he wrote to a friend: "Less and less do I see any difference now between research and adoration."

At times scientific understanding coincides with the appreciation of beauty. When Einstein was assessing a theory, he would ask himself whether—had he been in God's place—he would have made the universe in a certain way, and one of his frequently repeated statements was "This is so beautiful, God could not have passed it up." When he didn't know how to solve a scientific problem, Einstein would play the violin. Then, guided by the music, he would come up with a solution. Einstein said that "music has no effect on research work, but both are born of the same source and complement each other by the satisfaction they bestow." Referring to Bohr's atomic model, Einstein claimed that it was "the highest form of musicality in the sphere of thought."

For other scientists inspiration comes from nature. According to Hermann von Helmholtz, the great German physiologist who had his best ideas while walking in the country, "the scientist must have something of the poet in him." Inspiration came, not when he was at his laboratory but when out in nature:

> One needs the feeling of life and power, and these are best provided by pure mountain air. When the silent peace of the forest draws the traveller away from the restlessness of the world, when he is able to contemplate the rich plain at his feet, with its meadows and villages, and when the setting sun sends out its golden rays through the air, at that very time new ideas are germinated in the obscure depths of the soul, bringing light to the inner world, where, to begin with, there was nothing but obscurity and chaos.

Beauty and elegance are favorites of the scientist. There are scores of examples:

- ◇ Heisenberg would mention the Latin motto "Beauty is the splendor of truth" (*pulchritudo splendor veritatis*), claiming that even before demonstrating the validity of a theory with rational arguments, he was able to know whether the theory was true by evaluating its beauty.
- ◇ Paul Dirac, the English physicist, knew he was on the right track when he began to come up with "beautiful" equations.
- ◇ According to Jules Poincaré, the French mathematician, beauty is a filter for separating the rare ideas that have validity from the myriad of useless ones.
- ◇ The British physicist Ernest Rutherford considered Einstein's theory to be "a magnificent work of art."
- ◇ Ludwig Boltzmann said he could recognize mathematicians by the beauty of their styles, just as a musician can distinguish Mozart from Beethoven or Schubert.

Often the beauty of a law is due to its simplicity. Einstein loved to say that "God is shrewd, but he is not malicious" (*Raffiniert ist der Herrgott, aber boshaft ist er nicht*), meaning that the apparent complexity of the universe was not created to confuse our minds, but to give them the opportunity of discovering its underlying simplicity. If we accept this idea, we become convinced that even the most difficult theories can be explained to everyone, because such theories illustrate elementary facts. One morning, we are told by one of his fellow workers, Einstein mentioned that he had spoken about unified field theory to his sister, who was completely unfamiliar with such matters, "and she also thinks that it is a very good idea." English mathematician and physicist Isaac Newton, like Einstein, concentrated into a single short formula the essence of all his discoveries. His words almost sound like a statement by an Oriental mystic:

> Truth is ever to be found in simplicity, and not in the multiplicity and confusion of things. . . . The world, which to the naked eye exhibits the greatest variety of objects, appears very simple in its internal constitution when surveyed by a philosophical understanding, and so much the simpler by how much the better it is understood.

Another form of transpersonal experience in the Way of Science, perhaps the most representative of this Way, is the moment of discovery or invention, the "eureka" experience. This moment is invariably an explosion of joy and certainty. Like creative inspiration, it too is closely related to enlightenment, and there exist various well-documented examples. French geneticist and Nobel Prize–winner François Jacob said that discovery

> comes unexpectedly, as if by spontaneous generation. It can happen at any time, in any place, like a flash of lightning. What guides the mind at such times is not logic. It is instinct, or intuition. It is the need to see things clearly. It is an eagerness for life. In the interminable inner dialogue, and among the innumerable conjectures, comparisons, combinations and associations that are forever crossing the mind, sometimes a fiery

> trail cuts through the darkness. It lights up the surrounding landscape with a blinding, terrifying light which is brighter than a thousand suns.

What value is there, then, in knowing how the scientific mind works and what it aims to accomplish? What does this path have to teach to someone who sees science as an alien, perhaps even frightening, universe? It offers scope for new, fertile attitudes and mental habits which are not limited to scientific practice but are the birthright of all intelligent minds:

the honesty inherent in confronting facts
the discipline of precision and focus
the resolve never to take anything for granted
the ability to see hidden resemblances
a feeling for conceptual elegance
the art of thinking in a coherent way
wonder in the face of mystery

HONESTY

Two boys were playing badminton. The older boy kept beating the younger one. The weaker player was taking it badly and after a while threw down his racket saying, "I'm not playing anymore," and went to sit on a tree stump. The stronger boy was nonplussed. He had been enjoying himself and hadn't noticed his friend's increasing frustration. He now had to confront this problem. His face registered a sequence of expressions—surprise, concern, reflection—that outwardly signaled a change in his mental assessment of the situation. Then an idea came to him. "I know what we should do!" he said to his friend. "Instead of trying to beat each other, let's try to see how long we both can keep the shuttlecock in the air."

This was a clever solution and it worked. The German psychologist Max Wertheimer, who had witnessed the scene, regarded it as an example of "productive thinking." The key to the solution, according to Wertheimer, lay in the fact that the stronger boy forgot what interested him most at the time—namely, winning—and thereby perceived the game in a new perspective. Only by giving up one's mind-set is it possible to move from an inadequate to a more satisfactory view of reality.

Wertheimer had spent a number of days interviewing Einstein with the purpose of studying the stages whereby he had arrived at his theory of relativity. Wertheimer discovered that the process used by Einstein was essentially the same as in the young boy's insight: In order to have new ideas, we have to open ourselves to life as it is, not as habit would have it. We need to surrender to reality.

What children do in a moment and call a game, adults spend more time on and call scientific revolution. Consider the controversy between the Italian astronomer Galileo and the Aristotelians. Galileo stated that there were a number of large spots on the sun. The Aristotelians, in contrast, maintained that heavenly bodies are pure and perfect; the sun is a heavenly body, therefore it cannot have any spots—a coherent theory, and one that held sway for centuries yet proved utterly wrong.

Using the telescope he had recently invented, Galileo had seen sunspots. The Aristotelians countered that these spots were merely optical illusions or, as Jesuit father Cristoforo Scheiner interpreted them, swarms of small planets between the earth and the sun seen against the light. This was a clever argument to save the theory of the sun as a perfect heavenly body, but if one carefully observed the sunspots through the telescope one would easily realize that their shapes were too unstable to be true planets.

Aristotelian intellectuals preferred to deny uncomfortable facts that contradicted their ideas, and retained their coherent view of the universe. Galileo, who continued to see the anomalies and insist on them, brought about his own downfall. He was persecuted and reduced to loneliness and despair. Yet he established the basis for modern science.

The scientific method is only a few centuries old, but intellectual honesty—that is, the ability to eliminate firmly entrenched mental patterns and to see things as they really are—is timeless. People capable of intellectual honesty are adventurers. They are convinced that everything is possible, even realities that are uncanny or in opposition to what everyone else accepts as true. They never close their accounts with reality.

Consider the discovery of radioactivity. At the end of the nineteenth century, French physicist Henri Becquerel was working on the phosphorescence of potassium sulfate and uranium sulfate crystals. He exposed them to sunlight, then wrapped them in black paper and put them on a photographic plate that recorded the traces of their emissions. Becquerel wanted to show that the crystals absorbed radiation from the sun and as a result emitted energy.

One day, however, it was cloudy, and Becquerel, unable to repeat his usual experiment, placed the crystals in a drawer where there also happened to be some photographic plates. The following day when Becquerel took the crystals out of the drawer, he noticed these plates. According to his theory, no traces should have been recorded on them because the crystals had not been exposed to sunlight and should not emit energy.

Becquerel might have disregarded the plates, but instead he took the time necessary to examine them. What he found did not please him at all: the plates showed a strong, clear impression of the salts. Yet the salts had not been exposed to sunlight. How then could they have emitted energy? Evidently, his theory was wrong, and he had to admit it to himself. What happened next is history. Becquerel discovered that uranium emits an energy of its own—that it is radioactive. This breakthrough occurred because he was prepared to admit that reality belied his preconceptions.

How many of us are able to recognize our mistakes? It is inconvenient, because we are obliged to reorganize all our beliefs; it is painful, because our pride is hurt; it is tiring, because we have to start all over again. But when error no longer carries the dismal weight of failure, new opportunities open up for discovery.

Thanks to this paradoxical reframing, a mistake is not an occasion for self-reproach or guilt, but a *method* to find new facts and ideas. This point is fundamental not only on the Way of Science; for in all the Ways we make mistakes, and as long as we do not recognize them and do not learn what they can teach us, we are imprisoned by them. When, instead, we take full advantage of them, we are less afraid of erring and readier to risk.

This mental flexibility was Bohr's greatest strength. He actually collected his mistakes, studied them, selected those bearing similar aspects, and tried to understand what theory lay implicit in them. Then he formulated an alternative theory from which new, fertile opportunities would be born. By following this method he arrived at the formulation of the atomic model in 1912 to 1913 and the principle of complementarity in 1918.

The Way of Science is full of quandaries and deadly temptations. A fine, coherent theory is so reassuring—why throw it all away because of one tiny fact that contradicts it? The French historian Jacques Bossuet said that the greatest perversion of the human spirit was to believe in something because one wanted it to be so. Louis Pasteur, who loved to quote these words, would always act as his own devil's advocate whenever he thought he had made a discovery. He became the most critical and astute enemy of his own findings. For days, sometimes for years, Pasteur would try his hardest to demolish his own discoveries. When he had exhausted all possible opposing hypotheses, he would attain certainty and would experience "one of the greatest joys known to the human soul."

According to the great French chemist Antoine Lavoisier, a process of self-delusion is at work in scientists whereby a sort of complacency causes them to see and record only those facts that fit in with their ideas. Charles Darwin indicated how easy it was to gloss over the facts that contradicted one's ideas without realizing it, and made a point of writing them down. Otherwise, the perverse mechanism of self-deception would make him forget them.

When we surrender to reality, our mental framework may become disorganized. It is a costly operation, and few are prepared to pay the price. Sometimes the risk of surrendering to reality is greater than merely relinquishing attachment to our ideas, because a person's entire identity may be disrupted. Jung took this risk in confronting his unconscious mind. He frequently had visions, and he used them to explore unknown layers of the psyche. Jung imagined descending to cosmic depths, where he encountered beings and scenarios of every description. He claimed that he felt "defenseless in the presence of such a strange world where everything seemed difficult and incomprehensible." Terrified, he would force himself to continue his inquiry in the face of what seemed to be increasingly strange, immoral, senseless, or ridiculous material. Only by persevering despite the personal risk could Jung come to reach a more comprehensive understanding of the unconscious.

What happens in scientific inquiry is a model for what happens in ordinary life. Our subjective world is built on illusion. Various research projects have shown that we form a misshapen image of our past life, of ourselves and our bodies, of time, of other people and other countries. The lies we continually tell ourselves serve the purpose of giving coherence and continuity to our world and of protecting us against the threats to our personal stability. Without them our lives would be far more chaotic, impersonal, and painful.

Psychologist Anthony Greenwald spoke of the "totalitarian ego": our personality—censoring and manipulating what it perceives and records—resembles a dictatorial society, which subordinates truth to the regime propaganda. Our self-deception, however, costs us fatigue and tension, and produces unreal perceptions of the world. Maturity, and perhaps enlightenment, consists in seeing reality as it is, even when it is at variance with our dearest hopes and most firmly held convictions.

Our personality, however, frightened of incongruity, does not want to admit its mistakes. Like the individual who must be right at all costs in an argument, the personality identifies itself with its opinions, placing itself at center stage. It tries to arrange the universe to function according to its own preferences, for how else could it survive? In each one of the transpersonal Ways we find methods that help us to dismantle this mechanism. In the Way of Science one learns to adapt one's schemes to the world, instead of trying to make the world conform to one's own schemes.

Every Way is an invitation to unlearn. In the Way of Science one needs to put aside both the officially accepted explanations and one's own hypotheses. The French physiologist Claude Bernard wrote that "it is that which we do know which is the great hindrance to our learning, not that which we do not know." The British biophysicist Francis Crick, speaking on the importance of standing back from one's ideas, said: "Just as important as having ideas is getting rid of them." Darwin shared this view:

> I have steadily endeavored to keep my mind free so as to give up any hypothesis, however much beloved (and I cannot resist

forming one on every subject), as soon as facts are shown to be opposed to it.

Darwin also pointed out a fact relevant to all who are accustomed to formulating hypotheses. With the exception of his theory of coral reefs, he always had to abandon—or significantly modify—the first formulation of a theory.

By putting our own ideas to one side, we achieve nakedness of mind. One day Pasteur knocked at Fabre's door. Neither had yet reached a position of fame, although Pasteur had already made some important discoveries and had been commissioned by the government to research the causes of a serious plague affecting silkworms. Pasteur knew nothing about silkworms. He had called, he explained, so Fabre could show him a cocoon.

Fabre writes that Pasteur did not even know that a cocoon contains a chrysalis. Indeed, he was tackling the problem from a position of complete ignorance. Fabre could have considered Pasteur incompetent. What struck him instead was Pasteur's eagerness to consider a fact without the interference of explanations:

> Encouraged by the magnificent example of Pasteur, I have made it a rule to adopt the method of ignorance in my investigations of the instincts. I read very little. Instead of turning over the leaves of books, an expensive method which is not within my means, instead of consulting others, I set myself obstinately face to face with my subject until I contrive to make it speak. I know nothing. So much the better; my interrogation will be all the freer.

Stripping the mind is not only a cognitive act, but it also overcomes self-affirmation. In order for realization to take place, it is necessary that the will of the individual be left behind. Only then is it possible to glimpse an immensely greater and more intelligent will. Replying to a letter of condolence on the death of his four-year-old son, the English biologist Thomas Huxley wrote:

> Science seems to me to teach, in the highest and strongest manner, the great truth which is embodied in the Christian concept of the entire surrender to the will of God. Sit down before fact like a little child, and be prepared to give up every preconceived notion, follow humbly wherever and to whatever abysses Nature leads or you shall learn nothing.

ANALOGY

Drawing an analogy consists in seeing similarity in two distinct entities or processes. We are so accustomed to analogies that we no longer give them a second thought. For instance, to recognize a person from a photograph means to see the resemblance between a living being in flesh and blood, and black and white marks on a piece of paper—an instant recognition of analogy. And when we call a Pekinese, a Great Dane, a poodle, and a Saint Bernard by the generic term *dog*, it is because we see some essential common characteristics in these animals—namely, the ability to bark, wag their tails, and show affection to their masters. This too is analogy.

There are also *new* analogies, those which enable us to create concepts or invent devices. In order for this to happen, skillful observation is not enough; one also needs boldness to make an imaginative jump from one reality to another. Alexander Graham Bell invented the telephone, for instance, by thinking of the ear's internal structure:

> It struck me that the bones of the human ear were very massive, indeed, as compared with the delicate thin membrane that

> jated them, and the thought occurred to me that if a membrane so delicate could move bones relatively as massive, why should not a thicker and stouter piece of membrane move my piece of steel. And the telephone was conceived.

An analogy brings about a transfer of useful information—in this case, the fact that a delicate membrane can move a large mass is transferred from human physiology to acoustic mechanics. This is how an invention comes about.

The example of René Laënnec is well known. This shy Belgian doctor was embarrassed by auscultating his women patients' hearts (in those days doctors would place their ears directly on the patient's chest). One day while walking through a park, he saw some children playing with tubes that had been left lying around. One child spoke into the end of a tube, while another listened to his friend's amplified voice at the other end. Laënnec was impressed by this game. He ran home, rolled up a piece of paper, and placed one end over the heart of his next patient and his own ear to the other end. Laënnec had thus invented the stethoscope.

The invention of the hot air balloon was also the result of an analogy. The wife of one of the Montgolfier brothers had stretched out a skirt to dry over the fire. After a while the skirt fell from the wire to which it had been affixed. Everyone expected it to fall into the flames, but instead it rose into the air. The Montgolfiers realized that hot air, being lighter than cold air, could lift concave objects, and this insight enabled them to invent the hot air balloon.

These are simple domestic examples. More fascinating instances of analogy come from the study of nature. The flight of birds, for instance, led to the invention of the airplane. As Leonardo da Vinci had done centuries before and as the Wright brothers were to do in more practical terms a few years later, the American astronomer Samuel Langley created at the end of the nineteenth century the first flying airplane models as a result of observing birds in flight. Langley started out from a vivid childhood memory. Years back, lying in a meadow in New England, he had watched a hawk rising higher and higher into the sky. Langley vividly recounts his experience:

> I well remember how, as a child, when lying in a New England pasture, I watched a hawk soaring far up in the blue, and sailing for a long time without any motion of its wings, as though it needed no work to sustain it, but was kept up there by some miracle. . . . After many years and in mature life, I was brought to think of these things again, and to ask myself whether the problem of artificial flight was as hopeless and as absurd as it was then thought to be.

The practice of drawing analogies from natural forms also appears in the work of Gregory Bateson, the English biologist, anthropologist, ethologist, and cyberneticist. Bateson was particularly gifted in transferring models of thought from one discipline to another. Since childhood, he had experienced a "vague mystical feeling" in looking for similar processes in different natural phenomena: laws governing the structure of a crystal and a human society, patterns in the segmentation of a worm and in the formation of basalt pillars. Margaret Mead, married to Bateson for fourteen years, wrote that he took his models from various fields—"one minute from embryology, the next from geology, the next from anthropology, back and forth, very freely, so that the illustrations from one spot illuminated, corrected, and expanded the one from another."

In Nikola Tesla's case we have a far less direct analogy. For some time Tesla had been thinking of building an efficient alternating current engine. Everyone thought this was an impossible task. But Tesla had been considering the problem since his university days, despite the fact that his professor had repeatedly tried to dissuade him from the venture. On a late afternoon in February of 1882, Tesla was walking through a park with his friend Amital Szigety. The sun was setting, and Tesla began to recite some lines from *Faust* brought to mind by the sunset:

> The glow retreats, done is the day of toil;
> It yonder hastes, new fields of life exploring;
> Ah, that no wing can lift me from the soil,
> Upon its track to follow, follow soaring . . .

At this point, to the great astonishment of his friend, Tesla muttered some incomprehensible words and waved his arms around as though he were flying, gripped by a wild enthusiasm. It took some time for Szigety to understand the explanation that Tesla traced out on the ground with his walking stick: he had discovered a way of making an alternating current engine work.

This breakthrough marked the birth of an invention that was a technological milestone. The idea of a rotating magnetic field, an original and very elegant solution, came to Tesla as he quoted Goethe's verses on the setting sun. The analogy here is between the light of the sun moving beyond the horizon and a magnetic field which, rather than remaining static, rotates just as the sun appears to turn around the earth. Tesla later described how at the moment of this discovery he experienced the happiest state of his life. For two months following the event, Tesla was euphoric, and, according to his biographer John O'Neill, this sudden discovery was a true enlightenment that revealed to him the whole cosmos as a symphony of energy streams.

The Italian physicist Galileo Ferraris, however, had also invented the rotating magnetic field. Tesla, who did not patent his invention until 1888, was accused of plagiarism by his opponents. Actually it was Tesla who first put his invention to practical use. Nevertheless, it is of interest to note how Ferraris, quite independently and acting in equally good faith, arrived at his own discovery. Again, it was an analogy that brought the idea to his mind. As it happened, Ferraris too was walking after a day's work:

> In the evening of 17th August 1885 I went out for a walk, as was my custom. I walked along, daydreaming, and the natural succession of my thoughts brought me to the analogy of electromagnetic phenomena with optical phenomena. Certain obscure points, related to the latter, had figured in my research for some months. Suddenly an idea flashed through my mind, presenting me with a possibility which startled me when I thought of its consequences.

The possibility that had "startled" Ferraris was that of seeing the similarity between optical and electromagnetic events. During those same years another great inventor, Guglielmo Marconi, was considering the analogies between the same two realms. The idea of wireless telegraphy came to Marconi as a "consequence of the observation and study of the methods used by nature." The sun sends out light and heat in all directions through space, covering great distances. If this can happen with light, Marconi mused, is it not possible to produce the same effect with electromagnetic waves? These are his words:

> Just as the heat and light of the sun—on which life on our planet depends—are transmitted to us across millions and millions of miles through space, just as light reaches us from the most distant stars, and as countless electrical and magnetic disturbances of nature come to us after crossing unimaginable distances, it occurred to me that, using means similar to those employed by nature, it should be possible to

transmit our own selected messages and pick them up over any distance.

The experience of an English physician and anatomist illustrated another case in which the sun provided a useful analogy. William Harvey arrived at the discovery of blood circulation by drawing an analogy between the solar system and the human body. The heart is for the human body what the sun is for the solar system: the central life source. Might it not be possible that, just as the planets circulated around the sun, the blood circulated around the heart? The British Museum still contains Harvey's hastily written note, beginning in Latin (the language used by scientists of his day) and ending in English, almost as though his enthusiasm would not allow him to wait any longer before committing his discovery to paper.

Harvey's example clearly shows the heuristic function of analogy. Scientific theory at the time held that the blood fluctuated, and the idea of circulation was completely unknown to science. It took an external, and apparently unconnected, point to act as a lever—the movement of the planets around the sun—to disengage the old, false mental habit and create room for a correct explanation.

The analogy used by Harvey is also interesting for another reason: it draws similarities between the universe and the human body, between the macrocosm and the microcosm. There are a number of analogies of this type in the history of science. Crick, for instance, was aided in his speculations on the structure of DNA by the thought of a "perfect biological principle" similar to the "perfect cosmological principle" formulated by the astronomer Thomas Gold—an analogy between galaxy and cell structure. Rutherford and Bohr came up with the structure of the atom by comparing it to the solar system. In this connection their colleague Max Born wrote:

> A remarkable and alluring result of Bohr's atomic theory is the demonstration that an atom is a little planetary system . . . the thought that the laws of the macrocosmos reflect the terrestrial world obviously exercises a great magic on mankind's mind.

Furthermore, analogy is not only confined to science or technology. We come across it in all expressions of creative thought.

In literature, analogy becomes metaphor. In the *Divine Comedy*'s *Paradiso*, Dante said that the angels' beauty laughed; Goethe compared human destiny to the blowing of the wind, and the beloved to the embers of the sun glimmering in the sea; Shakespeare likened old age to a flame about to be extinguished. All of these images aimed at producing an aesthetic emotion.

Likewise, Andrea Palladio in his architectural works endeavored to reproduce the harmony of the heavenly bodies in orbit. And Austrian composer Joseph Haydn used images as a guideline for composing the various movements of his symphonies—for example, the vicissitudes of a sea voyage: a favorable wind, arrival in unknown places, commercial exchanges with a foreign country, the homeward journey, a storm on the high seas, the roaring of the waves, the calm after a storm, arrival in the port, and the joy of reunion with one's family.

Analogy is also useful in philosophical thought. Heraclitus, for instance, used the metaphor of a flowing river to illustrate unending change as the essence of the universe. For Plato, the Idea of the Good is the source of reality and truth, just as the sun is the origin of growth and light. In order to illustrate the arbitrary nature of language, Ludwig Wittgenstein used the metaphor of placing differently shaped grids over an array of black spots, thus giving different descriptions of the array.

Rituals, too, as we have seen in a previous section, use analogies—in fact, they are an *embodiment* of analogies. Movements, gestures, vestments, and architecture symbolize basic religious truths, the laws of nature, the hierarchies of the celestial worlds, or the order of the cosmos.

The great spiritual guides have also been inspired by analogies. The Chinese Taoist sage Lao Tse pointed out the usefulness of void by using the analogy of the central, open part of a wheel. The *Bhagavad Gita* compared a yogi who achieves union with the Self to a still flame protected by the winds. Sankara said that, just as the sky is not limited by the clouds, the human spirit is not confined by the body.

All of these analogies have different results. Some make discovery or invention possible; others facilitate aesthetic experience; others help bring about intellectual understanding; and yet others evoke spiritual insight. In all cases a fundamental phenomenon takes place—one perceives a reality from an external reference point and frees the mind from the old unproductive points of reference.

This freeing produces in those who experience it a transpersonal event that is variously perceived as the joy of discovery, the happiness of beauty, the embodiment of the sacred, or the enlightenment of the mind.

CHANCE

Even inventors play. Indeed, they play more than anyone else. Thomas Alva Edison made a cardboard toy—a little man who sawed wood—and attached it to a diaphragm in a funnel; when a person sang into the funnel, vibrations moved the diaphragm which, in turn, by means of a device, moved the little man, causing him to saw the wood. That is how geniuses amuse themselves.

At the same time, Edison was working on a technique for recording telegraphic signals onto the spiral grooves of a paper disk. Then an insight flashed: What if he combined the two ideas—conversion of sound into movement, and recording of signals on a disk? In that felicitous moment Edison had invented the record player.

In the sixteenth century, Ambroise Paré treated shotgun wounds with boiling elder-tree oil and theriac, an old antidote to poison. But this method of cauterization—presumably used because such wounds were thought to be poisoned—actually spread the infection and caused great suffering. During the French siege of Turin, Paré ran out of elder-tree oil and used the first thing that came to hand—a digestive remedy consisting of egg and turpentine—and no cauterization. The next day he discovered that the cauterized patients were infected and feverish, whereas those treated with the new method were cured. He had discovered the phenomenon of disinfection.

Samuel Morse, an American painter who had come to Europe to perfect his art, was returning to the United States in 1832 by ship. One day he took part in a conversation in the presence of some scientists who happened to be on board. Someone asked whether the speed of electrical impulses was reduced by the length of the conducting wire through which they passed. One of the scientists answered that speed was independent of wire length. Suddenly Morse had the idea of using electrical impulses for instantly transmitting information over great distances. Telegraphy and the Morse code developed from that insight.

In the autumn of 1837 the French painter and physicist Louis-Jacques Daguerre threw some silver iodide plates into a drawer, thinking they were defective. After some weeks, he discovered when he opened the drawer that the sheets were perfectly developed. He then looked into the drawer to discover what substance had favored this process. Eventually, Daguerre discovered, between the cracks in the wood, a few mercury pearls that had escaped from an old broken bottle. Clearly, the best way to develop plates was by means of mercury vapor, and this was the start of photography.

In 1855 Giuseppe Ravizza, a dreamy Italian lawyer, was

inspired by the toy piano he had given his daughter to build a "writing harpsichord." This is how the first typewriter came into being.

In the spring of 1879 Pasteur was studying cholera in hens. One day he injected cultures into some hens, but the cultures, though active, were not strong enough to cause infection. Pasteur then prepared a new and much more active culture and injected it into some new hens he had just brought from the market, as well as into those he had previously injected with the ineffective culture. The new hens died—a sign that the culture was very active. The old hens, however, did not even become ill. Pasteur then realized that they had been immunized by the first injection of weak cultures. He had discovered vaccination.

Mistakes, distractions, toys made during spare time, shortage of necessary materials, casual observations, mix-ups: these examples—and we could mention many others—might seem sufficient grounds for compiling a mocking, perhaps even grotesque, history of the scientific discoveries on which our civilization stands, showing that they were not the result of logical sequences of experiments, but rather the outcome of random events.

We think of science as an organized, rational task performed by means of systematic research in aseptic laboratories. We find instead that scientists have to feel their way, relying at times on chance or on a series of favorable circumstances. We can almost see these scientists at work in a domestic setting; we can almost smell a homey atmosphere around them.

Leopold Auenbrugger, for instance, was the son of an innkeeper who had taught him to gauge the quantity of beer in a barrel by striking it on the top. Several years later, he began to use the same method with the human body and thus started the percussion technique used in medicine to ascertain the condition of various organs.

During a mass in the Pisa Cathedral, seventeen-year-old

Galileo was distracted by a swinging chandelier. Galileo measured the duration of each swing against his own pulse and discovered that, as the arc gradually diminished, the time of each oscillation nevertheless remained the same. This observation led him to discover the laws of pendular motion—and to devote himself to the study of physics (against the wishes of his father, who wanted him to become a doctor).

The first research on electricity developed because the wife of the Italian physiologist Luigi Galvani, seeing that frogs' legs, affixed to a metal wire, were twitching, cried out in fright to her husband and interrupted his class. Although Galvani's theory of animal electricity was soon refuted by Alessandro Volta, it nevertheless provided a decisive impetus to the new science of electrophysiology.

Indeed, insight can happen in no other way, for the instruments and processes used by scientists are an embodiment of the old theories—the very ones that must be overcome. They obstruct discovery because they make no provision for it. In the less-structured universe of daily life and chance, in contrast, new ideas have full play to emerge in a less direct or even accidental fashion. Chance discovery and invention are the very essence of the creative mind, fertile in its ability to see a microcosm of meaning and beauty in any event. Uncreative people tend to dismiss the fortuitous or the unexpected as of little interest because they are so preoccupied with prearranged ideas and aims. Instead, creative people overlook not even the smallest detail. They are capable of finding significance in everything.

If it is true, as Einstein maintained, that all science is nothing more than a refining of everyday thought, we should rethink our everyday lives, whether we are scientists or not. How are we to react to chance and the unexpected? Do we banish them to a dusty storehouse ever more cluttered with meaningless items, or do we accept their invitation to think and to imagine? A chance encounter, a magazine article, an unusual coincidence, an overheard conversation, a fact mentioned in the news, a delay, a dream—everything can have deeper import and wider connections than we expect.

Yet again we find the *principle of economy* fundamental to many of the Ways—namely, that one makes use of the material offered in a given moment. This method requires the humility to let oneself be led by the signals along life's pathway. And those who believe they already know for sure what is significant and what is not are the losers in this game.

These examples of chance discoveries should not deceive us, however. The fact that many scientific discoveries and inventions are the result of chance in no way diminishes the importance of the human mind. On the contrary, it shows its very ingeniousness. Creative scientists allow events to take them by the hand and lead them into strange, unexplored territory. This intelligent passivity, this ability to make use of circumstances, is the distinguishing mark of many an explorer.

Pasteur used to say that "chance only favours the prepared mind." But what does *prepared mind* mean? At least three senses (not mutually exclusive) can be given to this expression.

First of all, a prepared mind may simply mean an informed mind. For instance, when the German physicist Wilhelm Röntgen stumbled upon a fluorescent light that enabled him to discover X rays, he immediately thought of rays capable of passing through matter, because he still remembered a research paper written two years before in which Helmholtz had suggested that there might exist rays with so short a frequency that they could pass through solid objects.

Second and more profoundly, a prepared mind is one which has devoted its energy to the same subject for many years, patiently sifting every detail and allowing the unconscious to elaborate on the assimilated material. In other words, it is a finely tuned mind that acts like a magnet, attracting to itself any thought or datum bearing some relation to the research topic. Every event is seen in terms of the relevant subject—even an apple falling on one's head, as happened to Newton, or an object floating in a bath, as in Archimedes' case.

There is also a third meaning to "prepared mind": an open mind, which, when stripped of all previous assumptions, is able to ascribe meaning to apparently insignificant events. It is a mind with the ability to conduct an intelligent dialogue with things, to ask the right questions, and to allow the universe—through its succession of apparently casual circumstances—to provide the answer. Jung coined the word *synchronicity* for the meaningful connection of random events. Neurophysiologist John Eccles wrote:

> This is essentially the way in which I have made discoveries. They arose from the happenings that I was not expecting, where eventually I was tuned in enough to listen to what nature was trying to tell me. The good research workers are those who can recognize and appreciate the significance of the unexpected.

There is also imperfect synchronicity—things speak but no one listens, at least not at first. This was the case with Alexander Fleming, mistakenly referred to as the discoverer of penicillin. It is an amazing story. In 1928 Fleming was working on certain staphylococcus cultures in connection with his research on the treatment of war wounds. On one occasion he went away on vacation and left everything as it was on his workbench. When he came back a month later, Fleming found the small plates containing the cultures covered with mold and did what he should have done before leaving: he threw everything out.

At this point a colleague happened to come in to ask how Fleming's work was progressing. The two of them began talking. In order to make a point with his colleague, Fleming picked up one of the cultures he had thrown away. He noticed that the mold had destroyed some of the staphylococci around it. That meant it had the property of killing bacteria. "Funny," he said, pointing this out to his colleague.

Fleming called the mold *penicillium* and wrote about it in a publication, but later he came to the conclusion that it did not have any particular relevance for the treatment of bacterial infection and put the whole thing out of his mind.

Several years later at the beginning of World War II, the need to treat war wounds led to a more intense and systematic research program in this field. An Australian doctor, Edward Florey, began to experiment with penicillin and realized its great therapeutic potential. So if by "discovering" we mean fully understanding the function and value of an entity or process, the real discoverer of penicillin was Florey, for it was he who really listened to what the facts, through their chain of chance circumstances, had tried in vain to convey to Fleming.

The chance element is not always external. We can also look on it as an inner impulse guided by no apparent logic. The same ability is demonstrated here as in the previously mentioned cases—namely, recognizing that one is on the right track. Enrico Fermi, the Italian physicist, wrote:

> I will tell you how I came to make the discovery which I suppose is the most important one I have made [how to produce a nuclear chain reaction]. We were working very hard on the neutron-induced radioactivity and the results we were obtaining made no sense. One day, as I came to the laboratory, it occurred to me that I should examine the effect of placing a piece of lead before the incident neutrons. Instead of my usual custom, I took great pains to have the piece of lead precisely machined. I was clearly dissatisfied with something: I tried every excuse to postpone putting the piece of lead in its place. When finally, with some reluctance, I was going to put it in its place, I said to myself: "No, I do not want this piece of

> lead here; what I want is a piece of paraffin." It was just like that, with no advance warning, no conscious prior reasoning. I immediately took some odd piece of paraffin and placed it where the piece of lead was to have been.

This is how creativity happens—when the mind is fertile; when everything is seen as having value and each event is welcomed as an opportunity; when strange and unforeseen accidents are met with confidence; when the unpredictable dance of life, rather than causing fear or annoyance, stimulates interest; and when there is always a "why" to ask, always a game to play.

DISCIPLINE

The goal is not for the weak. It is not for those who remain on the surface or for those who give up easily. Nor is it for those who are content with little, or those who think they already have the solution.

The goal is discovery. It may be another goal along another Way, but the same principle applies. In order to reach a goal one must use all of one's resources. One must neither be distracted nor give up. One must struggle with passion and challenge the impossible. And all this means discipline.

The most fundamental aspect of discipline—as everyday life teaches us—is concentration. Without concentration we could not even iron a shirt or tidy a desk, at least if we want the job well done. Concentration is necessary in all the Ways to the Self—indeed, for every kind of success. It is a focus so intense it may verge on madness:

◊ Isadora Duncan would stand immobile for hours, as if in a trance, her hands on her solar plexus. She was trying to find the origin of movement, the "music of the soul." Once she was in contact with this energy, she allowed it to flow through her body, "filling it with vibrating light."

◊ One day, Pierre Auguste Renoir was painting. Monet asked him repeatedly for a cigarette, but Renoir did not notice. Leaning over his friend, Monet began to search in Renoir's pocket where his cigarettes were usually kept. It was not until Monet's beard began to brush against Renoir's cheek that he noticed the other's presence. He continued painting as though nothing had happened.

◊ The Indian yogi Swami Viveknanda complained to the sage Ramakrishna, his teacher, that the noise from a nearby jute factory disturbed his meditation. Ramakrishna advised him to concentrate on the noise itself—and the problem was solved.

◊ When he had to come to terms with an idea, Napoleon would seize it "by the neck, by the arse, by the feet, by the hands, by the head," until he had fully worked it out.

◊ In his treatise on prayer, the Spanish mystic Pedro de Alcantara suggested keeping a tight control of the mind, just as one uses a bridle to control a horse.

◊ The South Tyrolean mountaineer Reinhold Messner wrote that his ability to concentrate—crucial if one is not to end up at the bottom of a precipice—manifested itself "from the fingertips to the soles of the boots."

We see the greatest need for concentration in science, where one's whole attention has to be given to a single subject. In this way the mind is released from its usual mechanisms and becomes capable of understanding. When asked how he had discovered the law of universal gravitation, Newton replied: "By thinking about it continuously. I keep the object of my research constantly before me, waiting until the first light begins to dawn, little by little; finally it changes and at last the light is complete." On one occasion he said that the discovery of scientific truth is "the offspring of silence and unbroken meditation."

Light and meditation are recurring metaphors in the writings of scientists. The French naturalist Georges-Louis de Buffon once made a useful remark for anyone who wants to learn how to think. "When you have an idea," stated Buffon, "consider it for a long time until it radiates, that is, until it presents itself clearly to you, surrounded by images of corollaries, of consequences."

Marie Curie, the Polish physicist who discovered radium, wrote that during the period of discovery she and her husband lived in their "single preoccupation as if in a dream," in an atmosphere of "peace and meditation, which is the true atmosphere of a laboratory." She further explains that it was also a question of faith:

> Life is not easy for any of us. But what of that? We must have perseverance and above all confidence in ourselves. We must believe that we are gifted for something, and that this thing, at whatever cost, must be attained.

Concentration is a consuming enterprise, an obsession. It goes on not only during working hours but all the time. Poincaré's nephew described his uncle's concentration:

> He would think in the street while going to the Sorbonne, on his way to some scientific gathering, or during the long walks he was used to taking after meals. He would think in the foyer or in the assembly rooms at the Institute, or when walking with short steps, an intense expression on his face, fumbling with his bunch of keys. He would think at the meal table, and often he would suddenly interrupt a conversation in mid-sentence in order to develop a thought that had just crossed his mind.

Concentration is a battle against distractions, discouragement, and other people's interruptions. It therefore requires perseverance and the ability to go deeply into a subject without losing one's way, without ever giving up. During the period from 1902 to 1910, when Russell was writing his monumental *Principia Mathematica*, the experience of finding the slightest contradiction in his work meant that he had to go right back to the beginning of his undertaking—and contradictions continued to emerge.

Russell would often spend days in front of a blank page—just thinking; but after a day of "severe intellectual work," as he called it, the sheet was often blank. On many occasions during that period, Russell would stand on the railway bridge watching the trains on the Oxford line and would feel like jumping under. But he explains why he did not:

> The difficulties appeared to me in the nature of a challenge, which it would be pusillanimous not to meet and overcome. So I persisted, and in the end the work was finished, but my intellect never quite recovered from the strain.

Einstein's struggle was perhaps less dramatic, but his determination was equally intense. American mathematician Ernst Straus recounts how one day he and Einstein had finished writing a certain document and were looking for a paper clip to hold the pages together. They found one but it was twisted, so they looked for some tool to straighten it. After searching through several drawers they found a whole box of paper clips. Einstein then took one from the box and began to use it to straighten out the twisted one. When Straus pointed out that it was no longer necessary to do this, Einstein replied that once he had set his mind on a certain goal, nothing could deflect him. Einstein later confided to his friend that this incident could aptly represent his way of working.

When we concentrate, we lose touch with the passing of

time and forget the world around us. The stereotype of the absentminded professor and corresponding stories (many of which are authentic) are good illustrations of this phenomenon. For instance:

◇ Einstein and a geologist friend were so engrossed in a conversation about earthquakes that neither noticed a big earthquake was actually happening and that the entire building had been evacuated.

◇ Newton only realized he was boiling his watch when he tried to tell the time by looking at an egg.

◇ Poincaré's sister sewed bells to his wallet so that the mathematical genius would be alerted not to lose his money.

◇ Edison, lost in his experiments, forgot to attend his own wedding.

These anecdotes are far less frivolous than they may appear. They tell us much about the individuals concerned—namely, that they were people dedicated to their work who withdrew their attention from the outer world and entirely concentrated on their particular interest, people who knew how to forget themselves.

We encounter this gift for self-forgetfulness in all of the transpersonal Ways. Paradoxically, one loses oneself—in the ecstasy of dance, in artistic creation, in service. As though in a spell thoughts and emotions are transcended and one's everyday personality vanishes. Barbara McClintock, American geneticist and recipient of the Nobel Prize, spoke of her work at the microscope, examining neurospora (a red mold) chromosomes:

> I found that the more I worked with them the bigger and bigger [they] got, and when I was really working with them I wasn't outside, I was down there. I was part of the system. I

> was right down there with them, and everything got big. I even was able to see the internal parts of the chromosomes. . . . It surprised me because I actually felt as if I were right down there and these were my friends.
>
> As you look at these things, they become part of you. And you forget yourself. The main thing is that you forget yourself.

This statement challenges all the clichés about the detachment of the scientist. We see here the ability to enter into the very heart of a subject, and the intense desire to know it intimately. And we also see a full identification with the research subject which, Barbara McClintock continues, led her to "ecstasy" and to an "exceedingly strong feeling" for the oneness of all things.

Concentration is not only applied to hypotheses and thoughts but may be also directed to the outside world and used in observation. Observation is necessary because the human eye does not always see what is right in front of it. In the ordinary act of seeing, the essence is often visible only to a trained eye, an eye which, for months or years, has been penetrating the heart of appearances.

According to the French physicist Augustin Fresnel, nature contains an order hidden beneath an inextricable net of confusion. "Simplicity lies concealed in this chaos, and it is only for us to discover it!" Pasteur would spend hours at the microscope examining a single plate, noting imperceptible movements and variations. His colleagues would joke that he was watching microbes growing. Pasteur would say that "nature . . . requires a great deal of work; she favours calloused hands and furrowed brows."

The technique for getting nature to reveal its secrets consists of patient, accurate observation. Whether it be a question of a nebula or a flower, a cell or a form of animal behavior, observation leads to full and true perception. At one point in a letter to his son Horace, Darwin mused: What is it that enables an individual to make discoveries? Not intelligence, since a good many intelligent people never discover anything, but observation. And in his autobiography Darwin wrote: "On the favorable side of the balance, I think that I am superior to the common run of men in noticing things which easily escape attention, and in observing them carefully."

Fabre would spend whole days without moving, as if rooted to the spot, in order to observe the behavior of insects. The peasants, passing by at dawn on their way to work and returning in the evening to find him in the same position, thought he must be mad.

The same can be said of Goethe, who, for the sake of both science and poetry, was a meticulous observer of nature. He liked to study rocks, plants, and stars. All you had to do to make him happy, wrote a friend, was to send him "a lion's tooth or a strangely twisted antelope's horn" as an object of contemplation. Goethe maintained that he could see the laws of nature in the veins of a rock; and when contemplating a palm in the botanical gardens of Padua, he perceived in it the fundamental, original form of the plant (*Urpflanz*) from which, he thought, all vegetable forms have come into being through various metamorphoses. He wrote to Jacobi that only in the contemplation of individual objects was he able to perceive the divine being.

Concentration can be extended over long periods of time. It then becomes tenacity. In the field of science this may mean the patient, methodical repetition of an experiment. Streptomycin, for instance, was discovered among ten thousand other microorganisms. Its discoverer, the Russian microbiologist Selman Waksman, recounts:

> It was the story of the ten thousand microbes. We isolated ten thousand microbes and tested them for ability to inhibit the growth of pathogenic bacteria. We found that ten percent had that quality. We tried to grow that thousand microbes in cultures and found that ten percent lent themselves to that process.

> From that one hundred we tried to extract the active substances, and we ended with ten chemical compounds. We tested them in animals, and one is the antibiotic known as streptomycin.

Edison performed 1,600 experiments in an attempt to find the most suitable filament for a light bulb, and 50,000 experiments to develop the accumulator battery. He said that his methods were akin to those used in seed selection—namely, he would try thousands of possibilities, then select the most promising one, and work on it in depth.

Here we see the difference between the amateur and the professional. The amateur will stop at the first satisfactory idea, while the professional will generate a large number of ideas, even if most are useless, and only then make a choice. According to the British mathematician and philosopher Alfred North Whitehead, we must try to come up with the maximum number of ideas:

> We need to entertain every prospect of novelty, every chance that could result in new combinations, and subject them to the most impartial scrutiny. For the probability is that nine hundred and ninety-nine of them will come to nothing, either because they are worthless in themselves or because we shall not know how to elicit their value; but we had better entertain them all however skeptically, for the thousandth idea may be the one that will change the world.

We can sum up the substance of these examples in one word—discipline. It is discipline never deflected by success or failure; discipline devoting itself to a subject and exploring it to its depths; discipline which is not only a guarantee of success but also a way of being. As American physicist Robert Oppenheimer wrote to his brother, we should gratefully acknowledge any circumstances that favor it:

> I believe that through discipline . . . we can achieve serenity, and a certain small but precious measure of freedom from the accidents of incarnation, and charity. . . . Therefore I think that all things which evoke discipline: study, and our duties to men and to the commonwealth, war, and personal hardship, and even the need for subsistence, ought to be greeted by us with profound gratitude; for only through them can we attain to the least detachment; and only so can we know peace.

CURIOSITY AND WONDER

In "Twilight," a science-fiction short story by John W. Campbell, a man succeeds in projecting himself seven million years into the future. All around him the signs of a magnificent past are still present. Both art and technology have reached their peak, and the triumph of the human spirit is everywhere to be seen. People in this civilization show evidence of the enormous biological and cultural transformation that took place over the eons: They have huge foreheads, live to an age of three thousand years, and speak in a musical language—a sort of mysterious, poignant song. Yet something shows that an irreversible decline has taken place. The eyes of these people betray a total inner sterility. Suddenly the protagonist understands: These beings have already discovered all there is to discover, invented all there is to invent. Humankind has reached its sunset. No one is able any longer to experience curiosity.

The death of curiosity is the death of humanness. When everything is obvious, spiritual evolution stops, in science fiction as in real life. The converse is also true: It is thanks to curiosity—this propensity for always asking troublesome questions and never feeling satisfied—that so many human achievements have come about. More specifically, many creative scientists feel an intense urge to *know*. Einstein stated so in very explicit terms:

> I want to know how God created this world. I am not interested in this or that phenomenon. . . . I want to know His thoughts, the rest are details.

Curiosity is a passion permitting no respite until these people have found an answer. It prevents the mind from falling asleep and obliges it to concentrate. It stimulates unconscious elaboration, eventually leading a person to discovery. And, as Helmholtz wrote in his autobiographical discourse, curiosity may also be quite disturbing:

> [The] passion to gain mastery of reality with one's mind, or, though in my case it is the same thing, to discover the connection between different phenomena, has been with me all my life; at times its intensity has been a cause of annoyance to me, because I could allow myself no respite in what appeared to be solutions, until I was aware of some obscure points connected with the problem in hand.

Curiosity's close companion is wonder, but there are differences between the two. Curiosity is born out of ignorance; wonder, out of understanding. In the one you are skeptical; in the other, surprised. Curiosity obsesses, while wonder uplifts. Curiosity is an accepted condition in scientific research. On the other hand, wonder—if acknowledged at all—is admitted grudgingly, as if it were an intruder in the aseptic edifice of science. Yet, upon further consideration, wonder must be seen as a most natural response—both on the part of scientists and the rest of us—for we all live in the same surprising universe. Wonder is intrinsic to all transpersonal experience. Perhaps even more than the absence of obsession or fear, wonder is the fundamental characteristic of true mental health.

Science is much more frequently associated with certainty and arrogance than with humility and wonder. Yet, if we study the lives of great scientists, the scene radically changes. We see that wonder is often present in their lives and that they freely acknowledge it. Galileo, for instance, spoke of it on a number of occasions. In a letter about his latest invention, the microscope, he wrote:

> I have contemplated a great many animals with infinite wonder: among them the flea is most horrible, the mosquito and the moth are extremely beautiful and I have had great pleasure from watching flies and other small creatures walk on mirrors, or even upside-down. There is infinite scope for contemplating the grandeur of nature, as well as the subtle and incredibly diligent fashion in which she operates.

On another occasion Galileo wrote about his discoveries in the field of astronomy, made with the help of the device he invented "after receiving divine inspiration" (the telescope). He spoke of the "wonder" he felt in discovering Jupiter's four moons and the "infinite awe" produced in him when he observed heavenly bodies hitherto unknown to humanity.

Another Italian astronomer, Giovanni Schiapparelli, wrote of similar experiences, recounting in a letter how his father had introduced him to astronomy when he was four years old, teaching him the constellations:

> The sense of the Infinite and of the Eternal, glimpsed by the child, was reinforced in the man: even now these are the forms through which God speaks to my mind with greatest effect. By that unconscious feeling I was guided to

astronomy—the science of long periods of time and immense distances.

Astonishment in the face of immensity can also be experienced in geology. At Niagara Falls, the great Scottish geologist Charles Lyell reflected on the eons of time required for the genesis of the coralline limestone beneath the waterfalls—a period, Lyell thought, comparable to the space that divides one galaxy from another. Over such a time span of millions of years the Alps, the Pyrenees, and the Himalayas were formed. Lyell noted that

> the geologist may muse and speculate on these events until, filled with awe and admiration, he forgets the presence of the mighty cataract itself, and no longer sees the rapid motion of its waters, nor hears their sound, as they fall into the deep abyss. But whenever his thoughts are recalled to the present, the tone of his mind, the sensations awakened in his soul, will be found to be in perfect harmony with the grandeur and beauty of the glorious scene which surrounds him.

In speaking of wonder, it is impossible to leave out Darwin, who wrote in a diary entry his impressions of the Brazilian forest: "It is not possible to give an adequate idea of the higher feelings of wonder, admiration, and devotion which fill and elevate the mind."

There are other aspects in Darwin's case. In his old age he actually rejected these feelings, declaring that, contrary to what he had thought when he experienced them, they could not be regarded as proof of the existence of God. Our subject here, however, is not the old Darwin's belief system, but the young Darwin's experience. For this purpose we need only read the journal of his trip to South America, filled with pages of descriptions full of wonder at the spectacular sights of nature—the cloud of Magellan, icebergs, waterspouts, glaciers, coral atolls, an erupting volcano, the flora in general, and more particularly the fauna. Indeed, some very peculiar finds were included in Darwin's fauna discoveries—among them, fishes emitting harsh sounds and birds with scissors beaks; oxen with exposed teeth; butterflies that ran on legs and made clicking noises; musical frogs; gregarious spiders; phosphorescent crustaceans; plantlike bodies that made eggs and swam about.

It was like being on another planet. Darwin said that his satisfaction came not only from the beauty around him but also from the knowledge of the individual elements of what he was seeing, just as a person who has an intimate knowledge of music and its principles is better able to appreciate a symphony. His moment of greatest wonder became the "sublimity" he found in the primeval forests of Brazil and Tierra del Fuego. "No one," Darwin claimed, "can stand in these solitudes unmoved, and not feel that there is more in man than the mere breath of his body."

It is not only the immeasurable expanses of space or the astonishing beauty of the fauna and of natural landscapes that may arouse wonder, but also the most humble laboratory. At the end of a day's work, Pierre and Marie Curie would remain in the doorway of the shed that housed their experiments, and in the dark they would look in fascination at the phosphorescent forms contained in bottles and test tubes.

Finally, it is possible to experience wonder in the moment of discovery itself. At some point François Jacob was able to define certain mechanisms of genetic blueprinting. His words beautifully sum up some of the highest points reached in scientific research. He felt

> wonder . . . at having discovered one of the mysteries of life, at having reached the very essence of things. At having gained access to a primordial mechanism of nature—a fundamental mechanism which, ever since living beings have existed, has helped them to live and would always help them as long as

> they exist. The idea that the very essence of things, a permanent yet hidden phenomenon, had suddenly been unveiled, made me feel freed from the law of time. More than ever before, scientific research seemed to me to be one and the same with human nature—in expressing the longing, the desire to live. This was the best way discovered by man to challenge the chaos of the universe. To master death itself.

For Jacob, wonder is the emotion accompanying discovery; for Einstein, it was the outcome of a contrast between experience and the tight system of accepted convictions. When Einstein was a child his father showed him a compass, and what the compass did was at variance with his childish image of the world. At this early point in Einstein's life, a strong feeling came over him: there *must* be some hidden structure behind the visible universe. This state of mind remained with him throughout his life.

Wonder, then, is the result of breaking the hold of existing convictions. Perhaps we should regard wonder not only as the result but also as the precondition for breaking that hold. We need a *questioning* way of thinking—an attitude that is not certain of anything and that perceives the extraordinary even in the ordinary. Rather than proclaiming "That's how it is," this attitude asks "What if?" It is able to find a source of wonder in the simplest of concepts, such as time, light, space, number, and gravity, issues which, if we give them a moment's thought, all possess what is necessary to fill us with puzzlement, even awe.

An affirmative way of thinking, by contrast, meets reality with ready-made conclusions that reflect the "I-already-know-what-I-need-to-know" attitude; it is a sort of King Midas in reverse, transforming everything it touches, even the wondrous, into banality.

Wonder in science derives from yet another factor. Once one goes beyond the usual way of looking at the world, one is confronted with a strange, unimaginable reality that cannot help but be alien. To study the structure of matter or the functioning of the brain, the behavior of insects or the formation of stars, the composition of rocks or the meandering processes of the unconscious means entering a visionary world, remote and alien from everyday experience.

Wonder is at times accompanied by the pain of not being able to comprehend. John and Antoinette Lilly, for instance, spent many years exploring the world of dolphins and other cetaceans—their awareness and their ways of thinking and communicating, so alien to our human modes and yet perhaps just as evolved. Speaking of himself and his fellow research workers, John Lilly wrote:

> This opening of our minds was a subtle and yet a painful process. We began to have feelings which I believe are best described by the word "weirdness." The feeling was that we were up against the edge of a vast uncharted region in which we were about to embark with a good deal of mistrust in the appropriateness of our equipment. . . . We felt that we were in the presence of Something, or Someone, who was on the other side of a transparent barrier which up to this point we hadn't even seen.

After the unease of severing from their normal thought patterns followed wonder at the unknown. Antoinette Lilly describes her encounter with a whale:

> I had the feeling I was perceiving, *and being perceived by*, an immense presence. I was simultaneously speechless and trying to absorb a vast amount of information that I was unable to fit into adequate patterns of past experience. It somehow transcended the human experience, going deeply into unknown mysteries. There were a few eternal moments of recognition . . . the frequency between us was like a brightly lighted tunnel of happiness. Everything else around me dimmed in the white light that soothed and pervaded my very essence.

Then came the point when the whale lifted its head out of the water, looked her in the eye, and shot out a jet of water:

> The joy of the next few minutes can only be described as absurd. . . . This whale's invitation to share her world gave me a glimpse through a cosmic crack between species . . . a oneness of all living beings as we will know them someday in the future . . . a place we have been before and will return to again . . . a peaceful promise . . . *the* "peaceable kingdom."

6

◇

◇ **The Way**

◇ **of Devotion**

◇

The starting point is always the same: dissatisfaction. It takes a thousand forms and we try to escape from it in a thousand ways, but it is always present. Like an unending sense of loss, it accompanies us throughout our lives and gives us no peace. We feel an emptiness we try in vain to fill; we sense how precarious our destiny is; we see that we will never manage to know and do all we would like to; we realize that sooner or later we must die. We feel weak and disappointed. Something is not quite right.

Some people put forward a surprising argument. We are already complete and fulfilled, they say, but ironically we destroy our completeness by being self-centered and foolish. We close our eyes to a wholeness that exists right before our eyes. The great poet Kabir, who was both a Muslim and a Hindu, followed the Way of Devotion but practiced no asceticism, because he loved God whenever he encountered Him. He once said:

> You sense that there is some sort of spirit that loves
>   birds and animals and the ants—
> perhaps the same one who gave a radiance to you in
>   your mother's womb.
> Is it logical you would be walking around entirely
>   orphaned now?

The truth is you turned away yourself,
and decided to go into the dark alone.
Now you are tangled up in others, and have
forgotten what you once knew,
and that's why everything you do has some weird
failure in it.

Every transpersonal Way begins from a state of incompleteness and has as its goal the achievement of unity. In this endeavor, the Way of Devotion is based on the feeling which, more than any other, personifies desire for unity—love. In this sense, the Way of Devotion is the most human, because it starts out from the most basic emotion of all.

We all love someone or something—a person or an idea, power or pleasure, money or health, beauty or truth. Our love may be greedy, inconstant, or faltering, but nonetheless it is love, and that already is a start. Indeed, however limited this love, it contains a more or less hidden need for unity and happiness, and for this reason it must be taken seriously.

If we accept this hypothesis, a profoundly important principle follows. We may call it the *principle of the hidden longing*: our yearnings and affections are not what they appear to be —they are mainly what they conceal. In our desires and affections—even the most senseless or destructive ones, such as fetishism or the urge to take drugs—surface aspects are what count *least*, and at their core is concealed a far greater need, a desperate longing for the eternal. We each conceive and express this desire according to our ability. Each of us, then, however remotely and unconsciously, is already on the right track, is already on the Way of Devotion—because we are all devoted to something.

The next step consists in deliberately redirecting our love toward that which is highest and most beautiful and in making this love increasingly purer and stronger.

Love of self, desire, erotic passion, the need for friendship, tenderness between parents and children—this is the raw material. These feelings are redirected toward an ideal or a divinity—be it Christ, Ishvara, Jehovah, Allah, the Great Mother, or God—and their energy acts as a propelling force for the ascent toward the transpersonal stratosphere. This does not mean, of course, that one no longer loves other people; rather, one loves them in this wider context. Every encounter becomes a vehicle for perceiving and serving God—be it through preparing a meal for children, visiting the sick, helping a friend, or even giving directions to a stranger on the street.

For many people in our delirious, splendid society, God does not matter. But many others, including children, have a beautiful and intimate relationship with God. Perhaps they may be nervous about discussing it, given the cynical climate surrounding them, and may fear that their feeling will be ridiculed. Yet it is an immensely important support for them. When they are in difficulty, they take refuge and find strength in God. They also turn to Him in moments of great joy, to express gratitude. They perceive God in the beauty of nature, in selfless love, or in the happiness of music. The absence of God is emptiness and fear for them. His presence, on the other hand, means joy. Throughout their lives God is a guide. When they die, He is their peace. Always, He is the Way. Indeed, God has a much greater effect on their mental stability than all the psychotherapies and drugs of our modern age. We would do well to remember: God does not so easily die.

In this chapter we will take a look at the "Olympic champions" of devotion. Some might consider these examples as the highest and most desirable models or, on the contrary, as alien to their way of living and feeling. As usual, each person must choose the path with which he or she can most readily identify. Yet one thing is certain: Devotion is an essential aspect of the human psyche. All of us, whatever life we may lead, can understand much about ourselves by simply asking, What do I really hold close to my heart?

When emotions are redirected toward the highest levels, they converge, sharpen, intensify. The language in which they are expressed, however, often betrays their origins. The words of tenderness and passion are often taken from everyday interactions. Instead of an impersonal cosmic Intelligence, as in the Way of Science, we have here a personal relationship with a divinity that retains human characteristics. There is warmth in this relationship, intimacy too, even sensuality. Sometimes the boldest human dream comes true—sexual union with God, the mystical marriage.

Intimacy, however, does not entail symmetry. The foundation of this relationship is an acknowledgment of one's own limitations and the impossibility of struggling through life alone. This is the only Way that is based on weakness rather than on qualities and talents. Individuals who accept their limitations no longer need to try to be what they are not. A profound relief sweeps over them.

This admission of weakness is a return to a childlike state of being. In all of us—however forgotten or neurotically camouflaged—lives a desire to become a child again, to let go of all responsibilities and have someone stronger and wiser to protect and take care of us. Of course, this need must be overcome if we are to reach full emotional maturity. It is overcome as well in the devotional attitude, but in a peculiar way. Instead of fighting this dependence, you acknowledge it, and no sooner have you recognized your smallness in the face of the difficulties and mysteries of existence than you are ready to invoke help from a greater source of wisdom and power. And with unexpected abundance, that help arrives.

The Way of Devotion is the most effervescent of all. Here we find the great mystics—Saint Teresa and Saint John of the Cross, Rumi and Hafiz, Narada and Kabir. Their lives are shining beacons; their transpersonal adventures are filled with events of unsurpassed variety and richness. Let us look at some phenomena we can expect to see in this Way.

First, we find manifestations of sublimated affection and

emotional surrender such as passionate love, fervor, and ecstasy. These feelings are often accompanied by physiological phenomena, for instance, the "gift of tears." Saint Catherine spoke of the spiritual tears that come to those who reach the state of perfect love. These tears, "full of gentleness and great peace," are in contrast with the "tears of death and fear," filled with torment, of those as yet unpurified.

An emotional revolution is started in this path, affecting the unconscious and manifesting itself in dreams. The *Philokalia*, a collection of Orthodox Christian mystical texts written between the fourth and fifteenth centuries, says that dreams "with great gentleness . . . approach the soul and fill it with spiritual gladness."

Sometimes one has an altered perception of one's own organism—such as in the state of rapture—when the body vanishes from consciousness. At other times it is transfigured, as in the case of Julian of Norwich, who saw the City of God in her own heart:

> Then our Lord opened my spiritual eyes, and showed me the soul in the middle of my heart. The soul was as large as if it were an eternal world, and a blessed kingdom as well. Its condition showed it to be a most glorious city.

It is not unusual to hear sounds. Richard Rolle heard his own thoughts transformed into music. The same happened to Saint Francis one night when he was praying. He heard a zither playing a wonderful melody and thought he had been transported to another world. And Shamsoddin Lahiji saw the whole universe made of light and heard every atom in it proclaiming in unison—yet each in its own way—"I am God."

Visions are most frequent. Henry Suso's account of the many hours he had spent contemplating the bliss of paradise includes a description of dancing angels, who "made the highest wildest leaps and bounds. . . . They sang and danced with

jubilant hearts. . . . It was like a heavenly flowing forth and back again in the lonely abyss of the divine mystery [*i.e.*, God]."

The Way of Devotion culminates in contemplation of a white light beyond all mythological or cultural images. The experience of Ramakrishna is a good example. At one point in his life he was in such anguish that nothing held meaning for him. On the verge of suicide and in a moment of madness, he ran to fetch a sword. But at that very moment his mind was enlightened:

> It was as if houses, doors, temples and everything else vanished altogether; as if there was nothing anywhere! And what I saw was an infinite shoreless sea of light; a sea that was consciousness.

Devotion offers great riches, but it also demands total poverty. When all vital energies are concentrated on one point, everything else loses its appeal. In order to proceed on this path, one must learn to be detached. Detachment, however, does not necessarily mean asceticism; rather, it means the freedom to regard nothing but the highest as absolutely essential. This state can give a sense of lightness and joy unavailable to those weighed down by a thousand desires, with the corresponding burden of worries and fears. Detachment is an inner state, valid in all life circumstances and necessary in all paths to the Self. In the Way of Devotion, it is a central aspect.

Like all of the Ways, this too has its moments or periods of darkness. Since the Way of Devotion is particularly intense at all stages, it is not surprising that darkness is often described in an extremely dramatic fashion. Openness to the divine world implies vulnerability to hell, its direct opposite. In the vision of Saint Teresa of Avila, hell was a long, narrow, dark underground tunnel: agony of the body, because she needed to stoop beneath the cramping walls; but, above all, agony of the soul, because hell was a place without hope and with no way out. This was a sudden and momentary vision that came to her as she was praying, but it was enough to cause her tremendous and lasting pain.

According to Saint John of the Cross, the soul suffers in the darkness of night because the divine light reveals imperfection and reduces it to powerlessness. It is like being walled up, hands and feet tied, in a dark prison cell. In the Way of Devotion, suffering is due to a vibrant, direct confrontation with higher planes of consciousness as well as to the work of purification that has to take place if one is to be ready for such levels.

The main danger in this path is fanaticism in its various forms. When a person's entire emotional life is channeled in a single direction, it is easy for him or her to become fanatical, and this fanaticism is expressed primarily toward others. Think of the people who want to save you at any cost—who attempt to convert you, pester and hassle you, try to prevent you from doing what they see as contrary to their own faith, ask for money, and express amazement if you are not as enthusiastic as they are. They oppress you if you show disagreement, and threaten you if you want to leave their sect, church, or party. They even send you to the stake in order to purify you from your sins—and they are always convinced they are doing nothing but the highest good.

There is also the type of fanaticism directed against oneself, primarily at one's own body, which is seen as the paradigm of evil. I am not speaking here of purification or asceticism (fasting, vigils, poverty, chastity, or solitude); many mystics have adopted these techniques or attitudes in a balanced and sound fashion on their spiritual journeys. I am referring instead to outright aggression against oneself, and attitudes of indignity and self-destruction.

We must not, however, judge a Way by its excesses. The

Crusades, the Inquisition, religious wars, witch-hunts, the burning of heretics, and terrorism all are frightful examples of how this Way can be perverted. Actually the Way of Devotion is full of love, passion, joy, and surrender. It is also full of fire—and this is where its risk lies. But is that any reason to give up fire altogether?

The plan of this chapter is to illustrate the process in this path as it can be observed in its purest and finest forms. After looking at the fundamental virtue of devotion, we survey the various forms of prayer, move on to detachment as a state of being, and conclude with its natural development: surrender.

Before considering these aspects in more detail, let us note the relationship between two of the Ways that have much in common—the Way of Devotion and the Way of Illumination (particularly in Christianity, where every aspect is colored by devotion). There are many similarities between these two ways: Both focus on inner work; both have been thoroughly investigated and documented throughout human history; both involve the systematic practice of detachment; and both are aflame with love.

There are some differences, however. In the Way of Illumination, love includes all creatures; in the Way of Devotion, love is directed vertically toward the Supreme Being. In the Way of Illumination, love is also a mental attitude, and it looks objectively into people's hearts and into the nature of reality. In the Way of Devotion, love is passionate and full of fervor. In the Way of Devotion, detachment is usually more pronounced, whereas in the Way of Illumination, love is often a consequence of freedom rather than a means of attaining it. Finally, in the Way of Illumination rationality—though it must in the end be transcended—is sometimes accepted and even used as an instrument for expanding consciousness. The Way of Devotion, on the other hand, is based on nonrational self-surrender.

But the higher one climbs along these two Ways—as well

as along the other Ways—the more they resemble each other. And just as the colors of the rainbow merge into white, so these Ways unite, at their highest point, in one single light.

DEVOTION

Devotion—what an old-fashioned word! Think of its trite connotations: the smell of incense, pious pictures of saints with their eyes looking heavenward and hearts pierced by divine darts, relics and idols, bigots and dogmas; and perhaps also the religious exaltation that makes God a personal property, a political banner, or an excuse for killing people. Let's face it—devotion has had quite bad press. Used and abused over the last two thousand years, adopted to both uplifting and sinister ends by religious leaders, exploited for political purposes, like all powerful forces devotion has been the cause of endless trouble.

But in order not to throw out the baby with the bathwater, we must distinguish between a transpersonal quality's essential form and its debased versions. Then we discover true devotion—this purest of feelings, the very essence of disinterestedness. Devotion is the ability to give oneself without asking anything in return—in a profound and total sense—and then to remain faithful, whatever the cost, through good times and through bad, be it to a person, a spiritual principle, or divinity.

Perhaps we can best understand devotion by reflecting on occasions when it was directed to us—when others have been loyal in times of trouble; when they have stood by us, though they had nothing to gain, and perhaps something to lose; or we can understand it by recalling times when it was absent, when others on whom we relied suddenly turned their backs on us, or people we thought were faithful friends betrayed us and disappeared when we needed them most.

Devotion is a basic human affection. As always, a spiritual

Way begins from a primary aspect of our being. We start from a feeling of love and faithfulness. Human nature, however, is weak, changeable, and self-contradictory. Thus devotion must be gradually strengthened and refined if it is to rise to the heights of the feelings—joy, peace, serenity, and love—that often accompany the most beautiful of human experiences. These vibrant, clean, free sentiments are to common emotions what mountain air is to town smog.

In order to understand devotion we need to understand the heart. The heart is located at the center of the soul, its most intimate and vital part. But who or what is really in our hearts? Perhaps a little of everybody and everything. Especially in this age of haste and busyness in which we are constantly bombarded with stimuli of all kinds, the heart is distracted and fragmented. The result is that our feelings become superficial, flimsy, and self-centered.

Devotion is the rediscovery of the heart. It entails removing all emotional clutter and finding the purest spring of feeling. It is also the realization that beneath all our fragmentary desires lies a fundamental need—the longing for that which transcends us.

Concrete, familiar metaphors have often been used to symbolize devotion. The first metaphor, perhaps the foremost, is passionate love, the most delightful and satisfying of erotic relationships, with its attendant features: ecstatic surrender, deep sadness in the absence of the beloved, and the game of love (*ludus amoris*), in which the beloved at first plays hard-to-get and finally yields, at the high point where passion is becoming more and more intense until it is incandescent. There are caresses, kisses, embraces, and ultimately union. Angela da Foligno, the Italian mystic, wrote:

> I could see and feel Christ within me, embracing my soul. . . . And I experienced in Him a joy far more certain than the one I ordinarily feel. Since then my soul has known a joy which has enabled me to understand how it is that this Man, Christ,

is in heaven, and how it is that our human flesh can be in such close union with God.

A second metaphor is fire. Love, as we have just seen, becomes fiery, and its heat is often felt in the area of the heart. The *incendium amoris* ("fire of love") shows us a basic phenomenon of our emotional lives: when all our feelings are channeled in the same direction, they overheat. This was the experience Rolle described with candor and wonder:

> I cannot tell you how surprised I was the first time I felt my heart begin to warm. It was real warmth too, not imaginary, and it felt as if it were actually on fire. I was astonished at the way the heat surged up, and how this new sensation brought great and unexpected comfort. I had to keep feeling my breast to make sure there was no physical reason for it! But once I realized that it came entirely from within, that this fire of love had no cause, material or sinful, but was the gift of my Maker, I was absolutely delighted, and wanted my love to be even greater. And this longing was all the more urgent because of the delightful effect and the interior sweetness which the spiritual flame fed into my soul.

Two other metaphors, madness and drunkenness, illustrate the intensity of the experience as well as the violent overthrow of the whole personality. The enemy to overcome here is rationality, which, with its slow measured steps and its need to sift and weigh everything, becomes an obstacle to the warmth of love. The *Cloud of Unknowing*, a work written by an anonymous fourteenth-century English monk, maintains that "God can well be loved, but not known," and more than the affirmation of a fact, this is the suggestion for a method. Do not attempt to know God, we are instructed, because the finite cannot even begin to comprehend the infinite. The attempt is as arrogant as it is pathetic. But to love God—yes, this is always possible.

Without the intellect one becomes mad, but this is a most beautiful, divine madness—the madness of love. Or one becomes drunk. "Get drunk on love," says Rumi, "because love is all there is."

Another image is flight, which represents the gap between the human and the divine, and the lightness produced by devotion, but also refers to specific phenomena encountered along the Way of Devotion. Saint Teresa of Avila speaks at several points in her writings about the "flight of the spirit," in which a person suddenly feels lifted up toward heaven:

> [The soul] feels itself being transported as a whole into a world completely different from the one we are used to; it is shown things greater than it could ever imagine, even if it were to work on them for an entire lifetime. In this way an infinite number of secrets is explained to the soul in a moment, a thousand times more than it could find out by itself even after many years of work by the imagination and the mind to get hold of them all.

None of the ways toward the Self is more direct and more explicit in its direction—to love the Spirit, to desire it, to think it at all moments, to give oneself to it totally. In a vision, Christ told Saint Catherine of Siena, "I, who am the Infinite God, wish to be served by you with infinite service, and the only infinite thing you possess is the affection and desire of your souls." This attitude perpetuates itself: Love expressed to the source of all good produces warmth, conviction, enthusiasm, and certainty. It is a virtuous circle.

The intensity of this Way is not only a result but a prerequisite. In one story from India, a disciple asks his master what he needs to reach true realization. The master takes him to a lake and pushes his head under the water, holding him there until the disciple can endure it no longer. The master then asks him what he longed for when his head was under water. "To breathe," answers the disciple. "And how intensely?" asks the master. "With all my strength," replies the disciple. The master says, "When you will feel the same desire to reach the divine, you will be on the right track."

An essential condition of this Way is that the object of devotion be numinous. Usually this is not the case. There are many idols to which a person can be devoted—money, pleasure, success, and so forth. Devotion tunes in to its object and enters its world; it is assimilated into it, opening not only to its benefits but also its problems and weaknesses.

If, for example, I devote myself to money, I become greedy; if I devote myself to justice, I become just; if I devote myself to God, I become divinelike. If individual consciousness is to rise above itself, it must aim at the highest level it can envisage. In a passage that highlights the loyalty and persistence characteristic of devotion, the *Theologia Germanica* says:

> That which is best should be the dearest of all things to us; and in our love of it, neither helpfulness nor unhelpfulness, advantage nor injury, gain nor loss, honor nor dishonor, praise nor blame, nor anything of the kind should be regarded; but what is in truth the noblest and best of all things, should also be the dearest of all things, and that for no other cause than that it is the noblest and best.

Undoubtedly there is risk here. Even devotion to God may be devotion for a vindictive, hostile, capricious God—in other words, devotion to an unrecognized aspect of oneself projected onto the cosmos. The danger then becomes fanaticism and intolerance. Only devotion to a boundless, infinitely loving, beatific, and luminous being can truly liberate.

Why does devotion liberate? First, when one is devoted to God one no longer thinks of oneself. Attention is withdrawn from personal preoccupations, plans, and desires—they are all forgotten. "He who loves, runs, flies, and exults," says the *Imitation of Christ*, a late medieval text whose authorship is often attributed to German ecclesiastic Thomas à Kempis. Hard tasks become easy and difficulties are faced joyfully.

Devotion also liberates because it makes a person generous in the absolute sense. One gives one's very life and essence—nothing is withheld. Generosity, like love and gratitude, is a sentiment that frees and raises individual consciousness. Moreover, devotion liberates because it integrates the whole psyche around a single focus, generating immense inner certainty. Conversely, people lacking devotion may be overwhelmed by anxiety because they do not know to whom or what—or even whether—to give themselves. Thus, finding someone or something to which to devote oneself wholly can turn out to be a most fertile therapeutic boon.

Finally, devotion liberates because individual consciousness tends to become assimilated into the object of love: in loving the infinite, it becomes infinite itself.

Devotion shows us that reaching the Self is in no way an artificial operation; rather, it is supremely natural. To be faithful to another—whether a person, principle, or divinity—means being faithful to oneself, transparent to oneself. Indeed those who are incapable of sincere devotion, whatever their faith or path may be, are forced to wander in a maze of mental reservations, collide with the walls of their own selfishness, flounder in muddy compromise, and fall into the traps of self-deception. On the other hand, people capable of devotion inhabit a transparent, natural world where energy is never dissipated in pointless conflicts and calculations.

For such people, this attitude succeeds, little by little, in permeating every aspect of their life. They refer everything to God. Like a magnet, Divinity attracts everything to itself and therefore acts as a unifying focal point for the mind. Thus, not only are the inner life, relationships with others, and one's overall behavior transmuted and reorganized, one's whole perception of the world is also altered. The *Srimad Bhagavatam*, an Indian scripture, considers as the most evolved individual the one who "with his whole being sees Divinity in all existing things, and all existing things in Divinity."

Here, then, we have all the paradoxes: concentrated, single-minded love for one being spreads out toward all beings; through hard discipline it discovers a boundless liberty; by directing itself at the most sublime and distant goal, it discovers that goal in the humblest and nearest of situations; stripping itself of all possessions, it grows immensely rich; foregoing the possibility of comprehension, it receives the most profound knowledge—the knowledge of the heart.

PRAYER

Prayer is not a request for God's favors. True, it has been used to obtain the satisfaction of personal desires. It has even been adopted to reinforce prejudices, justify violence, and create barriers between people and between countries. But genuine prayer is based on recognizing the Origin of all that exists, and opening ourselves to It. The Abbé Bremond wrote that in prayer we acknowledge God "as the supreme source from which flows all strength, all goodness, all existence, acknowledging that we have received our being, life itself, from this supreme Power." One can then communicate with this Source, worship it, and ultimately place one's very center in It.

Prayer is a passive relationship because, despite the commitment and presence that it requires, it is—at its highest—a surrender of any initiative, and the creation of an empty space into which forces and revelations greater than one's own individuality can flow.

It is a natural relationship, because we enter it as we are, without expedients or disguises.

It is also an asymmetrical relationship: facing the infinity of God, a human being is zero.

It is an intimate rapport, because it generates a flow of life, affection, and warmth toward the divinity one encounters.

Prayer, then, is a relationship. And each one of our relationships is defined by what the other is like. If the other is aggressive, for instance, we will be on our guard; if he is interesting, we will perhaps be curious; if she is gentle, we are more likely to be gentle ourselves. In the case of prayer, the other is divinity itself—an unimaginable, infinite being. The state of mind produced in us by this Presence will vary from person to person, but one general condition applies to everybody: in this relationship you cannot be only partially involved—you must participate with your whole being.

In such a relationship we can do nothing other than be ourselves—for what else is there to do? All pretense is impossible, let alone duplicity or one-upmanship. We will then experience an unconditional state—the state of one who has nothing to lose or hide or prove. All we can do, as Saint Francis of Sales tells us, is be. We will be open and defenseless, aware of a greater presence penetrating our being, understanding us, loving us. Then, as we let down our guard and admit what we are, we will be flooded by an immense relief.

For many people prayer is the time when they are most genuine, because they are brought back to the Source of their being; for them nothing is more necessary and more obvious. A life without prayer, they feel, is like a tree without roots or a child without a family.

Prayer is the most natural of relationships, but it is also an impossible one. How else could one describe this relationship between the finite and the infinite? One might think it a situation designed to dissolve all sense of security, revolutionize one's thought patterns, and shatter any self-confidence at a stroke. Just think about it. This being in space and time which I call "myself," with its history and its constraints, faces the Unknowable, Infinite Mystery—an absurd challenge, were it not that this relationship contains one fundamental factor: awareness and acceptance of one's own limitations.

In the Way of Devotion, more than in any other transpersonal Way, we surrender all independence. To start with, we are weak. And our weaknesses, inexorable as they are, follow us everywhere: old age and death grow ever nearer; attempts to change end in failure; life keeps wounding us with its rough edges; and the unknown surrounds us with its unfathomable mystery. We feel inadequate and alone. The Way of Devotion makes of this painful awareness a point of strength. "Come to God," said Madame Guyon, "as a weak child, one who is all soiled and badly bruised—a child that has been hurt from falling again and again. Come to the Lord as one who has no strength of his own."

This is a wise choice. By entrusting ourselves to a higher Being we are at once empowered to transcend our limitations. Of course, this encounter is most demanding—how could it be otherwise? We relate with invisible realms, we have no guarantees, and everything is expected from us. But this is also an ideal relationship, because we know that this Being to whom we commit ourselves is able to know us far better than we can ever know ourselves, and to love us the way we have always dreamt of being loved.

This, then, is the essence of prayer. And it remains the same at all times and in all places. The form it takes, however, varies greatly, depending on circumstances—one prays with words and song; with the body and the emotions; with one's attention, mind, and imagination; with inner dialogue, with one's own naked presence; or with silence. One uses the faculties and methods most suited to one's particular character.

We should not underestimate purely verbal prayer. Rather than degenerating into a mere repetition of formulas, verbal prayer can elicit the highest level of attention. Simone Weil, the contemporary French mystic and philosopher, would recite the Lord's Prayer every morning in Greek with absolute concentration. If her attention wavered for a fraction of a second, she would start all over again:

> On occasions the very first words tear my mind from the body and transport it outside space, where there is no perspective, no point of reference. Space opens up. The infinity in the ordinary space of perception is replaced by an infinity at the second or even third power. At the same time this infinity of infinities fills itself everywhere with silence, a silence which is not the absence of noise, but the object of a positive sensation, indeed more positive than the experience of sound. Noises, if there are any, only reach me after crossing this silence.

Verbal prayer may also consist of repeating a mantra. According to the science of mantras, each sound—whether internal or external—opens the mind to a corresponding level of consciousness. Thus the repetition of God's name enables one to come into contact with Him. Swami Ramdas, an Indian devotee (*bhakti*), lived in a cave repeating the name of Ram all day long. His life consisted in this prayer, and nothing else. On one occasion he became conscious of an inner circle of bright light, which caused him to cry out in joy:

> Continuing his experiment [Ramdas is speaking of himself in the third person] for some days, he saw a blinding light, like a flash of lightning, which dazzled him, entering and spreading throughout his body, filling his whole being with an inexpressible transport of joy. When this began he could no longer feel his hands or feet; then, little by little, he lost all sense of feeling in his body.

Ramdas remained in this state of consciousness for about three hours. One day, as he came out of ecstasy, he saw that a snake had entwined itself around his right leg, licking his big toe with its forked tongue. The serpent came to visit him on the three following mornings and then stopped coming. Instead of being afraid, Ramdas saw God in the serpent and interpreted this episode as a manifestation of God's eternal playfulness.

Of course, the continuous repetition of a name can become a mechanical, even hypnotic, practice. This method nevertheless demonstrates prayer to be a testimony of God's supreme importance, by the repeated affirmation of His name.

One can also combine verbal prayer with body consciousness. The Russian Pilgrim, a nineteenth-century mystic, repeated the name of Jesus as he breathed, concentrating on his heart. This ancient technique, taken from the teachings of the *Philokalia*, was supposed to be used throughout the day. As he breathed in, the pilgrim would say "Lord Jesus Christ," and as he breathed out, he would say "Have mercy on me":

> Sometimes my understanding, which had been so stupid before, was given so much light that I could easily grasp and dwell upon matters of which up to now I had not been able even to think at all. Sometimes that sense of a warm gladness in my heart spread throughout my whole being and I was deeply moved as the fact of the presence of God everywhere was brought home to me. Sometimes by calling upon the Name of Jesus I was overwhelmed with bliss, and now I knew the meaning of the words "The Kingdom of God is within you."

The expansion of the heart can take the form of inner dialogue. We can speak to God of our troubles, ask His advice, thank Him. Saint Teresa of Avila describes such dialogue:

> [The soul] should imagine itself to be in the presence of Jesus Christ, to talk with Him often, and should seek to fall in love with His Humanity, keeping it always alive within. It should ask Him for help in times of need, weep with Him in pain, rejoice with Him in joy, and be careful not to forget Him in sperity, and all this has to be done not with contrived orations: it should be expressed in simple words, in tune with one's

> wishes and needs. This is an excellent method for reaping great benefits in a short time.

This attitude is profoundly liberating. In her autobiography, Teresa relates how she suddenly felt overwhelmed by such a vivid feeling of the divine Presence that she could not doubt God was in her, and she in God. In this state the soul is suspended, memory fades away, the intellect is present but silent. Full of astonishment, it simply witnesses the experience.

One prays with what one has. If our emotions are the most vital part of what we are, then we pray with our emotions. This process can be likened to thinking of a person who means much to us, whereby at once feelings of affection and gratitude arise. "Prayer is an outflowing of the heart," said Thérèse of Lisieux, "a simple look cast heavenward, a cry of gratitude and love, in hard times and in happy times; in short it is something great and supernatural which expands my soul and unites me with God."

It is also possible to pray with the mind and the imagination. In the Christian tradition, meditation itself is often considered part of prayer. Indeed, for people with an intellectual bent, prayer is very close to meditation. Saint Ignatius of Loyola, for instance, reflected on the meaning of the words in a prayer or imagined scenes from the life of Christ as intensely and realistically as he could. It was after one such time of prayer that Saint Ignatius had the enlightenment in which, as he writes, he was able to understand in a few moments more than he had ever understood in his entire life. This is how he describes his experience, speaking in the third person:

> As he went along occupied with his devotions, he sat down for a little while with his face toward the river which was running deep. While he was seated there, the eyes of his understanding began to be opened; though he did not see any vision, he understood and knew many things, both spiritual

> things and matters of faith and learning, and this was with so great an enlightenment that everything seemed new to him.

One also prays with the watchfulness of an attentive mind. As Jeanne de Chantal perceives it, we are like a blind man who does not realize he is in the king's presence and therefore acts inappropriately; but everything changes when he realizes where he is. According to Jeanne, realizing we are in God's presence is in itself prayer, quite irrespective of our inner or outer state. In this prayer the conscious mind is aware of God at all times and stands guard lest distractions crowd into the mind. The Islamic tradition calls it *dhikr*, the Hebrew *deveqùth*, meaning a constant awareness and love of God—and the supreme value against which all other values are measured. In the *Philokalia*, Hesychios said that

> watchfulness is a spiritual method which, if sedulously practised over a long period . . . leads, in so far as this is possible, to a sure knowledge of the inapprehensible God, and helps us to penetrate the divine and hidden mysteries.

It is also possible to pray with silence. Indeed, silence may be the highest form of prayer. "When you are praying," says Evagrios in the *Philokalia*, "do not shape within yourself any image of the Deity, and do not let your intellect be stamped with the impress of any form; but approach the Immaterial in an immaterial manner, and then you will understand." Prayer, for Evagrios, meant getting rid of thoughts by stepping back from the mind until he was inwardly naked and silent.

God lives within us. The path toward Him is a return to the Center of our being. This too is a prayer of silence, or rather *is* silence. In the "prayer of simplicity" described by Madame Guyon, you withdraw into yourself and trust in the presence of God within your own heart. Everything else comes by itself, because God is like a magnet that attracts you. In the central silence you encounter God, the experience of love:

> There is no way to describe this experience, this encounter. I would only say that this love which the Lord pours into your depths is the beginning of an indescribable blessedness.

For Saint Francis of Sales and his followers, prayer consisted of finding the "fine point of the soul," that part of us which exists far above the turmoil of passions and desires, an "unassailable, unconquerable stronghold." The fine point of the soul is the Self, and it has been compared to a mountain peak, to an inner castle, and to a sanctuary, because it is the most silent place in the soul, distinct and independent of all that goes on at its periphery. Prayer, very similar to meditation in this case, is an inner act of geometric precision. It takes the form of retiring to the most secret room of the inner castle, or reaching to the "fine point of the soul," the place where it is possible to communicate with God and allow one's will to be brought into line with God's will.

The fine point of the soul is the emptiest state and at the same time the fullest and richest one. According to Saint Francis of Sales' disciple Jean-Pierre Camus, faith, hope, and charity—the supreme virtues—"have their true seat and their most natural residence in this supreme point of the soul from which, like a happy spring of living water, they are able to spread out, in the form of brooks and streams, over the parts and faculties of the inner being."

DETACHMENT

What is it we desire—pleasure for ourselves or happiness for everybody, nirvana or a new car, union with a lover or union with God, the disgrace of our enemies or the well-being of our friends? And how do we desire—secretly or publicly, with shame or with joy, with ambivalence or with enthusiasm? Answer these two questions about someone, and you will say a lot about that person—about what one thinks and feels, how one behaves, what one's problems are, and how likely one is to succeed in solving them. The reason is simple: desire is the element around which emotions, ideas, and motivation are constellated. They are the personality's dynamic vectors.

Because of its importance, desire has often attracted the attention of those seeking spiritual liberation. They ask themselves, What role does desire play in our quest? Is it a help or hindrance? The answers have been many, but we can generally say that desire, particularly in the form of craving, has been seen as the primary hindrance to transpersonal development.

Let us look at the reasons for this belief. First, too many desires pull us in countless directions and crowd our life with commitments, fears, fantasies, obligations, and setbacks. We thus lose touch with what really counts. We worry and we hasten, forgetting how to play and laugh. In addition, the objects of our attachments—material things that offer us well-being, people who give us security, roles in which we can hide—provide us with a false sense of identity. They become an artificial support and distract us from looking at the deeper and more disturbing aspects of life.

Desire prevents us from living in the present and focuses our attention on regrets about the past or on hopes for the future. We become unbalanced and therefore incapable of objective knowledge, for the moment we have interests to safeguard we easily fall prey to prejudice.

It is a short step from prejudice to hostility. When many people want the same things, struggle and competition ensue —and so do fear, suspicion, and violence. These can easily lead to all sorts of conflicts and wars. We want too many things, and we want them all to ourselves.

Other problems arise when desire is fixed on a single object: one's life is impoverished (as with the miser who can think of nothing other than counting money); one becomes narrow-minded (like those who place business before friendship); or downright ridiculous (like those who take their cars as an object of faithful devotion); or pathetic (like the people who, overcome by nostalgia, continually try to relive the past); or even self-destructive (like those who, for love of money or security, sell their own dignity). In extreme cases greed can lead to perdition, compelling a person to crime or the destruction of mind and body, as with alcohol and drug addiction.

Now let us imagine the absence of desire. Preoccupation, enslavement, and a sense of separation from others disappear. Because we no longer expect anything, we are more present and sincere; whatever turn life takes, we accept it without regrets or protests. True objectivity is possible because the mind—no longer agitated by this or that craving—is as transparent as the cloudless sky.

Detachment also has another gift in store: simplicity. In our affluent society it is possible to adopt voluntary simplicity as an intelligent response to the excessive wealth and waste around us. By discovering that what we thought necessary is superfluous, we experience great relief. In this attitude of disinterest, love is genuine and stripped of expectations. Knowing how to be detached means taking life with humor, accepting the rules of the game, being flexible—the characteristics of any truly sane person. Finally, freed from supports, distractions, and anxieties, we discover the simplicity of just being. It is then far easier for the reality of the Self to be manifested.

Someone, however, might object that this all sounds nice and straightforward but that desire is part of the human condition—you cannot get rid of it, and any attempt to do so produces only torment, a sense of guilt and frustration. This is true. However, there are those who have attained a certain detachment from the compulsion of desires, and we can learn much from their serenity. To loosen the hold of desire, these people did not tackle it head-on; instead, they created situations in which its urgency would diminish quite naturally. There are many different methods for working with desire in a creative way, and they are encountered in each of the spiritual paths we are examining. In dealing with desire one can

- ◇ redirect it to the highest and most beautiful goal imaginable;
- ◇ detach oneself from it and observe it as something different and distinct from one's true essence, so that one is not drawn in by it;
- ◇ live in the present (rather than the future of imaginary fulfillment), and realize that each moment is the Eternal Now;
- ◇ train one's mind in discipline and tranquillity, freeing it from the tyranny of the inner forces that unsettle it;
- ◇ become increasingly aware of hidden beauty—not only in a few objects or people, but everywhere;
- ◇ get in touch with the compelling, dramatic needs of the poorest, in comparison with which our desires appear as absurd whims;
- ◇ love deeply and strongly, so that the heart stops looking for satisfaction in illusory possessions;
- ◇ face death in all its aspects and possibilities, thereby banishing all greed.

The mechanism is ever the same. In order to enter the transpersonal world it is necessary for the structure of the personality, so solid and weathered, to be dismantled and then restructured around a higher Center. Desire is the personality's dynamic organizing principle. It colors the way we perceive reality, intensifies and feeds the emotions, influences our ideas and mental images, and determines our behavior. Eliminate or weaken desire, and the whole personality will be stripped of its most powerful element and prepared for transformation.

As the transpersonal world becomes visible, an individual will gradually feel a sense of fullness, a peace, a joy, and a unity with everything, and will forget the frantic search for other forms of satisfaction. Detachment, then, is a natural, physiological process, like leaves falling from trees in autumn, a snake throwing off its old skin, or a flower blossoming.

There are those who disagree, however. They see in desire the finest aspect of human potential. They feel in it the very heartbeat of life, to be saluted with enthusiasm. Goethe, for example, states in his autobiography that "our wishes are presentiments of the capabilities which lie within us, and harbingers of that which we shall be in a condition to perform." This is a wonderful thought. Seen in this light, desires are not irritating demands or shameful impulses, but mines of future possibilities. Woe betide anyone who represses or ignores them! On the other hand, those who respect and listen to them will experience success and fulfillment.

In Blake's view, desires that are not transformed into action will fester within us. Blake maintained that religion wrongly teaches us of God's intention to torment people in eternity if they enjoy and rely on their own vital energy and pleasure. But for him it is in this very source that we can find happiness: "energy is eternal delight." Desire restrained is weak in the first place; suffocated, it becomes passive and is reduced to a shadow of what it once was.

This idea resembles the Indian system of Tantra, where all aspects of life are regarded as sacred and therefore all pleasures are permitted as long as they are entered with total involvement and no ego. *Yoga* (union with the divine) is *bhoga* (unconditional enjoyment).

We see, then, that there are very different opinions on desire and detachment. In the Way of Devotion, however, nothing could be clearer and more certain: In order that our hearts might receive God, say all the great mystics, they must first be emptied of all appetites.

For instance, Saint John of the Cross says in his work, *The Ascent of Mount Carmel*, that desires tire, torment, blind, degrade, and weaken us. They tire us, like children whining continually around their mother's legs; they torment us, like torture instruments; they blind us, like dust in the eyes; they degrade us, because the greedier a soul, the less beautiful it becomes; and they weaken us, like too many buds on a feeble tree that prevent it from bearing fruits. Surely, then, we should free ourselves from desires.

Such an attitude makes this path seem one of the hardest. It may even seem absurd and unnatural to our hedonistic mentality. But we should not forget that there is a Way for every type of person, and for many people, making their lives simple and poor can be a perfect and liberating choice. In any case, each one of us, busy citizens of a consumer society, would do well to reexamine our desires from time to time, asking ourselves which ones are essential and which are artificial and empty.

In order to illustrate detachment, the metaphor of acting as if one were foreign has often been adopted. As *Imitation of Christ* says:

> Live on earth as a pilgrim, as a guest for whom the affairs of this world hold no interest: keep your heart free and set it on high, on God, because down here you have no fixed abode.

Linked to this thought of being an alien is the thought of death. When we die we will leave everything, and, like an alien, we will be distant from the people and objects that are now so close and familiar to us. So why not become accustomed to this idea here and now? Evagrios says:

> Remember the day of death, visualize the dying of your body, reflect on this calamity, experience the pain, reject the vanity of this world, its compromises and crazes, so that you may continue in the way of stillness.

As desire grows weaker, so does the sense of ownership, the mental attitude that views objects and people as an extension of oneself. The *Theologia Germanica* suggests a truly revolutionary thought in this regard:

> We must refrain from claiming anything for our own. When we do this, we shall have the best, fullest, clearest and noblest knowledge that a man can have, and also the noblest and purest love, will and desire.

Desires should not be repressed and cannot be destroyed. In the Way of Devotion they are redirected: all the energy once employed in selfish satisfaction is channeled into timeless goals and made a powerful, propelling force, projecting the soul to worlds of great splendor and beauty. According to the *Cloud of Unknowing*, anyone who genuinely desires paradise is, in spirit, at that very moment already in paradise.

SURRENDER

You allow yourself to let go because you were first holding on tightly, and in that clinging you felt both desire and anxiety. And to what were you clinging? To everything you had—the sense of existing, a way of life, a role, a goal, the promise of happiness. In remaining attached to these things you had to struggle, because you always felt in danger of losing what was closest to your heart. It was a question of hold on or die. This struggle became part of your being, your habits, your muscular structure, your cellular existence.

Then you allowed yourself to let go.

You had no idea what would happen. You abandoned every point of reference. The burden of suspicion and effort you had carried around with you vanished. You realized you had always been part of the plans of an Intelligence far greater than your own, and the weight of your separate, personal identity was lifted. Suddenly you felt a lightness you had never known before. Suddenly you found peace.

This is the highest form of surrender, an experience we find in the lives of many creative and enlightened people. Few are capable of their feats, and yet all of us are familiar with some form of surrender—in sleep, when we yield to the darkness of night and unconsciousness; in sexual orgasm, when in an explosion of pleasure we let ourselves go in the arms of the beloved; in laughter, when we momentarily relinquish all anxieties. Surprising ourselves with our own spontaneity, we forget all our well-rehearsed plans.

Surrender refreshes and regenerates. Failure to surrender strains and wearies. Behind every genuine surrender lives a faith fulfilled; behind every failure to surrender lies confidence betrayed, a wound that will never be forgotten, a fear of disintegration and death. Without surrender one becomes hesitant and rigid. Laughter is fake and sleep disturbed, spontaneity is lost, and orgasm is nothing more than mechanical contractions.

Despite all our fears and resistances, the search for surrender is universal. How relieving it would be to do away with all care and responsibility! Deep down we know that such relief is possible—and we desperately long for it. But surrender can be unconscious or conscious. Some people let go with joy, while others give up in despair. One might seek release by taking alcohol or drugs, sitting in front of television for hours on end, or listening to loud music. These forms of surrender are full of darkness; they dull and bewilder the mind.

Conscious surrender yields to a greater Will, and stems naturally from detachment and devotion. It is the most complete absence of calculation and pretense—an attitude unclouded by preferences, which greets all inner and outer possibilities with openness and generosity.

For Madame Guyon, surrender "is . . . *the key* to *the inner court*—the key to the fathomless depths. Abandonment is the key to the inward spiritual life." Surrender is a basic event in all the transpersonal Ways. But here it has a central role, because the Way of Devotion is built around a personal relationship with God. Here is Someone in whom we can place a limitless, unconditional trust that comes only from sincere love. Surrender is easier when there is someone to whom we can surrender.

Many analogies have been drawn to capture the essence of surrender. It has sometimes been described as becoming an instrument in the hands of God. Rumi, for instance, compared himself to a harp upon which the Divinity played wonderful melodies. Other images are more passive. According to Jeanne de Chantal, we must become like an empty container, ready to be filled. For others, surrender means dissolving like a drop that falls in the ocean. For Veronica Giuliani, the soul in a state of ecstasy feels itself transported by waves into an immense sea of love. The most frequent metaphors belong to the biological realm. For Saint Thérèse of Lisieux, surrender is like the sleep of a child in its mother's arms. At other times, spiritual letting go has been likened to erotic ecstasy.

Yet others have thought of surrender in terms of death. In dying one becomes inanimate, like a stone or a piece of wood. Ramakrishna said, "Live in the world like a dead leaf. As a dead leaf is carried by the wind into a house or on the roadside and has no choice of its own, so let the wind of Divine Will blow you wherever it chooses."

What prevents us from total surrender is also the cause of our other troubles. It is our selfish will, originating in the belief that we are separate from everything and act accordingly. This incapacity to let go is the source of hatred, anger, separateness, and the fear of death. We go through life constantly looking for guarantees, endeavoring to control people and circumstances, striving to conform the world to our plans. How absurd! And how tiring!

But what if we were to sign a blank contract with the universe? What if we fully surrendered? Such an attitude entails courage, generosity, and the truthfulness that enables us to call ourselves into question, risking everything we are. When we do this we are able to see—in the terrifying unknown confronting us—a Will that is infinitely good and wise, and to this Will we can give ourselves without reservation.

Happiness, then, is available here and now. But it is a completely different happiness from anything our minds imagine or our hearts desire. "What is Paradise?" asks the *Theologia Germanica*, and it replies "All things that are . . . this world is verily an outer court of the eternal . . . for the creatures are a guide and a path unto God and Eternity."

Surrendering to the divine Will, therefore, consists in accepting whatever happens as part of the divine plan. All personal preferences and projects are forgone. Everything that happens is right. Then the Power to which we have surrendered enters our being and performs a work we would have been incapable of doing alone, a work of purification and release. It is a hidden, wonderful work that brings not only joy but also at times deep pain. In talking about this Will, de Caussade says:

> . . . one can do nothing but allow it to have its way and surrender to it blindly and in perfect trust. It is infinitely wise, powerful, beneficial to the souls who hope in it without reservation, love and care for it alone; and who believe with complete faith and unshakeable trust that whatever it does at every moment is for the best.

The only time in which surrender is possible is the present. The past of fond memories or recriminations, and the future full of anxieties and desires no longer have any meaning once we have given ourselves completely to a higher Will. Only the present counts. And we do not strive to change it, because each moment is perfect as it is. The only change is internal: we align our will with what is happening.

Surprisingly, this attitude does not entail fatalism; neither does it mean that we are at the mercy of events. Even for those not traveling along the Way of Devotion, accepting reality as it is gives freedom. What happens around us is not something to fight against, complain about, be ashamed of, or escape. Suddenly we see the events of our lives in a new light. Even when they are ugly, unfair, chaotic, or cruel, they are what they are.

This attitude of acceptance—not adding to or taking away from anything that is already there—is the most economic response and also the noblest, because it does not fret or struggle. This complete assent is the foundation for any truly whole state of mind to which human beings can aspire, because not a fiber of our being says "no," and life becomes ours to live 100 percent.

The result of this mental attitude is the quiet of the Center, the equanimity and detachment that pave the way for transpersonal development. De Caussade continues:

> We live in this superior region of the soul, in which God and His will create an unchanging eternity. . . . In this entirely spiritual abode, where the uncreated, the indistinct and the inexpressible keep the soul infinitely distant from everything belonging to a world of shadows and appearances, one remains calm, even when the senses are in the storm.

The surrender of which mystics speak is not random. It is surrender to the "Divine Providence." It is not merely a leap in the dark or an attitude of carelessness. Rather, this surrender of the personal will to the universal will is preceded by strenuous training and spiritual purification. Letting go is not equivalent to throwing oneself away but instead is a conscious offering to God of what is dearest to us. According to the *Imitation of Christ*, perfection consists in

> offering yourself to the divine will with your whole heart, seeking your own advantage neither in big things nor in small ones, neither in time nor in eternity, so that, with an un-

swerving attitude of mind, you are able to be equally grateful in prosperity and in adversity.

Once the gift has been made, as Madame Guyon reminds us, it cannot be taken back: what has been given has been given and no longer belongs to us. A real transfer of ownership has taken place. The "I" which existed before, no longer belongs to myself, but to God. Nothing has changed, everything has changed.

Above all, complete surrender is the result of systematic discipline. We need to let go not only of our most obvious points of reference but also of the thoughts and the memories we take for granted and from which it is so difficult to disentangle ourselves. For Saint John of the Cross it is a matter of attaining the "nakedness of memory." By this, he meant that before we come face-to-face with God we must free ourselves from our most deeply held mental assumptions—in fact, from everything we have learned in our lives.

The following guidelines may strike us as cryptic and laborious. But look again, and you will find nothing simpler. This is wisdom for our everyday lives:

◇ Accepting things as they are, we save effort and energy.
◇ Finding our good in the present, not in the past or in the future, we experience fulfillment.
◇ By not clinging to our ideas, we become more flexible.
◇ By not demanding that the world work as we wish, we are freed from innumerable worries.
◇ Letting go, we find the joy of living.

7

◇

◇

◇

◇

The Way of the Will

The survival instinct is the oldest and most deeply entrenched aspect of our nature, the boundary beyond which we disintegrate. Existence inside this boundary feels good and safe. But approach the danger zone and you are overcome by anxiety, bewilderment, and terror.

There are some people, however, who enjoy the experience of going beyond, of reaching into this solitary zone between life and death. They discover that by challenging their attachment to survival they are transformed and regenerated. Their whole life is rattled by a violent tremor, and in the aftermath of this revolution a profound renewal takes place. These people tread the Way of the Will.

We find all types of individuals on this path: pioneers and explorers who dare to go beyond the frontiers of the known; political leaders who dangerously stand up against society's dominant forces; athletes who push beyond the limits of the impossible; and, in general, all those who risk their lives for some worthy cause.

Let us take the example of the great Norwegian pioneer Fridtjof Nansen. Throughout his life Nansen was consumed by a desire to explore the unknown. First, he tried to satisfy this need with scientific research. In studying the structure of the nervous system, he sought to understand what he felt to be the greatest enigma—the origin of thought itself. Nansen wrote in his diary that he was searching for a splendid reality. Then he interrupted his career and devoted himself to exploring the Arctic. This was a different area of research, fraught with risk and uncertainty, but born of the same need to know:

> I found the great adventure of the ice, deep and pure as infinity, the silent, starry arctic night, the depths of Nature herself, the fullness of the mystery of life, the eternal round of the universe and its eternal death.
>
> In this silent, starry arctic night around me I stand in all my naked simplicity face to face with nature. I sit down devoutly at the feet of eternity and listen, and I know God, the all-commanding, the center of the universe.

The people who follow the Way of the Will, as we have noted, are quite diverse. Yet they share one basic characteristic: All of them triumph over fear, push themselves beyond a given threshold, and look death in the eyes. And in order to overcome their deeply rooted inclinations, all of them make use of the function that most clearly expresses what we truly are—the will.

The Way of the Will is the most direct of all the transpersonal Ways. In order to reach the mountaintop it ignores safe paths and gentle slopes; untroubled by snow and ice, by storms or precipices, it aims straight for the peak. At its most decisive phase, the Way of the Will proceeds without hesitation, ignoring the complexities of the subjective world. Those who travel along this path are often gifted with imagination, sensitivity, and intelligence, but when a crucial moment comes they set aside all superfluous ideas, images, and feelings and act incisively and resolutely.

Each transpersonal Way is lonely, because it is paved with problems and difficulties that must be overcome with one's own resources. But the Way of the Will is the loneliest. Help is often available in the other paths in the form of general guidelines, encouragement, and the experiences of others. But the Way of the Will offers no support and no precedents. One is always the first—to carve a track through the jungle, to break a record, to fight the establishment, to disobey a law or a social convention, to fly into space. Indeed, those who travel along this Way become a law unto themselves.

The Way of the Will is also the most literal. In the other Ways one is confronted with death in a metaphorical sense; here, one's life is actually at risk—perhaps in coming face-to-face with an angry mob, hanging over a precipice, or venturing into unknown territory. In the other Ways one may be probing inner space; here, one explores outer space too—geographical or cosmic. In the other Ways one metaphorically climbs toward ever greater heights; here, the peaks are real, with rock and ice. In each of the other Ways one comes up against all kinds of inner obstacles; here, there are external obstacles, too, which can be seen or touched—a wall of granite, a police charge, an immense ocean, a dark abyss, or cosmic space.

Finally, the Way of the Will is the hardest. In every path toward the Self, individual consciousness moves beyond its previous sphere of experience and extends into vaster worlds. There are many different methods by which this expansion can be actualized. The network of automatic responses that imprison us can be analyzed, traced back to its origin, transformed, deautomated, ignored, or transcended. In the Way of the Will it is shattered. Head-on, one confronts generally accepted opinions, powerful interests, commonsense rules, or physiological limits. With nothing more than will and courage, one overcomes limits and breaks new ground.

Although it is of crucial importance on all the Ways, in this Way the will plays the decisive role. Indeed it is the will that sets apart a free person from one who is unaware, fearful, or weak. The will is choice: the basic expression of what we are. When our choice is strong and clear, without indecision or ambiguity, our whole being is strong and clear. And precisely when the will faces a force apparently greater than itself, it finds its greatest realization: willing the impossible, even at the cost of life itself, not for personal satisfaction, but because it is right.

Individuals traveling along this Way—alone as they so often are—may feel a deep sense of identity with other people. Take, for example, Russell Schweickart, the first astronaut who floated in space without an umbilical, during the Apollo 9 flight. The Earth appeared as a "small spot" in space. Yet that small object, Schweickart wrote, contained everything that had any meaning for him—"all of history and music and art and death and birth and love, tears, joy . . ." And in that silence, there were "no frames . . . no boundaries."

Schweickart realized that he was not so much a privileged loner, enjoying the honor of a wonderful sight, but humanity's sensory organ: "You look down and see the surface of that globe that you've lived on all this time, and you know all those people down there and they are like you, they are you." Thus Schweickart, at that moment the most isolated man ever, felt "a piece of this total life."

In the extreme situations in which they find themselves, people who travel on the Way of the Will not only cross uncharted territory, but also meet at times with frightening and mysterious phenomena. What they are doing has never been done before; as a result, their actions can sometimes seem senseless. They venture where no one has dared go before—and are therefore extremely vulnerable. They are alone; no one is there to encourage them. They have no sure criteria for reference and may therefore border on madness.

The French oceanographer Jacques-Yves Cousteau spoke of the *ivresse des grandes profondeurs* ("the intoxication of the great depths"), a very dangerous state of euphoria that induces a false sense of safety, even of omnipotence, in the most perilous of circumstances. To describe it, Cousteau quotes Dumas, another explorer:

> I experience a strange sensation of bliss. I feel carefree as though I had been drinking. My ears buzz and my mouth tastes bitter. The stream makes me sway from side to side as though I had had several drinks.

Another example is provided by the French speleologist Michel Siffre, who once spent a long period living in the depths of a cave, alone. In a book he recounts his adventure: In that silence so different, so much deeper than the silences with which we are familiar, in a dark, eternally motionless place, he was overcome with melancholy and despair, sometimes panic. He had hallucinations and lost awareness of time.

A person who travels along this perilous Way is the archetype of the warrior or hero. We would be mistaken if we thought that the transpersonal world contains only the quieter qualities, such as love, peace, and serenity. Force, fire, and power are transpersonal qualities as well, and those who are ready to embody them are warriors. They are ready to step forward when others hold back, to speak when everyone else, through indifference or fear, remains silent. Warriors put their own life at risk for the sake of others and fight valiantly for what they believe to be right and necessary. They see life from the viewpoint of death.

In the Japanese samurai tradition, warriors are trained to enter the state of *ai-uchi*, serene indifference to the outcome of the fight, for the moment fear of death or wish for victory appear, they are already defeated. In the *Bhagavad Gita*, Krishna exhorts Arjuna not to be afraid, because the true Self was never born and will never die—weapons cannot touch it, fire cannot burn it, nor can water drown it. Anyone who realizes this truth is indestructible and timeless.

At this point a very obvious objection can be raised. War is murder and destruction; it creates misery and evil. What does that have to do with a spiritual search? The answer is that although war should in no way be considered a transpersonal path, the emotions and impulses from which it originates, such as brute force, aggressiveness, enmity, greed, and cunning, can be transmuted into the archetypal qualities of the warrior—courage, heroism, power, resolution, will, even generosity.

These qualities have universal validity. They can be *transferred* to the struggles of everyday life, primarily with a view to conquering internal enemies—such as fear, discouragement, or lethargy—and also for tackling the difficulties of existence, other people's hostility, social injustices, a rough environment, or dangers of any kind. They can be fully manifested, not in order to deny life but to affirm it. Can there be a warrior without weapons? The answer is a resounding yes: the noblest warrior fights not with the feeble. He—or she—is tirelessly involved in the most strenuous wars of all, wars against ignorance, injustice, or indifference.

The main danger in the Way of the Will lies in the distortions of the warrior's essential quality—the destructive use of force. Warriors of all kinds often enjoy a position of power in society. They can be overcome with feelings of omnipotence and, becoming indifferent to other people, use force to further their own interests, become tyrants, display their might, get revenge, turn other people into objects, and destroy life. Such has been the fate of many powerful individuals over the centuries of human history.

We can see, therefore, that the risks inherent in this Way, particularly in the areas of politics and human relations, are enormous. Yet this path is not only a valid avenue for transpersonal development but also an indispensable quality for social evolution. Those who tread it redefine our reality—physiological, geographical, political, or cosmological. In taking risks, in following the most difficult route, such people broaden all of our outlooks, succeed in glimpsing worlds that are invisible to those who prefer a more reassuring existence, and generate a force that encourages and inspires many. In so doing, such people rise to universality.

You may think that the Way of the Will is the monopoly

of a few exceptional individuals. Indeed, according to a strict definition, this is true. But the experiences of these few are symbolic representations of the human spirit. Even if we are not astronauts, speleologists, or parachutists, we can all learn how to be more adventurous. Even if we do not actually sacrifice our lives in the struggle against injustice and cruelty, we have the chance to overcome hypocrisy and indifference. Even if we are not prepared to risk death, we can die to all that is old and stale in our life.

This chapter presents a composite of topics. We start with the will—the basic function in this path. The following two subjects, risk and the unknown, show how people who tread this Way put their own survival at stake to honor values dear to their heart. The next section—the voice—covers a phenomenon that, although recurrent in the other Ways, reaches its highest frequency and intensity in the Way of the Will: the inner voice reassures and guides us in the moments of gravest danger and greatest meaning. Sacrifice, the next theme, is the attitude that often accompanies the nudity of selflessness. Finally, confrontation with death—the ultimate act of will—points the way to the transcendence of personality limitations.

Studying the exploits of those who have gone along this path is like hearing an inner voice. And this voice forewarns that whatever path you follow, you will come up against seemingly insurmountable obstacles; in the battle of life you will at times feel confused and frightened; when you need it most, there will be no one there to understand you, to encourage or guide you. You are alone. You will be tempted to believe that your highest values are worthless, that your most beautiful dreams are impossible. You will be tempted to give up. But you must not succumb. The time has come for you to take a risk. This will require a great deal of courage and offers no guarantee. Perhaps you will be beaten. But in the process you will have discovered a force of great beauty within yourself. It is your own strength, the strength of your real Self.

THE WILL

Three hundred yards from the end he had jumped commandingly into the lead. The finish line lay before him. Now he only had to race against himself. Roger Bannister had trained for months; his aim was a feat many experts thought physiologically impossible: to run the mile under four minutes—to go, as he later said, "where no man had yet ventured."

Months of hard work had brought him to the peak of fitness; each movement had become automatic, so his mind was left free to concentrate wholly on the goal. Bannister had thought of this race for months, and every evening before going to sleep he had visualized himself going through it. Now the great moment had come.

The race had begun well, and Bannister felt strong. He felt as if he were running without resistance, as though his legs were being "propelled by some unknown force." After three quarters of a mile, the announced time was encouraging—three minutes, seven seconds. The crowd roared with excitement. This was his last chance. By now Bannister was nearing the end of his career; another opportunity as favorable would be rare. He was pinning all his hopes on this one race. This is his description of the last yards.

> My body had long since exhausted all its energy, but it went on running just the same. The physical overdraft came only from greater willpower. This was the crucial moment when my legs were strong enough to carry me over the last few yards as they could never have done in previous years. With five yards to go, the tape seemed almost to recede. Would I ever reach it?
>
> Those last few seconds seemed never-ending. The faint line of the finishing tape stood ahead as a haven of peace, after the struggle. The arms of the world were waiting to receive me if

> only I reached the tape without slackening my speed. . . . I leapt at the tape like a man taking his last spring to save himself from the chasm that threatens to engulf him.
>
> [After victory] I felt suddenly and gloriously free of the burden of athletic ambition that I had been carrying for years. No words could be invented for such supreme happiness, eclipsing all other feelings. I thought at that moment I could never again reach such a climax of single-mindedness. I felt bewildered and overpowered.

Bannister had redefined the possible. No one before him had ever managed to run the mile in less than four minutes. But in the months following his record, several other athletes accomplished the same feat. Bannister had not only run faster but had actually changed a subjective reality, and what had once been considered a physiological impossibility was now brought within the reach of many. An act of will is not effort alone; it is choice—the choice of one belief over another belief.

When Admiral Richard Byrd remained alone in a hut in his Antarctic base, with the stove emitting carbon monoxide and slowly poisoning him, he could do nothing but wait for spring, when rescuers would be able to reach him. But how was he to survive in the meantime? Byrd decided to reinforce within himself the will to live, and to eradicate any negative ideas as soon as they came into his mind, at the same time cultivating those that fostered serenity and faith. Thus, alone in a hut, surrounded for hundreds of miles by ice, snow, and storms, in cold and darkness, inaccessible, and half poisoned by fumes, Byrd decided to live:

> I was able again to fill my mind with the fine and comforting things of the world that seemed irretrievably lost. I surrounded myself with my family and my friends; I projected myself into the sunlight, into the midst of green, growing things. I thought of all the things I would do when I got home.

Thus Byrd was able to win over death in the same way as concentration-camp survivors or people recovering from grave illness have been able to pull through their predicament. As recent research bears out, this is accomplished to a great extent by stimulating positive thoughts and emotions, thereby strengthening ourselves and reinforcing our immune defenses. It all depends, it appears, on which universe of thought we decide to feed.

There is much we can learn from these people. How often—even before we began—have we declared a task "impossible"? And how often have we construed a picture of ourselves as being inadequate? In these cases a great deal depends on the thought patterns we choose and on the persistence with which we affirm them.

But however positive our thoughts may be, we cannot ignore obstacles and difficulties. Any undertaking will have negative conditions. We must neither be slaves to inertia nor victims of intimidation. We must not allow ourselves to be blocked by the density of life or duped by its deceptions. Instead, we need to be freed from the dictates of chance and impulse. We must not give in when encountering opposition or misfortune. We should not allow ourselves to be paralyzed by fear or led astray in momentary satisfactions. This is true for any important endeavor and is especially true for a Way to the Self.

In each Way we catch a glimpse of a distant, shining vision, a thing of great beauty. But the vision lasts a moment, then disappears; suddenly we are left in the dark. All we have is our will—the will to believe, to focus on the next step, and to move forward.

Make no mistake: The will we are speaking of here is not "willpower"—the moralistic, frowning dictatorship that negates without creating. Old-fashioned willpower is based on repression and splits the personality in two parts struggling against each other. Instead, genuine will is the capacity to say *yes* 100 percent, without doubts or compromises—be it to ideas, possibilities, or people—and also to say *no* with equal strength, because wrong moves are much more numerous than right ones.

Will means applying to one's life—even in the small, insignificant circumstances—the values in which one believes most. It means having clear, well-defined goals, and pursuing them with energy and determination. Will also implies knowing how to act autonomously, at the cost of appearing a rebel, rather than thinking and doing as everyone else thinks and does. It may also mean risking one's emotional, social, and, at times, even physical survival. Will is pushing oneself beyond one's bodily, emotional, and mental limits.

Concentration and discipline are also essential aspects of the will: knowing how to go forward day after day with patience and endurance, disregarding boredom or uncertainty, discouragement or the desire to do something else. With will we are able to model what we wish to become; without will we are modeled by events, carried at random by the stream of life.

Some might challenge the relevance of will by asking whether the opposite is not the case: Do we not need to *lose* our personal will, surrendering to a greater, transpersonal will? The ultimate answer is yes. Those who have had transpersonal experiences have often referred to the death of the personal will. But the transition from personal to transpersonal will does not take place at the same time and in the same way for all people. In some cases, it is found at the start of a Way toward the Self. One need only think of the Zen discipline of archery, in which "the shot will only go smoothly when it takes the archer himself by surprise." All aim, all choice is surrendered. In these cases the work consists in downplaying any claim on decision and control. At other times, however, the death of the personal will takes place only in the later stages of a transpersonal Way.

Moreover, some of the Ways adopt attitudes that seem to dissolve the will—for instance, acceptance of any feeling or spontaneous impulse, unfocused panoramic attention, surrender, or emptying of the self. In all these operations the personal will appears to be negated. In a sense this is true, but deep down underneath we discover a choice, a goal, and concentration of the highest degree. Indeed the loss of one's will in order to surrender to a greater will does not imply slackness, disorganization, or sheer impotence; rather, it is the result of steady, careful discipline. In order to surrender one's will one must have it in the first place.

In the Way that bears its name, the will is used in its most explicit and extreme sense. It is will in its purest form, consisting of the aspects we have already examined, but it is also something more: the indomitable dynamic force that channels all powers in a single direction, is determined to surpass itself, and perseveres until it reaches the chosen goal.

In this extreme form, the will becomes an element of severance—first and foremost, severance from the body, because in this Way one ignores the most elementary needs and impulses. Whereas other Ways, especially the Way of Dance, play themselves out *through* the body, the subjective experience here is victory over the opacity and inertia of matter, so much so that the body is at times subjected to extreme stress, even to the point of endangering its survival.

Second, there is a severance from emotions and desires. Rather than following their lead, the will overcomes them, sometimes forcing a way through the complex world of feelings, without dwelling on them, acting as though they did not exist. The other Ways are quite different. The Way of Devotion, for instance, uses feelings as propulsive power; the Way of Beauty adopts them as an instrument of aesthetic sensibility; and the Way of Illumination acknowledges feelings as the channel for union with all beings: Different ways for different people.

And third, the will can even oppose the mind and everything that seems logical and sensible. After all, it is good sense which, in the guise of a reassuring, benevolent presence, imprisons us in an impoverished vision of reality. The will can sometimes, despite penalty or ridicule or ostracism, forge ahead by ignoring everything others think and say—their claims, demands, and protests.

We have looked at the stories of Bannister and Byrd. Another example of will taken to its extreme limits, a will capable of choosing adventure over survival, is that of Herbert Tichy, the Austrian mountain climber. Tichy had decided to move onto the final section of the Cho Oyu, one of the Himalayan peaks, although his frozen hands could not even grip the rock. This is how he described the experience of reaching the top:

> The world seemed to me to be instilled with a hitherto unknown benevolence and goodness. The barrier between me and the rest of creation was broken down. The few phenomena, sky, ice, rock, wind and I which now constituted life, were an inseparable and divine whole. I felt myself—the contradiction is only apparent—as glorious as God and at the same time no more than an insignificant grain of sand.
>
> I had broken through a metaphysical barrier and entered a world where other laws were in force. I recalled Blake's words: "If the doors of perception were cleansed, everything would appear to men as infinite."
>
> Here the doors were all thrown wide open and an indescribable, impersonal bliss filled me. It did not prevent my believing that we should all die that very day.

Robert Peary was the first to reach the North Pole after many before him had tried and failed, either turning back in disappointment or dying in the expanse of eternal ice. Peary made several attempts and succeeded in reaching the Pole only after seven abortive efforts and twenty-three years of work. During that period Peary had spent twelve years in the Arctic desert; the rest of the time he devoted to preparing for subsequent expeditions. Reaching the Pole involved weeks of forced marching, physical fatigue, lack of sleep, and tormenting anxiety. Here nature unveiled herself only to those who had come through the hardest tests. It is easy to understand how, when Peary reached the Pole, he experienced an extraordinary state of "mental exaltation":

> For more than a score of years that point on the earth's surface had been the object of my every effort. To its attainment my whole being, physical, mental, and moral, had been dedicated. Many times my own life and the lives of those with me had been risked. My own material and forces and those of my friends had been devoted to this object. . . . The determination to reach the Pole had become so much a part of my being that, strange as it may seem, I long ago ceased to think of myself save as an instrument for the attainment of that end. To the layman this may seem strange, but an inventor can understand it, or an artist, or anyone who has devoted himself for years upon years to the service of an idea.

We have far fewer details on another, older example, but it is nonetheless worth mentioning. Portuguese explorer Ferdinand Magellan arrived at the critical point in his circumnavigation of the world after more than a year of hardship at sea. He was faced with a partial mutiny of his crew in a region where snow, wind, hail, and storms prevailed. With only ocean and unknown lands ahead and having exhausted all supplies, he decided to carry on through the strait between Patagonia and Tierra del Fuego. Magellan commented: "Even if we have to eat the leather strips on the masts and the yards, I will go on to discover what I set out to discover." When his ship reached the Pacific Ocean, Magellan wept for joy.

This forceful way of treating oneself—excess carried to the point of method, perhaps fanaticism—may upset us even if we just think about it. Our reaction is natural, because in such instances the will is used to counteract the normal and reasonable attitudes. Where survival mechanisms are at risk, we naturally react with terror. But the challenge is not absurd or destructive. In this path the will is expressed as the triumph of the human spirit without concession to mediocrity or compromise; it is an affirmation of the invincibility of the spirit in the face of matter, of freedom from its inertia and opacity. We all know that matter can be like a prison, can make us feel blinded, slowed down, trapped. Many people know what it is to aspire to freedom from such constrictions. A few of them have actually attained it.

RISK

An all-inclusive guarantee, from birth to death, perhaps even beyond—that is what we long for. For what is more desirable than total security when we are surrounded by nuclear threat, economic uncertainty, the horrors of pollution, the unknown perils of technology, terrorism and the innumerable dangers created by human folly, the hazardous jungle in which we struggle to survive, and a universe in which each day ten thousand suns like ours explode?

We know, of course, that total security from cradle to grave is impossible. We know that uncertainty, change, and mystery are the stuff of life. We know too that in the long run security—if we ever think we have it—kills curiosity and wonder. Risk, on the other hand, has a spiritual value. Only by detaching ourselves from the safety and comfort of our supports can we discover what we truly are. Only when, naked and alone, we have nothing to lose, are we ready for truly knowing and loving. Only by taking risks can we truly *be*.

In the Way of Will, risk is a central aspect of the path. By challenging our most ingrained personality structures we earn a salutary shake-up. It is impossible to take risks and remain what we were. According to Professor Rosenthal of Illinois University, the existence of dangerous sports, such as mountain climbing or parachuting, indicate that risk is a fundamental need of the human species. His research shows that participating in dangerous sports makes people more efficient and productive, more creative, and more able to enjoy their sex life.

In order to take risks we do not need to climb mountains or jump out of planes. Risk is all around us in everyday life. It can take the form of shaking off our roles and being transparent, of questioning issues, daring new behaviors, doing the unexpected, or even exposing ourselves to ridicule or rejection. We are often too shy to be what we are and instead prefer a quiet and reassuring life. Sometimes it seems that we almost seek to be excused for existing. Conversely, rather than continuing to be a pale imitation of ourselves, we can risk being what we are, with our feelings, our convictions, and our dreams.

Risk, by definition, can lead to danger and death—that is what makes it so terrifying. But it can also offer great opportunities for regeneration and growth. If we are regimented by our habits and our conditioning, our thoughts and emotions will be limited and predictable; but if we take risks, we generate new possibilities. Recounting the time when he was on the north face of the Eiger, an almost totally smooth and deadly surface, the French mountaineer Lionel Terray said: "I had now reached the condition of divine madness which makes a man oblivious of danger and renders all things possible."

Martin Buber wrote that play is "the exultation of the possible." We could say the same about risk: precisely because it is playful, risk resides at the heart of a hopeful spirit and defies the humdrum of life. Also, when we take risks we are confronted with our doubts and fears, and become stronger for it. Through risk we transcend our predicament, leaving behind our old self like some prehistoric fossil that no longer belongs to us.

Risk liberates. However, it also exposes us to innumerable forms of hardship and danger. What motivates us to forgo our security? To answer this question we need to examine a recurring—though implicit—theme in most of contemporary psychology: the idea of homeostasis, the principle whereby an organism seeks to maintain its own stability and integrity.

Every need—be it hunger, thirst, sex, or security—is a threat to our psychophysical balance; by satisfying it, we experience pleasure and temporarily regain stability. At first this concept appears quite satisfactory, because it extrapolates from the description of bodily functions where homeostasis continually takes place. Body temperature, blood sugar level, blood pressure, and so forth, are regulated in this way. Also, we easily identify with this process. We all have needs and we all enjoy relieving them.

However, this model leaves out one basic factor—the underlying dissatisfaction that human beings experience, which leads them to venture into the unknown. This need—which has been called the "Ulysses factor"—is a mystery. Why on earth should we want to exchange comfort for danger and hardship? The only convincing answer is that we long for a fulfillment which ordinary satisfactions cannot give us. We yearn for infinity, and nothing finite will lastingly satisfy us.

That is where the transpersonal search begins. And that is also why some human beings decide to take risks. Risk costs much, but it yields great rewards. "Courage," said Seneca, the Roman philosopher, "carries us to the stars; fear leads us to death." *Animus* in Latin means both "soul" and "courage," indicating that this quality is an intrinsic part of our being.

People who perform acts of courage place themselves in situations where they are no longer protected. Thus they reveal themselves for what they are:

◊ They are generous, because they put their full presence at stake.

◊ They are open to life, rather than shut in the stronghold of comfort and immobility.

◊ They are able to put up with uncertainty and are revitalized by danger, whereas more rigid temperaments are unable to tolerate precariousness.

◊ Instead of being ruled by fear, they are able to look around and choose, even choose what they dread most.

◊ They are alert, because in a high-risk situation vigilance is a must.

◊ They have faith that life, with all its richness of new, unforeseeable circumstances, will in some way come to their aid.

When Charles Lindbergh made his great flight from Boston to Paris, he was risking his life. No one had ever attempted such a feat before. Crossing the Atlantic Ocean alone meant living each moment with the possibility of death and entering a world in which the rules and experiences of a familiar world no longer applied. Guided by the spirit of adventure, he penetrated into this rarified universe. Lindbergh described the advanced stages of his flight in terms that resemble those of Oriental mysticism:

> Consciousness grows independent of the ordinary senses. You see without assistance from the eyes, over distances beyond the visual horizon. There are moments when existence appears independent even of mind. The importance of physical desire and immediate surroundings is submerged in the apprehension of universal values.
>
> For unmeasurable periods, I seem divorced from my body, as though I were an awareness spreading out through space, over the earth and into the heavens, unhampered by time or substance, free from the gravitation that binds men to the heavy human problems of the world.

This was undoubtedly a true yogic experience. Solitude removed Lindbergh from any interpersonal influence and led him into introspection and inner bareness; the monotonous roar of the engine numbed his thought-processes; lack of food altered his body chemistry, preparing the ground for expansion of consciousness; continuous concentration on the flight conducted him to a higher plane of reality. All of these factors undoubtedly worked together within Lindbergh to produce extraordinary transpersonal experiences. More than anything else, however, it was his willingness to risk that brought him to a realization of the Self.

Let us pursue planes and pilots. Lindbergh made his flight in 1927. In 1947 the fastest planes had not yet reached the speed of sound, Mach 1. As one approached this speed, the machine's instability increased and the framework creaked, threatening to give way and thereby creating an aura of terror around the sound barrier, as it came to be called. Just as the pillars of Hercules, before the time of Columbus, marked the boundary beyond which lay worlds populated with monsters, the sound barrier marked the limit beyond which lay disintegration and death; indeed, more than one pilot had already died in the attempt to surpass it.

Chuck Yeager succeeded in breaking the sound barrier with the Bell X-1, whereupon a whole series of pilots followed him shortly after. They began to speak of "pilot heaven": it was like the entrance to a new, silent dimension (sound had been left behind). It was also a break through the barrier of fear, hesitation, disbelief, the recollection of dead companions, and attachment to life. This is how William Bridgeman, one of the first pilots to surpass the speed of sound, described his experience:

> I have an awareness that I have never experienced before, but it does not seem to project beyond this moment. Every cell, fluid, muscle of my body, is acutely awake. Perception is enormously exaggerated—black is blacker, white is whiter. Silence is more acute. It is the tender edge of the unknowable.

> I have the unshakeable feeling that no matter what the instruments read, it will have no effect on the power that is making this ship fly. An independent, supernatural power she has. She is alive with her own unknowable and unmovable power.

The silence of supersonic flight resembles underwater silence—another dimension, as alluring as it may be deadly. Here, too, one risks by entering unfamiliar spaces. Enzo Maiorca, the man who several times broke the world record for deep-water free diving without oxygen equipment, stated in an interview that he had had significant spiritual experiences in the silent world underwater:

> The God I meet down there, in the depths, is different from the God we pray to in this world. It is a God without organ music, without liturgy, blue and immense. I remember Him by the absolute silence, the mysterious message of eternity.
>
> These are not mere words . . . my God is down there at the bottom of the sea. He is present in my solitude, in my life hanging by a thread.
>
> Swimming at a depth of thirty meters, I once entered a cave through a low, narrow opening. Caution should have stopped me, but something pushed me on: a certain curiosity, perhaps, or a call, I don't know. The cave was pink and at the bottom there were two unusual columns. It was like a temple. One of the caves was open—there was a slit through which an unreal light shone in, a coral pink ray which gradually merged with the water and was diluted into a deep blue color. I had my aqualung and stayed there for a while. It was a subaqueous church. It was there I found my God.

Mahatma Gandhi took risk to its extreme. In him courage was found in its highest state, based on nonviolence (*ahimsa*) and absence of ego. According to Gandhi, nonviolence does not imply a mere abstention from acts of aggression; it is a profound attitude of the heart, involving the whole person in a continuous spiritual exercise, which Gandhi compared to the art of a tightrope walker. It is abstention from any hostile thought, and, in positive terms, what he called "perfect love," goodwill toward every living being.

The term *ahimsa* does not signify a passive indifference to offenses but instead involves confronting any injustice and fighting it until it is eliminated. Its strength, said Gandhi, is born out of an "indomitable will." But it is a force that harms no one and leads to inner release. When the adversaries, who have been expecting some form of violent reaction, find themselves faced with *ahimsa* over which they have no power, they are taken by surprise and are forced to surrender. But this defeat, instead of humiliating, frees and elevates them. Gandhi wrote:

> The more I work at this law [of nonviolence] the more I feel the delight in my life, the delight in the scheme of the universe. It gives me a peace and a meaning of the mysteries of Nature that I have no power to describe.

This was how Gandhi, unarmed, confronted police charges, beatings, prison, the colossal power of the British Empire and, finally, the man who killed him.

For Gandhi, "fearlessness is the first requisite of spirituality. Cowards can never be moral." He viewed courage as an essential vitamin for each individual's spiritual growth—in contrast with cowardice, which reduces a person's sense of value and self-respect. Without courage, love and the search for truth are impossible. Courage, however, must be based on nonviolence: "I want . . . the greater bravery of the meek, the gentle, and the non-violent, the bravery that will mount the gallows without injuring, or harboring any thought of injury to a single soul."

The illusory foundation of our normal outlook, said Gandhi, is fear. But fear has no place in our hearts once we have eradicated the most ingrained attachments, particularly those involving wealth, pleasure, and safety. Gandhi also said that we become intrepid when we no longer consider ourselves owners, but "trustees" of what life has assigned to us, and no longer masters making demands on others, but servants who have nothing to lose. Then "all fears will roll away like mists."

THE UNKNOWN

When faced with the unknown, we find ourselves back to step one. This is our original condition in the universe, and the sincerest one, because what we have learned over the course of our lives, however significant it may be, is but a speck in comparison with the infinite mystery that surrounds us. Faced with the unknown, we can do nothing other than stand open-mouthed. Boredom or distraction are out of the question. Like a baby, we are newly born in a world we do not comprehend.

We are all destined to come up against the unknown—above all, the unknown within ourselves. As research into altered states of consciousness has shown, there exist within us amazing landscapes, jungles and oceans, monsters and chimeras, peaks and abysses, galaxies and entire universes. The unknown pervades even the familiar setting of our everyday lives. It surfaces in unexpected events, in the riddle that other people are, in chance, in ever-impending death.

Our attitude to the unknown will affect the way we respond to such important issues in life as beauty, awareness, love, and creativity. Are we prepared to accept what we do not know? Or do we stop short at the edge of the mystery, only feeling at ease with ready-made explanations that are anathema to true understanding? Indeed, making friends with the unknown is a prerequisite in any transpersonal search.

That is precisely why the various transpersonal paths use

different methods for cultivating intelligent ignorance. In the Way of Illumination, for instance, we train ourselves in awareness without concepts; in the Way of Science, valid research is possible only when all assumptions are questioned; in the Way of Beauty, one must rediscover innocent perception.

In the Way of the Will, everything is even more intense and immediate: innocence and awe are not cultivated but rather emerge as an inevitable result of contact with the unknown. One goes straight to virgin perception, because what one meets has never been encountered before. One reaches down to the depths of the ocean or the earth, or up into the air, or out in the cosmos. Here the familiar models one has habitually used for steering a steady course through everyday life become obsolete, ridiculously useless devices. One faces sublime, terrifying, or grotesque forms, whose grandeur evokes awe and the numinous.

Let us take the example of descent to the abysses of the sea. William Beebe descended a half mile beneath the ocean's surface in his bathysphere, the "Arcturus." At that depth, he wrote, one discovers unimaginable beings, compared with which the Notre Dame gargoyles or the demons in Dante's *Inferno* are household items: fishes with telescopic eyes or luminous teeth, dragon fish, lantern fish, flame-throwing fish that emit a luminous purple jet, rainbow fish, fish with luminous tentacles, parachutes with tentacles, dancing sparks. This is the unknown—a dream world, improbable, and marvelous to the eye. Who can remain unchanged after witnessing such a spectacle?

People who explore the unknown find themselves in an indifferent, impersonal world. It is a world that is completely alien to them—one that not only leaves them permanently affected but makes it impossible for their thought processes to function normally. Far from the known world, in this silence, in this vast space, wrote Beebe, "[I feel] like an infinitesimal atom lost in boundless space." For him, the spectacle of this eternally silent dark night in the underwater abysses was supernatural. Here one could truly sense the terror of infinity—a terror which is the counterpart to wonder. All alone deep below the sea surface, Beebe recalled an experience from his childhood when he had hastily pulled down a kite, terrified at the thought of leaving it so alone up in the sky and of it being carried off into infinite space.

Similar feelings are experienced by speleologists. After they have spent a certain period in the caves, they often lose the familiar rhythm of day and night. Underground silence contrasts sharply with the usual noise in which we all live. Here, too, there is the enchantment of an otherworldly landscape. French speleologist Norbert Casteret describes such an experience:

> Just when we thought we had exhausted our powers of admiration, we stepped into a fairy palace. Hundreds of caverns and countless strange stories and pictures had not prepared me for marvels like these.
>
> Stalactites and crystals sparkled everywhere; their profusion, their whiteness, their shapes were fantastic beyond belief. We were inside a precious stone; it was a palace of crystal. . . . Even in coloring and delicacy the formations surpassed the most gorgeous flowers of nature.
>
> There were microscopic stalactites and flawlessly transparent giant crystals. There were shiny formations, dull formations, milky, red, black, crude green formations. . . . Finally, there were two entirely new phenomena, still unexplained: huge needles as fine as cobwebs, which trembled and broke at a breath, and silver strings with the brilliance of silk yarn, which dangled from roof and walls.
>
> Amid all these wonders we advanced but slowly. We went several hundred yards through chambers and vestibules. Constant new splendors kept us breathless.

Let us leave the magical setting of underground caves and return to the dazzling white Arctic landscape. How is an individual affected by this white—the most visionary of all colors, and the one that symbolizes innocence itself? Between 1903 and 1907 explorers Roald Amundsen and Godfred Hansen, together with twelve dogs, explored the Arctic. This is how Amundsen ends the account of their adventures:

> It seemed to me that the infinite wastes gave birth to conceptions of greatness, beauty, and goodness. This was to be my theme. I desired so to write that those who would read might enrich their ideas and gain some impressions, at least, of the Stupendous, such as were conveyed to me in those pathless regions.

Anything can happen when one enters a world far removed from the dramas and dreams of ordinary human experience. Mountain climbing is a complete form of yoga involving altered physiological conditions, the continual vigilance required in risk taking, teamwork in perilous circumstances (fostering a sense of solidarity with fellow explorers), the search for situations at the edge of human experience, and the symbolism of ascent to higher levels. All of these elements work together to elicit transpersonal states. To these factors we should add the rediscovery of nature's innocence and the confrontation with an alien world—almost another planet.

Here too the unknown has its destabilizing, vision-inducing effect. The following words by Maurice Herzog describe the last part of his climb—together with Louis Lachenal—of the Annapurna in the Himalayas:

> I felt as though I were plunging into something new and quite abnormal. I had the strangest and most vivid impressions, such as I had never before known in the mountains. There was something unnatural in the way I saw Lachenal and everything around us. I smiled to myself at the paltriness of our efforts, for I could stand apart and watch myself making these efforts. But all sense of exertion was gone, as though there were no

longer any gravity. This diaphanous landscape, this quintessence of purity—these were not the mountains I knew: they were the mountains of my dreams.

The snow, sprinkled over every rock and gleaming in the sun, was of a radiant beauty that touched me to the heart. I had never seen such complete transparency, and I was living in a world of crystal. Sounds were indistinct, the atmosphere like cotton wool.

An astonishing happiness welled up in me, but I could not define it. Everything was so new, so utterly unprecedented. It was not in the least like anything I had known in the Alps, where one feels buoyed up by the presence of others—by people of whom one is vaguely aware, or even by dwellings one can see in the far distance.

This was quite different. An enormous gulf was between me and the world. This was a different universe—withered, desert, lifeless; a fantastic universe where the presence of man was not foreseen, perhaps not desired. We were braving an interdict, overstepping a boundary, and yet we had no fear as we continued upward.

And what of going up in a balloon? As in the case of water, air can evoke a sense of vastness and freedom of movement: it is symbolic of a condition in which all ties have been severed, all restrictions transcended. And far more so than with water, its connotations suggestive of the regressive, the embryonic, whereas air is transparent and luminous. Moreover, the absence of reference points is perhaps greater than in any other situation. Once balloon travelers have passed through the clouds, they are unable to perceive their own motion. In pure space one feels as if one were everywhere.

During the nineteenth century, balloon travelers were pioneers of a technology they thought would become the means of communication of the future. The leading figures have left us many descriptions of their adventures. The following two accounts contain some late-nineteenth-century rhetoric, but their enthusiasm is nonetheless sincere:

> Here we are, now, in the light, in the clean sky. The earth and its misty veil has sunk far below. Here light reigns; here warmth blazes; here the atmosphere is full of joy. Coming into this new world is like leaving behind the dark shores of pain.
>
> The most enchanting, majestic view of nature, seen from the top of a mountain, does not even approach the beauty of that place seen perpendicularly from space. Only here does one become aware that the earth is beautiful, the life of nature grand, that air surrounds this world with living radiance, and all creation is one harmonious whole.

Finding oneself confronted with extraordinary, unexpected sights cannot only surprise, but also open one's mind to the awareness of a superior Intelligence in the universe. Admiral Byrd stayed alone for four-and-a-half months at the Bolling Advanced Base Camp during his second expedition to the Antarctic. In this period he experienced "mystical" states (as he refers to them in his book *Alone*) and an "exalted sense of identification" with nature. He also felt at times a sensation of transcending his body, so that his mind would "go voyaging through space as smoothly and felicitously as it passes through the objects of its reflections. The body stood still, but the mind was free." Here, in this freezing, desert land, alone and in danger of losing his life, Byrd became aware of a greater Mind:

> For those who seek it [harmony], there is inexhaustible evidence of an all-pervading Intelligence.
>
> The human race, my intuition tells me, is not outside the cosmic process and is not an accident. It is as much a part of

the universe as the trees, the mountains, the aurora, and the stars.

Why is it that, in exploring the unknown, many of these explorers become aware of an Intelligence that transcends them? The answer is simple: When they venture where they know nothing and abandon the familiar geometries of their minds, a greater order is more likely to appear to them. When Edgar Mitchell reached the moon and saw the planet Earth from a distance, he was overcome by its beauty:

> It began with the breathtaking experience of seeing planet Earth floating in the immensity of space—the incredible beauty of a splendid blue-and-white jewel floating in the vast, black sky. I underwent a religious-like peak experience, in which the presence of divinity became almost palpable, and I *knew* that life in the universe was not just an accident based on random processes. This knowledge, which came directly, intuitively, was not a matter of discursive reasoning or logical abstraction. It was not deduced from information perceptible by the sensory organs. The realization was subjective, but it was knowledge every bit as real and compelling as the objective data the navigational program or the communication system was based on.

These otherworldly sceneries seem to evoke equally extraordinary worlds *within* those who contemplate them. As if they found the right wavelength, these unknown landscapes evoke, in the pioneers who see them for the first time, corresponding inner landscapes, far removed from the conventions of the world. Nature in its virgin state draws them to that part of themselves which has never been affected by mental habits or cultural conditioning. Paradoxically, it is only when these pioneers push themselves far beyond known territories into weird worlds—be it the darkest abyss, the most frightening peak, or the far reaches of space—that they win the most intimate and personal discovery they could ever hope to make: their own true face.

THE VOICE

Men and women traveling along the Way of the Will, more than other people, tend to hear their inner voice. Lost and alone—in the desert, in the sky, in the sea, in the midst of a hostile society—they, more than anyone else, have both the need and the possibility to listen to the voice within. But the inner voice can also be heard by seekers traveling along the other Ways, and inner listening is a supremely useful skill. The basic principle here is that every inner reality has a sound or a voice—though not, of course, a sound as we know it in the concrete world. We have become too externalized, perhaps, so that we have grown accustomed to the harsh noises of traffic, television, pneumatic drills, and rock music. And who, amid such a cacophony, is able to hear the subtle voice of the innermost core?

The task is far from easy. Many voices strive to be heard: the voices of other people who seduce, threaten, demand, preach, or shout; and the voices within us, equally varied and contrasting—the voice of neurosis, which criticizes, mocks, or condemns us as we try to do our best. Or the voice of loneliness, for when no one else encourages us, we do it for ourselves, like a child talking in the dark. Then, again, there are also the voices of our doubts, a thousand anxious questions assailing us. Maybe we listen to the voice of common sense—calm, sensible, and somewhat tedious. Or perhaps it is the voice of our regret we hear, pursuing us with hammering persistence.

Often the voices belong to people in our lives. Outer voices have become inner, and continue to speak to us. All these voices have an emotional impact. From the first time we were soothed by a lullaby or wounded by a reproach, voices have had the power to penetrate our beings, touch us deeply, and give shape to our personality. These are basic matters: Tell me what voices you listen to, and I will tell you who you are.

The Self has a voice too. On occasions it prevails over other voices by dint of its power and clarity. Unlike other inner or outer voices, it has no need to dictate or rationalize. Like a vibration mysteriously springing from silence, it reaches us with a life and will of its own. It is a categorical imperative: Once we have heard it, we know what we must do. It guides, inspires, and regenerates us. This is the voice of the inner master which, in the most complex of situations, shows us the solution with simplicity. Thus, contact with the numinous presence of the Self can take place through the vibrations of the voice within. Much more often, however, other, more familiar voices speak more loudly. Then the voice of the Self is choked by a din of grosser sounds.

Actually we can think of every inner state as sounding its own note. Thus is the whole history of humankind represented —as though in some vast, ever-changing chorus—by our inner voices, all the way from the ancestral cries of hunger and fear, to the utterances of emotion and reason, right up to the supermundane voice of the transpersonal levels.

Sometimes the transpersonal voice is clearly audible, almost like a physical voice, as in the case of Joan of Arc. From an early age, this peasant girl heard invisible beings who exhorted her to liberate France. These voices guided her, dressed and armed like a man, in leading the French troops into the Battle of Orléans, putting the English army to rout.

When testifying at her trial some time later, Joan said that she had begun to hear voices—with mixed feelings of fear, wonder, and surprise—in Domremy, the village where she was born, and then in the woods, when alone. Usually, she explained, the voice came from the right: "If I were in a wood

I could easily hear the Voice which came to me. It seemed to me to come from lips I should reverence. I believe it was sent me from God. . . . There was abundance of light from every side."

The voice, or voices, are most easily heard when one is physically distant from society. Reinhold Messner, the mountain climber, said that when up in the Himalayas he had been aware of "strange sounds" and hallucinations that led him to an "innocent awareness" of his "unity with the cosmos." Lindbergh, too, during his flight across the Atlantic, felt benevolent presences that spoke to him:

> The phantoms have human voices—friendly, vaporlike shapes, without substance, able to vanish or appear at will, to pass in and out through the walls of the fuselage as though no walls were there. Now, many are crowded behind me. Now, only a few remain. First one and then another presses forward to my shoulder to speak above the engine's noise, and then draws back among the group behind. At times, voices come out of the air itself, clear yet far away, travelling through distances that can't be measured by the scale of human miles; familiar voices, conversing and advising on my flight, discussing problems of my navigation, reassuring me, giving me messages of importance unattainable in ordinary life. . . . The spirits have no rigid bodies, yet they remain human in outline form—emanations from the experience of ages, inhabitants of a universe closed to mortal men.

Neurophysiologists speak of the "cocktail party effect," the marvelous ability of the human brain that enables us, among the confusion of various external sounds (such as one hears at a cocktail party), to focus on only one. This selective ability can also be employed in the context of the inner world. Before being able to listen to one's own inner voice, one must be able to exclude all other voices—those of the body demanding comfort, the beguiling voice of power, the voice of threats or the voice of one's own fear, other people's protests, the voice of doubt, or even the voice of rationality.

We also need to discern the one true voice from the other gratifying voices, which tell us what we want to hear but do nothing other than reinforce our prejudices and complexes. In this context, the analogy of a wavelength is helpful. A radio can be tuned to different wavelengths within the same narrow band. With the slightest movement of a knob we can find ourselves listening to a car advertisement, the news, a sermon, a comedy sketch, the weather forecast, a political speech, or a wonderful melody—different universes in a confined space, yet light years apart. The voices within us, varied as they may be, are also close together. They can overlap and, at times, interfere with one another. Yet they sound from essentially different parts of our being. We need to learn how to tune into the right one.

In addition to guiding us, the voice of the Self encourages us in times of danger or low morale. People on the Way of the Will hear it when in the throes of fear, despair, or physical exhaustion. Christopher Columbus was on his fourth journey to America. He was on his way back but had lost hope of reaching home, and he was sick, tired, prey of adverse circumstances, and worn down by a desperate crew. Then Columbus heard, as he writes in a letter, a voice chiding him for being discouraged by external conditions, a voice that filled him with courage and hope and infused him with a faith that enabled him to bring his voyage to an end.

At a peak moment during an intense period of his struggle for justice, Martin Luther King experienced great fear. It was the time when the blacks in Birmingham, Alabama, had decided to make a peaceful protest against discrimination on buses, which obliged them to give their seats to whites. They boycotted the bus company by going to work on foot, making everyone more aware of an injustice they were no longer prepared to suffer. The initiative was successful, but King—who had promoted it—became the target for the anger of the white conservatives.

During that period King received between thirty and forty "hate" letters and a dozen threatening phone calls each day. In many cases the threats were not only directed at him but also at his wife and daughter. This destructive pressure had a temporary success: King became frightened, began to doubt his own abilities, and thought about giving up and going off to live somewhere else with his family. At this point, however, having admitted to himself his feeling of powerlessness, he heard the voice of the "inner Christ" within him saying "Martin Luther, stand up for righteousness. Stand up for justice. Stand up for truth. And lo, I will be with you, even unto the end of the world."

King says that the "inner Christ" promised He would not forsake him and filled King with a power and confidence he had never known before, giving him the strength to advance along the path he had chosen. From that moment on, King truly understood the reality of a personal God who could be close to him and transform "the fatigue of despair into the buoyancy of hope." It was a milestone, and King often referred to this experience in his later life.

For Gandhi, the precondition for receiving the inner voice was rigorous purification:

> For me the Voice of God, of Conscience, of Truth, or the Inner Voice or "the Still Small Voice" mean one and the same thing. I saw no form. I have never tried, for I have always believed God to be without form. But what I did hear was like a Voice from afar and yet quite near. It was as unmistakable as some human voice definitely speaking to me, and irresistible. I was not dreaming at the time I heard the Voice. The hearing of the Voice was preceded by a terrific struggle within me. Suddenly the Voice came upon me. I listened,

> made certain it was the Voice, and the struggle ceased. I was calm.

Gandhi also said:

> For me the Voice was more real than my own existence. It has never failed me, or for that matter, anyone else. And everyone who wills can hear the Voice. It is within everyone. But like everything else, it requires previous and definite preparation.

The voice of the Self reaches with greater force those who follow the Way of the Will, because in this path—where situations are often extreme and dramatic—everything acquires more intensity. But the inner voice is nonetheless a resource that we can all draw upon. In a psychosynthesis exercise, the Italian psychiatrist Roberto Assagioli suggests visualizing an old and wise person, then having a dialogue with him or her and asking for advice. Help often comes, because, if the exercise is done correctly, the wise old person represents the Self and speaks its voice.

Inner listening, like inner seeing or visualization, is a function one can call upon for guidance and inspiration. Many creative people on all the Ways have availed themselves of it. Brahms wrote in a letter to Marie Schumann:

> Deep in the human heart, in a rather unconscious way perhaps, something often whispers and moves, which with time can resonate in the form of poetry or music.

A musician, quite obviously, listens to his inner sounds. But how about a painter? According to Kandinsky, the voice can guide to new and unexplored territories. Here obedience to one's inner voice is synonymous with spontaneity:

> Often while working one hears a voice which "dictates within"; in this case nothing is left but to obey carefully. This voice leads us on a different road, a hard one to figure out at first: the result ends up being different from one's "intention."

For Søren Kierkegaard, the Danish philosopher, the voice was an inner music allowing him to give a rhythm to his prose, to the extent that he recommended his books be read aloud in order for the reader to better appreciate them. There is a music to be heard:

> I listen to my inner forum, the happy accents of music and the deep tone of the organs; to combine them is a task that belongs to me—not to a composer, but to a man who, without great expectations from life, limits himself to this very simple one: to understand himself.

In the case of the Austrian poet Rainer Maria Rilke, the voice came from a deep level and could be heard only when all other levels were transcended:

> These days it sometimes happens that I discover how much I am listening within, so that, hesitant and modest, I learn from dialogues with myself. Something resonates deep in my being which, beyond these pages [his journal], beyond my cherished songs and all plans for future action, wants to reach the man in me. It is as if I should speak now, in this moment of lucid strength, when in my intimate being something greater than I sounds its voice: my bliss.

In still other cases, the unsought voice seeks us, comforts and leads us. This happens mainly in supreme moments of choice, or in crisis, when all has been tried again and again, and one feels lost. Then the voice points the way to follow. Annie Besant had been a feminist, free thinker, and socialist and had fought a thousand social battles, always in search of a way to achieve solidarity among all human beings. She felt she had not yet found an answer. One day, on the verge of desperation, she heard a voice: a short time later she found an answer to her questions in Theosophy and soon became a leader of the movement:

> Sitting alone in deep thought as I had accustomed to do after the sun had set, filled with an intense but nearly hopeless longing to solve the riddle of life and mind, I heard a Voice that was later to become to me the holiest sound on earth, bidding me to take courage for the light was near.

SACRIFICE

In January 1981, on a cold, misty morning, an Air Florida aircraft took off from Washington Airport full of passengers, most of whom were dreaming of a sunny holiday. The plane did not get far. Still low in the air, it struck a bridge over the Potomac River and was precipitated into the water with its crew and passengers. Help was soon on the scene. In a race for survival, the rescuers had to lift out of the icy water those who were barely managing to stay afloat. They threw life rings from helicopters—in particular, to one man in the water who, as soon as he caught them, readily passed them on to other people around him. Instead of fighting for his own ring, he passed it on at once to someone else, as though it were the most natural thing in the world—and with the life rings he passed over life itself. When the rescuers, having saved those who could be saved, were about to throw the last life ring to the man himself, there was no longer anyone to be seen. The "man in the water," as he was later called, had drowned in the icy January waters. He had sacrificed himself for others.

What is it that prompts an individual to offer his or her life with such extraordinary naturalness? What factor convinced the man in the water to pass on the life ring, instead of desperately grasping it for himself, thereby casting doubt on all the theories on human nature that affirm the innate selfishness of the human being? And what did the man in the water experience in those few moments in which, snatched away from a journey to the sun and thrown into the reality of ice and death, he sacrificed his own life?

These are difficult, perhaps impossible, questions to answer. But one thing we can say: sacrifice is the truest act a human being can perform. There is no turning back—this is the final act par excellence.

When we are feeling generous we can give something of ourselves: skills, money, time, presence. But for those who give their life, the gift is absolute. They are saying good-bye to the possibility of loving and suffering, of enjoying their existence, of having a future, of continuing to hope.

People who make such a sacrifice no longer possess anything, not even their own life. They are unimaginably light. What do they experience, and what do they think? According to the German philosopher Arthur Schopenhauer, in certain emergency situations the illusion of separate individuality is replaced by an instinctive, immediate recognition of the oneness of all beings. This is an interesting explanation, because it eliminates from sacrifice all rhetoric of self-immolation, all sentimentalism, and all secret feelings of superiority. There is no calculated motive, just a natural act.

Research was carried out on several hundred people in various European countries who had saved Jews from concentration camps during World War II. These people broke the rules imposed by the Germans—whereas the majority of the population obeyed them—and put their own lives at stake. The research shows that none of them thought they were doing anything exceptional. They were moved by principle or by care for the potential victims. Contrary to the psychoanalytical theory on this subject, none of these people were trying to act out grandiose fantasies or satisfy masochistic needs.

Another example: in 1918 the Italian explorer Umberto Nobile disappeared on an airship flying toward the North Pole. When the call for assistance came, Amundsen was at a dinner celebration. Although Amundsen's relationship with Nobile had previously been strained, he nevertheless unhesitantly offered his services. His immediate response to the appeal—"At once!"—is the archetype of absolute availability.

Many acts of sacrifice are instantaneous and are characterized by the spontaneous certainty to which we all aspire in the relationships most precious to us. But in addition to these immediate acts, there are also the sacrifices of those who risk their lives over a long period of time. In such cases, there is time to think, to be afraid, perhaps to withdraw. This type of sacrifice may happen not only on behalf of other people but also in the name of an ideal like liberty, truth, or justice. It is in such cases that we see how these ideas, apparently so abstract, are able to exert on certain people a power even greater than the force of attachment to their own life.

A memorable book collected letters written by people condemned to death because of their involvement in the European Resistance movement. They fought against Nazism, risked their lives, and lost. Imprisoned and awaiting execution, these individuals wrote letters—some full of accusations and bitterness, some serene and moving, a few showing a transpersonal awareness. One forty-eight-year-old German primary school teacher, for example, experienced in his last hours of life a feeling of unity with the All, which he described to his wife:

> I sat on the hard bench in my cell, as I had done for hundreds of hours before, and found myself deeply immersed in the All: the world, human beings, art. The difference between life and death had disappeared in a single joy, that of existence itself.

How can we explain this experience? We can think and feel in two main modes. According to the first mode, the easiest to understand and the most common, my life is my own; my survival is a victory; my individuality is a success at the expense of others; I am a prisoner of time, alone and separated from everyone and everything by dense barriers of fear and suspicion.

But according to the second mode, the one underlying sacrifice, the universe in which we live does not contain any barriers between one being and another, between living and dying, between the past and the future. My life does not belong to me: it is one with the life of plants and flowers, animals, human beings, planets, and stars. Each act we perform comes under one or the other of these two modes. It either reinforces separation or affirms unity. The heroic act of sacrifice is but one clear and extreme illustration of a choice that is open at each moment to everyone—even to those who do not wish to play the hero.

Indeed sacrifice is an attitude that all can cultivate, even when their lives are not actually at stake; but sacrifice should not be confused with any act even faintly smacking of self-inflicted hardship, moral superiority, bitter renunciation, self-aggrandizement, reproach, or blackmail. Sacrifice means having no claim and making one's very existence available to others. It is a revolutionary attitude, and its principal characteristic is never to exalt the ego, but rather to transcend it. As Cesar Chavez put it,

> when we are really honest with ourselves we must admit that our lives are all that really belongs to us. So it is how we use our lives that determines what kind of men we are. It is my deepest belief that only by giving our lives do we find life.
>
> I am convinced that the truest act of courage, the strongest act of manliness is to sacrifice ourselves for others in a total non-violent struggle for justice. To be a man is to suffer for others.

In contrast with selfishness, which greedily accumulates riches only to reap spiritual impoverishment, sacrifice leads to an unusual state of lightness. Indeed, people who sacrifice themselves do not consider anything a possession, reject privilege, and shun comfort. Sacrifice is a demonstration of the will because it requires a resolute disposition, often calling for a quick decision on vital issues. This attitude is not accompanied by loud claims of greatness or self-immolation; rather, it is ready, quick, and clean. And yet sacrifice is far from easy, because it involves the effort of assuming a position that is often against one's own interests, and possibly of facing one's own end.

Dag Hammarskjöld was the secretary general of the United Nations from 1953 to 1961. During this time he had to deal with various critical situations, and the United Nations enjoyed a period of greater importance in international affairs. Hammarskjöld based his work on a vision of the ideal, a strong sense of duty, an impressive diligence, and much humility. According to him, international problems should be treated from the standpoint of personal ethics:

> I inherited a belief that no life was more satisfactory than one of selfless service to your country—or humanity. This service required a sacrifice of all personal interests, but likewise the courage to stand up unflinchingly for your convictions concerning what was right and good for the community, whatever were the views in fashion.

Hammarskjöld died while working, when the airplane on which he was traveling crashed to the ground. Although the crash may have been an accident, it was widely believed to have been sabotage, given that this man had challenged the powerful. Whatever the truth, the fact remains that his life was lived on the basis of sacrifice, and these words—from *Markings*, his posthumously published diary—bear transparent testimony to the fact:

The ultimate surrender to the creative act—it is the destiny of some to be brought to the threshold of this in the act of sacrifice rather than the sexual act; and they experience a thunderclap of the same dazzling power.

The etymology of the word *sacrifice* is revealing: *sacer facere*, to make sacred—to rise up vertically in a single act from the profane world of greed and fear, up into the serene, still dimension of the sacred, and to transfigure one's whole life in one moment.

DEATH

A man once heard two people speaking. One of the speakers was the Angel of Death, and he was saying, "I've got several calls to make in Baghdad today." Terrified, the listener felt sure his last hour had come: Could he perhaps escape his fate? Could he run away as death was seeking him out? He suddenly jumped on a horse and galloped off to faraway Samarkand.

Meanwhile the Angel of Death was continuing his conversation. "Where is so-and-so?" he asked the other, mentioning the name of the man who had just run off. "I believe he's in the city somewhere," came the reply. "That's strange," said the Angel of Death. "I've got his name down on my list here: I am supposed to meet him in four weeks' time in Samarkand."

Inexorable—that is what death is like. We hide and run away from it; we use every trick and illusion we know to fend it off. But death will find us, whatever corner of the world we run to. Seconds, hours, years pass by; destiny runs its course; our time is limited. Yet in this brief season allotted to us, we try to forget death. Some claim that our whole existence is an organized attempt not to think about its own end. We allow ourselves to become lost in our games, and forget. But time is running out, and we are approaching the complete cessation of all we believe we are.

Nothing is more terrifying than this prospect. Yet, if we can for a moment get beyond terror and despair, we may perhaps see that there is no better time than death to free ourselves. And that nearness to death, or even the mere thought of it, can liberate.

Let us imagine approaching the point of death. The conviction that we hold the reins to our own lives—as the naïve man in the oriental story thought—is shattered. We are close to an absolute separation, a farewell to our loved ones, to our favorite projects, to all we love. Good-bye to springs full of flowers and scents, good-bye to music, to friends, to everything beautiful. And good-bye also to all the anxieties and worries that weigh us down.

Everything that seemed so serious and stable now takes on the insubstantial consistency of a dream. We no longer wear a mask, for death cannot be deceived. We are confronted with a mystery we cannot grasp, and thus become aware of the uselessness of our opinions. We live in the present, for there is no future as we know it. As we have seen in our discussion of the various Ways, these attitudes all facilitate access to the transpersonal world.

Time, too, takes on a whole new meaning and may even disappear entirely. People who almost died and then came back to life say that in the moments near death everything slows down until it stops. Those on the brink of drowning, for instance, are aware of their arms thrashing the water, of the bubbles of air rising to a distant, luminous surface—all in slow motion as in a dream. Those who have fallen into a precipice recount that their brief time in the air seemed like millennia, and it is not uncommon for them to see their whole life unroll before their eyes in a flash. These people have reached the end of time: in that moment a gleam of timelessness appears. A serious accident, a brush with danger, a critical illness, the death of a loved one, or simply the thought of death can sometimes awaken similar emotions and feelings in each one of us.

Among all the accounts of those who have reached the boundary between life and death, Jung's is one of the richest. After a heart attack, and on the point of dying, Jung felt as if he were floating far above the earth's surface, and about to leave this planet. He knew it was all over, and although this feeling was painful, it gave him a great sense of satisfaction, because there was no longer anything to desire. When Jung subsequently realized that he must return to the world of the living, he felt an unbearable oppression, which he called the "little box system"—the return to a life made up of small watertight compartments, an incomprehensible prison endowed with a hypnotic power to attract and ensnare.

In the following weeks Jung remained in a near-death state, and had the most beautiful visions and experiences. "I felt as though I were suspended in space," Jung recounted, "as if I were securely cradled in the womb of the universe, in a measureless void, but overcome with an intense feeling of happiness. I thought: 'This is eternal bliss, it cannot be described, it is too wonderful!' " This bliss, Jung went on, may be described as "a state outside of time, where present, past and future are one."

Those who practice the Way of the Will find themselves in this situation more often than others, because the risks they run confront them with the possibility of not surviving. As Hammarskjöld wrote in his diary, "death was always one of the party." Death is in the air—the possibility of extinction, which is ever present in human life, becomes palpable, like the presence of another person. Perhaps the most explicit metaphor of this state is free-falling in empty space. When death is near, there is nothing to hold onto—an invitation to total surrender.

This is a concrete possibility for mountain climbers, some of whom have survived such a free-fall and have been able to speak of their experiences. Zürich geologist Albert von St. Gallen Heim, for instance, was climbing one day when a gust of wind blew off his hat. He instinctively raised his hand to his head to catch it, lost his balance, and fell some twenty meters through space. During the fall Heim had a transpersonal experience. Subsequently he looked into this subject and collected accounts by people who had been in similar situations.

In ninety-five percent of the cases, their experiences had many of the following common factors: the absence of anxiety, despair, or physical pain and instead feelings of serenity, acceptance, and an underlying sense of security; disidentification from the body; accelerated mental activity; inner clarity; and slowing down of time. Heim wrote an article and dedicated it to the parents of victims of mountaineering deaths in the hope that, knowing about the beauty of those moments, they might in some small measure be consoled over the loss of their loved ones. Here is how Heim described his own fall:

> Everything was transfigured as though by a heavenly light and everything was beautiful without grief, without anxiety, and without pain. The memory of very tragic experiences I had had was clear but not saddening. I felt no conflict or strife; conflict had been transmuted into love. Elevated and harmonious thoughts dominated and united the individual images, and like magnificent music a divine calm swept through my soul. I became ever more surrounded by a splendid blue heaven with delicate roseate and violet cloudlets. I swept into it painlessly and softly and I saw that now I was falling freely through the air and that under me a snow field lay waiting. Objective observations, thoughts, and subjective feelings were simultaneous. Then I heard a dull thud and my fall was over.

Death was also "one of the party" in the lives of the aviation pioneers. Alone on board the *Spirit of St. Louis* during the last hours of his flight, Lindbergh looked for pockets of clear air away from rain and fog. In those moments he felt as if he had reached the very boundary of life:

> I'm on the border line of life and a greater realm beyond. . . . For twenty-five years, [my mind has] . . . been surrounded by solid walls of bone, not perceiving the limitless expanse, the immortal existence that lies outside. Is this death? Am I crossing the bridge which one sees only in last, departing moments? Am I already beyond the point from which I can bring my vision back to earth and men? Death no longer seems the final end it used to be, but rather the entrance to a new and free existence which includes all space, all time.

Those who travel along the Way of the Will acquire a special familiarity with death, and certainly many other people besides Jung have had first-rate intuitions as the result of close contact with death. The Italian poet Giuseppe Ungaretti made a number of unsuccessful attempts at writing poems in the period leading up to World War I. His poetry actually came to life in the trenches. There, surrounded by death, Ungaretti had to be quick to say what he wanted to say—with the fewest and most extraordinarily intense words:

> That is how I found my language: few words full of meaning to describe my situation at that moment—this lonely man among other lonely men, in a naked land, a terrible stoney land in which each of these men individually felt his own fragility. And at the same time they felt something far more important than war being born in their hearts: they felt the birth of affection, love for one another. They felt so small in the face of danger, so disarmed in spite of their weapons, and they knew that they were brothers.

Sometimes even thinking about death can be enough in itself to liberate and inspire. Schweitzer said of Bach that "in death he saw release from all ills, and in wonderful spiritual songs he described the calm that entered his spirit at that thought."

That this was a true spiritual experience for Bach and not just an occasional theme for artistic elaboration is shown by numerous themes he chose for his cantatas: the lullaby *Schummert ein ihr müden Augen* ("Close, tired eyes"); Cantata no. 82, *Ich habe genug* ("I have had enough"); Cantata no. 8, *Liebster Gott, wann werd' ich sterben*?" ("Dear God, when shall I die?"); Cantata no. 53, *Schlage doch gewünschte Stunde* ("Sound out, long desired hour"); and Cantata no. 156, *Ich steh' mit einem Fuss in Grabe* ("I stand with one foot in the grave").

Mozart must have felt something similar. In 1778 at the age of thirty-one, he wrote in a letter to his sick father:

> ". . . since death, when you come to think of it, is actually the ultimate purpose of our life, I have got to know this true, best friend of man so well that his image not only no longer frightens me, but calms and comforts me! And I thank God that He has given me the boon of providing . . . an opportunity to know Him as the key to our true happiness—I never go to bed without considering that, young as I am, perhaps I shall not see the next day.

It makes sense that the thought of death should evoke the numinous, as well as the idea of nothingness, of infinity, human destiny and human fragility, the meaning of life and the order of the universe. Marcus Aurelius, the philosopher emperor, suggested that one apply to one's life the thought of death on a daily basis:

> Take it that you have died today, and your life's story is ended; and henceforward regard what further time may be given to

> you as an uncovenanted surplus, and live it out in harmony with nature.

Sixteenth-century French essayist Michel de Montaigne adopted a similar attitude:

> The premeditation of death is the premeditation of liberty. A person who has learned how to die has learned how not to be a slave. Knowing how to die frees us from all subjection and constraint.

Theravada Buddhism suggests the attentive and detailed observation of decaying corpses as a means to understand the precarious and illusory nature of existence. According to the *Maha Satipatthna Sutta* (from the teachings of Buddha), contemplation consists of observing corpses in a cemetery after one, two, and three days, "swollen, bluish, and festering," and then reflecting that one's own body will meet the same fate.

In a precise progression toward nothingness, the disciple is then invited to successively contemplate corpses devoured by vultures, dogs, and jackals; skeletons with flesh and blood still attached to them; skeletons held together only by tendons; skeletons reduced to bones scattered around the cemetery ("here a bone of the hand, and there a bone of the foot, a shin bone, a thigh bone, the pelvis, a vertebral bone, the skull"); and finally, bones discolored and eventually decaying into dust.

Convincing ourselves in this brutal way of the impermanence that is the lot of every living being, and thus of the temporary conglomerate of which our personality is composed, we are released from illusory attachments and see the world for what it is—not immutable entities, but continually changing relationships. We make progress toward the victory over suffering and toward ultimate insight into the nature of things.

The Buddhist meditation on death has a hard, merciless quality: one has to look at what one least wants to see, the termination of existence. But when one courageously faces it, the very origin of anxiety disappears.

Even the death of a loved one can liberate consciousness if one is open to the transpersonal world. The Buddhist saint Milarepa wrote some very interesting pages on this subject in his autobiography. One of the most important moments of his life came from an anguishing experience. Several years after leaving home, Milarepa had returned to his birthplace and found it deserted and crumbling. He went in to explore:

> Then groping my way towards the outer rooms I found a heap of earth and rags, over which a large quantity of weeds and grass had grown. On shaking it up I found it to be a heap of human bones, which instinctively I knew to be my mother's. A deep and unutterable yearning seized me. So unbearable was the thought that I should never more see my mother that I was about to lose consciousness, when I remembered my Guru's teachings; and, communing spiritually with my mother's spirit and the divine spirits of the saints of the Kargyupta Sect, I made a pillow of my mother's bones and remained in an undistracted state of tranquillity, in clear and deep meditation, whereby I realized that it was indeed possible to save both my father and mother from the pain and miseries of *sangsaric* existence [the life of those prey to illusion]. After passing seven days and nights thus, I rose from the *samadhi*.

Chuang Tzu also lost someone dear to him—his beloved wife. Yet when the philosopher Hui Tzu came to the house to take part in the funeral, he found Chuang Tzu singing and drumming with his fingers on an upturned bowl. Hui Tzu expressed his astonishment, to which the Taoist sage replied:

> You misjudge me. When she died, I was in despair, as any man well might be. But soon, pondering on what happened,

> I told myself that in death no strange fate befalls us. . . . For not nature only but man's being has its seasons, its sequence of spring and autumn, summer and winter. If someone is tired and has gone to lie down, we do not pursue him with shouting and bawling. She whom I have lost has lain down to sleep for a while in the Great Inner Room. To break in upon her rest with the noise of lamentation would but show that I knew nothing of nature's Sovereign Law. That is why I ceased to mourn.

Artistic inspiration, inner guidance, the intensification of experience, freedom, illumination, and an awareness of the great rhythms in the universe: these are some of the possible gifts a human being may receive from the most terrifying reality of all.

8

◇
◇
◇
◇

The Characteristics of Transpersonal Experience

In this book we have examined various Ways to the Self and the corresponding experiences in the lives of creative, inspired people. These Ways are more reminiscent of a blurry mountain path than of a wide, speedy freeway—the mountain path branches off, joins another path, changes its appearance, or disappears altogether. Those ascending the mountain can choose this or that track as they climb, and even carve a new one of their own. Depending on which way they go and what heights they reach, they will see different vistas. Only from the top will their view be complete.

The same is true for transpersonal experiences. We have come across many of them along the different Ways, and, as with mountain views, it is easy to notice great differences. Some of them are little more than intense bursts of emotion; others are little short of nirvana. We have seen many different paths, but do they all lead to the same peak?

In this chapter and the final one, we shall be asking what all these experiences and ways have in common. Does it make sense to speak of a transpersonal world, qualitatively different from our normal one? Or are these phenomena merely a hodgepodge of isolated, idiosyncratic events? The answers to these questions are crucial, because if we find that the experiences we have seen do indeed have something in common, that means there is in us a single, superior source of high-grade knowledge, strength, love, and beauty.

Indeed, the transpersonal world is a vast and multifarious reality, difficult to define or to categorize. Its many manifestations in the human psyche seem, at first, unrelated. At a closer glance, however, one can see that they have certain fundamental aspects in common and that the multiplicity of phenomena we have qualified as "transpersonal" actually stem from one and the same source. These common aspects are amazement, rightness, knowledge, unity, universality, and social relevance. In the following sections we will examine these one by one.

One difficulty nevertheless remains: these characteristics are not *all* present in *all* cases. It may help us to remember that we are not dealing with inanimate objects that simply need to be cataloged, such as colored marbles, coins, or chemical substances. Ours is a far subtler task. We are attempting to identify a matrix of possible experiences. We therefore have to be flexible, and in our analysis we must resist the temptation to divide up the material into watertight hierarchical structures.

We would do well to adopt here Wittgenstein's family resemblance model. Let us imagine, says the Viennese philosopher, a family in which the many members have various traits in common but none has them all. For instance, some members, but not all, have red hair; many, but not all, have blue eyes; several have aquiline noses, but some have straight, pointed ones; almost all are tall, but here too there are exceptions. Should we conclude that these individuals have nothing in common? Of course not. Rather there is a family resemblance, and anyone meeting several members can easily see it.

Likewise, the family of transpersonal states and phenomena is extremely wide. And while its members share certain characteristics, each experience does not necessarily have all the characteristics of the others. There is a continuum of resemblances whose diversity compares less to the clear separation of floors in a building, than to nature's huge variety and wondrous richness. And yet, throughout this dazzling diversity, all transpersonal experiences bear testimony—sometimes a faint echo, sometimes a portentous presence—to the origin from which they stem: our Center, the transpersonal Self.

AMAZEMENT

At the end of *Purgatory* in the *Divine Comedy*, after having encountered the horrors of hell and having reached the top of the mountain of purification, Dante again meets Beatrice, his lover. It is a dramatic meeting: Beatrice reproaches him for having forgotten her, and Dante, devastated by her words, freezes; but then, like the icy snow in the Apennines, he melts and bursts into tears. Soon after, he is "pure and ready to leap to the stars."

In this episode Beatrice represents the highest truth a human being can conceive—that truth which the cares and distractions of life so easily eclipse. Being oblivious to the transpersonal world may be an unavoidable fact. But when, lost in futile pursuits, we are suddenly reminded of the Self, like Dante we are shocked. How could we ever have forgotten?

Compared with ordinary experience, the transpersonal world has an immeasurably greater voltage. Testimonies often speak of being dazzled, of dizziness, weeping and laughter, mental disorientation, fainting, fear, dismay, madness, and even the conviction that one is the victim of a demonic trick. These phenomena indicate that the transpersonal world is a dimension fundamentally different from the world of ordinary experience.

Amazement and wonder can be evoked by the transpersonal vision of nature. In the summer of 1816 Percy Bysshe Shelley visited the Mont Blanc valley. In those days, when mass tourism had not yet trivialized those glorious landscapes, traveling was a far more exciting adventure than it is now, because everything was viewed through innocent eyes. This is how Shelley described the emotion he felt when he first saw the Alps (which at once inspired him to write the poem "Mont Blanc"):

> Pinnacles of snow, intolerably bright, part of the chain connected with Mont Blanc shone through the clouds at intervals on high. I never knew, I never imagined what mountains were before. The immensity of these ariel summits excited, when they suddenly burst upon the sight, a sentiment of ecstatic wonder, not unallied to madness.

Similarly, Gauguin felt intense emotions in Tahiti, as he noted in his diary:

> The landscape, with its pure, shining colors dazzled and stunned me. In the past I had always been uncertain and anxious. . . . But now it was easy to paint what I saw, putting a red or a blue on the canvas without much calculation. Why would I hesitate over letting all that golden, sunny joy flow across the canvas?

We have seen that a transpersonal experience is often responsible for destructuring the mind. Completely new, unexpected elements come onto the scene, and amazement follows. According to an Indian saying, the bursting of transpersonal elements in the mind is like the moment at the theater when the curtain is raised for the show to begin, and suddenly the buzz of voices in the public melts away. When confronted with the Spirit, there is no longer any room for chatter. In the words of Nietzsche, describing his composition of *Thus Spake Zarathustra*, we see how imperiously the Self can make its way into one's mind:

> Something profoundly convulsive and disturbing suddenly becomes visible and audible with indescribable definiteness and exactness. One hears—one does not seek; one takes—one does not ask who gives: a thought flashes out like lightning, inevitably without hesitation—I have never had any choice about it. There is an ecstasy whose terrific tension is sometimes released by a flood of tears, during which one's progress varies from involuntary impetuosity to involuntary slowness. There is the feeling that one is utterly out of hand, with the most distinct consciousness of an infinitude of shuddering thrills that pass through one from head to foot; there is a profound happiness in which the most painful and gloomy feelings are not discordant in effect, but are required as necessary colors in this overflow of light.

These experiences come at the right moment. They are the response to a search, or the seal to a transformation that has been going on quietly for years. But it can also be said that from the ordinary personality's point of view, such experiences may be felt as inappropriate, like an unexpected guest or a person speaking out of turn. The transpersonal world easily breaks the rules of the personal world. It has a will of its own that takes one by surprise.

The conscious "I" can either resist or yield and cooperate with the new events. Because of its numinous content, transpersonal experience is discontinuous with the preceding mental situation. It transforms those who come into contact with it and authoritatively presents itself to consciousness, affecting every aspect of an individual's life. The result, as the German philosopher Rudolf Otto put it, is amazement (*stupor*), utter astonishment at the majesty and power of a new reality: *Mysterium tremendum et fascinans*, a mystery that fills us with awe and fascination.

RIGHTNESS

The experience of the Self does not require further confirmation, testing, or comparisons. It has its own intrinsic value and authority—not because it is a dogma but because it renders any explanation superfluous, and because it is as immediate as happiness.

Transpersonal experience is a response to profound questions, the fulfillment of a measureless need. When it comes, and as long as it lasts, we feel there is nothing else we need. We have the impression, after journeys and wanderings in remote lands, of having finally come home.

Let us take Rousseau's example. In the last years of his life, the Geneva philosopher was troubled by the recurrent idea that everyone was plotting to harm him. He became severely depressed and felt completely alone. He had found a certain relief from his torment through writing his *Confessions*, where he was able to expose himself fully and sincerely on paper. But only on his walks in the midst of nature did Rousseau succeed in attaining some degree of serenity. His words are an eloquent indication of transpersonal rightness:

> If there is a condition in which the soul finds a poise so still that it is truly able to rest and gather its whole being, without the need of remembering past or aiming at future; in which time is nothing, and the present lasts forever, beyond trace of rhythm or sequence, without any feeling of lack or of enjoyment, of pleasure or pain, of desire or dread, except the sense of one's own existence, and with only this awareness

> filling it completely; if there is such a condition, then, as long as this state lasts, whoever experiences it can be called happy. And this is not an imperfect, needy, or relative happiness such as the one we encounter with in life's pleasures, but a happiness which is plentiful, perfect, and complete, and does not leave in our soul any empty space crying to be filled. Such is the state I experienced on the island of Saint Pierre, in my solitary daydreaming, now lying on my boat as it drifted on the water, now sitting by the restless surface of a lake, or elsewhere, on the bank of a river or a stream murmuring as it flows over stones. What does one enjoy in such a situation? Nothing external, nothing except oneself and one's own existence; and as long as this state lasts, one is as self-sufficient as God is.

Rightness implies certainty, an infinitely deeper certainty than any material security can offer. There is no room for guilt, hesitation, or anxiety in this state. Here the fundamental weaknesses of every human being disappear for a time—even the fear of death.

From childhood Tennyson was in the habit of repeating his own name as a mantra, or magic formula. This practice, as he describes here, transported him to a state of transpersonal consciousness:

> The individuality itself seemed to dissolve and fade away into boundless being; and this not a confused state, but the clearest of the clearest, the surest of the surest, the weirdest of the weirdest, utterly beyond words, where death was an almost laughable impossibility, the loss of personality but the only true life.

Rightness is deeply connected with the sense of self. One feels that it is right and good to be alive. But this realization does not concern only oneself. Rightness can also be seen in the lives of other people, in nature, or in the order of reality, which is seen to be governed by an Intelligent law. This rightness does not exist in a world apart, or in spite of the sufferings and horrors to which humankind is subject. Instead, it sees these as forming a necessary part of the whole. This is no reassuring, fatalistic theory; rather, it is an intuitive knowledge of the fundamental, inexplicable "all-rightness," beyond good and evil, of all that exists, exactly as it is.

KNOWLEDGE

The person who has had a transpersonal experience stands before panoramas of outstanding significance. As the French philosopher Maine de Biran wrote, such a person reaches another level of consciousness:

> It seems that there is within me a higher sense—like a face to my soul—which at certain moments . . . turns its attention to another dimension. It is an order of things and ideas higher than anything to do with common life, or with the interests of this world which occupy men so exclusively. I then have the intimate feeling, a strong impression of certain truths, that I am in contact with an invisible order, with a superior state of existence, that is completely different from the one in which we normally exist.

Transpersonal knowledge is complete, immediate, relevant, surprising, and profound. It is, first of all, complete knowledge. It is not the acquisition of information bit by bit, in the way one might become familiar with the workings of a machine, the composition of a substance, or the events of history—by breaking a subject down into fragments. Transpersonal knowledge comes whole and indivisible.

It is immediate. No words, deductions, or explanations of any sort are needed as intermediaries. Often transpersonal knowledge arrives unexpectedly; but even when it emerges slowly, it is never part of the logical realm.

It is relevant. However supermundane it may be, that which has been understood takes root in the heart and makes sense in the light of the questions and the fundamental problems of human life.

It is surprising. Because it is completely different from the formerly adopted mental outlook, it can throw us into a state of crisis, because it obliges us to revolutionize our way of thinking.

Finally, it is profound. A transpersonal experience brings us into contact with a richness our minds are ill-equipped to handle. Indeed there are more things in heaven and earth than are dreamed of in our philosophy.

In addition to the kind of intuition to which de Biran refers, full-blown enlightenment is also possible. Intuition is seeing a truth for a moment at a distance; enlightenment means complete fusion of the I with the Self—gnosis. It is a form of knowledge that transforms the knower more than any other. Realities that once terrified or preoccupied us, such as death and illness, are now seen with serenity and humor. It has the effect of waking us up, or of unmasking a deception to which we had been a victim for a long time.

Experiences of this kind are described in the accounts of Narendra (who later took the name of Swami Vivekananda)—a brilliant, young, and somewhat skeptical student of Ramakrishna. Narendra was predisposed to visionary phenomena: for instance, from early childhood he would fall asleep seeing a wonderful point of light that changed, assuming various colors, grew into a large, luminous ball and then exploded, covering his whole body with a bright white liquid. Narendra would then fall asleep. The same thing happened each night.

Narendra first heard about Ramakrishna at the university when an English literature professor, speaking of Wordsworth, compared the poet's ecstatic perception of nature with enlightenment often referred to in the Indian tradition, and mentioned Ramakrishna as the person who was most familiar with these phenomena. Narendra then went in search of Ramakrishna. When they met, Ramakrishna turned to him and, following an ancient Indian custom of physical contact between master and disciple, placed his right foot on the young man. Recounting the experience, Narendra stated:

> Immediately, I had a wonderful experience. My eyes were wide open, and I saw that everything in the room, including the walls themselves, was whirling rapidly around and receding, and at the same time, it seemed to me that my consciousness of self, together with the entire universe, was about to vanish into a vast, all-devouring void. This destruction of my consciousness of self seemed to me to be the same thing as death.

This was the beginning of Narendra's enlightenment. But he was not ready for it, and soon cried out "Ah, what are you doing to me? Don't you know I have my parents at home?" Ramakrishna laughed, touched him on the chest, and Narendra returned to his normal state of consciousness.

After this incident Narendra had an ambivalent attitude toward Ramakrishna and suspected that he had been hypnotized by him. A short time later, however, when Narendra and a friend were making fun of Vedanta teachings, Ramakrishna approached, touched him once again, and this time it was unquestionably the real thing:

> And then, at the marvellous touch of the Master, my mind underwent a complete revolution. I was aghast to realizethat there really was nothing whatever in the entire universe but God. I remained silent, wondering how long this state of mind would continue. It didn't pass all day. I got back home, and I felt just the same there; everything I saw was God.

UNITY

Our minds formulate distinctions that turn into such dichotomies as ugly/beautiful, good/bad, light/dark, pleasure/pain, before/after, I/you. These differences, necessary as they are, bring about comparisons and choices, and thus anxiety and conflict.

They are inner dichotomies—the contrast between reason and instinct, for instance, or between the real and the ideal. They are also outer dichotomies, appearing in our relationship with the world: we feel separate from external reality and people, and this outlook is at the root of fear and hostility toward everything that is other than ourselves. Finally, this fragmentation may be carried to the very structure of reality. It is then that all people, things, and events appear chaotic, conflicting, or meaningless.

Unitive consciousness has a different outlook. First of all, desire is absent, so there are no preferences. If preferences do not exist, there is no need to make choices. Without choices there are no distinctions. And where no distinctions are present, everything is one.

Let us take an example. One evening the Italian poet Giovanni Pascoli was returning home alone under the starry sky. Solitude, the thought of his father's tragic murder by gunshot, and a longing for his mother evoked a daydream in which his dear ones were surrounding him with love, taking him with them to the "world beyond, so quiet and gentle." The contrast between dream and reality, however, filled Pascoli with pain. Then, quite unexpectedly, something happened that carried the poet to a world beyond his own personal reality of longing and memories. He saw a shooting star:

> Suddenly I saw a globe of gold, a ball of fire very slowly falling from the sky. And it plunged into the great green expanse, softly silent. Oh! That globe from the sky! It was not the puny

> shot from your gun, mortal man. It came down from the deep blue, calm and soundless. . . . I forgot so many misfortunes; as in a dream I saw the falling stars ablaze, and I see them still, like a shepherd sitting on a rock. . . . It caused me no pain to be a star, which, shining, was descending into the darkness. . . . And I felt my life merge into the great All.

In other cases, the realization of unity comes from observation and research. Goethe spent much time contemplating the reality of biological evolution. At the age of thirty-five, he identified the intermaxillary bone in the human skeleton, a discovery that not only marked the separation between human being and ape but at the same time revealed the continuity uniting human beings with the whole of nature.

Why so much fuss over a bone? Goethe explained in a letter:

> Man is very closely related with animals. Only the harmony of the whole makes each being what it is, and man's being is due as much to the form and nature of his upper jaw, as to the shape of the last phalanx in his little toe. Each creature is but a note, a nuance in a great harmony, which must be studied as a whole, otherwise each individual part becomes a lifeless object.

Goethe wrote to his friend, the German philosopher Johann Gottfried Herder: "I have found it—not gold, nor silver, but what gives me unspeakable joy—the *Os intermaxillare* in man!" The jubilation Goethe experienced in discovering the intermaxillary bone came from having found the missing piece in a great mosaic, and that made it possible to see the whole in which every part has its own place and its own dignity.

Seeing unity, then, gives joy, just as multiplicity weighs down and disorients. In multiplicity attention is divided, feelings are tormented, desires are in conflict, and the mind is crowded. Divisions consume mental energy as well as emotional energy, whereas unity restores and lightens the mind.

Feeling that one has become merged "with the great All," as Pascoli experienced, means no longer yearning for lost love. Perceiving human beings as entities—separate from the rest of nature—generates mental tension. Seeing them as a note in a great symphony, as did Goethe, relieves tension and generates joy.

When in this state, we no longer feel that what we ardently desire is elsewhere, we no longer feel deprived or excluded. Poet Rabindranath Tagore recounts an experience:

> I had so long viewed the world with external vision only, and so had been unable to see its universal aspect of joy. When of a sudden, from some innermost depth of my being, a ray of light found its way out, it spread over and illuminated for me the whole universe, which then no longer appeared like heaps and things and happenings, but was disclosed to my sight as one whole.

UNIVERSALITY

Henry David Thoreau felt freer and more lucid in the moments between sleep and waking:

> I am conscious of having, in my sleep, transcended the limits of the individual, and made observations and carried on conversations which in my waking hours I can neither recall nor appreciate. As if in sleep our individual fell into the infinite mind, and at the moment of awakening we found ourselves on the confines of the latter.

This is a good example of universality as a characteristic of transpersonal experiences. In the transpersonal world one is not restricted by the narrow confines of one's private experience, or overwhelmed by desires, or oppressed by the dramas of one's life. Selfishness is seen as awkward and pathetic.

There is an end to the distinction between "yours" and "mine," the obsession with owning things, and partisanship. The most besetting of problems loses its urgency, and our greatest accomplishments seem like children's games. Sometimes an awareness of infinity shines through and expands the mind, revolutionizing our outlook. Once the particular has been transcended, universality can be glimpsed. This is true catharsis.

Becoming aware of universality can sometimes lead to a radical change in the way one sees oneself. This was the case for the French writer and pilot Antoine de Saint-Exupéry, who experienced his most beautiful moments when flying:

> And so you feel yourself carried away by this internal migration no one ever spoke to you about. . . . Suddenly, by virtue of a midnight test which stripped you of all accessories, you discovered in yourself a person of whom you were unaware. . . . Someone great and whom you will never forget. And it is yourself. . . . He has opened his wings, he is no longer bound to the perishable goods of this world, he has agreed to die for all men and thus entered into something universal. A mighty breath sweeps through him. And here he is, shed of his matrix, the sovereign lord that lay dormant within you: man. You are the equal of the musician who composes, of the physicist who broadens the horizons of knowledge. . . . You have reached that altitude where all loves have but a common measure. You may have suffered, you may have felt lonely, your body may have found no refuge, but into its open arms today you have been received by love.

Coming into contact with the universal provides relief because it helps to transcend the contradictory, shaky world of individual reality and to enter transpersonal certainty. Moreover, it vivifies because of the encounter with a reality that belongs to all beings, and which therefore possesses a force that our private ideas and emotions do not have. Universality clarifies the way we see things, because it lifts us above individual limited and distorted points of view. Finally, universality gives sense to our existence; for human life, if seen as an episode separate from everything else, loses its significance. Hell consists in being stuck with this feeling of deep, terrifying loneliness.

In many cases universality and particularity mutually exclude each other: the former frees, the latter binds and oppresses. But it is also possible for the particular and the universal to coincide. Then the infinite can be seen in the smallest detail of everyday life. It was in this sense that the poet Leopardi was conscious of the infinite in a voice or a distant sound, echoing in vast spaces, like thunder in the country, or in the song of farm workers, or even in the lowing of the oxen. Blake saw the universe in a grain of sand. And Pasteur said he could see everywhere the inescapable expression of the infinite in the world.

SOCIAL RELEVANCE

Johann Sebastian Bach, like all great artists, knew happy moments of inspiration. This inspiration was converted into musical notes written down on paper, and over the following centuries they were transformed into sound by countless interpreters. These sounds were then recorded, among others, onto the tape which I am now hearing through my portable cassette recorder as I wait for the bus. The sounds recorded on the tape in the form of magnetic information become electrical impulses that travel through the wires of the stereo headphones, and the sounds reach my ears. Through this highly improbable route Bach comes to me, enlarging my vision of life, giving me beauty and happiness.

A basic principle is at work here. Transpersonal influence spreads beyond its own happening and, in some cases, lives on in the form of a work of art, a scientific discovery, an invention, a social or religious movement, a humanitarian initiative. The action of the Self becomes concrete: it stretches out into space and time, transforming people's ideas and emotions, sometimes even their whole lives. No experience takes place in a vacuum. And no experience is purely individual. A person's inner state is transmitted to others. It is communicated not only by words and actions, but through a person's whole being.

The beneficial effect of an individual living in the transpersonal world is intense and is visible to those who are physically close to him or her. Those in contact with the world of the Self radiate charisma, which many people—especially simple people—notice at once, and to which they are attracted as a thirsty person is attracted to water.

In Indian culture, where greater attention is paid to the subtle levels of reality, there is a custom known as *darshan*—the transmission, through mere presence, of transpersonal consciousness. The American journalist William Shirer tells how the Indian crowds sought *darshan* from Gandhi. Once, in 1931 during a train journey from Delhi to Ahmedabad, thousands of people at every stop crowded around the compartment in which Gandhi was traveling:

> They were fulfilled by the sight of him and especially by receiving his darshana. . . . They felt in the presence of the great man that something immense was suddenly happening in their drab lives.

Those in contact with the transpersonal world see and experience a reality that is valid for all men and women. They inevitably transmit something of this reality to those around them. It is an extension of themselves, rather like the scent of a flower or sun radiance. Everyone knows that being close to a creative, loving, or serene person makes us feel more creative, loving, or serene. That person's presence enriches and uplifts us. This is what the crowds were seeking in Gandhi. And many individuals who have been in close contact with inspired people testify to this fact. There is an emanation that heals, regenerates, and gives hope to those exposed to it, and reminds them of something precious they had forgotten.

Let us take a spectacular example of transpersonal radiation. The Russian noble Motovilov was a disciple of the great mystic Russian, Seraphim of Sarov, and has left a most valuable testimony of a meeting he had with him. Motovilov had asked Seraphim how to recognize the Divine Spirit. Seraphim gave him some answers, but Motovilov remained unsatisfied. Seraphim then took him by the shoulders and continued to speak to him. Motovilov recounts:

> Picture to yourself the center of the sun in the most dazzling brightness of its noonday rays, and in this center the face of the man who is conversing with you. You see his lips move, you watch the changing expression of his eyes, you hear his voice; you are conscious that someone is holding you by the shoulders. Yet not only do you not see the hands which hold you, but you do not see yourself, nor the man's figure, only the dazzling sphere of light spreading in a radius of many feet, flooding the snow on the field, and the falling sleet, and myself, and the great stars.

Motovilov continued by saying that he felt on that occasion a peace no words could describe—a warmth, a wonderful sweetness, and an extraordinary joy in his heart. And he smelled a perfume unimaginably finer than any one might buy in the best shops of Kazan.

Not only inner states but also exceptional capacities may be transmitted. Take the case of Ramana Maharshi and the English journalist Paul Brunton. Brunton had reached the Maharshi after a long exploratory trip in the Middle East and the Orient, in search of wizards, gurus, miracle workers, and mysteries of all sorts. At his first meeting with Ramana, Brunton asked him the typical questions of an eager student: What must I do to attain freedom? Why do I not make any progress in meditation? Do I need a guide? etc. The written accounts show that Ramana's answers were not particularly original either. However, Brunton extended his stay and on several occasions meditated with Ramana. After a few days he wrote:

> During these daily meditations in the potent neighbourhood of the sage, I have learnt how to carry my thoughts inward to an ever-deepening point. It is impossible to be in frequent contact with him without becoming lit up inwardly, as it were, mentally illumined by a sparkling ray from his spiritual orb.

One evening something very beautiful happened:

> The brain has passed into a state of complete suspension, as it does in deep sleep. . . . Yet my sense of awareness has been drawn out of the narrow confines of the separate personality.
>
> I find myself outside the rim of world-consciousness. The planet, which has so far harbored me, disappears. I am in the midst of an ocean of blazing light.
>
> I have drunk the Platonic Cup of Lethe, so that yesterday's bitter memories and tomorrow's anxious cares have disappeared completely.

9

◇

The Self

◇

◇

◇

A Persian poem from the twelfth century—Attar's *Conference of the Birds*—celebrates the Simurgh, a wonderful and mighty bird, living in its abode, inaccessible to mortals. The Simurgh is able to answer all questions, solve all problems, heal all evil. No one, however, has ever seen it. Only once, in China—a faraway country—a passerby picked a feather that had fallen from the sky, a feather so beautiful it made everybody put up all kinds of hypotheses about the extraordinary bird from which it had come. Meanwhile the Simurgh was flying, free and invisible, in some distant, unknown region of the cosmos.

In speaking about the transpersonal Self we may end up with just that—an exquisite feather and a bunch of hypotheses. We have data on peak experiences, but the Self remains elusive and paradoxical. It can be illustrated by a thousand theories without being fully explained by any. And yet the Self is there, everywhere around us, for all of us alike—geniuses and nongeniuses, children and grown-ups, rich and poor, male and female—available if we simply ask, visible if we only look. We could say about its discovery what Russian novelist Vladimir Nabokov wrote about the birth of mind in a child: "[It] is the stab of wonder that accompanies the precise moment when, gazing at a tangle of twigs and leaves, one suddenly realizes that what seemed a natural component of that tangle is a marvelously disguised insect or bird."

In spite of the difficulties, it may still be worthwhile to try to make some sense of the Self—even theoretical sense. Let us begin by looking at a few certainties we can count on.

The experiences we have seen in this book show that throughout human history certain individuals have realized abilities and states of consciousness of exceptional value. They are the peaks of human possibilities and form the basis for the greatest accomplishments of all civilizations: masterpieces of art, scientific discoveries, ethical and social renewal, philosophical systems, geographic discoveries, and religious movements.

These transpersonal phenomena have an intrinsic existence of their own. They are not a mere product of the imagination. Since they are found in all cultures, they are not simply local or random events. They are too genuine and immediate to be considered compensations or delusions. They are often rich in positive consequences, so they cannot be dismissed as excesses or as madness. Finally, transpersonal experiences do not belong to the same level of consciousness as other phenomena of the mind: they are numinous and universal.

These facts are, I believe, self-evident. From them we may derive a number of hypotheses.

First hypothesis: The abilities and experiences we have seen in a limited number of exceptional people are not isolated events, but form part of the potential heritage of all humankind. Studies of near-death experiences, investigations into altered states of consciousness, information from comparative religion and cultural anthropology, anecdotal but well-documented evidence of religious awareness, psychotherapeutic practice, the experiences of those involved in various forms of meditation, dance and prayer, the study of transpersonal states in sport and in extreme situations, sociological research, the material on states accompanying childbirth—these and other factors tell us that transpersonal experiences are fairly common, even if those who have them lack the means to describe them fully.

In this book we have concentrated on the most creative and enlightened people because their experiences, in addition to carrying great power and beauty, are often better documented. These people have succeeded in putting into words the abilities and potentials that are present in all of us. A study of what they have felt and perceived is concretely and practically relevant for all of us and for our possible future.

Second hypothesis: All transpersonal abilities and experiences form part of a single family and stem from the same source, which we have called the "Self" in order to indicate the most authentic identity of each human being. In other words, in the biopsychospiritual makeup of a human being there exists a higher transpersonal Center from which these experiences and abilities originate, and this Center is our truest being.

From the evidence we have gathered in this book, there are several points we could make about this Center. While our ordinary sense of identity is founded on boundaries, attachment, possession, competition, and anxiety over death, the Self has a sense of identity based on the pure awareness of being and unity with the All. Its very essence is a consciousness free of all contents, beyond time and cultural conditioning of culture. From it radiate higher qualities such as love, peace, joy, and strength. It is the source of creative inspiration and higher intelligence. It has a serene, broad perspective, originating in a cosmic viewpoint. It is the ultimate life principle, possibly the deathless nucleus of each human being.

The Self, however, is almost always invisible. At rare times it causes particularly intense experiences, such as those we have seen in this book. For some people it may become the Center around which the personality is organized. Nevertheless, it remains unconscious for the vast majority of us, concerned as we are with more mundane matters, far removed from the transpersonal levels.

Third hypothesis: It is possible to achieve some awareness of the Self, express it in one's life, and recognize it in others. Certain attitudes and techniques make this undertaking possible for a great number of human beings. In this connection we speak of Ways: journeys made of attempts, errors, learning experiences, and achievements. Human life is, or can be, *in motion*—a journey toward greater meaning and awareness. One cannot arrive at a full realization of the Self by accident, by mistake, or unexpectedly, but only through a systematic approach that mobilizes all of one's attention and every resource at one's disposal.

The *fourth hypothesis* is that the Self represents the next stage in human evolution—a stage that various exceptional individuals have already glimpsed, but which may one day become the heritage of all people. From this perspective, evolution is a process of self-organization and self-renewal occurring at physical, biological, sociocultural, psychological, and spiritual levels. Many recent and crucial developments in science are relevant to this theme. In the study of various subjects—ranging from chemical substances to social behaviors, from vortices in fluids to economic fluctuations to meteorological phenomena—order has been discovered to emerge spontaneously from chaos. Mathematical models such as Mandelbrot's fractal geometry or Thom's catastrophe theory, chemical models like Prigogine's dissipative structures or Eigen's hypercycles, biological models such as Maturana and Varela's concept of *autopoiesis*, and general models such as Haken's synergetics, show that order may spontaneously be produced from disorder.

In his day Freud had adopted hydraulic models as metaphors in psychodynamics. Transpersonal psychology can see in the phenomena of spontaneous order a useful analogy to illustrate the emergence of coherence and unsuspected harmony from preexisting chaos in the human psyche. Intuitions, creativity, aesthetic enjoyment, the feeling of unity with nature and the cosmos, illuminations, and all the experiences we have studied in this book are understandable, less by Doctor Freud's panting old pistons and anxious compressions then through the splendid geometries of the new science.

A corollary of these hypotheses is that forgetting the Self —our truest and most genuine being—in our own lives and in the lives of others, will cause us to struggle with countless problems, and to lead a false, miserable, or pathological existence. We may become like the rich beggar who lived in the small attic of a grand palace, without knowing that he was the owner of the whole building. Denying, ignoring, or mocking our own or others' supreme capacities for intelligence, love, and creativity, and allowing this attitude to form the basis for a whole society—its institutions, educational system, relationships between people, work and living conditions—can only result in unhappiness, disharmony, and sickness.

It is essential therefore that the Self be recognized in all its areas of expression, especially those which have to do specifically with the development, health, and well-being of all individuals.

First, this task applies to the field of *education*. Recognizing the existence of the Self in a child (and in students in general) means giving life to all that is valid in that person. Education in its truest sense means helping an individual along the path to the Self. All the abilities and experiences we have studied in this book can be recognized and stimulated: inventiveness, empathy, courage, concentration, aesthetic appreciation, intuition, attention to detail, analytical and synthetic thought, the ability to evoke joy through the body, awareness of invisible worlds and the expansion of consciousness, a constructive attitude toward pain—just to mention a few. In this way, education is no longer purely a transfer of information, but an evocation of the "universal human being."

Psychotherapy is another vast field where recognition of the Self is decisive. ("Psychotherapy" should be understood here not only as the practice of curing neurotic or psychotic patients, but more generally as the counseling of anyone who wants to learn and grow.) The transpersonal dimension in psychotherapy offers enormous benefits:

- ◇ It changes our self-image and gives us a wider and more truthful sense of identity.
- ◇ It heals wounds and past traumas, evoking beneficial energies, and redeeming wrongs and violations that our personal psychological equipment would not ordinarily be able to handle.
- ◇ It changes our perspective and helps us perceive reality in an entirely different context.
- ◇ It gives guidance in the basic choices of our life, a guidance such as only the wisest of sages could offer.
- ◇ It integrates experience and transforms a chaos of piecemeal, free-floating fragments into a cosmos, a harmonious order.
- ◇ It reveals meaning and value in our life, even in the most trying or apparently absurd situations.
- ◇ It helps us to transcend our narrow sphere of petty concerns and to adopt a universal outlook.

In *medicine*, too, the recognition of the Self can have revolutionary results: the human organism is seen not only as a complex system of biochemical balances but also as the embodiment of a Self—a living, timeless being much vaster and higher than an ill organism. The medicine of drugs and tests, of anonymous hospitals and institutionalized loneliness, of transplants and artificial hearts, is not enough. Only a relationship between an "I" and a "thou," as Buber said, can truly heal.

Seen from a transpersonal perspective, illness takes on a new significance: the reality of pain is no longer an overwhelming presence but an opportunity for reviewing one's life and changing one's outlook. Patients can learn not to identify themselves solely with a sick body, but to understand that their identity extends to regions of their being where sickness and pain never reach. When they are gravely ill or close to death, the membrane separating them from the higher levels of consciousness becomes more and more tenuous.

Moreover, the period of confinement—so often characterized by loneliness, boredom, confusion, or despair—can be used creatively. When everyday life is interrupted by illness, when the normal roles cannot be played and one's sensitivity becomes more acute, new perspectives open up before the patients, which they can be helped to recognize and use. Finally, in conjunction with newly acquired knowledge about psychosomatic medicine, psychoneuroimmunology, the work with terminal patients, and the therapeutic effect of positive emotions, the vision of the Self can transform the very way in which medicine is understood today.

Religion, too, can be helped by an empirical study of transpersonal states. All religions are based on the transpersonal experiences of their founders and other inspired individuals. However, they are also public institutions with all their shortcomings, beginning with failure in their central task: to bring human beings into contact with the sacred. The study of transpersonal experiences leads to the core of religion, shows beyond dogmatism the universality of the Self, and can therefore foster religious unity.

There are many other spheres in which recognition of the Self would lead to openness and facilitate revolutionary changes: politics, for example, or sport, art, entertainment, or business. But the necessary condition for such a transformation in any field is recognition of the Self *in ourselves*. Accepting this reality—in whatever form we might choose to verbalize or interpret it—will lead to a radical revision of many aspects in our lives that we deceivingly thought we knew so well, and will set off a time bomb beneath various mental assumptions we previously took for granted.

First, there will be a revision of our self-image: we will realize that we are more than we thought ourselves to be and that under our surface identity there lives a deeper and richer sense of who we are. The models with which culture and society provide us for our self-understanding, we discover, do not correspond to what we feel. They are like the washing-machine instructions which consistently refer to a button that is not there. We do not recognize ourselves in these models. We know they do not describe us as we really are, so we have a vague but persistent feeling that something is just not right.

In addition to transforming our self-image, recognition of the Self also enables us to see our needs and aspirations in a new light: are they as they appear—the needs for security, love, recognition, wealth—or do they not hide a deeper and all-encompassing need, the need for wholeness and happiness which only transpersonal realization can give?

We also come to see our problems in a different way. Depression, anxiety, and dissatisfaction are not pathological states to be eliminated or anesthetized as soon as possible—they are signals that we are not heading in the right direction in our lives, and that we need to look elsewhere or redefine what we are seeking. Or they may be signs of a transformation, a hidden work that will lift our personality onto a new plane of existence.

In other words, the entire way in which we interpret reality is changed. It is as in the Jewish story of the mad prince: he believed himself to be a turkey and would scratch around, naked, on the ground, picking up breadcrumbs under the table. The court physicians had tried everything they could to cure him, but all in vain. Finally, a little old man stepped forward. "Let me do it my way," he said. The king, in despair, accepted his offer.

The little old man at once undressed and went under the table himself. He then started behaving like a turkey and befriended the prince. For a while things continued in this vein. The little old man then had two pairs of trousers brought. "Why are you putting on trousers?" the prince asked in astonishment. "One can quite easily wear trousers and still be a turkey," answered the old man. So the prince also put on a pair of trousers. After a time the same thing happened with two shirts: "Anyone can wear a shirt and still be a turkey." Little by little, without his views ever being questioned, the prince assumed a type of behavior more in keeping with human reality. More time passed, and the little old man invited him to sit at the table to eat: "One can eat at the table and still be a turkey." Finally, the prince forgot all about being a turkey. He began to think and act with the qualities and the dignity that were truly his.

As in the prince's case, there exists in us a whole identity, endowed with qualities and abilities of the highest order, which we do not recognize we have. We therefore live a life far below our psychological and spiritual means. Also, there are ways of discovering—or rediscovering—who we are and of what we are capable. Sometimes this is an easy process that is carried out in an elegant fashion, as in the case of the prince and the little old man. At other times it is fraught with trials and errors, doubts and sheer hard work.

But it is always worth it.

References

THE WAY OF BEAUTY

14. Plato. *Banquet*, 211a.

15–16. Chekhov, Anton. *Selected Letters*. L. Hellman, ed. London: Picador, 1955, p. 142.

16. *Leopardi autobiografico*. M. Bonifazi, ed. Ravenna: Longo, 1984, p. 108.

17. Matheopoulos, Helena. *Maestro—Encounters with the Conductors of Today*. London: Hutchinson, 1982, p. 11.

18. Ruskin, John. *Viaggi in Italia 1840–45*. A. Brilli, transl. Firenze: Passigli, 1985, p. 163.

18. Schumann, Robert and Clara. *Journal Intime*. Yves Hucher, ed. Paris: Buchet/Chastel, 1967, pp. 265–267.

19. Geffroy, Gustave. *Claude Monet: sa vie, son oeuvre*. Paris: Macula, 1980.

19. Van Gogh, Vincent. Letter 380 to Theo, october 1984, in Van Gogh, Vincent. *Self-Portrait*. London: Thames & Hudson, 1961, p. 222.

19. Hamilton, Nigel. *The Brothers Mann*. London: Secker Warburg, 1978, p. 99.

19. Zamoyski, Adam. *Chopin*. London: Granada, 1979, p. 239.

19. Berlioz, Hector. *Autobiography*, in *Warner's Library of the World's Best Literature*. Vol. IV. New York: 1896, pp. 1817–1818.

21. Flaubert, Gustave. *Correspondance*, II, p. 19.

22. Fitzgerald, F. Scott. *Letters*. A. Turnbull, ed. New York: Penguin, 1963, p. 612.

23. Hanson, Lawrence. *Gaugain*. Milano: Rizzoli, 1958, p. 254.

23–24. Petrarca. *Epistole Familiari*, XV, 11.

24. On Courbet: De Miceli, Mario. "Courbet," in *I Protagonisti*. Vol. 10. Milano: C.E.I., p. 185.

24. Goethe, Wolfgang von. *Autobiography (Dichtung und Wahreit)*. Trad. J. Oxendorf. Vol. II, Book XII, p. 165.

25–26. Saba, Umberto. "Quello che resta da fare ai poeti," in Saba, Umberto. *Prose*. Milano: Mondadori, 1964, pp. 756–757.

27. Van Gogh, Vincent. Letter 347 to Theo, 16 december 1883, in Van Gogh, Vincent. *Self-Portrait*. London: Thames & Hudson, 1961, p. 192.

28. Shelley, Percy Bysshe. *Shelley's Prose: or, The Trumpet of a Prophesy*. D. L. Clark, ed. University of New Mexico Press: 1966, pp. 282–283.

29. Keats, John. Letter to Richard Woodhouse, 27 october 1818.

30. Maurois, André. *Prometheus—The Life of Balzac*. Trad. N. Denny. New York: Harper & Row, 1965, pp. 57–58.

30–31. Valéry, Paul. *Degas Manet Morisot*. D. Paul, transl. New York: Pantheon Bollingen, 1960, pp. 54–55.

31–32. Neruda, Pablo. *Memoirs*. H. Martin, transl. New York: Penguin, 1977, p. 171.

34. Lamartine, Alphonse de. *Confidences*. Book VI.

34–35. Wordsworth, William. Letter to Dorothy Wordsworth, 6–12 september 1790, in *Letters of William Wordsworth*. A. Hill, ed. Oxford: Oxford University Press, 1984, p. 3.

35. Thoreau, Henry David. *A Writer's Journal*. New York: Dover, 1960, pp. 93–94.

36. Renoir, Jean. *Renoir mio padre*. Milano: Garzanti, 1962, p. 420.

36. Elsen, Albert. *Rodin*. New York: Museum of Modern Art, 1963, p. 163.

37. Da Vinci, Leonardo. *Codice Atlantico*, 141.

37. Panofsky, E. *La vita e le opere di Albrecht Durer*. Milano: Feltrinelli, 1979, p. 361.

37. Sullivan, Michael. *Symbols of Eternity—The Art of Landscape Painting in China*. Stanford: Stanford University Press, 1979, p. 48.

37. Shikes, Ralph E. *Pissarro: His Life and Work*. New York: Horizon, 1980, p. 23.

37. Cézanne, Paul. Letter CXCIII to Emile Bernard, 8 september 1906, in Cézanne, Paul. *Letters*. J. Rewald, ed. London: Bruno Cassirer, 1941, p. 262.

38. Leslie, Charles Robert. *Memoirs of the Life of John Constable*. Oxford: Phaidon, 1951, pp. 323, 327.

38. Petrarca. *Epistulae Metricae*, I, 6.

38. Delacroix, Eugène. *Diary 1822–1863*. 6 may 1852 and 13 july 1855.

39. Tchaikovsky, Modeste. *The Life and Letters of Peter Ilich Tchaikovsky*. Letter 24 november. London: John Lane, 1878, p. 325.

39. Lockspeiser, Edward. *Debussy—la vita, le opere*. Milano: Bocca, 1946, p. 214.

39. Wagner, Riccardo. *Autobiografia*. Trad. Sergio Varini. Milano: Dall' Oglio, 1983, p. 498.

40. Panofsky, E. *La vita e le opere di Albrecht Durer*. Milano: Feltrinelli, 1979, p. 361.

40–41. Wolfe, Thomas. *The Autobiography of an American Novelist*. Cambridge: Harvard University Press, 1983, pp. 30–31.

41. Allason, Barbara. *Goethe a colloquio*. n. 249, 4 novembre 1823, Cancelliere Muller. Torino: Da Silva, 1947.

42. Delacroix, Eugène. *Diary 1822–1863*. 28 april 1854.

43. Hanson, Lawrence. *Gaugain*. Milano: Rizzoli, 1958, p. 154.

43–44. Da Vinci, Leonardo. *Codice Urbinate*, 5 r.

44. Lisle, Laurie. *Portrait of an Artist—A Biography of Georgia O'Keeffe*. New York: Washington Square Press, 1980, p. 81.

44. Rothenberg, Albert. *The Emerging Goddess*. Chicago: University of Chicago Press, 1979, p. 114. See also Miller, Arthur. *Imagery in Scientific Thought*. Boston: Birkhauser, 1984, p. 244.

44–45. Watson, James. *The Double Helix*. New York: Signet, 1968, p. 118.

45. O'Neill, John. *The Life of Nikola Tesla, Prodigal Genius*. London: Granada, 1968, p. 276.

45–46. Blofeld, John. *The Tantric Mysticism of Tibet*. New York: Dutton, 1970, p. 86.

46. On Corot: *Landowska on Music*. D. Restout, ed. New York: Stein & Day, p. 368.

46. Jung, Carl Gustav. *Ricordi Sogni Riflessioni*. Milano: Il Saggiatore, 1965, p. 211.

46. Fouquet, Jacques. *La vie d'Ingres*. Paris: Gallimard, 1930, p. 170.

46. Westernhagen, Curt von. *Wagner—L'uomo, il creatore*. Milano: Mondadori, 1983, p. 63.

46. Weil, Alexandre. *Schiller*. Paris: Dentu, 1855, p. 98.

47–48. Seiberling, Grace. *Monet's Series*. New York: Garland Publishing, 1981, p. 274.

48. *Conoscere De Chirico*. I. De Chirico and D. Porzio, eds. Milano: Mondadori, 1979, p. 15.

48. Moore, Henry. *My Ideas, Inspiration and Life as an Artist*. London: Ebury Press, 1986, p. 25.

49. Micheli, P. "Ricordi Pascoliani," in *Pan*, 1932.

50. On Baudelaire: Huisman, Philippe. *Lautrec visto da Lautrec*. Milano: Garzanti, 1964, p. 200.

50–51. Schiller, Johann Cristoph. Letter 1, december 1788.

51–52. Keats, John. Letter to George and Thomas Keats, 21 december 1817.

52–53. Hocquard, Jean-Victor. *La Pensée de Mozart*. Paris: Editions du Seuil, 1958, p. 39.

53. Wordsworth, William. *The Borderers*, III, 1539.

55. Beethoven, Ludwig van. Letter to Franz Gerhard Wegeler, 29 june 1801, in *Beethoven—A Documentary Study*. H. C. Robbins Landon, ed. London: Thames & Hudson, 1970, p. 71; and "Heiligenstadt testament," ibid., p. 84.

55–56. Beethoven, Ludwig van. Letter to Countess Erlody, 27 october 1818, in Magnani, Luigi. *Beethoven lettore di Omero*. Torino: Einaudi, 1984, p. 68.

56. Schauffler, Robert Haven. *Franz Schubert: The Ariel of Music*. New York: Putnam, 1949, p. 126.

56. Casals, Pablo. *Joys and Sorrows*. New York: Simon and Schuster, 1970, p. 111.

57. Kandinski, Vassilij. *Tutti gli scritti*. Milano: Feltrinelli, 1973, p. 156.

57–58. Shykes, Ralph E. *Pissarro—His Life and Work*. New York: Horizon, 1980, p. 175.

58. Renoir, Jean. *Renoir mio padre*. Milano: Garzanti, 1962, pp. 168–169.

58. Goodrich, Lloyd, and Bry, Doris. *Georgia O'Keeffe*. New York: Whitney Museum of American Art, 1970, p. 23.

59. Yarmolinsky, Adam. *La vita e l'arte di Dostojevskij*. Milano: Mursia, 1959.

59–60. Wordsworth, William. Letter to John Wilson, 7 giugno 1802, in Wordsworth, William. *Letters of William Wordsworth*. Oxford: Oxford University Press, 1984, pp. 51–52.

60. Hanson, Lawrence. *Gaugain*. Milano: Rizzoli, 1958, p. 320.

60–61. Sand, George. *Oeuvres autobiographiques*. Paris: Gallimard, 1971, p. 446.

62. Tchaikovsky, Peter Ilich. Letter to N. F. von Meck, 24 giugno (6 luglio) 1878, in Tchaikovsky, Modeste. *Peter Ilich Tchaikovsky*. London: John Lane, p. 309.

62. Huisman, Philippe. *Lautrec visto da Lautrec*. Milano: Garzanti, 1964.

62. Vallier, Dora. *L'intérieur de l'art—Entretiens avec Braque, Léger, Villon, Miró, Brancusi*. Paris: Editions du Seuil, 1982, p. 47.

62. Thayer, Alexander. *Thayer's Life of Beethoven*. Rev. E. Forbes. Princeton: Princeton University Press, 1969, pp. 372, 380.

63. Keats, John. Letter to George and Georgiana Keats, 3 may 1819.

63. Panofsky, E. *La vita e le opere di Albrecht Durer*. Milano: Feltrinelli, pp. 19–20.

63. Stravinsky, Igor, and Craft, Robert. *Colloqui con Stravinsky*. Torino: Einaudi, 1977, p. 6.

63. Stevenson, Robert Louis. "A Chapter on Dreams." *Memories and Portraits, Random Memories, Memories of Himself*. New York: Scribner, 1925.

64. *Great Short Biographies of the World*. C. Barett, ed. New York: Robert McBride, 1929, p. 1226.

64. Eckermann, Johann Peter. *Colloqui con Goethe*. 11 march 1828. Firenze: Sansoni, 1947, p. 608.

65. Erb, Lawrence. *Brahms la vita le opere*. Milano: Bocca, 1946, p. 103.

65. Beethoven, Ludwig van. Letter to Louis Schlosser, 1823, in Scott, Marion. *Beethoven*. London: Dent, 1974, p. 121.

65. Renoir, Jean. *Renoir mio padre*. Milano: Garzanti, 1962, p. 198.

65. Vallier, Dora. *L'intérieur de l'art, entretiens avec Braque, Léger, Villon, Miró, Brancusi*. Paris: Editions du Seuil, 1982, p. 128.

66. Wagner, Richard. *Autobiografia*. Varese: Dall'oglio, 1983, p. 521.

66. Hayman, Ronald. *Kafka*. Milano: Rizzoli, 1983, p. 23.

66. Schumann, Robert and Clara. *Journal Intime*. Parigi: Buchet/Chastel, 1967, p. 114.

THE WAY OF ACTION

72. Haas, Louis. *Practical Occupational Therapy*. Milwaukee: The Bruce Publishing Company, 1944, p. 3.

74. Huxley, Elspeth. *Florence Nightingale*. London: Chancellor Press, 1975, p. 27.

74–75. Chuang Tzu. *The Complete Works*. New York: Columbia University Press, 1968, p. 97.

78. Tooley, Sarah. *The Life of Florence Nightingale*. London: Cassell, 1910, p. 298.

78–79. Brother Lawrence. *The Practice of the Presence of God*. Flaming Revell, 1958, pp. 30–31.

80–81. Schweitzer, Albert. *Thoughts for Our Times*. Erica Anderson, ed. New York: Peter Pauper Press, 1975, p. 21.

82–83. Mother Teresa of Calcutta. *A Gift for God*. New York: Harper & Row, 1975, p. 43.

84. Brabazon, James. *Albert Schweitzer: A Biography*. New York: Putnam, 1975, p. 223.

84–85. Manton, Jo. *Mary Carpenter and the Children of the Streets*. London: Heinemann, 1976, pp. 32, 79; and ibid., p. 74.

85–86. Yinger, Winthrop. *Cesar Chavez, The Rhetoric of Nonviolence*. Hicksville: Exposition Press, 1975, p. 29.

87. Bosco, Teresio. *Raoul Follerau*. Torino: Elle Di Ci, 1982, p. 8.

89. Huxley, Elspeth. *Florence Nightingale*. London: Chancellor Press, 1975, p. 107.

89–90. Day, Dorothy. "Abbé Pierre and the Poor." *The Commonweal*, 30 October 1959, p. 147.

90–91. Mother Teresa of Calcutta. *A Gift for God*. New York: Harper & Row, 1975, pp. 56–57.

92–93. Whitney, Janet. *Elizabeth Fry*. New York: Benjamin Blom, 1972, pp. 198–199.
94. Brabazon, James. *Albert Schweitzer: A Biography*. New York: Putnam, 1975, p. 178.
95. S. Tereṣa di Gesu Bambino. *Storia di un'anima—Scritti autobiografici*. Roma: Postulazione Generale dei Carmelitani Scalzi, 1980, p. 296.
96–97. Chuang Tzu. *The Complete Works*. New York: Columbia University Press, 1968, p. 75.
97–98. "Epitome of Zen Master Han Shan's Autobiography," in Carma Chang. *The Practice of Zen*. New York: Perennial Library, 1959, p. 135.
98. Sri Aurobindo. *Letters on Yoga*. Parts II and III. Pondicherry: Sri Aurobindo Ashram, p. 717.
99. Suzuki, Deitaro. *Zen Buddhism*. New York: Anchor Books, 1956, p. 130.
99–100. Nightingale, Florence. *Notes on Nursing*. Edinburgh: Churchill Livingstone, 1980.
100. Cook, Sir Edward. *The Life of Florence Nightingale*. New York: Macmillan Company, 1942, p. 245.

THE WAY OF ILLUMINATION

104–105. Gopi Krishna. *Kundalini*. Berkeley: Shambala, 1970, p. 62.
105–106. Buber, Martin. *Ecstatic Confessions*. New York: Harper & Row, 1985, p. 43.
106–107. Kaluahana, David and Indrani. *The Way of Siddharta*. Boulder: Shambala, 1982, p. 32.
107. Dhammapada, II, 21.
107. Huxley, Aldous. *Letters*. New York: Harper & Row, 1969, p. 527.
108. Ouspensky, Peter Demianovich. *In Search of the Miraculous*. New York: Harcourt, 1949, p. 120.
108–109. Suzuki, Shunryu. *Zen Mind, Beginner's Mind*. New York: Weatherhill, 1960, p. 21.
109. Krishnamurti, Jiddhu. *Notebook*. New York: Harper & Row, 1976, pp. 196–197.
110–111. Watts, Alan. *In My Own Way*. Pantheon: New York, 1972, p. 367.
111. *Milindapanha*, 25–28.
113. Patañjali. *Yoga Sutra*, I, 1.
113. *Nada-bindu Upanishad*, 31–41.
114. Montaigne, Michel de. *Essais*, III, 3.
115. Emerson, Ralph Waldo. *Saggi*. Torino: Boringhieri, 1962, p. 53.
115–116. Tolstoy's letter to Aleksandra Andreievna Tolstoy, 3 may 1859,

in Rolland Romain. *Vita di Tolstoy*. Torino: UTET, 1972, pp. 285–286.

116. Herold, Cristopher. *Mistress to an Age*. New York: Harmony Books, 1958, pp. 188, 222.

117. Zolla, Elémire. *I Mistici*. Milano: Garzanti, 1963, pp. 940–941.

117–118. On Boehme: Foster Case, Paul. *The Tarot*. Richmond: Macoy, 1947, p. 99.

118–119. Teresa d'Avila. *Life*, XXVIII, 5.

119–120. Mahadevan, T. M. P. *Ramana Maharshi*. London: Unwin, 1977, p. 17.

121. Madhava Vidyaranya. *Sankara Digvijaya—The Traditional Life of Sri Sankaracharya*. Madras: Sri Ramakrishna Math, 1980, p. 60.

121. *Meister Eckhart*. Raymond Blakney, transl. New York: Harper & Row, 1941, p. 87.

121. Sankaracharya. *Crest Jewel of Discrimination*. Swami Prabhavananda and Cristopher Isherwood, transl. New York: Mentor, 1947, p. 85.

123. Ramakrishna, Sri. *Alla Ricerca di Dio*. Jean Herbert, ed. Roma: Ubaldini, 1963, p. 270.

123–124. Lash, Joseph. *Helen and Teacher—The Story of Helen Keller and Anne Sullivan Mac*. New York: Delacorte Press/Seymour Lawrence, 1978, p. 781.

124–125. Schelling, Friederich Wilhelm. *Werke*, I, 318.

127–128. *Teachings of Tibetan Yoga*. Trad. Garma Chang, New York: University Books, 1973, p. 94.

128–129. Marcus Aurelius. *Meditations*, XII, 24.

129. De Caussade, Jean Pierre. *Abandonment to the Divine Providence*, I, 4.

129. *Theologia Germanica*, V.

129. Tommaso da Celano. *Vita Prima di San Francesco d'Assisi*, VII, 17.

129. *Tibetan Yoga and Secret Doctrines*. W. Y. Evans Wentz, ed. London: Oxford University Press, 1951, pp. 71, 86.

130. *Lankatavara Sutra*, 154.

131. Aurobindo, Sri. *Tales of Prison Life*. Calcutta: Sri Aurobindo Pathamandir, 1974, p. 64.

133. Froebel, Friederich. *Autobiography*. E. Michaelis, transl. London: Swan Sonnenschein, pp. 107–108.

134–135. Rousseau, Jean Jacques. Letter 2 to Malesherbes, in *Lettere Morali*. Roma: Ed. Riuniti, 1978, pp. 200–201.

135. Froebel, Friederich. *Autobiography*. E. Michaelis, transl. London: Swan Sonnenschein, p. 109.

135. Silber, Kate. *Pestalozzi, The Man and His Work*. London: Routledge & Kegan Paul, 1960, p. 76.

136. Maroger, Dominique. *Le idées pédagogiques de Tolstoy*. Lausanne: Edition L'Age d'Homme, 1974, p. 164.

136–138. Standing, E. M. *Maria Montessori—Her Life and Work*. London: Hollis & Carter, 1957, p. 34.

138. Cenker, William. *The Hindu Personality in Education*. Manohar, 1976, p. 50.

138–139. De Guimps, Roger. *Pestalozzi, His Life and Work*. London: Swan Sonnenschein, 1980, p. 72.

139–140. *Froebel's Chief Writings on Education*. Trad. S. Fletcher and J. Welton. London: Edward Arnold, 1912, p. 110.

140. De Guimps, Roger. *Pestalozzi, His Life and Work*. London: Swan Sonnenschein, 1980, p. 75.

140. Standing, E. M. *Maria Montessori—Her Life and Work*. London: Hollis & Carter, 1957, p. 34.

142. Buber, Martin. *Between Man and Man*. New York: Macmillan, 1965, pp. 1–2.

143–144. Magidoff, Robert. *Yehudi Menuhin*. London: Robert Hale, 1955, p. 231.

144. Steiner, Rudolf. *La mia vita*. Milano: Istituto Tipografico Editoriale, 1937.

145. *La vie de Madame Guyon écrite par elle-meme*, XIII, 5. Paris: Dervy-Livres, 1983, p. 339.

145–146. Russell, Bertrand. *Autobiography*. London: Unwin, 1971, p. 149.

147. Plato. *Republic*, XI, 1, 611–612.

148. Spinoza, Baruch. *De intellectus emendatione*. Preface. Padova: R.A.D.A.R., 1969, pp. 45–54.

148. Da Celano, Tommaso. *Vita Prima di San Francesco d'Assisi*, XXIX, 80; and *Vita Seconda di San Francesco d'Assisi*, CXXIV, 165.

148–149. Burtt, E. A. *The Teachings of the Compassionate Buddha*. New York: Mentor, 1955, p. 47.

THE WAY OF DANCE AND RITUAL

155. Shawn, Ted. *Gods Who Dance*. New York: Dutton, 1929, p. 12.

156. Barrault, Jean-Louis. *Souvenirs pour Demain*. Paris: Editions du Seuil, 1972, p. 211.

157. Al Chung-liang Huang. *Embrace Tiger, Return to Mountain*. Moab: Real People Press, 1973, p. 70.

158. Reps, Paul. *Zen Flesh, Zen Bones*. New York: Doubleday, 1961, p. 166.

158. Eliade, Mircea. *Yoga—Immortality and Freedom*. London: Routledge & Kegan Paul, 1969, p. 97.

159. Nijinsky, Romola. *Nijinsky*. New York: Simon & Schuster, 1934, p. 113.

159–160. Hemery, David. *The Pursuit of Sporting Excellence*. London: Willow Books, 1986, p. 112.

160–161. *The Dance Experience*. M. H. Nadel and C. G. Nadel, eds. New York: Praeger, 1970, p. 32.
162–163. *The Dance Has Many Faces*. W. Sorell, ed. Cleveland: World Publishing Company, 1951, p. 13.
163. Cunningham, Merce. *The Dancer and the Dance*. London: Maryon Boars, 1985, p. 23.
163–164. Mara, Thalia. *To Dance, To Live*. New York: Dance Horizons, 1977.
164. Béjart, Maurice. "Danzare, come dire vivere," *Alfabeta*, N. 78, november 1985, supplement.
165. Bourguignon, Erika. "Trance Dance," *Dance Perspectives*, N. 35, 1968.
166. *The Mary Wigman Book—Her Writings Edited and Translated*. W. Sorell, ed. and transl. Middletown: Wesleyan University Press, 1973, p. 52.
166. Gopal, Ram. *Rhythm in the Heavens—An Autobiography*. London: Secker & Warburg, 1957, p. 36.
167. Lucian. *Dialogue on Dance*, VII.
167. Shawn, Ted. *Dance We Must*. London: Dennis Dobson, 1946, p. 11.
167. Nijinsky, Romola. *Nijinsky*. New York: Simon & Schuster, 1934, p. 159.
168. Reiss, Francoise. *Nijinsky—A Biography*. London: Black, 1960, p. 69.
168. *The Dance Anthology*. S. Cobbett, ed. New York: New American Library, 1980, p. 86.
168. Buckle, Richard. *Nijinsky*. Middlesex: Penguin, 1975, p. 267.
168–169. On Isadora Duncan: Murphy, Michael, and White, Rhea. *The Psychic Side of Sport*. Reading, Mass.: Addison-Wesley, 1978, p. 22.
169. *Nijinsky, Pavlova, Duncan*. P. Magriel, ed. New York: Da Capo Press, 1977, p. 11.
170–171. *I Mistici*. E. Zolla, ed. Milano: Garzanti, 1963.
171. On the dance of angels: Backman, Louis. *Religious Dances*. London: Allen & Unwin, 1952, pp. 66, foll.
172–173. On the river procession in Egypt: Wild, Henri. "Les Danses sacrées en Orient," in *Les Danses Sacrées*. Paris: Editions du Seuil, 1963, p. 33.
173. On shamanic dances: Ibid., pp. 281, foll.
174. Sarabhai, Mrinalini. *Longing for the Beloved*. Gujarat: Darpana, 1976.
174. On the Shakers: Fisk Taylor, Margaret. *A Time to Dance*. Philadelphia: United Church Press, 1967, p. 124.
174. On Rumi: Sachs, Curt. *La Storia della Danza*. Milano: Saggiatore, 1966, p. 22. See also Friedlander, Ira. *The Whirling Dervishes*. New York: Macmillan, 1975.
174–175. Burke, Michael. *Among the Dervishes*. London: Octagon Press, 1973, p. 50.

175–176. Neihardt, John. *Black Elk Speaks*. New York: Pocket Books, 1973, p. 36.

176–177. Ibid., p. 147.

177–178. Fisk Taylor, Margaret. *A Time to Dance*. Philadelphia: United Church Press, 1967, p. 124.

179. Suzuki, Shunryu. *Zen Mind, Beginner's Mind*. New York: Weatherhill, 1970, pp. 43–44.

180. Guardini, Romano. *Lo Spirito della Liturgia*. Brescia: Morcelliana, 1961.

180–181. On the Friar Giovanni episode: *Fioretti di San Francesco*, cap. 53.

181. Suzuki, Daisetz. *Zen and Japanese Culture*. Princeton: Princeton University Press, 1959, p. 314. See also ibid., pp. 271–314.

182. Hammitzsch, Horst. *Zen in the Art of the Tea Ceremony*. New York: Avon Books, 1982, p. 19.

183–184. Apuleius. *Metamorfoses*, XI, 23.

185. *Rig Veda*, VIII, 48, 3.

185–186. *Livre des morts tibétain*, I. 1. W. Evans-Wentz, ed. Paris: Adrien-Maisonneuve, 1933, p. 77.

187. On Mitterwürzer: Kjerbuhl-Petersen, Lorenz. *Psychology of Acting*. Boston: Expression Company, 1935, p. 210.

187–188. On David Garrick: *Actors on Acting*. T. Cole and H. Krich Chinoy. New York: Crown, 1949, p. 135.

188. Olivier, Laurence. *Confessions of an Actor*. London: Weidenfeld & Nicolson, 1982, p. 117.

191. Stanislavski, Konstantin. *La mia vita nell'arte*. Torino: Einaudi, 1963, pp. 198–199.

191. On Furtwängler: Jantsch, Eric. *The Self-Organizing Universe*. Oxford: Pergamon, 1980, p. 290.

192. Le Gallienne, Eva. *The Mystic in the Theatre—Eleonora Duse*. London: Feffer & Simons, 1965, p. 37.

THE WAY OF SCIENCE

196. Moszkowski, Alexander. *Conversations with Einstein*. London: Sidgwick & Jackson, 1970, p. 4.

196. Howard, Jane. *Margaret Mead—A Life*. New York: Fawcett Crest, 1985, p. 129.

197. Flammarion, Camille. *Dieu dans la nature*. Parigi: Librairie Academique, 1871, pp. 545–546.

198. Weyl, Hermann. *Il Mondo Aperto*. Torino: Boringhieri, 1981, p. 37.

198–199. Fabre, Augustin. *The Life of Jean Henri Fabre, the Entomologist*. London: Hodder & Stoughton, 1921, p. 263.

199. Frangsmyr, Tore. *Linnaeus—The Man and His Work*. Berkeley: University of California Press, 1983, p. 12.

199–200. Eccles, John, and Gibson, William. *Sherringston—His Life and Thought*. Locarno: Springer International, 1970, p. 142.

200. Hooper, Judith, and Teresi, Dick. *The Three-Pound Universe*. New York: Macmillan, 1986, p. 390.

200. Lukas, Mary and Ellen. *Teilhard*. New York: McGraw-Hill, 1981, p. 328.

200. Straus, Ernst. "Memoir," in *Einstein—A Centenary Volume*. A. P. French, ed. Cambridge: Harvard University Press, 1979, p. 31.

200. Clark, Ronald. *Einstein, the Life and Times*. New York: Avon, 1971, p. 141.

200. Moore, Ruth. *Niels Bohr*. New York: Knopf, 1966, p. 418.

200–201. On Helmholtz: Ostwald, W. *Les Grandes Hommes*. Paris: Flammarion, 1912, p. 104.

201. On Heisenberg: *Quantum Questions—Mystical Writings of the World's Great Physicists*. K. Wilber, ed. Boulder: New Science Library, 1984, p. 61.

201. Dirac, Paul. "The Evolution of the Physicist's Picture of Nature," *Scientific American*, May 1963, p. 47.

201. Poincaré. *The Foundations of Science*. Science Press, 1924, pp. 383–394.

201. Oliphant, Mark. *Rutherford—Recollections of the Cambridge Days*. Amsterdam: Elsevier, 1972, p. 65.

201. Straus, Ernst. "Memoir," in *Einstein—A Centenary Volume*. A. P. French, ed. Cambridge: Harvard University Press, 1979, p. 32.

201. Ibid., p. 71.

202. On Newton: Holton, Gerald. *The Scientific Imagination*. Cambridge: Cambridge University Press, 1978, pp. 272–273.

202–203. Jacob, François. *La statue interieure*. Paris: Seuil, 1987, p. 330.

204. Wertheimer, Max. *Il pensiero produttivo*. Firenze: Giunti, 1965.

204–205. On Galileo: Geymonat, Ludovico. *Galileo Galilei*. Torino: Einaudi, 1957.

205–206. On Becquerel: Badash, Lawrence. "Chance favors the prepared mind," *Archives des Sciences*, January–June 1965, pp. 56–66, nn. 70–71.

206–207. Cussy, Hilaire. *Pasteur: la vita il pensiero i testi esemplari*. Milano: Accademia, 1974, p. 168.

207. Lavoisier, Antoine. *Oeuvres*, I, 3.

207. Jung, Carl Gustav. *Ricordi sogni riflessioni*. Milano: Saggiatore, 1965, p. 204.

208. Greenwald, Anthony. "The Totalitarian Ego," *American Psychologist*, n. 35, 1980, pp. 603–618.

208. On Bernard: Beveridge, William. *The Art of Scientific Investigation*. New York: Vintage Books, 1950, p. 5.

208. On Crick: Judson, Horace Freeland. *The Eighth Day of Creation—The*

Makers of the Revolution in Biology. New York: Simon & Schuster, 1979, p. 41.

209. Fabre, Augustin. *The Life of Jean Henri Fabre the Entomologist*. London: Hodder & Stoughton, 1921, p. 121.

210. Huxley, Thomas H. Letter to Charles Kingsley, 23 september 1860, in Huxley, Leonard. *Life and Letters of Thomas Henry Huxley*. New York: Appleton, 1900, Vol. I, p. 235.

210–211. MacKenzie, Catherine. *Alexander Graham Bell*. New York: Houghton Mifflin, 1928, pp. 72–73.

211. On Laënnec: Sagredo. *Aneddotica delle Scienze*. Milano: Hoepli, 1960, p. 329.

211. On the Montgolfiers: Towle, George. *Heroes and Martyrs of Invention*. Boston: Lees and Shepard, 1903, pp. 104–105.

211–212. Thompson, Holland. *The Age of Invention*. New Haven: Yale University Press, 1921, p. 231.

212. Lipset, David. *Gregory Bateson—the Legacy of a Scientist*. Boston: Beacon, 1980, p. 148.

212. On Bateson's use of analogy: Hoard, Jane. *Margaret Mead—A Life*. New York: Fawcett Crest, 1984, p. 163.

212–213. O'Neill, John. *Prodigal Genius—The Life of Nikola Tesla*. London: Granada, 1968, pp. 54–56.

214. Savorgnan di Brazzà, Francesco. *Da Leonardo a Marconi—Invenzioni e scoperte italiane*. Milano: Hoepli, 1939, p. 198.

214–215. Masini, G. *Marconi*. Torino: UTET, 1975, p. 56.

215. On Harvey: Shrady, Maria. *Moments of Insight*. New York: Harper, 1972, pp. 63–65.

215–216. Watson, James. *The Double Helix*. New York: Signet, 1969, pp. 83–84.

216. Miller, Arthur. *Imagery in Scientific Thought*. Boston: Birkhauser, 1984, p. 129.

216. Dante Alighieri. *Paradiso*, XXXI, 134.

216. Shakespeare, William. Sonnet LXXIII.

216. Palladio. *I quattro libri dell'architettura*, chapter IV.

216. Stendhal. *Vita di Haydn*. Firenze: Passigli, 1983, pp. 94–96.

216. On Heraclitus: Fr. 91, Diels.

216. Plato. *Republic*, 508–509.

216. On Wittgenstein: *Tractatus*, 6.341.

217. Lao Tse. *Tao Te Ching*, XI.

217. *Bhagavad Gita*, VI, 19.

217. Shankaracarya. *Viveka Chudamani*.

217–218. Meadowcroft, William. *Edison*. Paris: Payot, 1929, pp. 108–109.

218. Aubery, M. *Le vittorie della medicina*. Milano: Longanesi, 1960.

218. On Morse: Larsen, Egon. *Storia delle invenzioni*. Roma: Editori Riuniti, 1968, p. 302.

218. On Daguerre: Ibid., p. 351.

219. Dubos, René. *Louis Pasteur, franc tireur de la science*. Paris: Presses Universitaires de France, 1955, p. 332.

219. On Auenbrugger: Aubery, M. *Le vittorie della medicina*. Milano: Longanesi, 1960.

220. On Einstein: Miller, Arthur. *Imagery in Scientific Thought*. Boston: Birkhauser, 1984, p. 13.

221. Cussy, Hilaire. *Pasteur—La vita le opere i testi esemplari*. Milano: Accademia, 1974, p. 170.

221. Nitske, Robert. *The Life of Wilhelm Conrad Röntgen*. Tucson: The University of Arizona Press, 1971, p. 94.

221–222. Beveridge, William. *Seeds of Discovery*. London: Heinemann, 1980, p. 18.

222–223. On the discovery of penicillin: Macfarlane, Gwyn. *Alexander Fleming, The Man and the Myth*. London: Chatto & Windus, 1984.

223–224. Segrè, Emilio. *Enrico Fermi, Physicist*. Chicago: The University of Chicago Press, 1970, p. 80.

224–225. Duncan, Isadora. *My Life*. New York: Liveright, 1927, p. 75.

225. Renoir, Jean. *Renoir mio padre*. Milano: Garzanti, 1963, p. 129.

225. *The Life of Swami Viveknanda by His Eastern and Western Disciples*. Vol. I. Calcutta: Advaita Ashrama, 1979, p. 132.

225. Cronin, Vincent. *Napoleon*. New York: Penguin Books, 1972, p. 235.

225. Cassarà, Emanuele. *Le quattro vite di Reinhold Messner*. Varese: Dall'oglio, 1981, p. 89.

225. On Newton: *Great Short Biographies of the World*. A cura di C. Barrett. New York: Robert McBride, 1929, p. 713; and Manuel, Frank. *A Portrait of Isaac Newton*. London: Frederick Muller, 1980, p. 86.

226. Dimier, Louis. *Buffon*. Paris: Nouvelle Librairie Nationale, 1919, p. 216.

226. Curie, Eve. *Madame Curie*. New York: Doubleday, 1938, pp. 158, 171.

226. Bellivier, André. *Henri Poincaré ou la vocation souveraine*. Paris: Gallimard, 1956, p. 216.

227. Russell, Bertrand. *Autobiography*. London: Unwin, 1975, pp. 154–155.

227. *Einstein—A Centenary Volume*. Cambridge: Harvard University Press, 1979, p. 31.

228–229. Fox Keller, Evelyn. *A Feeling For the Organism*. New York: Freeman, 1983, p. 117.

229. On Fresnel: Moszkowski, Alexander. *Conversations with Einstein*. London: Sidgwick & Jackson, 1972, p. 45.

229. Dubos, René. *Louis Pasteur, franc tireur de la science*. Paris: Presses Universitaires de France, 1955, p. 394.

230. Fabre, Augustin. *The Life of Jean Henri Fabre the Entomologist*. London: Hodder & Stoughton, 1921, p. 102.

230. Allason, Barbara. *Goethe a colloquio, n. 275 with J. D. Falk before 1826*. Torino: Da Silva, 1947, pp. 244–245.

230. Goethe, Wolfgang. *Viaggio Italiano*, 27 september 1786.

230–231. Orsag Madigan, Carol, and Elwood, Ann. *Brainstorms & Thunderbolts: How Creative Genius Works*. New York: Macmillan, 1983, p. 110.

231. Meadowcroft, William. *T. A. Edison*. Paris: Payot, 1929, pp. 181–182.

231. On Whitehead: Olson, Robert. *The Art of Creative Thinking*. New York: Barnes & Noble, 1980, p. 65.

231–232. Oppenheimer, Robert. *Letters and Recollections*. A. Kimball Smith and C. Weiner, eds. Cambridge: Harvard University Press, 1980, p. 155.

233. *Einstein: A Centenary Volume*. A. P. French, ed. Cambridge: Harvard University Press, 1979, p. 67.

234. On Galileo: Savorgnan di Brazzà, Francesco. *Da Leonardo a Marconi: invenzioni e scoperte italiane*, p. 82.

234. Segre, Emilio. *Personaggi e scoperte nella fisica classica*. Milano: Mondadori, 1983, p. 33.

234–235. Schiapparelli, Giovanni. "Lettera autobiografica," 29 april 1907, in Schiapparelli, Giovanni. *Le più belle pagine di astronomia popolare*. Milano: Hoepli, 1925, p. 4.

235. Lyell, Charles. *Travels in North America*. Vol. I. London: John Murray, 1845, p. 52.

236–237. Jacob, François. *La Statue Interieure*. Paris: Seuil, 1987, p. 331.

238–239. Lilly, John. *Communication between Man and Dolphin*. New York: Crown, 1978, pp. x–xii.

THE WAY OF DEVOTION

240–241. Bly, Robert. *The Kabir Book*. Boston: Beacon Press, 1977, p. 23.

244. *The Dialogue of Saint Catherine of Siena*. A. Thorold, transl. Rockford: Tan Books, 1974, p. 187.

244. The *Philokalia*. Vol. I. G. Palmer, P. Sherrand, and K. Ware, transl. London: Faber & Faber, 1979, p. 264.

244. Norwich, Julian of. *Revelations of Divine Love*. Middlesex: Penguin, 1966, p. 183.

244. Celano, Tommaso da. *Vita Seconda di San Francesco d'Assisi*. Cap. LXXXIX, 126.

244. On Shamsoddin Lahiji: *The Dream and Human Societies*. E. von Grunebaum and R. Callois, eds. Berkeley: University of California Press, 1966, p. 397.

244–245. Suso, Henry. *The Life of the Servant*. Trad. J. Clark. Cambridge: James Clarke, 1982, p. 29.

245. Isherwood, Cristopher. *Ramakrishna and His Disciples*. New York: Simon & Schuster, 1959, p. 65.

245–246. Teresa of Avila. *Life*. Chapter XXXII, 1–4.

246. John of the Cross. *The Dark Night*. Chapter VII, 3.

249–250. Angela da Foligno. *L'esperienza di Dio Amore*. Roma: Città Nuova, 1973, p. 106.

250. Rolle, Richard. *The Fire of Love*. Prologue. Middlesex: Penguin, 1981, p. 45.

250. *The Cloud of Unknowing*. Chapter VI, 3.

251. Teresa of Avila. *The Interior Castle*. Chapter V, 7.

251. *The Dialogue of Saint Catherine of Siena*. Algar Thorold, transl. Rockford: Tan, 1974, p. 198.

252. *Theologia Germanica*. Chapter VI.

252–253. *Imitation of Christ*. Chapter V, 4.

253–254. On the *Srimad Bhagavatam*: Danielou, Alain. *Yoga—The Method of Re-integration*. New York: University Books, 1949, p. 108.

254. Bremond, Henri. *Historire Littéraire du Sentiment Religieux en France*. Vol. VII. Paris: Armand Colin, 1968, p. 9.

256. Guyon, Jeanne. *Experiencing the Depths of Jesus Christ*. G. Edwards, transl. Augusta: Christian Books, 1980, p. 16.

257. Ramdas, Swami. *Carnet de Pelerinage*. Parigi: Albin Michel, 1973, pp. 138–139.

258. *The Way of a Pilgrim*. R. M. French, transl. New York: Seabury, 1968, p. 41.

258–259. Teresa of Avila. *Life*. Chapter XII, 2.

259. Thérèse of Lisieux. *Storia di un'anima*. Roma: Postulazione Generale dei Carmelitani Scalzi, 1980, p. 289, n. 317.

259–260. *The Autobiography of St. Ignatius Loyola*. J. Callaghan, transl. New York: Harper, 1974, p. 39.

260. Di Chantal, Giovanna. *Volerci come Dio ci vuole. Scritti spirituali*. Roma: Città Nuova, 1984, p. 165.

260. *Philokalia*. Vol. I. G. Palmer, P. Serrard, K. Ware, transl., p. 162.

261. On Camus: Bremond, Henri. *Historie Littéraire du sentiment religieux en France*. Vol. VII. Paris: Armand Colin, 1968, p. 58.

265. Goethe, Wolfgang von. *Autobiography* (*Dichtung und Wahreit*). Trad. J. Oxendorf. Vol. I. Chicago: University of Chicago Press, 1974, p. 420.

265–266. John of the Cross. *Ascent to Mount Carmel*. Chapter I, 6–11.

266. *Imitation of Christ*. Chapter XXIII, 9.

266. *Philokalia*. G. E. H. Palmer, P. Sherrard, and K. Ware, eds. London: Faber & Faber, 1979, p. 35.

266–267. *Theologia Germanica*. Trad. S. Winkworth. Cap. V. London: Stuart & Watkins, 1966, p. 41.

268. Guyon, Jeanne. *Experiencing the Depths of Jesus Christ*. G. Edwards, transl. Augusta: Christian Books, 1980, p. 33.

269. De Chantal, Giovanna. *Volerci come Dio ci vuole*. N. 61. Roma: Città Nuova, 1984, p. 95.

269. Veronica Giuliani. *I Mistici*. A cura di E. Zolla. Milano: Garzanti, 1963, p. 978.

269. Thérèse of Lisieux. *Storia di un'anima*. N. 241. Roma: Postulazione Generale dei Carmelitani Scalzi, 1979, p. 230.

269. M. *Gospel of Ramakrishna*. New York: Vedanta Society, 1947, p. 89.

270. *Theologia Germanica*. S. Winkworth, transl. London: Stuart & Watkins, 1966, p. 119.

270. De Caussade, Jean-Pierre. *Abbandono alla provvidenza divina*. I, 5. Roma: Astrolabio, 1951, p. 21.

271. Ibid., II, 1, p. 74.

272. John of the Cross. *Ascent to Mount Carmel*. Chapter III, 2, 4.

THE WAY OF THE WILL

273–274. Sorensen, Jon. *The Saga of Fridtjof Nansen*. New York: Norton, 1932, p. 146.

276–277. Cousteau, Jacques. *Il Mondo Silenzioso*. Milano: Bompiani, 1954, p. 37.

277. Siffre, Michel. *Beyond Time*. New York: McGraw-Hill, 1964.

277. Suzuki, Daisetz. *Zen and Japanese Culture*. Princeton: Princeton University Press, 1971, p. 177.

280–281. Bannister, Roger. *The Four-Minute Mile*. London: Dodd, Mead, 1955, p. 49.

281–282. Byrd, Richard. *Alone*. Los Angeles: Tarcher, 1986, p. 192.

285. *Quest for Adventure*. C. Bonington, ed. New York: Clarkson Potter, 1981, p. 225.

286. *Man against Nature—Tales of Adventure and Exploration*. C. Neider, ed. New York: Harper, 1954, p. 366.

286. Roditi, Edouard. *Magellano del Pacifico*. Milano: Mursia, 1977, p. 145.

287–288. On Rosenthal: Leonard, George. *The Ultimate Athlete*. New York: Avon, 1975, pp. 246–247.

288. Terray, Lionel. *Conquistadors of the Useless—From the Alps to the Annapurna*. London: Gollancz, 1963, p. 165.

290. Lindbergh, Charles. *The Spirit of St. Louis*. New York: Scribners, 1953, p. 352.

291–292. Bridgeman, William. *The Lonely Sky*. New York: Henry Holt, 1955, p. 303.

292. Maiorca, Enzo. *La Nazione*, 15 august 1973.

292–293. *The Mind of Mahatma Gandhi*. R. K. Prahbu and U. R. Rao, eds. Ahmedabad: Navajivan, 1967, p. 59.

293. Gandhi. *Lettres à l'Ashram*. Paris: Albin Michel, 1960, p. 158.

294. Gandhi. *Selected Writings*. R. Duncan, ed. New York: Harper, 1972, p. 45.

295–296. Beebe, William. *The Arcturus Adventure*. New York: Putnam's Sons, 1926, pp. 340–341; and Beebe, William. *Mille metri sott'acqua*. Milano: Bompiani, 1950, p. 151.

296. Casteret, Norbert. *Ten Years under the Earth*. Teaneck: Zephyrus, 1939, p. 143.

297. Amundsen, Roald. *The North West Passage*. Vol. II. New York: Dutton, 1908, pp. 363–364.

297–298. Herzog, Maurice. *Annapurna*. New York: Dutton, 1952, pp. 132–133.

298–299. Glaisher, J., Flammarion, C., de Fonvielle, W., and Tissander, G. *Voyages aériens*. Paris: Hachette, 1870, pp. 158, 192.

299–300. Byrd, Richard. *Alone*. Los Angeles: Tarcher, 1986, pp. 120, 129, 161, 183.

300. Mitchell, Edgar. "Outer Space to Inner Space," *Saturday Review*, 22 february 1975, p. 20.

302–303. James, Grace. *Joan of Arc*. London: Methuen, 1910, pp. 51–52.

303. Messner, Reinhold. *La mia strada*. Varese: Dall'Oglio, 1983, p. 190.

303. Lindbergh, Charles. *The Spirit of St. Louis*. New York: Scribners, 1953, p. 389.

304. Charcot, Jean-Baptiste. *Cristoforo Colombo Marinaio*. Firenze: Giunti Martello, 1982, p. 211.

304–305. Oates, Stephen. *Let the Trumpet Sound—The Life of Martin Luther King, Jr.* New York: Harper & Row, 1982, pp. 88–89.

305–306. *The Mind of Mahatma Gandhi*. R. K. Prahbu and R. U. Rao, eds. Ahmedabad: Navajihan, 1967, pp. 33, 34.

306. Holmes, Paul. *Brahms: His Life and Times*. London: Baton Press, 1984, p. 151.

306–307. Kandinsky, Vasilij. *Tutti gli scritti*. Vol. 2. Milano: Feltrinelli, 1974, p. 188.

307. Hohlenberg, Johannes. *Søren Kierkegaard*. Paris: Editions Albin Michel, 1956, p. 348.

307–308. Dinnage, Rosemary. *Annie Besant*. Harmonsworth: Penguin Books, 1986, p. 66.

309. On the research on rescuers of Jews: Fogelman, Eva, and Lewis Wiener, Valerie. "The Few, the Brave, the Noble," in *Psychology Today*, August 1985, p. 61.

309–310. On Nobile and Amundsen: Huntford, Roland. *The Last Place on Earth*. London: Pan Books, 1985, p. 540.

310. *Lettere di condannati a morte della resistenza europea*. P. Malvezzi and G. Pirelli, eds. Torino: Einaudi, 1954, pp. 371–372.

312–313. Hammarskjöld, Dag. *Markings*. New York: Knopf, 1980, pp. 115, 166.

315. Jung, Carl Gustav. *Ricordi, Sogni, Riflessioni*. Milano: Saggiatore, 1965, pp. 324–329.

315. Kelen, Emery. *Hammarskjöld*. New York: Putnam, 1966, p. 167.

316. St. Gallen Heim, Albert von. "Remarks on Fatal Falls," in Noyes, Russell, and Kletti, Roy. "The Experience of Dying from Falls," *Omega*, vol. 3, 1972, pp. 46–47.

317. Lindbergh, Charles. *The Spirit of St. Louis*. New York: Scribners, 1953, p. 390.

317. Ungaretti, Giuseppe. *Vita di un uomo*. M. Diacono, ed. Milano: Mondadori, 1974.

318. Schweitzer, Albert. *J. S. Bach, il musicista poeta*. Milano: Suvini Zerboni, 1952, p. 155.

318. Mozart, Wolfgang Amadeus. Letter of 9 july 1778 to his father.

318–319. Marcus Aurelius. *Meditations*. Cap. VII, 56.

319. Montaigne, Michel de. *Essais*, III, 13.

319. Conze, Edward. *Buddhist Meditation*. London: Allen & Unwin, 1956, pp. 103–104.

320. "Life and Hymns of Milarepa," in *A Buddhist Bible*. D. Goddard, ed. Boston: Beacon, 1966, p. 568.

320–321. Waley, Arthur. *Three Ways of Thought in Ancient China*. London: Allen & Unwin, 1969, pp. 21–22.

THE CHARACTERISTICS OF TRANSPERSONAL EXPERIENCE

324. Dante Alighieri. *Divina Commedia*. Purgatorio, XXXIII, 144.

325. Shelley, Percy Bysshe. *Letters*, I, N. 358.

325. Hanson, Lawrence. *Gaugain*. Milano: Rizzoli, 1958, p. 255.

326. Nietzsche, Friederich. *The Creative Process*. B. Ghiselin, ed. New York: New American Library, 1952, p. 202.

326–327. Otto, Rudolf. *The Idea of the Holy*. Oxford: Oxford University Press, 1980, p. 26.

327–328. Rousseau, Jean-Jacques. *The Reveries of the Solitary Walker*. Fifth walk.

328. Tennyson, Lord Alfred. *A Memoir by his Son*. London: Macmillan, 1897, p. 320.

329. Maine de Biran, Francois Pierre. *Journal Intime*. 16 april 1820. Paris: Plon, 1927, pp. 209–210.

330. Vivekananda. *The Life of Swami Vivekananda by his Eastern and Western Disciples*. Vol. I. Calcutta: Advaita Ashrama, 1979, p. 19.

330–331. On Vivekananda: Isherwood, Cristopher. *Ramakrishna and his Disciples*. New York: Simon & Schuster, 1970, pp. 197, 206.

332–333. Biagini, Mario. *Pascoli, il poeta solitario*. Milano: Mursia, 1963, p. 500.

333. Ludwig, Emil. *Goethe, storia di un uomo*. T. Gnoli, transl. Milano: Mondadori, 1932, pp. 208–210.

334. Ramaswami, Sastri. *Tagore*. Madras: Ganesh, pp. 39–40.

334. Thoreau, Henry David. *Journal*. 17 march 1852. New York: Dover, 1960, p. 85.

335. Cate, Curtis. *Antoine de Saint-Exupéry*. New York: Putnam, 1970, p. 332.

336. Dubos, René. *Louis Pasteur, franc tireur de la science*. Paris: Presses Universitaires de France, 1955, p. 396.

337. Shirer, William. *Gandhi, A Memoir*. New York: Simon & Schuster, 1979, p. 74.

338. *A Treasury of Russian Spirituality*. G. P. Fedorov, ed. London: Sheed & Ward, 1981, p. 274.

338–339. Narasimha Swami. *Self-Realization—The Life and Teachings of Sri Ramana Maharshi*. Tiruvannamalai: Sri Ramanasramam, 1976, pp. 243, 248.

THE SELF

340. Nabokov, Vladimir. *Speak, Memory*. Harmonsworth: Penguin Books, 1987, p. 228.

Bibliography

This bibliography refers only to subjects related to transpersonal psychology, not to bibliographical sources. The source material is too extensive to be presented in its entirety.

Tart, Charles (ed.). *Altered States of Consciousness*. San Francisco: Freeman & Company, 1972.

Achterberg, Joan. *Imagery in Healing*. Boulder: Shambala, 1986.

Adams, James. *Conceptual Blockbusting: A Guide to Better Ideas*. New York: Norton, 1974.

Alberti, Alberto. "Psicosintesi e immagine dell'uomo." In AA.VV., *Immagini dell'uomo*. Firenze: Rosini, 1986.

———. *La volontà di sintesi*. Firenze: Centro Studi di Psicosintesi, "R. Assagioli," 1986.

Angyal, Andras. *Neurosis and Treatment: A Holistic Theory*. New York: Viking Compass, 1965.

———. *Foundations for a Science of Personality*. New York: Viking Compass, 1969.

Anthony, Dick; Ecker, Bruce; and Wilber, Ken. *Spiritual Choices*. New York: Paragon House, 1987.

Arieti, Silvano. *Creativity: The Magic Synthesis*. New York: Basic Books, 1976.

Assagioli, Roberto. *Per l'armonia della vita la psicosintesi*. Firenze: Istituto di Psicosintesi, 1966.

———. *Jung and Psychosynthesis*. New York: Psychosynthesis Research Foundation, 1967.

———. "Symbols of Transpersonal Experiences," in *Journal of Transpersonal Psychology*, vol. 1, 1969, n. 1.

———. *Principi e metodi della psicosintesi terapeutica.* Rome: Astrolabio, 1973.

———. *The Act of Will.* New York: Viking, 1973.

———. *Per vivere meglio.* Firenze: Istituto di Psicosintesi, 1975.

———. *I tipi umani.* Firenze: Istituto di Psicosintesi, 1976.

———. *Intervista con Sam Keen.* Firenze: Centro Studi di Psicosintesi, "R. Assagioli," 1987.

———. *Interviste 1972–74.* Firenze: Centro Studi di Psicosintesi, "R. Assagioli," 1987.

———. *Lo sviluppo transpersonale.* Rome: Astrolabio, 1988.

Aurobindo. *The Synthesis of Yoga.* Pondicherry: Centenary Library, XX, XXI.

Austin, James. *Chase, Chance, and Creativity: The Lucky Art of Novelty.* New York: Columbia University Press, 1977.

Bancroft, Anne. *Modern Mystics and Sages.* London: Granada, 1978.

Bartoli, Sergio. "Joy," in *Psychosynthesis Digest*, vol. 1, n. 2, Estate 1982.

Bateson, Gregory. *Steps to an Ecology of Mind.* New York: Ballantine, 1972.

———. *Mind and Nature: A Necessary Unity.* New York: Dutton, 1979.

Benoit, Hubert. *The Supreme Doctrine: Psychological Studies in Zen Thought.* New York: Viking Press, 1959.

Berkowitz, Bill. *Local Heroes.* New York: Lexington Books, 1987.

Berti, Alessandro (curatore). *Assagioli 1888–1988.* Firenze: Centro Studi di Psicosintesi, "R. Assagioli," 1988.

———. *Roberto Assagioli: profilo biografico degli anni di formazione.* Firenze: Istituto di Psicosintesi, 1988.

Beveridge, W. I. B. *Seeds of Discovery.* London: Heinemann, 1980.

———. *The Art Of Scientific Investigation.* New York: Vintage.

Blofeld, John. *The Tantric Mysticism of Tibet.* New York: Dutton, 1970.

Blyth, R. H. *Zen in English Literature and Oriental Classics.* New York: Dutton, 1960.

Boggio Gilot, Laura. *Forma e sviluppo della coscienza: psicologia transpersonale.* Rome: Asram Vidya, 1987.

Bohm, David. *Wholeness and the Implicate Order.* London: Routledge & Kegan Paul, 1980.

Borysenko, Joan. *Minding the Body, Mending the Mind.* New York: Bantam, 1988.

Bos, Ben. *Je bent het Zelf.* Sfinx Boeken, Amersfoort: Sfinx, 1982.

Bremond, Henri. *Histoire littéraire du sentiment religieux en France.* 11 vols. Paris: Armand Colin, 1967.

Briggs, John. *Fire in the Crucible: The Alchemy of Creative Genius.* New York: St. Martin's Press, 1988.

Brown, Daniel, and Engler, Jack. "Stages of Mindfulness Meditation," in *Journal of Transpersonal Psychology*, vol. 12, 1980, n. 2.

Brown, Barbara. *Supermind: The Ultimate Energy*. New York: Harper & Row, 1980.

Buber, Martin. *I and Thou*. New York: Scribners, 1970.

———. (curatore). *Ekstatische Konfessionen*. Eugen Diederichs Verlag, 1909.

Bucke, Richard Maurice. *Cosmic Consciousness*. New York: Dutton, 1923.

Burckhardt, Titus. *Scienza moderna e saggezza tradizionale*. Torino: Borla, 1968.

———. *An Introduction to Sufi Doctrine*. Wellingborough: Aquarian Press, 1976.

———. *Principes et méthods de l'art sacré*. Paris: Dervy, 1976.

———. *Mirror of the Intellect: Essays on Traditional Science and Sacred Art*. Cambridge: Quinta Essentia, 1987.

Campbell, Joseph. *The Hero with a Thousand Faces*. Princeton: Princeton University Press, 1949.

Capra, Fritjof. The Tao of Physics. London: Wildwood House, 1975.

Carter-Haar, Betsie. "Identity and Personal Freedom," in *Synthesis*, vol. 1, 1975, n. 2.

———. *L'integrazione della personalità*. Firenze: Centro Studi di Psicosintesi, "R. Assagioli," 1986.

Chinen, Allan. "Fairy Tales and Transpersonal Development in Later Life," in *Journal of Transpersonal Psychology*, vol. 17, 1985, n. 2.

Cirlot, J. E. *A Dictionary of Symbols*. London: Routledge & Kegan Paul, 1962.

Conze, Edward. *Buddhist Meditation*. New York: Harper, 1956.

Coomaraswami, Ananda. *Time and Eternity*. Ascona: Artibus Asial, 1947.

Coppes, Dolf. *De Tijd van je leven*. Amersfort: Sfinx, 1982.

Cousins, Norman. *Anatomy of an Illness*. New York: Bantam, 1979.

———. *The Healing Heart*. New York: Avon, 1983.

Crampton, Martha. "Psychological Energy Transformations," in *Journal of Transpersonal Psychology*, vol. 6, 1974, n. 1.

———. *Psychosynthesis: Some Key Aspects of Theory and Practice*. Montreal: Canadian Institute of Psychosynthesis, 1977.

Daumal, René. *Rasa*. New York: New Directions, 1982.

David-Neel, Alexandra, and Lama Yongden. *The Secret Oral Teachings in Tibetan Buddhist Sects*. San Francisco: City Lights Books, 1967.

———. *Initiations and Initiates in Tibet*. Berkeley: Shambala, 1973.

Davis, Philip. *The Mathematical Experience*. Boston: Birkhauser, 1981.

De Sainte Colombe, Paul. *Graphotherapeutics*. Los Angeles: Paul de Sainte Colombe Foundation, 1972.

De Vries, Marco. *The Redemption of the Intangible in Medicine*. London: Psychosynthesis Monographs, 1981.

Deikman, Arthur. *The Observing Self: Mysticism and Psychotherapy*. Boston: Beacon Press, 1982.

Desoille, Robert. *Theorie et Pratique du Reve Eveillé Dirigé*. Genéve: Editions du Mont-Blanc, 1961.

———. *Entretiens sur le reve éveillé dirigé en psychothérapie*. Paris: Payot, 1973.

Deussen, Paul. *The Philosophy of the Upanishads*. New York: Dover, 1966.

Dodds, Eric. *The Greeks and the Irrational*. Berkeley: University of California Press, 1951.

Donnelly, Morwenna. *Founding the Life Divine: An Introduction to the Integral Yoga of Sri Aurobindo*. London: Rider, 1955.

Dossey, Larry. *Space, Time, and Medicine*. Boulder: Shambala, 1982.

Eastcott, Michal. *The Silent Path*. London: Rider, 1969.

———. *"I": The Story of the Self*. London: Rider, 1979.

Eigen, Manfred. *The Hypercycle: A Principle of Natural Self-Organization*. Heidelberg: Springer, 1979.

Eliade, Mircea. *Images et symboles*. Paris: Gallimard, 1951.

———. *Yoga, immortalité et liberté*. Paris: Librairie Payot, 1954.

———. *Mythes, reves, et mystères*. Paris: Gallimard, 1957.

———. *The Sacred and the Profane*. Trad. W. Trask. New York: Harcourt, Brace & World, 1959.

———. *Mephistophélès et l'Androgyne*. Paris: Gallimard, 1962.

———. *Le mythe de l'éternel retour*. Paris: Gallimard, 1969.

Engler, Jack. "Therapeutic Aims in Psychotherapy and Meditation: Developmental Stages in the Representation of Self," in *Journal of Transpersonal Psychology*, vol. 16, 1984, n. 1.

Epstein, Mark. "Psychiatric Complications of Meditation," in *Journal of Transpersonal Psychology*, vol. 13, 1981, n. 2.

———. "The Deconstruction of the Self: Ego and "Egolessness" in Buddhist Insight Meditation," in *Journal of Transpersonal Psychology*, vol. 20, 1988, n. 1.

Evans, Joan. "The Process and Principles of Empowering," in *Institute of Psychosynthesis Yearbook IV*, London, 1984.

Evans-Wentz, W. *The Tibetan Book of the Dead*. London: Oxford University Press, 1968.

———. *The Tibetan Book of the Great Liberation*. London: Oxford University Press, 1968.

———. *Tibetan Yoga and Secret Doctrines*. London: Oxford University Press, 1971.

Feldman, David, and Goldsmith, Lynn. *Nature's Gambit: Child Prodigies and the Development of Human Potential*. New York: Basic Books, 1986.

Ferguson, Marilyn. *The Brain Revolution*. New York: Bantam, 1975.

———. *The Aquarian Conspiracy*. Los Angeles: Tarcher, 1980.

Ferrucci, Piero. *Crescere*. Rome: Astrolabio, 1980.

Firman, John, and Vargiu, James. "Dimensions of Growth," in *Synthesis*, 3–4, 1976.

Fischle, Willy. *The Way to the Centre*. London: Robinson & Watkins, 1982.

Frankl, Viktor. *The Doctor and the Soul: From Psychotherapy to Logotherapy*. New York: Knopf, 1955.

Freeland Judson, Horace. *The Search for Solutions*. New York: Holt, 1980.

Fresia, Giorgio. "Terapia Psicosintetica," in *Psicosintesi*, December 1983.

Frost, Bede. *The Art of Mental Prayer*. London: SPCK, 1966.

Fugitt, Eva. *He Hit Me Back First*. Rolling Hills Estates: Jalmar Press, 1979.

Funk, Joel. "The Self and the Study of Art," in *ReVISION*, vol. 6, n. 1.

Gardner, Howard. *Art, Mind and Brain*. New York: Basic Books, 1982.

———. *Frames of Mind: The Theory of Multiple Intelligences*. New York: Basic Books, 1983.

Ghiselin, Brewster (curatore). *The Creative Process*. New York: New American Library, 1980.

Gleick, James. *Chaos: Making a New Science*. New York: Viking, 1987.

Globus, Gordon; Maxwell, Grover; and Savodnick, Irwin. *Consciousness and the Brain*. New York: Plenum Press, 1976.

Godel, Roger. *Essais sur l'expérience libératrice*. Paris: Gallimard, 1952.

Goldberg, Philip. *The Intuitive Edge: Understanding Intuition and Applying It in Everyday Life*. Los Angeles: Tarcher, 1985.

Goldstein, Joseph. *The Experience of Insight*. Boulder: Shambala, 1976.

Goleman, Daniel. *The Meditative Mind*. Los Angeles: Tarcher, 1988.

Goleman, Daniel, and Davidson, Richard (curatori). *Consciousness: Brain, Awareness, and Mysticism*. New York: Harper & Row, 1979.

Goleman, Daniel; Smith, Huston; and Ram Dass. "Truth and Transformation in Psychological and Spiritual Paths," in *Journal of Transpersonal Psychology*, vol. 17, 1985, n. 2.

Gordon, William. *Synectics*. New York: Harper & Row, 1961.

Gorman, Paul, and Ram Dass. *How Can I Help?* New York: Knopf, 1987.

Govinda, Lama Anagarika. *Foundations of Tibetan Mysticism*. London: Rider, 1968.

———. *Creative Meditation and Multidimensional States*. Wheaton: Theosophical Publishing House, 1976.

Graf Von Durckheim, Karlfried. *Altag as Ubung*. Berne: Verlag Hans Huber, 1962.

Grant, Patrick (curatore). *A Dazzling Darkness: An Anthology of Western Mysticism*. Glasgow: Fount, 1985.

Green, Elmer and Alyce. *Beyond Biofeedback*. New York: Delacorte, 1977.

Grof, Stanislav. *Realms of the Human Unconscious*. New York: Viking, 1975.
———. *The Human Encounter with Death*. New York: Dutton, 1978.
———. *Beyond the Brain*. New York: University Press, 1985.
Grof, Christina and Stanislav. "Spiritual Emergency: The Understanding and Treatment of Transpersonal Crises," in *ReVISION*, Winter/Spring 1986, vol. 8, n. 2.
Gruber, Howard (curatore). *Contemporary Approaches to Creative Thinking*. New York: Atherton Press, 1962.
———. *Darwin on Man: A Psychological Study of Scientific Creativity*. Chicago: University of Chicago Press, 1981.
Guenon, René. *L'uomo e il suo divenire secondo il Vedanta*. Trad. C. Podd. Torino: Edizioni Studi Tradizionali, 1965.
———. *Introduzione generale allo studio delle dottrine indù*. Trad. P. Nutrizio. Torino: Edizioni Studi Tradizionali, 1965.
Hadamard, Jacques. *The Psychology of Invention in the Mathematical Field*. Princeton: Princeton University Press, 1945.
Haken, Hermann. *Erfolgsgeheimnisse der Natur*. Stuttgart: Deutsche Verlag, 1981.
Hamel, Peter Michael. *Through Music to the Self*. Boulder: Shambala, 1976.
Happold, F. C. *Mysticism: A Study and an Anthology*. Harmondworth: Penguin, 1963.
Hardy, Jean. *A Psychology with a Soul*. London: Routledge & Kegan Paul, 1987.
Harman, Willis. "The New Copernican Revolution," in *Journal of Transpersonal Psychology*, vol. 1, 1969, n. 2.
———. *Global Mind Change*. New York: Knowledge Systems, 1988.
———. "How to Think About Peace," Sausalito: Institute of Noetic Sciences.
Harman, Willis, and Rheingold, Howard. *Higher Creativity: Liberating the Unconscious for Breakthrough Insights*. Los Angeles: Tarcher, 1984.
Haronian, Frank. *Repression of the Sublime*. New York: Psychosynthesis Research Foundation, 1967.
Heard, Gerald. "Can This Drug Enlarge Men's Minds?" in *Psychedelic Review*, Summer 1963, n. 1.
Hemery, David. *The Pursuit of Sporting Excellence*. London: Collins, 1986.
Hesse, Mary. *Models and Analogies in Science*. Notre Dame: University of Notre Dame Press, 1966.
Hindle, Brooke. *Emulation and Invention*. New York: New York University Press, 1981.
Hooper, Judith, and Teresi, Dick. *The 3-Pound Universe*. New York: Macmillan, 1986.

Horowitz, Mark. "Psychology in the Global Area," in *Institute of Psychosynthesis Yearbook III*, London, 1983.

Houston, Jean. *The Possible Human*. Los Angeles: Tarcher, 1982.

Hunt, Morton. *The Universe Within: A New Science Explores the Mind*. New York: Simon & Schuster, 1983.

Huntley, H. E. *The Divine Proportion*. New York: Dover, 1970.

Hurley III, Thomas. "The Perennial Puzzle of Untapped Potentials," in *Noetic Sciences Review*, Winter 1986, n. 1.

———. "The Exceptional Abilities Program," in *Noetic Sciences Review*, Winter 1987, n. 5.

——— (curatore). "The Greater Self," in *Noetic Sciences Review*, Spring 1988, n. 6.

Hurley III, Thomas, and O'Regan, Brendan. "Psychoneuroimmunology: The Birth of a New Field," Sausalito: Institute of Noetic Sciences, 1983.

———. "Placebo: The Hidden Asset in Healing," Sausalito: Institute of Noetic Sciences, 1985.

Huxley, Aldous. *The Perennial Philosophy*. New York: Harper & Row, 1944.

———. "Knowledge and Understanding," in *Tomorrow and Tomorrow and Tomorrow*. New York: Harper & Row, 1954.

———. *The Doors of Perception. Heaven and Hell*. New York: Harper & Row, 1954, 1955.

———. *Island*. New York: Harper & Row, 1962.

———. *The Human Situation*. New York: Harper & Row, 1977.

Huxley, Laura. *You Are Not the Target*. New York: Farrar, Straus, Giroux, 1961.

———. *This Timeless Moment*. New York: Farrar, Straus, Giroux, 1968.

Huxley, Laura; Ferrucci, Piero; and Ferrucci, Paola. *The Child of Your Dreams*. Minneapolis: Compcare, 1987.

James, William. *The Varieties of Religious Experience*. New York: Collier, 1961.

Jantsch, Erich. *The Self-Organizing Universe: Scientific and Human Implications of the Emerging Paradigm of Evolution*. Oxford: Pergamon Press, 1980.

———. (curatore). *The Evolutionary Vision: Toward a Unifying Paradigm of Physical, Biological, and Sociocultural Evolution*. Boulder: Westview Press, 1981.

Jaynes, Julian. *The Origin of Consciousness in the Breakdown of the Bicameral Mind*. Boston: Houghton Mifflin, 1976.

Jenny, Hans. *Cymatics*. Basel: Basilius Presse, 1967.

John-Steiner, Vera. *Notebooks of the Mind*. New York: Harper & Row, 1985.

Johnston, William. *Silent Music*. New York: Harper & Row, 1974.

Jung, Carl Gustav. *The Secret of the Golden Flower*. New York: Harcourt, Brace & World, 1931.

———. *Ricordi, sogni, riflessioni*. Milano: Il Saggiatore, 1965.
———. *Aion*. Princeton: Princeton University Press, 1968.
———. *The Archetypes and the Collective Unconscious*. Bollingen: Princeton, 1969.
Jung, Emma, and Von Franz, Marie-Louise. *The Grail Legend*. Trad. A. Dykes. Boston: Sigo Press, 1986.
Kapleau, Philip. *The Three Pillars of Zen*. Boston: Beacon Press, 1965.
Kayser, Hans. *Akròasis: die Lehre von der Harmonik der Welt*. Basel: Schwabe, 1964.
Kelley, Kevin (curatore). *The Home Planet*. San Francisco: Addison-Wesley, 1988.
Keys, Donald. "The Synthesis of Nations," in *Synthesis*, vol. 1, 1975, n. 2.
Koestler, Arthur. *The Act of Creation*. London: Hutchinson, 1964.
Kohn, Alfie. *No Contest: The Case Against Competition*. Boston: Houghton Mifflin, 1986.
Kolm, Serge-Cristophe. *Le Bonheur-liberté: bouddhisme profond et modernité*. Paris: Presses Universitaires de France, 1982.
Krippner, Stanley (curatore). "The Plateau Experience: A. A. Maslow and Others," in *Journal of Transpersonal Psychology*, vol. 4, 1972, n. 2.
Krishna, Gopi. *Kundalini: The Evolutionary Energy in Man*. Berkeley: Shambala, 1970.
Krishnamurti, J. *The First and Last Freedom*. Wheaton: Theosophical Publishing House, 1954.
Kubie, Lawrence. *Neurotic Distortion of the Creative Process*. New York: Noonday Press, 1958.
Kübler-Ross. *On Death and Dying*. London: Macmillan, 1969.
Kuhn, Thomas. *The Structure of Scientific Revolutions*. Chicago: University of Chicago Press, 1962.
Kull, Steve. *Evoluzione e personalità*. Firenze: Centro Studi di Psicosintesi, "R. Assagioli," 1986.
Laberge, Stephen. *Lucid Dreaming*. New York: Ballantine, 1985.
Laszlo, Ervin. *Evolution: The Grand Synthesis*. Boston: Shambala, 1987.
Leary, Timothy. "The Religious Experience: Its Production and Interpretation," in *The Psychedelic Review*, vol. 1, 1964, n. 3.
Lee, Whorf. *Language, Thought, and Reality*. Cambridge: MIT Press, 1956.
Leonard, George. *Education and Ecstasy*. New York: Delacorte, 1968.
———. *The Ultimate Athlete*. New York: Viking, 1974.
Leshan, Lawrence, and Margenau, Henry. *Einstein's Space and Van Gogh's Sky: Physical Reality and Beyond*. New York: Macmillan, 1982.
Leuner, Hanscarl. *Guided Affective Imagery*. New York: Thieme-Stratton, 1984.

Levine, Stephen. *Who Dies? An Investigation of Conscious Living and Conscious Dying*. New York: Doubleday, 1982.

Lilly, John. *Center of the Cyclone*. New York: Julian Press, 1972.

———. *Programming and Metaprogramming in the Human Biocomputer*. New York: Julian Press, 1974.

Linssen, Robert. *Living Zen*. New York: Grove Press, 1960.

Lukoff, David. "Transpersonal Perspectives on Manic Psychoses: Creative, Visionary, and Mystical States," in *Journal of Transpersonal Psychology*, vol. 20, 1988, n. 2.

Martinetti, Giovanni. *La vita fuori del corpo*. Leumann: Elle di ci, 1986.

Maslow, Abraham. *Motivation and Personality*. New York: Harper & Row, 1954.

——— (curatore). *New Knowledge in Human Values*. New York: Harper & Row, 1959.

———. *Toward a Psychology of Being*. New York: Van Nostrand, 1962.

———. *The Psychology of Science*. New York: Harper & Row, 1966.

———. *Religion, Values, and Peak Experiences*. New York: Viking Press, 1970.

———. *The Farther Reaches of Human Nature*. New York: Viking Press, 1971.

Matter, Joseph. *Love, Altruism, and World Crisis*. Totowa: Littlefield Adams, 1975.

Matthews-Simonton, Stephanie, and Simonton, Carl. *Getting Well Again*. New York: Bantam, 1978.

Maturana, Humberto, and Varela, Francisco. *The Tree of Knowledge: The Biological Roots of Human Understanding*. Boulder: Shambala, 1987.

May, Rollo. *The Courage to Create*. New York: Norton, 1975.

McKellar, Peter. *Imagination and Thinking*. New York: Basic Books, 1957.

Metzner, Ralph. "Metaphors of Self-transformation," in *Journal of Transpersonal Psychology*, vol. 12, 1980, n. 1.

Miller, Arthur. *Imagery in Scientific Thought*. Boston: Birkhauser, 1984.

Miller, Stuart. "Dialogue With the Higher Self," in *Synthesis*, vol. 1, 1975, n. 2.

Mitchell, Edgar. *Psychic Exploration: A Challenge for Science*. New York: Putnam, 1976.

Murphy, Gardner. *Human Potentialities*. New York: Basic Books, 1958.

Murphy, Michael. "Education for Transcendence," in *Journal of Transpersonal Psychology*, vol. 1, 1969, n. 1.

———. "The Future of the Body," in *Noetic Sciences Review*, Autumn 1987, n. 4.

Murphy, Michael, and White, Rhea. *The Psychic Side of Sports*. San Francisco: Addison-Wesley, 1978.

Murti, J. *The Central Philosophy of Buddhism: A Study of the Madhyamika System*. London: Allen & Unwin, 1955.

Myers, F. W. H. *Human Personality and Its Survival of Bodily Death*. New Hyde Park: University Books, 1961.

Naranjo, Claudio Ornstein. *On the Psychology of Meditation*. New York: Viking, 1973.

Needleman, Jacob. *The Encounter of Modern Science and Ancient Truth*. New York: Dutton, 1961.

Neumann, Erich. *The Origins and History of Consciousness*. Princeton: Princeton University Press, 1954.

———. *Eros and Psyche*. Trad. R. Manheim. Princeton: Princeton University Press, 1954.

Nicholson, Reynold. *The Mystics of Islam*. London: Routledge & Kegan Paul, 1963.

Nyanaponika Thera. *The Heart of Buddhist Meditation*. London: Rider, 1962.

O'Regan, Brendan. "Healing: Synergies of Mind and Spirit," in *Institute of Noetic Sciences Newsletter*, Spring 1986, vol. 14, n. 1.

Odent, Michel. *Bien Naitre*. Paris: Editions du Seuil, 1976.

Oliner, Samuel, and Oliner, Pearl. *The Altruistic Personality*. New York: Macmillan, 1988.

Olson, Robert. *The Art of Creative Thinking*. New York: Barnes & Noble, 1979.

Ornstein, Robert. *The Psychology of Consciousness*. New York: Viking, 1972.

Orsag Madigan, Carol, and Elwood, Ann. *Brainstorms and Thunderbolts: How Creative Genius Works*. New York: Macmillan, 1983.

Otto, Rudolf. *The Holy*. Trad. J. Harvey. London: Oxford University Press, 1923.

Parrinder, Geoffrey. *The Indestructible Soul*. London: Allen & Unwin, 1973.

Pelletier, Kenneth. *Mind as Healer, Mind as Slayer: A Holistic Approach to Preventing Stress Disorders*. New York: Dell, 1977.

Penfield, Wilder. *The Mystery of the Mind*. Princeton: Princeton University Press, 1975.

Perkins, D. N. *The Mind's Best Work*. Cambridge: Harvard University Press, 1981.

Perry, John Weir. *The Self in Psychotic Process: Its Symbolization in Schizophrenia*. Dallas: Spring 1987.

Pickering, George. *Creative Illness*. New York: Oxford University Press, 1974.

Pierrakos, John. *Core Energetics: Developing the Capacity to Love and Heal*. Mendocino: Liferhythm, 1987.

Polanyi, Michael. *Knowing and Being*. Chicago: University of Chicago Press, 1969.

Popper, Karl, and Eccles, John. *The Self and Its Brain*. New York: Springer International, 1977.

Priestley, J. B. *Man and Time*. London: Aldus, 1964.

Prigogine, Ilya. *From Being to Becoming: Time and Complexity in the Physical Sciences*. San Francisco: Freeman & Company, 1980.

Radakrishnan, Sarvepalli (curatore). *The Bhagavadgita*. London: Allen & Unwin, 1948.

Rainwater, Janette. *You Are in Charge: A Guide for Becoming Your Own Therapist*. Los Angeles: Peace Press, 1978.

Ram Dass. *Be Here Now*. San Cristobal: Lama Foundation, 1971.

———. *The Only Dance There Is*. New York: Anchor, 1974.

———. "A Ten-year Perspective," in *Journal of Transpersonal Psychology*, vol. 14, 1982, n. 2.

Remen, Naomi. "Spirit: Resource for Healing," in *Noetic Sciences Review*, Autumn 1988, n. 8.

Ring, Kenneth. *Life at Death*. New York: Morrow, 1980.

———. *Heading Towards Omega*. New York: Morrow, 1984.

Robertson, Chris. "Changing the Concept of Change," in *Institute of Psychosynthesis Yearbook III*, London, 1983.

Rosenfeld, Edward. *The Book of Highs*. New York: Quadrangle, 1973.

Rosselli, Massimo. "Psicoterapia: regressione e crescita," Atti dell'VIII Congresso Nazionale di Psicosintesi, Firenze, 1985.

Rossi, Ernest. *The Psychobiology of Mind-Body Healing*. New York: Norton, 1986.

Roszak, Theodore. *Unfinished Animal: The Aquarian Frontier and the Evolution of Consciousness*. London: Faber & Faber, 1976.

———. *Person/Planet*. London: Granada, 1979.

Rothenberg, Albert. *The Emerging Goddess: The Creative Process in Art, Science, and Other Fields*. Chicago: University of Chicago Press, 1979.

Satprem. *Sri Aurobindo or the Adventure of Consciousness*. Pondicherry: Sri Aurobindo Ashram Press, 1968.

Schimmel, Annemarie. *Mystical Dimensions of Islam*. Chapel Hill: University of North Carolina Press, 1975.

Scholem, Gershom. *Major Trends in Jewish Mysticism*. London: Schoken Books, 1968.

Shattock, E. H. *An Experiment in Mindfulness*. New York: Weiser, 1970.

Sheldrake, Rupert. *A New Science of Life: The Hypothesis of Formative Causation*. London: Blond & Briggs, 1981.

———. *The Presence of the Past: Morphic Resonance and the Habits of Nature*. London: Collins, 1988.

Shrady, Maria. *Moments of Insight: The Emergence of Great Ideas in the Lives of Creative Men*. New York: Harper, 1972.

Siddheswarananda, Swami. *La Méditation selon le Yoga-Vedanta*. Paris: Adrien-Maisonneuve, 1955.

Sivananda Sarasvati, Swami. *La pratique de las meditation*. Paris: Editions Albin Michel, 1950.

Sorokin, Pitimin. *Altruistic Love*. Boston: Beacon Press, 1950.

———. *The Ways and Power of Love*. Boston: Beacon Press, 1954.

Spangler, David. *Relationship and Identity*. Forres: Findhorn Foundation, 1978.

Spencer Brown, G. *Laws of Form*. London: Allen & Unwin, 1969.

Spielberg, Frederic. *Spiritual Practices of India*. New York: Citadel Press, 1951.

Stauffer, Edith. *Unconditional Love and Forgiveness*. Burbank: Triangle Publishers, 1987.

Sutich, Anthony. "Transpersonal Therapy," in *Journal of Transpersonal Psychology*, vol. 5, 1973, n. 1.

———. "The Emergence of the Transpersonal Orientation: A Personal Account," in *Journal of Transpersonal Psychology*, vol. 8, 1976, n. 1.

Suzuki, Daisetz. *On Indian Mahayana Buddhism*. New York: Harper Torchbooks, 1968.

———. *Essays in Zen Buddhism*. 3 vols. London: Rider, 1970.

Suzuki, Daisetz; Fromm, Erich; and De Martino, Richard. *Zen Buddhism and Psychoanalysis*. New York: Harper & Brothers, 1960.

Szent-Gyoergyi. "Drive in Living Matter to Perfect Itself," in *Synthesis*, vol. 1, 1974, n. 1.

Tart, Charles. *Altered States of Consciousness*. New York: Wiley, 1969.

———. "Transpersonal Potentialities of Deep Hypnosis," in *Journal of Transpersonal Psychology*, vol. 2, 1970, n. 1.

———. *States of Consciousness*. New York: Dutton, 1975.

———. *Waking Up: Overcoming the Obstacles to Human Potential*. Boulder: Shambala, 1986.

———. *Transpersonal Psychologies*. Boulder: Shambala, 1986.

Tarthang Tulku. "A View of Mind," in *Journal of Transpersonal Psychology*, vol. 8, 1976, n. 1.

———. *Time, Space, and Knowledge*. Emeryville: Dharma Publishing, 1977.

Teilhard de Chardin. *Le phénomène humain*. Paris: Editions du Seuil, 1955.

———. *Le milieu divin*. Paris: Editions du Seuil, 1957.

———. *L'activation de l'énérgie*. Paris: Editions du Seuil, 1963.

Thom, René. *Stabilità strutturale e morfogenesi*. Torino: Einaudi, 1980.

Tilli, Sebastiano. *Concetti della psicologia umanistica di Roberto Assagioli*. Firenze: Istituto di Psicosintesi, 1980.

Trungpa, Chogyam. *The Myth of Freedom*. Berkeley: Shambala, 1976.

Underhill, Evelyn. *Practical Mysticism*. New York: Dutton, 1955.

———. *Mysticism*. New York: Dutton, 1961.

Vachot, Charles. *Le yoga de l'art*. Paris: Dervy Livres, 1981.

Valiuddin, Mir. *Contemplative Disciplines in Sufism*. London: East-West Publications, 1980.

Vargiu, James. "Subpersonalities," in *Synthesis*, vol. 1, 1974, n. 1.

———. "Creativity," in *Synthesis*, 1976, nn. 3–4.

Vaughan, Frances. *Awakening Intuition*. New York: Doubleday, 1979.

———. *The Inward Arc*. Boulder: Shambala, 1985.

Vaughan, Frances, and Walsh, Roger. *Beyond Ego*. Los Angeles: Tarcher, 1980.

Vernon, P. E. (curatore). *Creativity*. Harmondsworth: Penguin, 1970.

Von Bertalanffy, Ludwig. *Teoria generale dei sistemi*. Milano: Mondadori, 1983.

Walsh, Roger. "Meditation Research," in *Journal of Transpersonal Psychology*, vol. 11, 1979, n. 1.

Watson, Lyall. *Lifetide*. London: Hodder & Stoughton, 1979.

Watts, Alan. *Nature, Man and Woman*. New York: Pantheon Books, 1958.

———. *This is It*. New York: Pantheon Books, 1958.

———. *Psychotherapy East and West*. New York: Pantheon Books, 1961.

———. *The Two Hands of God*. New York: Macmillan, 1963.

Weber, Renée. *Dialogues with Scientists and Sages*. London: Routledge & Kegan Paul, 1986.

Wechsler, Judith (curatrice). *On Aesthetics in Science*. Cambridge: MIT Press, 1978.

Weiser, John, and Yeomans, Tom. *Psychosynthesis in the Helping Professions: Now and for the Future*. Toronto: Ontario Studies in Education, 1984.

———. *Readings in Psychosynthesis: Theory, Process, and Practice*. Toronto: Ontario Institute for Studies in Education, 1985.

Welwood, John. "Exploring Mind: Form, Emptiness, and Beyond," in *Journal of Transpersonal Psychology*, vol. 8, 1976, n. 2.

White, John. *The Highest State of Consciousness*. New York: Doubleday, 1973.

———. *What is Enlightenment?* Boston: Tarcher/Houghton Mifflin, 1984.

Whitmore, Diana. *Psychosynthesis in Education*. Wellingborough: Thorsons, 1987.

Widmann, Claudio, and Caldironi, Bruno. *Le visualizzazioni guidate in psicoterapia*. Piovan, 1980.

Wilber, Ken. *The Spectrum of Consciousness*. Wheaton: Theosophical Publishing House, 1977.

———. *The Atman Project: A Transpersonal View of Human Development*. Wheaton: Theosophical Publishing House, 1980.

——— (curatore). *The Holographic Paradigm*. Boulder: Shambala, 1982.

——— *Up From Eden: A Transpersonal View of Human Evolution*. Boulder: Shambala, 1983.

——— (curatore). *Quantum Questions: Mystical Writings of the World's Great Physicists*. Boulder: Shambala, 1984.

Wilber, Ken; Engler, Jack; and Brown, Daniel. *Transformations of Consciousness*. Boulder: Shambala, 1986.

Woods, Richard (curatore). *Understanding Mysticism*. New York: Image Books, 1980.

Young Brown, Molly. *The Unfolding Self*. Los Angeles: Psychosynthesis Press, 1983.

Zimmer, Heinrich. *Kunstform und Yoga im indischen Kultbild*. Berlin: Frankfurter Verlag, 1926.

———. *Myths and Symbols in Indian Art and Civilization*. Washington: Bollingen, 1946.

———. *Philosophies of India*. Princeton: Princeton University Press/Bollingen, 1951.

Zolla, Elémire. *I Mistici*. Milano: Garzanti, 1963.

———. *Archetypes*. London: Allen & Unwin, 1981.

Zukav, Gary. *The Dancing Wu Li Masters: An Overview of the New Physics*. New York: Bantam, 1979.

Index of Names